Grand Blue Dreaming 15

PRESENTED BY KENJI INOUE & KIMITAKE YOSHIOKA

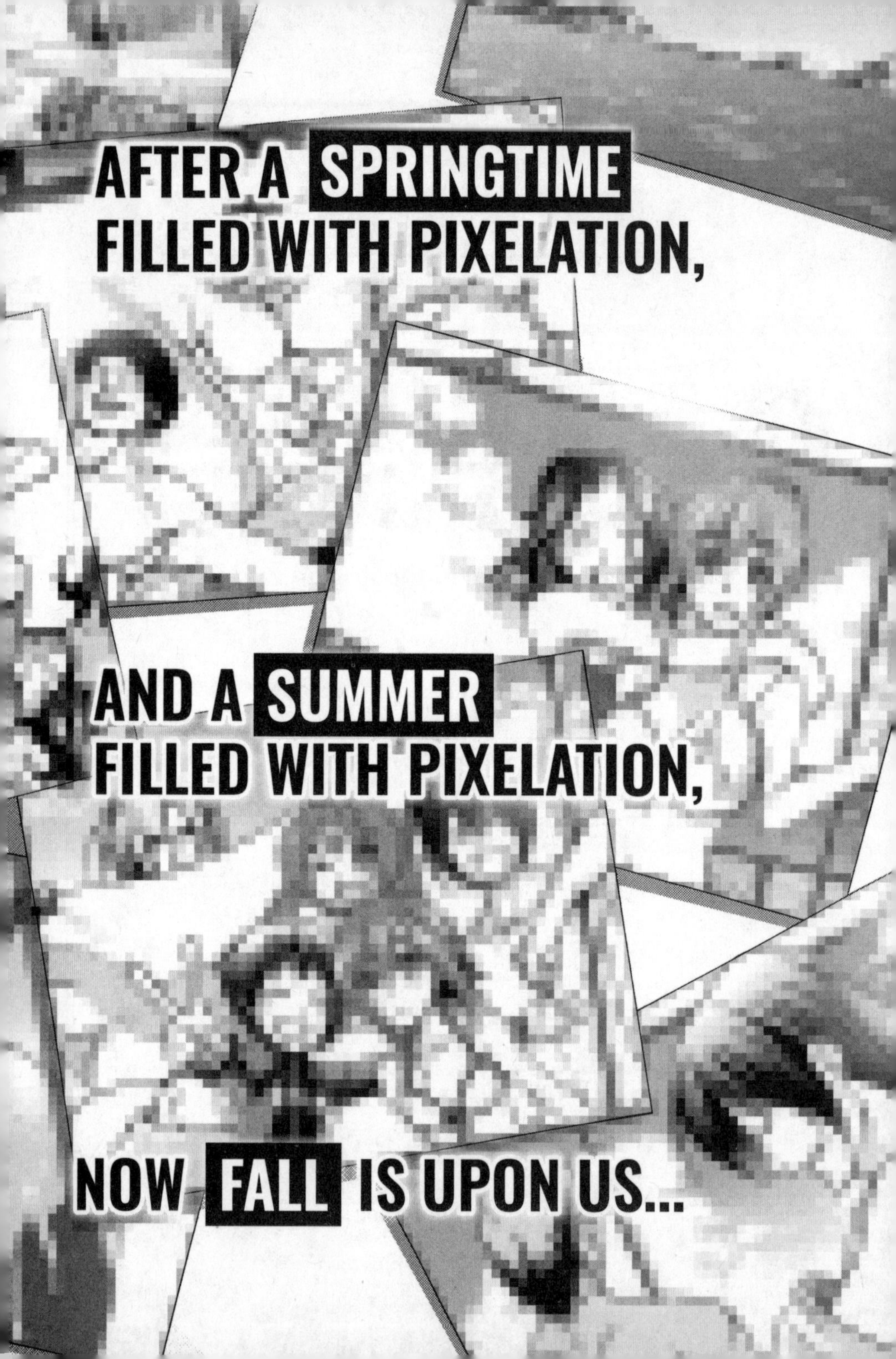
AFTER A SPRINGTIME FILLED WITH PIXELATION,
AND A SUMMER FILLED WITH PIXELATION,
NOW FALL IS UPON US...

Ch. 58: The End of Summer Vacation

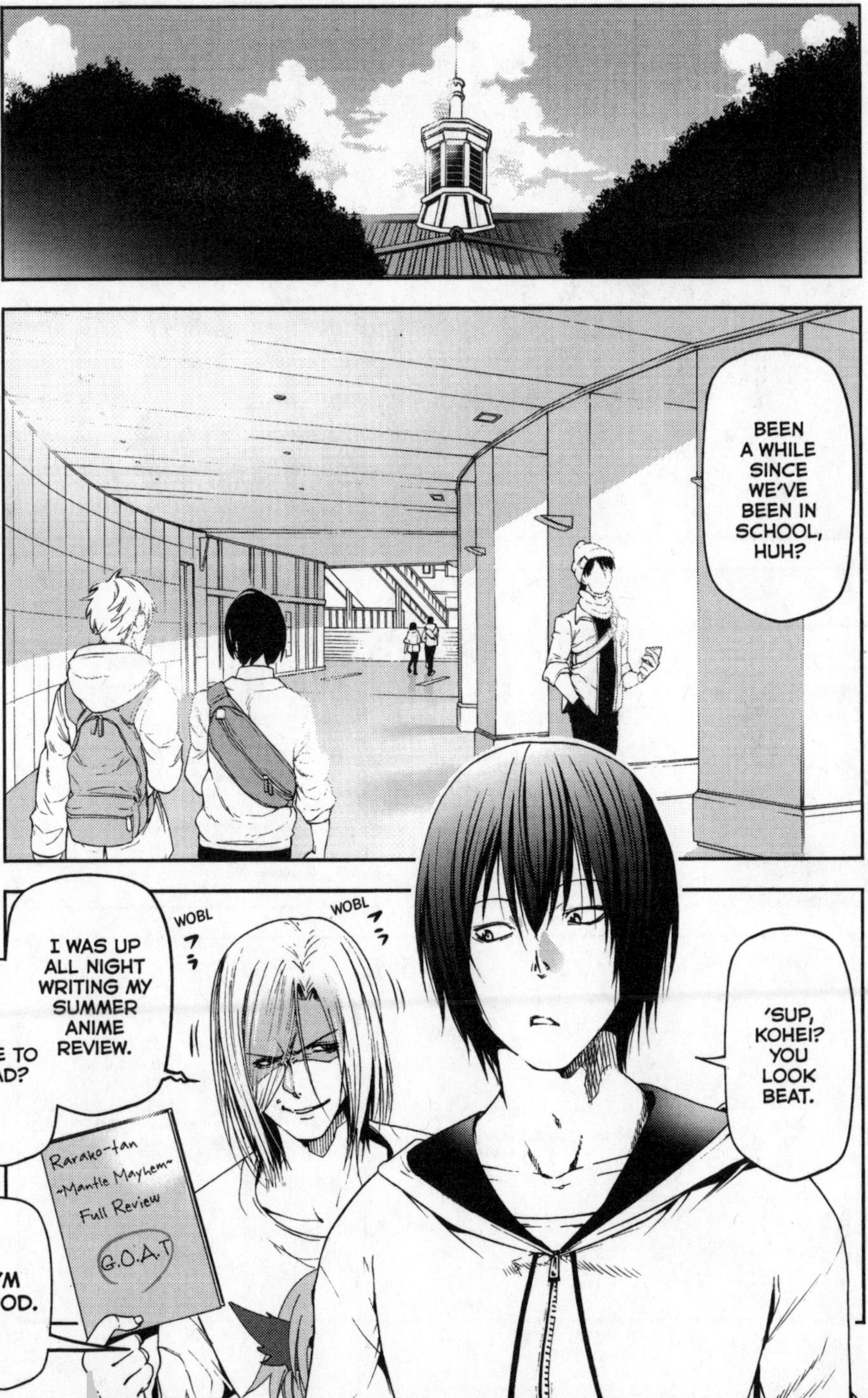
BEEN A WHILE SINCE WE'VE BEEN IN SCHOOL, HUH?
'SUP, KOHEI? YOU LOOK BEAT.
WOBL
WOBL
I WAS UP ALL NIGHT WRITING MY SUMMER ANIME REVIEW.
CARE TO READ?
Rarako-tan ~Mantle Mayhem~ Full Review
G.O.A.T
I'M GOOD.

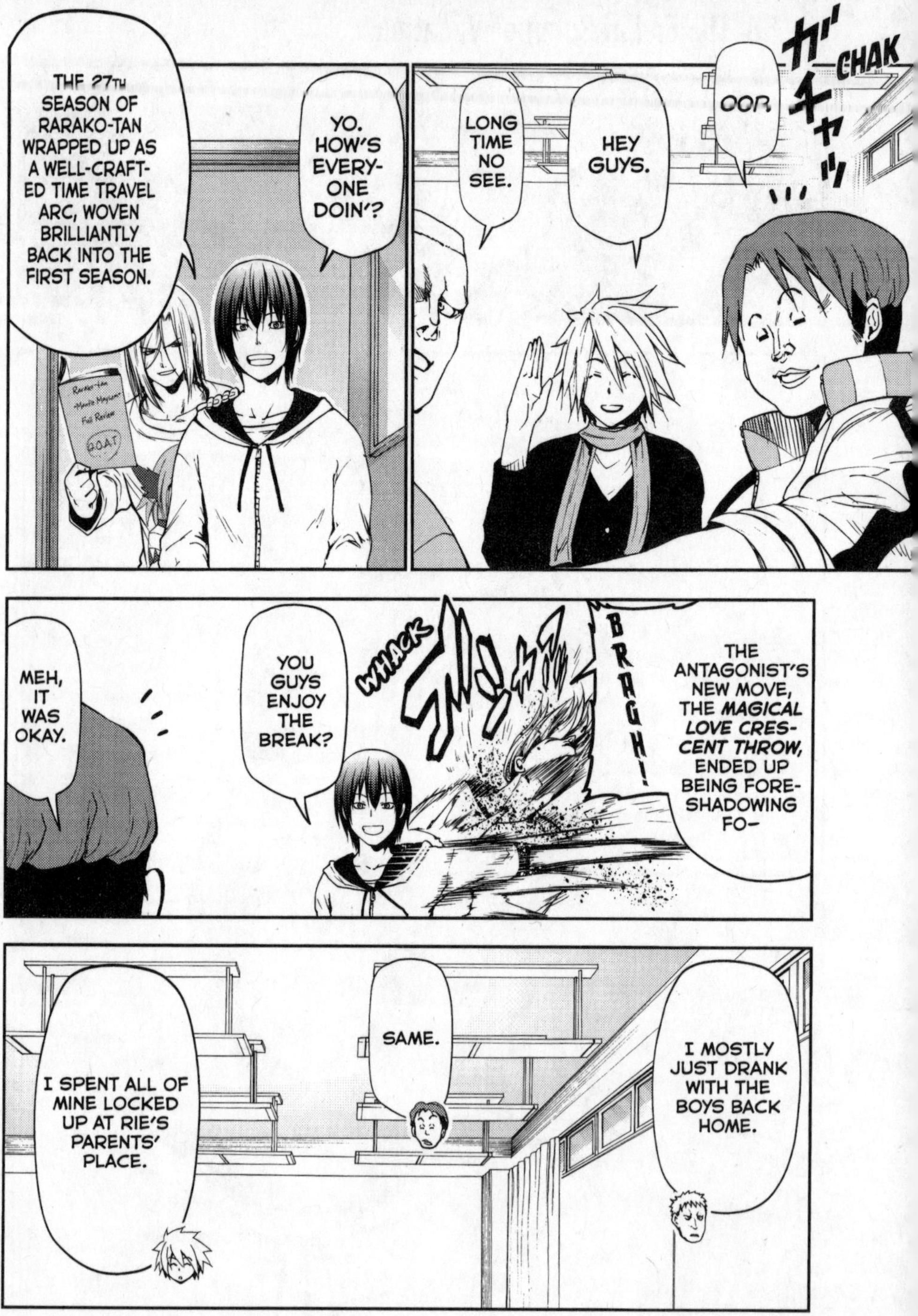

OOR.
カチャッ
CHAK
HEY GUYS.
LONG TIME NO SEE.
YO. HOW'S EVERYONE DOIN'?
THE 27TH SEASON OF RARAKO-TAN WRAPPED UP AS A WELL-CRAFTED TIME TRAVEL ARC, WOVEN BRILLIANTLY BACK INTO THE FIRST SEASON.
THE ANTAGONIST'S NEW MOVE, THE *MAGICAL LOVE CRESCENT THROW*, ENDED UP BEING FORESHADOWING FO–
BRAGH!
WHACK
YOU GUYS ENJOY THE BREAK?
MEH, IT WAS OKAY.
I MOSTLY JUST DRANK WITH THE BOYS BACK HOME.
SAME.
I SPENT ALL OF MINE LOCKED UP AT RIE'S PARENTS' PLACE.

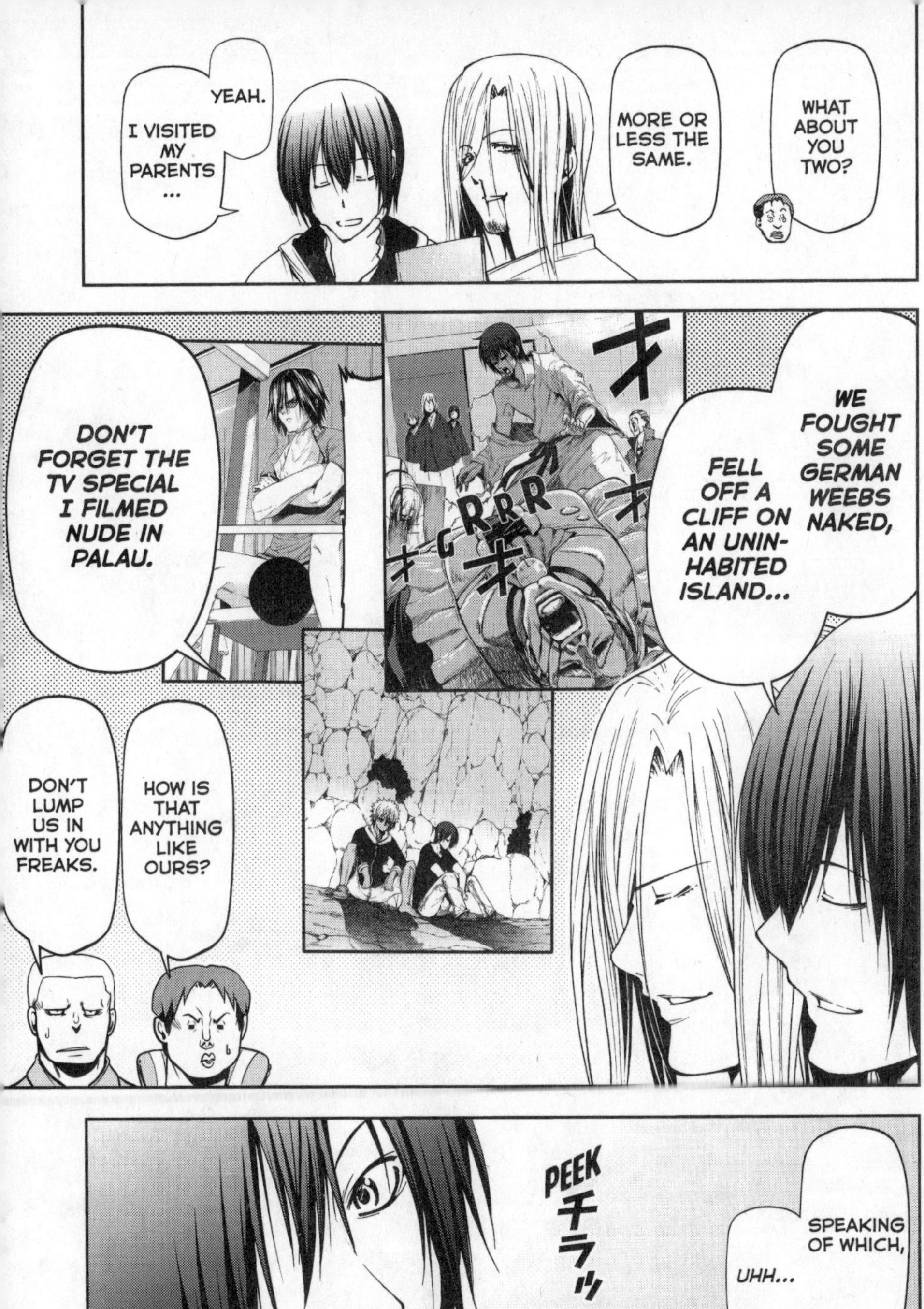

WHAT ABOUT YOU TWO?
MORE OR LESS THE SAME.
YEAH.
I VISITED MY PARENTS...
WE FOUGHT SOME GERMAN WEEBS NAKED,
FELL OFF A CLIFF ON AN UNIN-HABITED ISLAND...
GRRR
DON'T FORGET THE TV SPECIAL I FILMED NUDE IN PALAU.
HOW IS THAT ANYTHING LIKE OURS?
DON'T LUMP US IN WITH YOU FREAKS.
SPEAKING OF WHICH,
UHH...
PEEK
チラッ

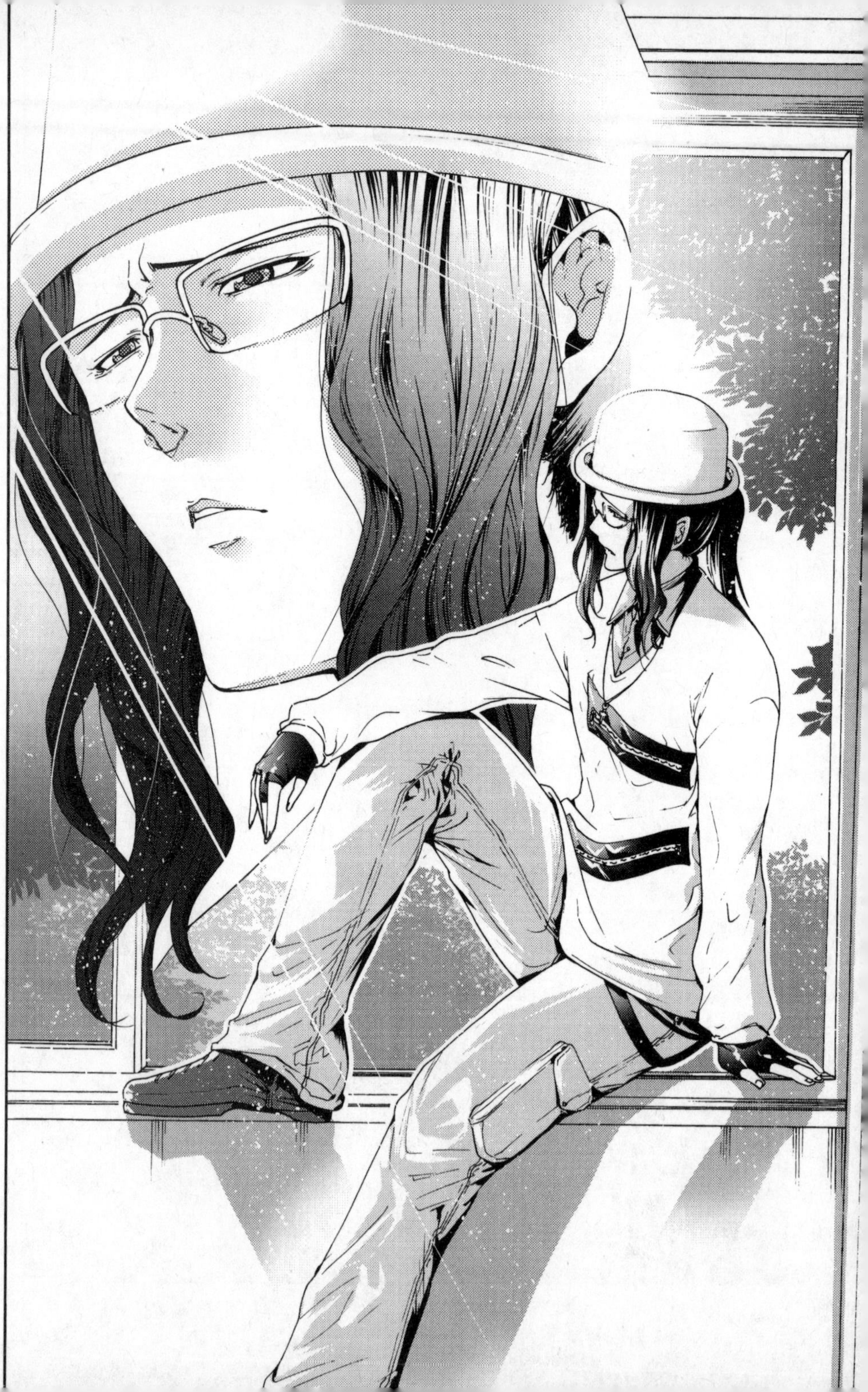

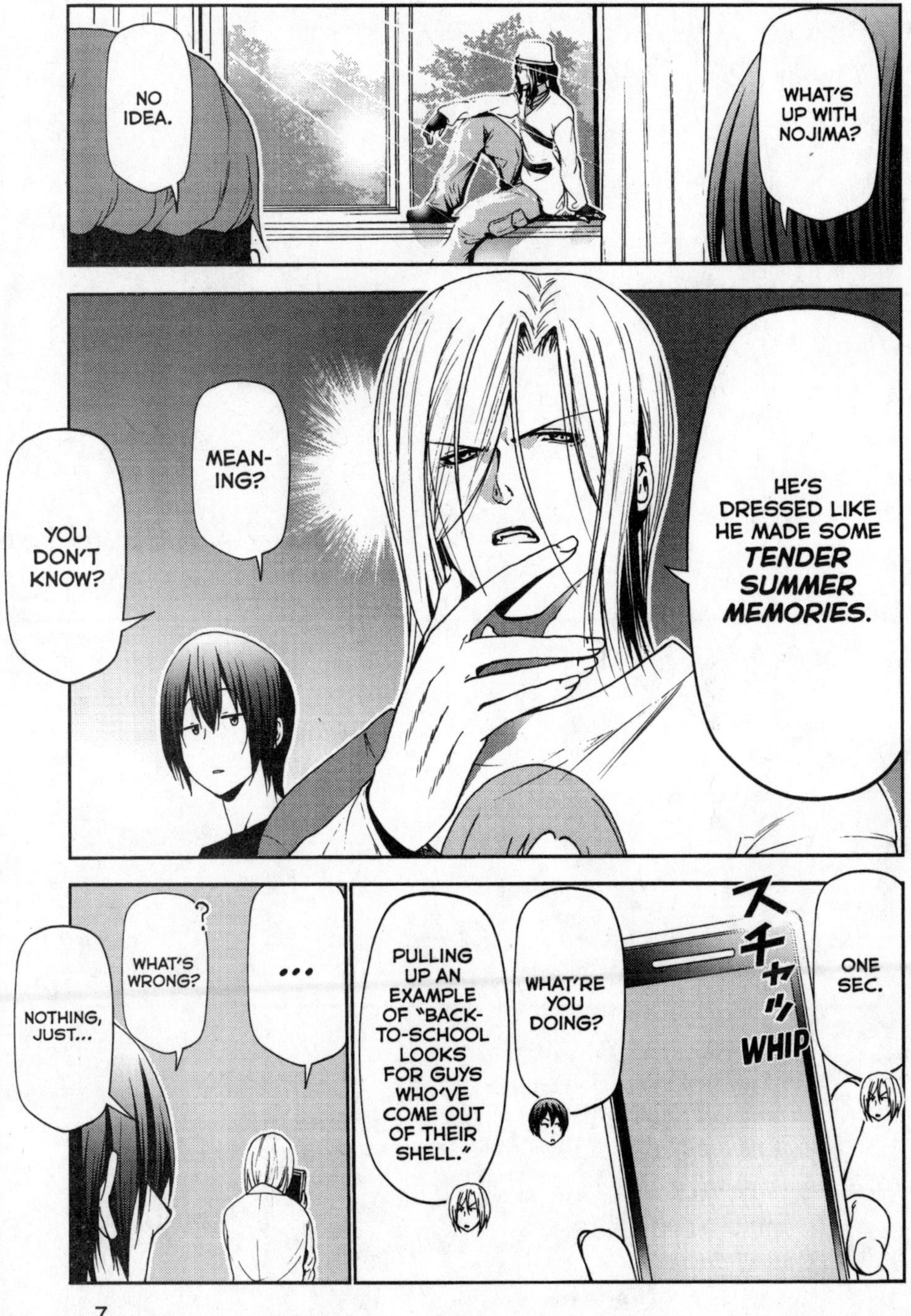
WHAT'S UP WITH NOJIMA?
NO IDEA.
HE'S DRESSED LIKE HE MADE SOME *TENDER SUMMER MEMORIES.*
MEAN-ING?
YOU DON'T KNOW?
ONE SEC.
スチャッ
WHIP
WHAT'RE YOU DOING?
PULLING UP AN EXAMPLE OF "BACK-TO-SCHOOL LOOKS FOR GUYS WHO'VE COME OUT OF THEIR SHELL."
...
?
WHAT'S WRONG?
NOTHING, JUST...

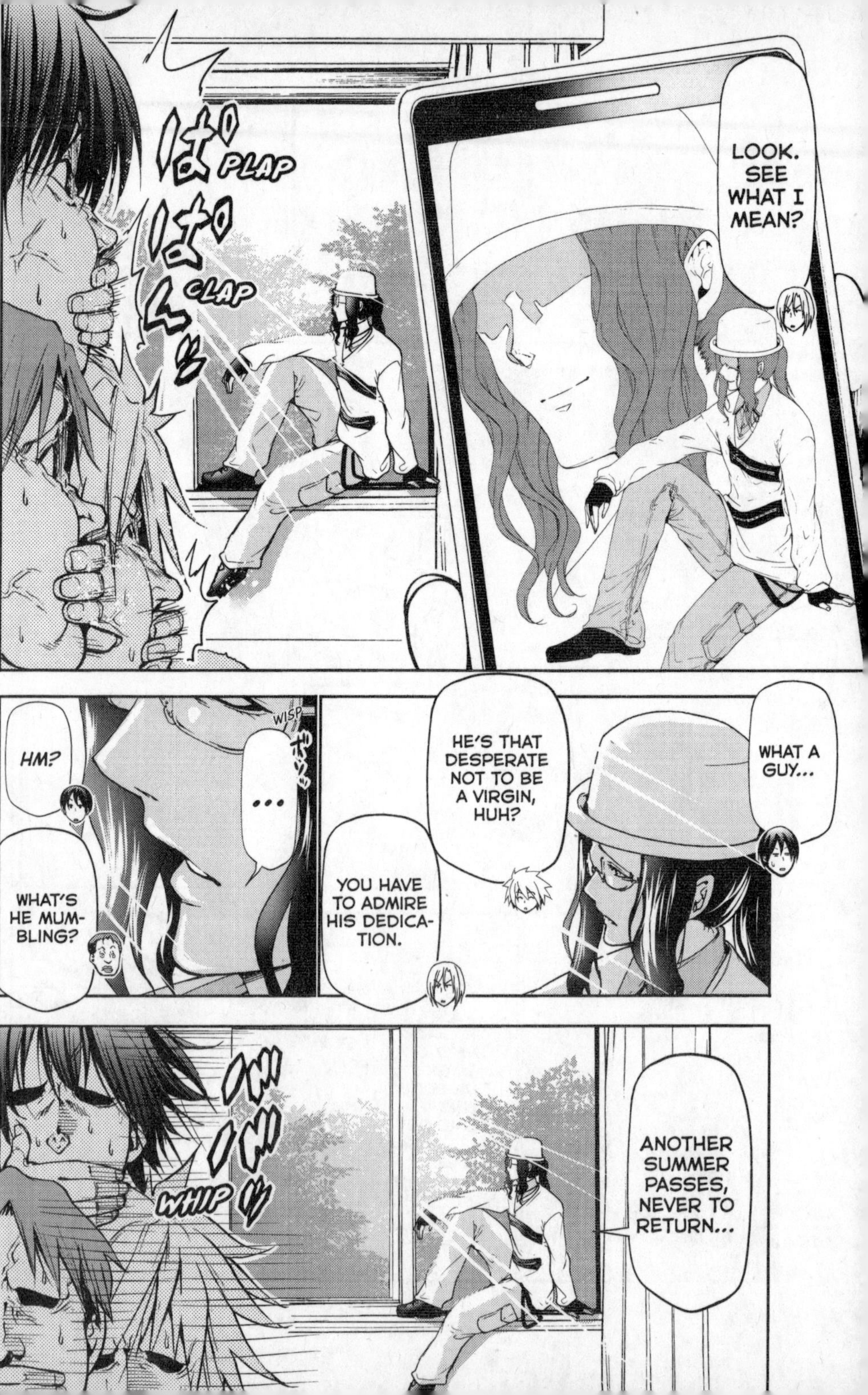
LOOK. SEE WHAT I MEAN?
PLAP
CLAP
WHAT A GUY...
HE'S THAT DESPERATE NOT TO BE A VIRGIN, HUH?
YOU HAVE TO ADMIRE HIS DEDICATION.
WISP
...
HM?
WHAT'S HE MUMBLING?
ANOTHER SUMMER PASSES, NEVER TO RETURN...
WHIP

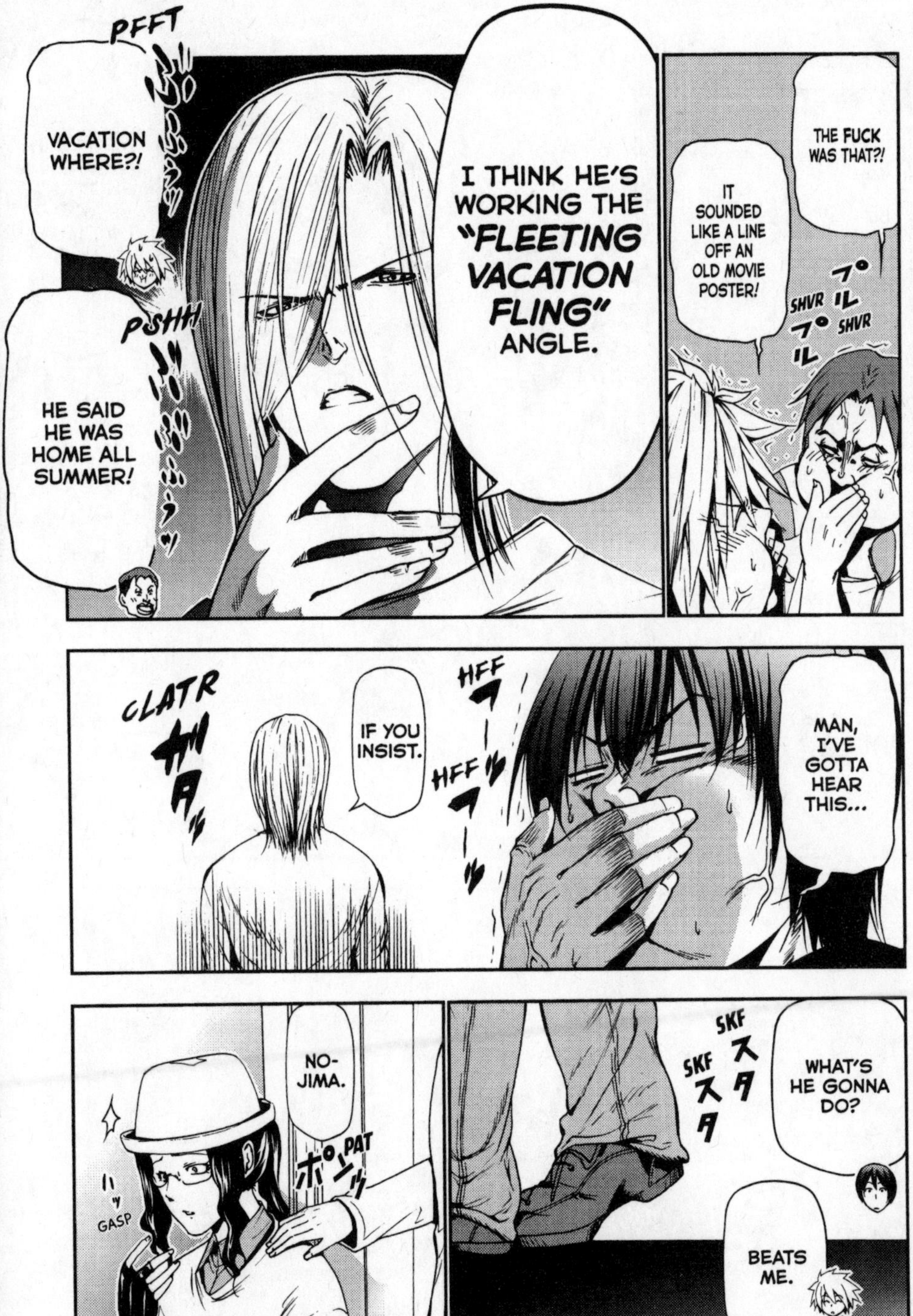
THE FUCK WAS THAT?!
IT SOUNDED LIKE A LINE OFF AN OLD MOVIE POSTER!
SHVR
SHVR
I THINK HE'S WORKING THE "FLEETING VACATION FLING" ANGLE.
PFFT
VACATION WHERE?!
PSHH
HE SAID HE WAS HOME ALL SUMMER!
MAN, I'VE GOTTA HEAR THIS...
HFF
HFF
IF YOU INSIST.
CLATR
WHAT'S HE GONNA DO?
SKF
SKF
BEATS ME.
NO-JIMA.
PAT
GASP

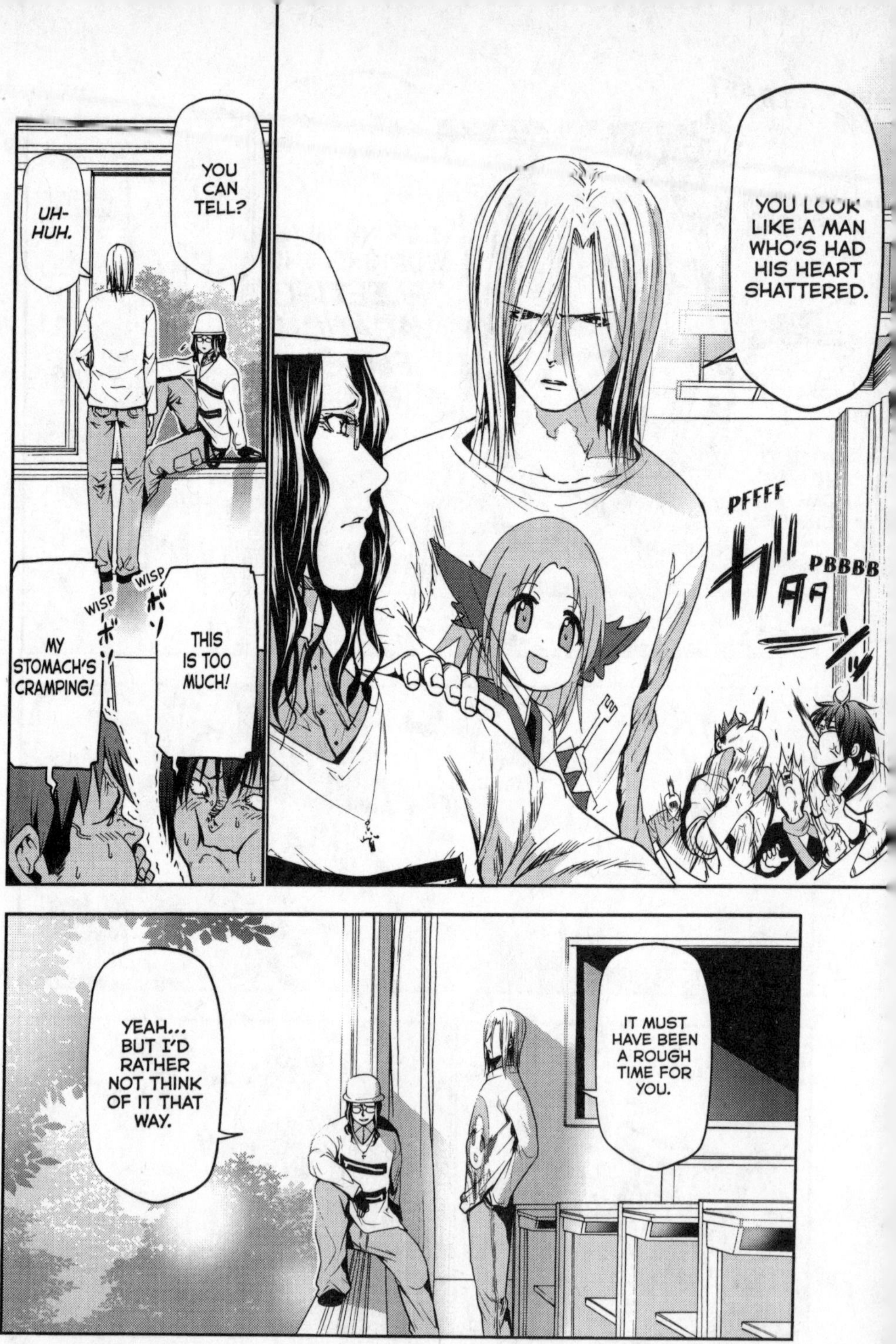
YOU LOOK LIKE A MAN WHO'S HAD HIS HEART SHATTERED.
PFFFF
PBBBB
YOU CAN TELL?
UH-HUH.
WISP
THIS IS TOO MUCH!
WISP
MY STOMACH'S CRAMPING!
IT MUST HAVE BEEN A ROUGH TIME FOR YOU.
YEAH... BUT I'D RATHER NOT THINK OF IT THAT WAY.

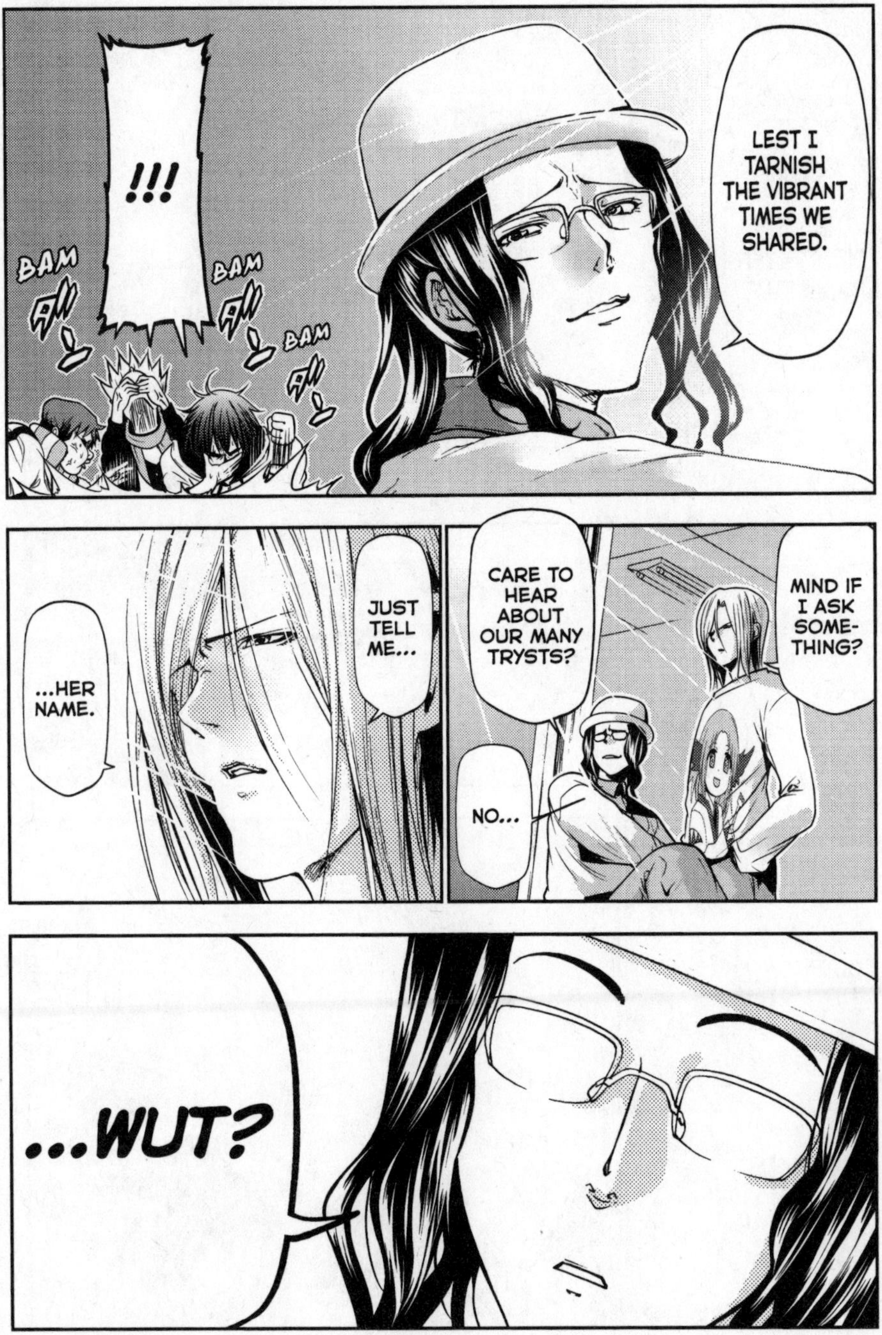
LEST I TARNISH THE VIBRANT TIMES WE SHARED.
!!!
BAM
BAM
BAM
MIND IF I ASK SOME-THING?
CARE TO HEAR ABOUT OUR MANY TRYSTS?
NO...
JUST TELL ME...
...HER NAME.
...WUT?

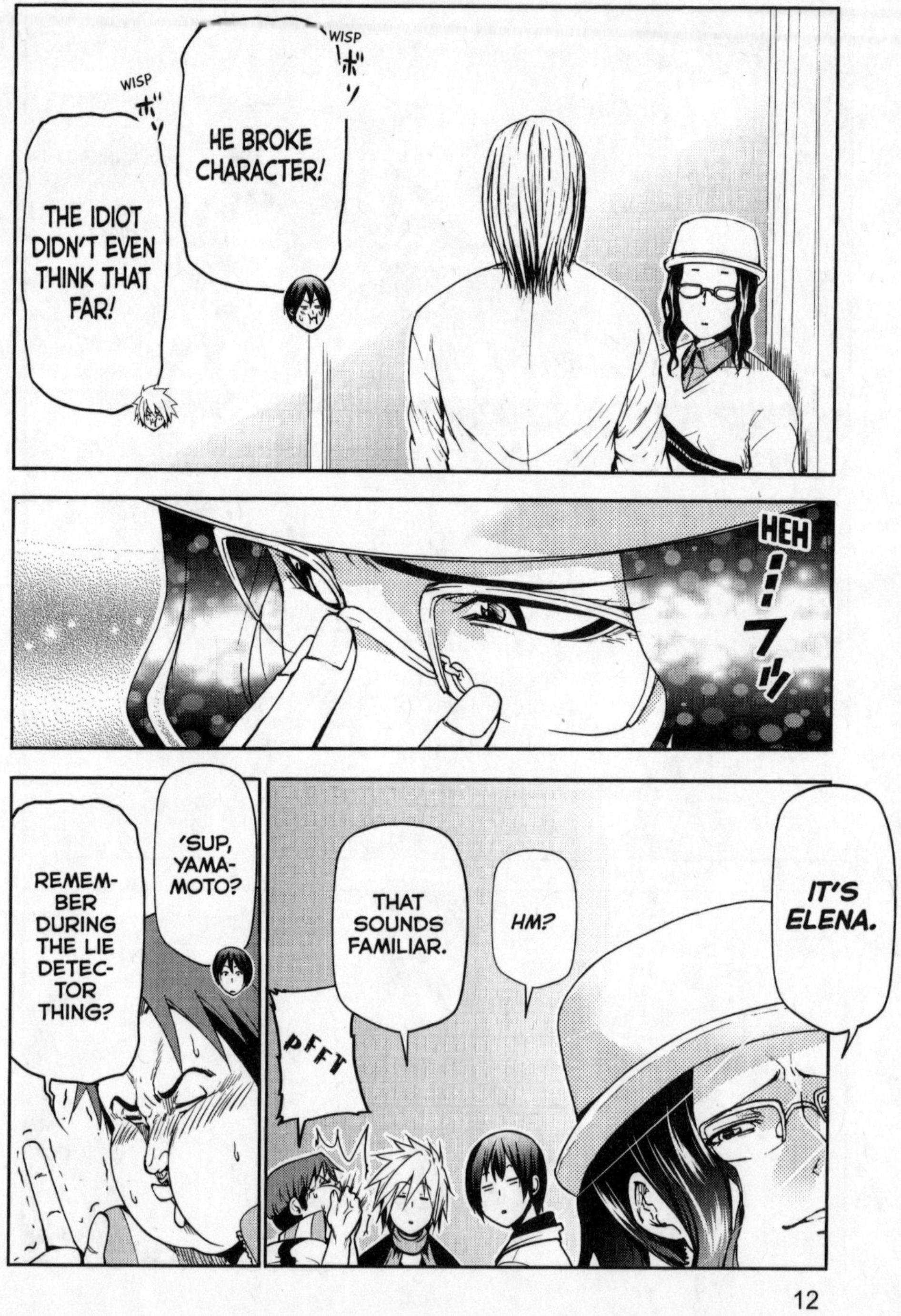
WISP
ボッ
HE BROKE CHARACTER!
WISP
ボッ
THE IDIOT DIDN'T EVEN THINK THAT FAR!
HEH...
フッ
IT'S ELENA.
HM?
THAT SOUNDS FAMILIAR.
PFFT
'SUP, YAMAMOTO?
REMEMBER DURING THE LIE DETECTOR THING?

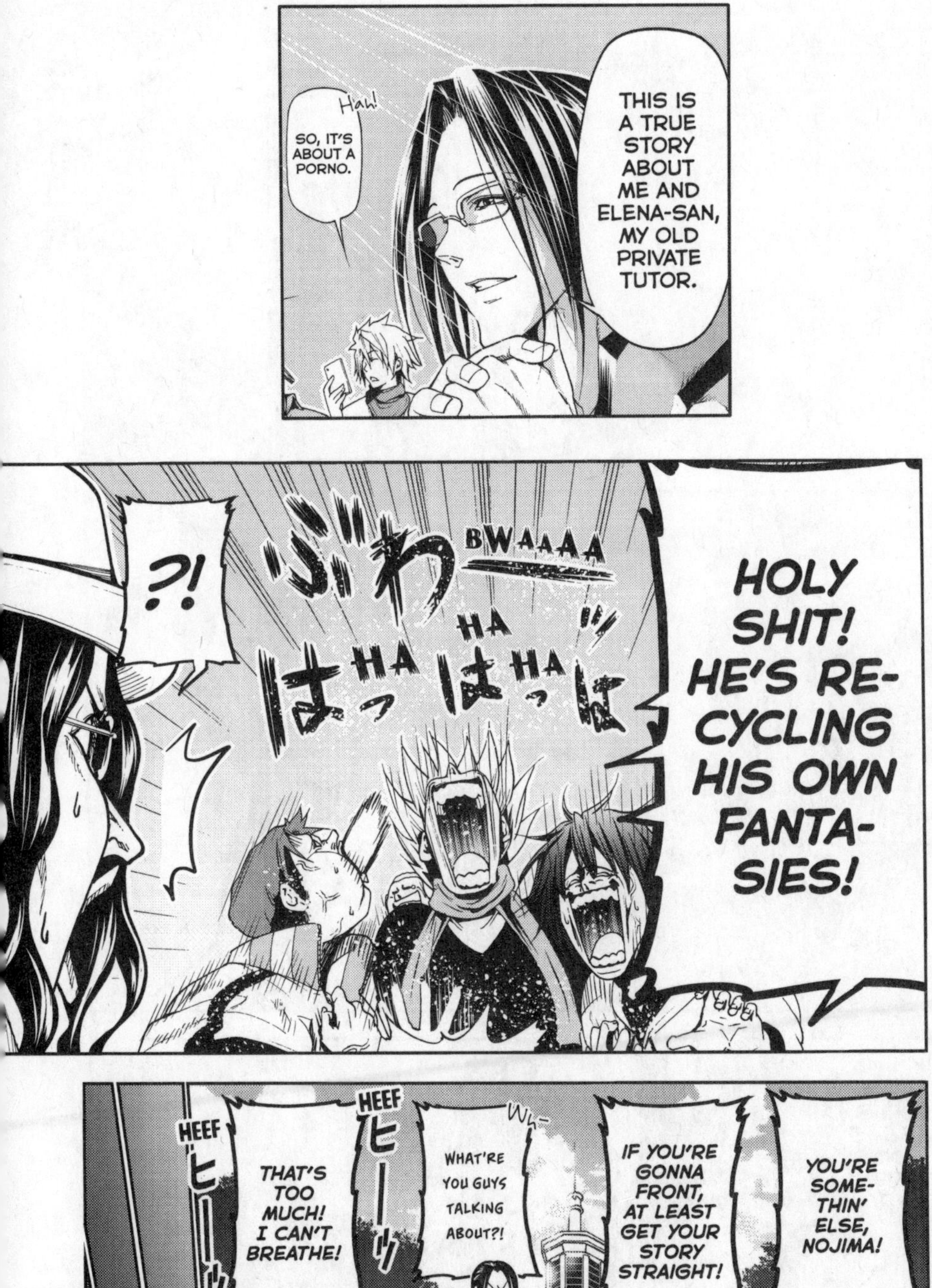
THIS IS A TRUE STORY ABOUT ME AND ELENA-SAN, MY OLD PRIVATE TUTOR.
Hah!
SO, IT'S ABOUT A PORNO.
HOLY SHIT! HE'S RE-CYCLING HIS OWN FANTA-SIES!
ぶわー BWAAAA
はっはっはっ HA HA HA HA
?!
YOU'RE SOME-THIN' ELSE, NOJIMA!
IF YOU'RE GONNA FRONT, AT LEAST GET YOUR STORY STRAIGHT!
WHAT'RE YOU GUYS TALKING ABOUT?!
ヒーッ HEEF
THAT'S TOO MUCH! I CAN'T BREATHE!
ヒーッ HEEF

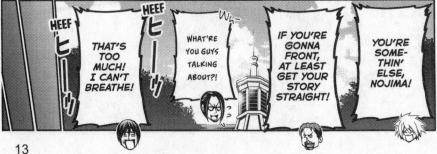

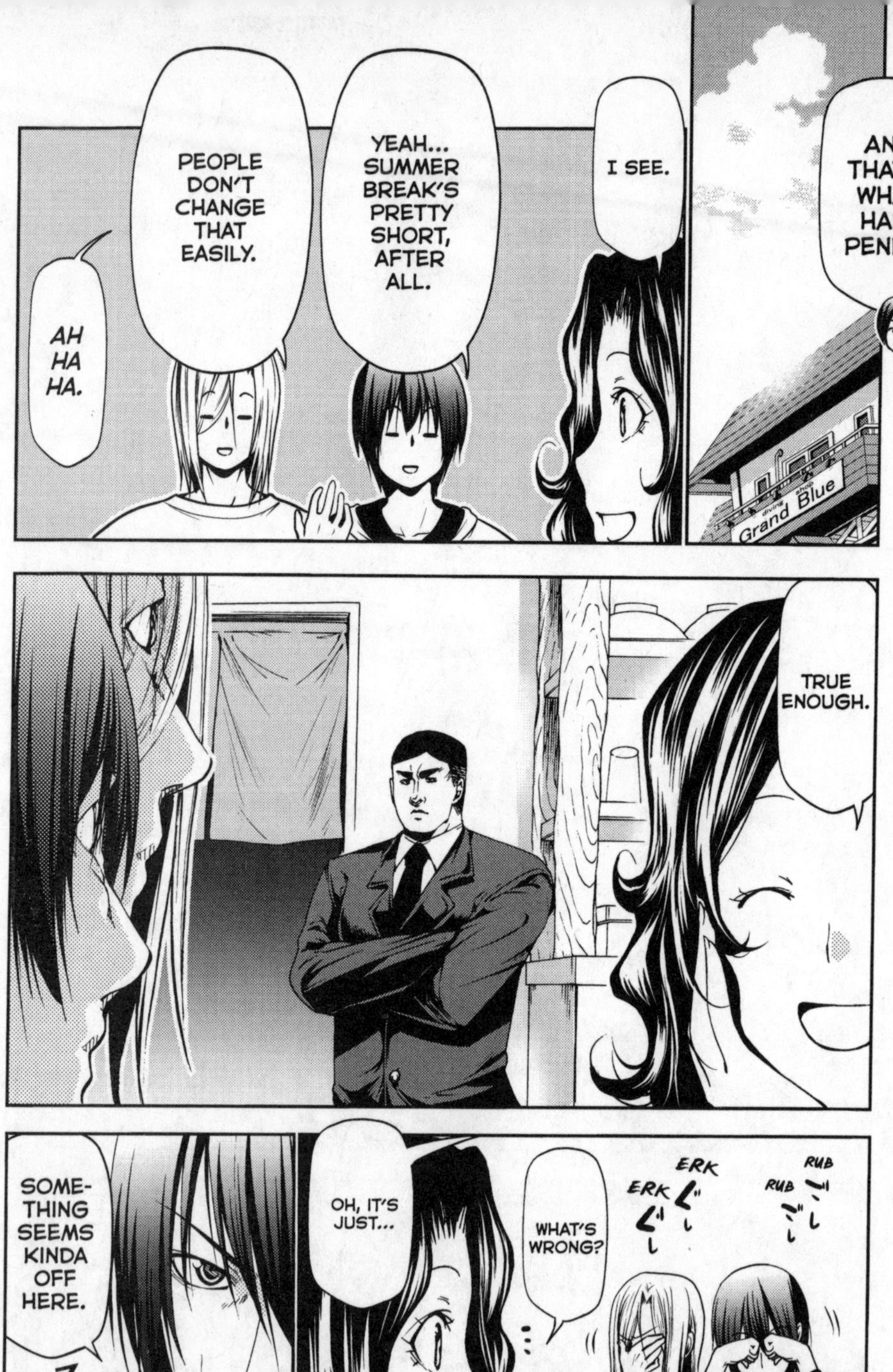
AND THAT'S WHAT HAP-PENED.
diving shop
Grand Blue
I SEE.
YEAH... SUMMER BREAK'S PRETTY SHORT, AFTER ALL.
PEOPLE DON'T CHANGE THAT EASILY.
AH HA HA.
TRUE ENOUGH.
RUB RUB
ごしごし
ERK ERK
ぐいぐい
WHAT'S WRONG?
...
OH, IT'S JUST...
SOME-THING SEEMS KINDA OFF HERE.
スッ
SWIF

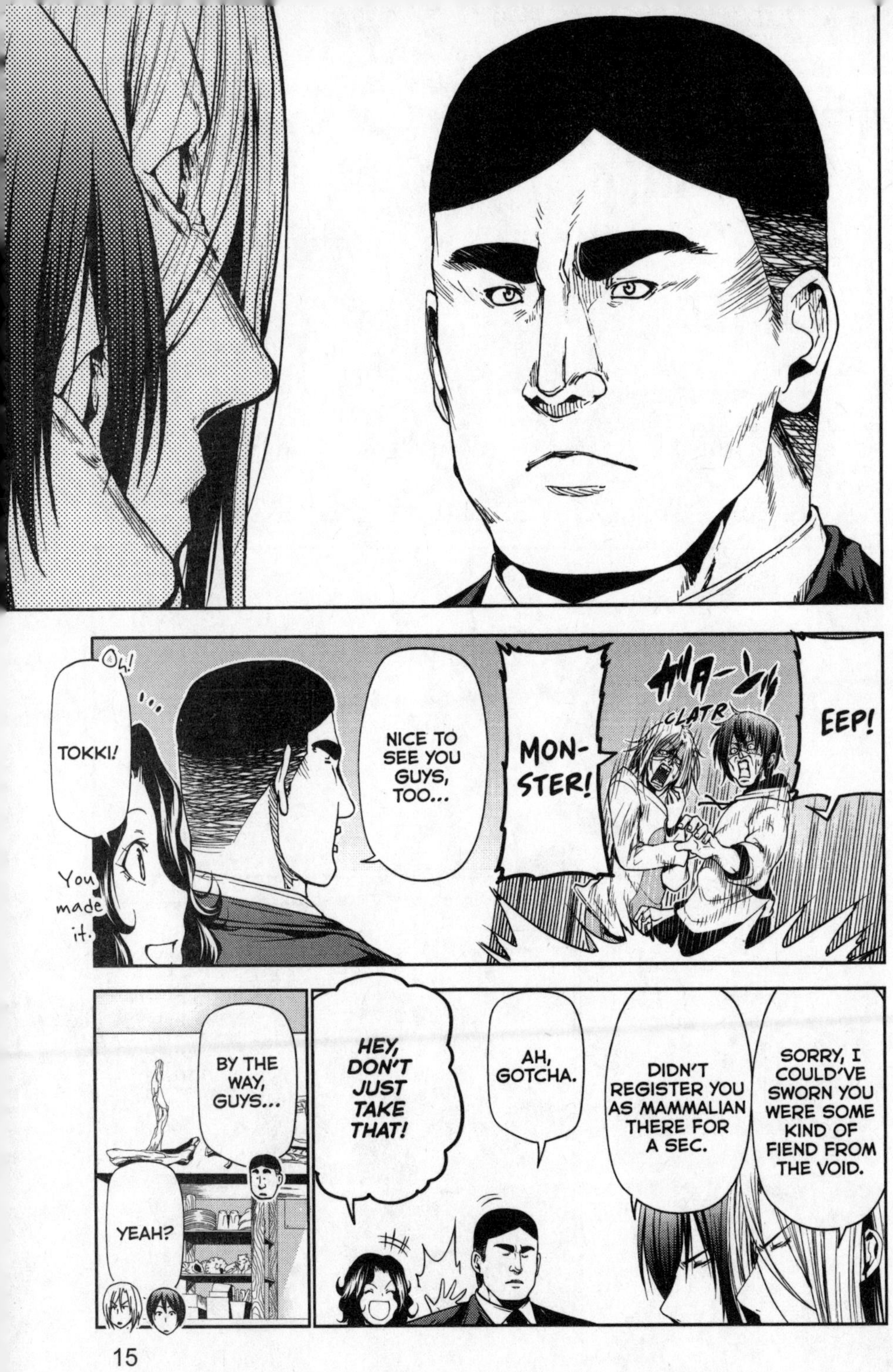
EEP!
ガターン
CLATR
MON-STER!
NICE TO SEE YOU GUYS, TOO...
...
Oh! TOKKI!
You made it.
SORRY, I COULD'VE SWORN YOU WERE SOME KIND OF FIEND FROM THE VOID.
DIDN'T REGISTER YOU AS MAMMALIAN THERE FOR A SEC.
AH, GOTCHA.
HEY, DON'T JUST TAKE THAT!
BY THE WAY, GUYS...
YEAH?

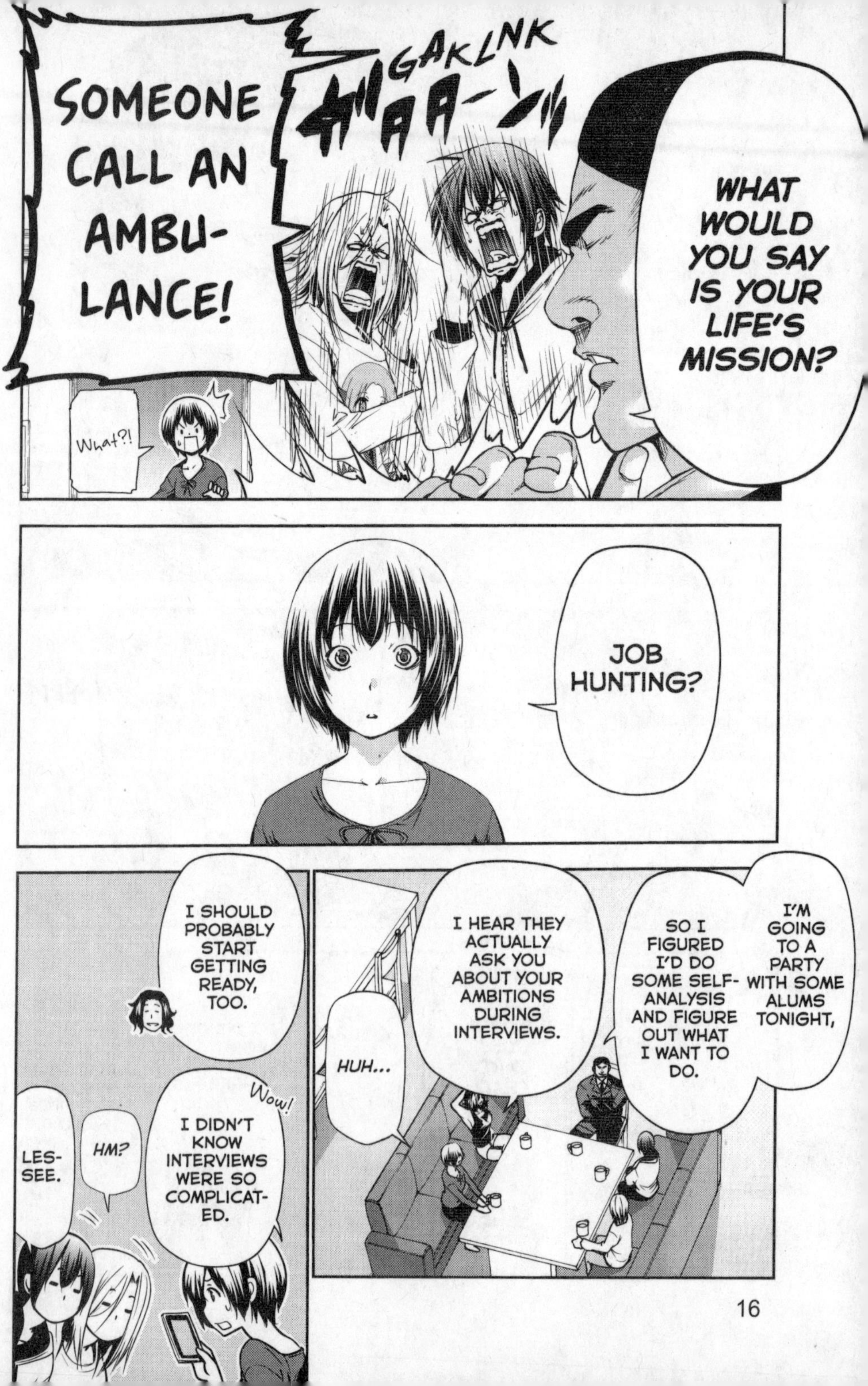
WHAT WOULD YOU SAY IS YOUR LIFE'S MISSION?
GAKLNK
SOMEONE CALL AN AMBU-LANCE!
What?!
JOB HUNTING?
I'M GOING TO A PARTY WITH SOME ALUMS TONIGHT,
SO I FIGURED I'D DO SOME SELF-ANALYSIS AND FIGURE OUT WHAT I WANT TO DO.
I HEAR THEY ACTUALLY ASK YOU ABOUT YOUR AMBITIONS DURING INTERVIEWS.
HUH...
I SHOULD PROBABLY START GETTING READY, TOO.
Wow!
I DIDN'T KNOW INTERVIEWS WERE SO COMPLICAT-ED.
HM?
LES-SEE.

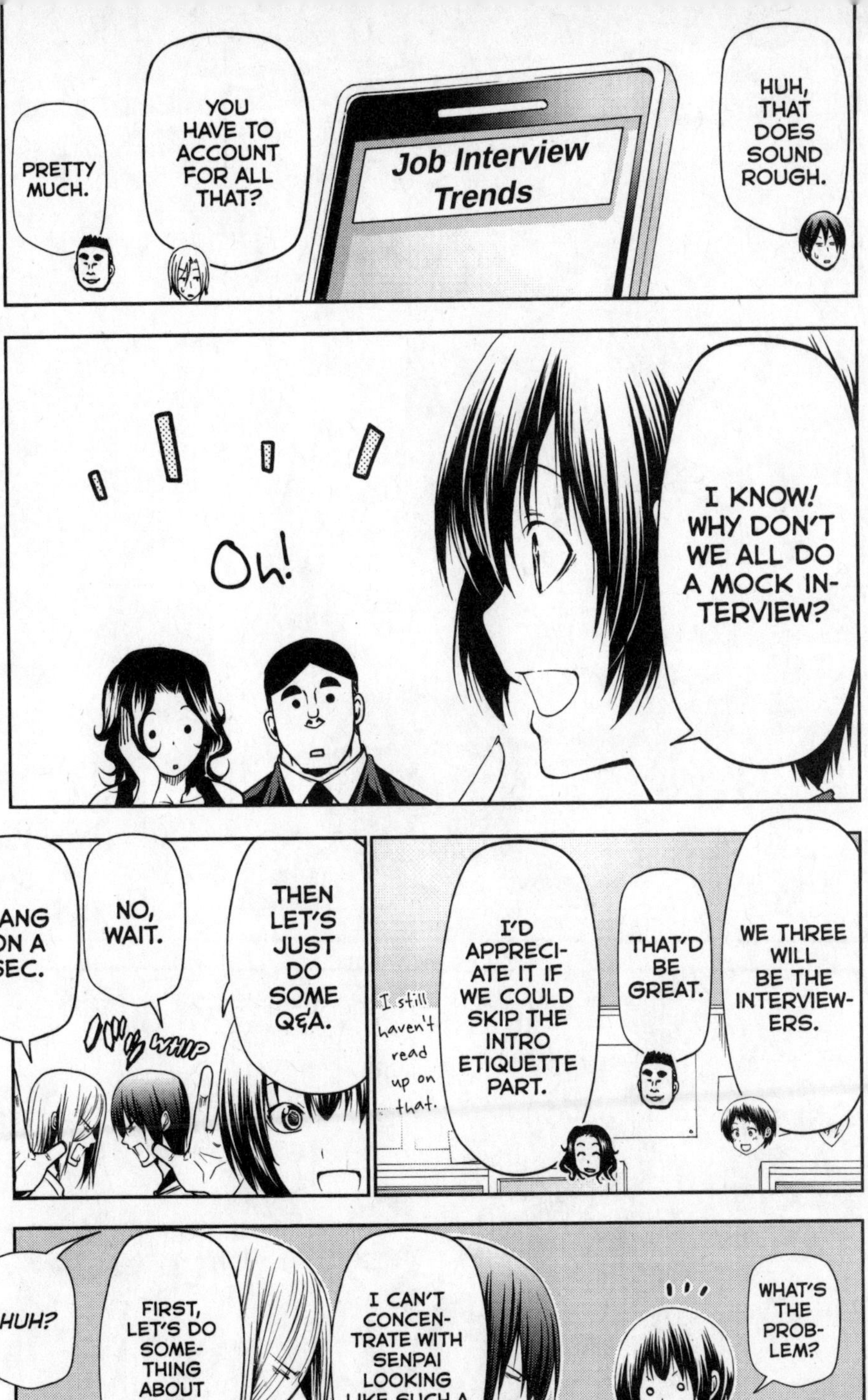
HUH, THAT DOES SOUND ROUGH.
Job Interview Trends
YOU HAVE TO ACCOUNT FOR ALL THAT?
PRETTY MUCH.
I KNOW! WHY DON'T WE ALL DO A MOCK INTERVIEW?
Oh!
WE THREE WILL BE THE INTERVIEWERS.
THAT'D BE GREAT.
I'D APPRECIATE IT IF WE COULD SKIP THE INTRO ETIQUETTE PART.
I still haven't read up on that.
THEN LET'S JUST DO SOME Q&A.
NO, WAIT.
WHIP
HANG ON A SEC.
WHAT'S THE PROBLEM?
I CAN'T CONCENTRATE WITH SENPAI LOOKING LIKE SUCH A CREEPER.
FIRST, LET'S DO SOMETHING ABOUT THAT.
HUH?

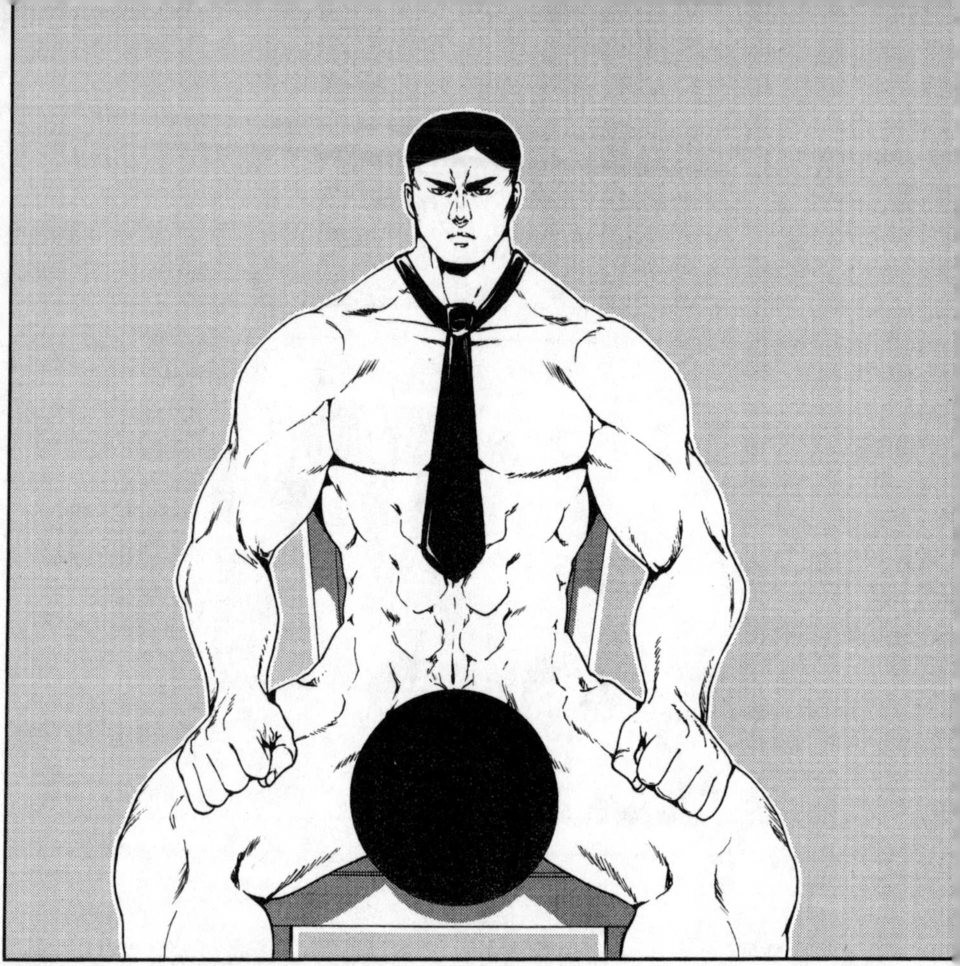

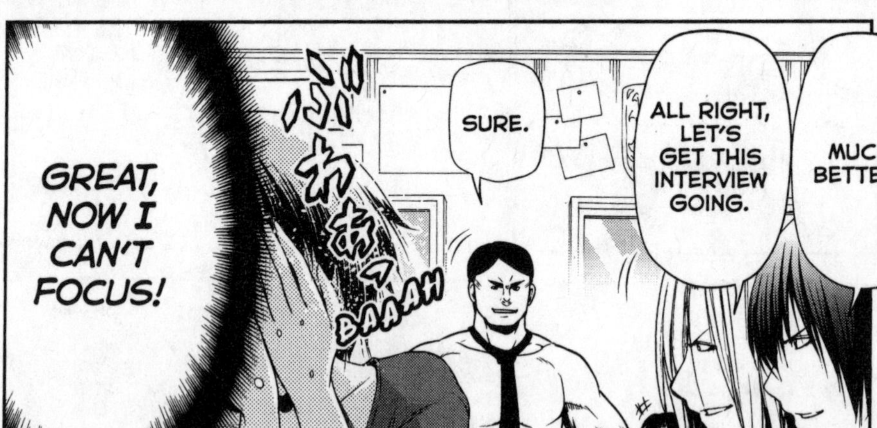
MUCH BETTER.
ALL RIGHT, LET'S GET THIS INTERVIEW GOING.
SURE.
ぶわぁ
BAAAAH
GREAT, NOW I CAN'T FOCUS!

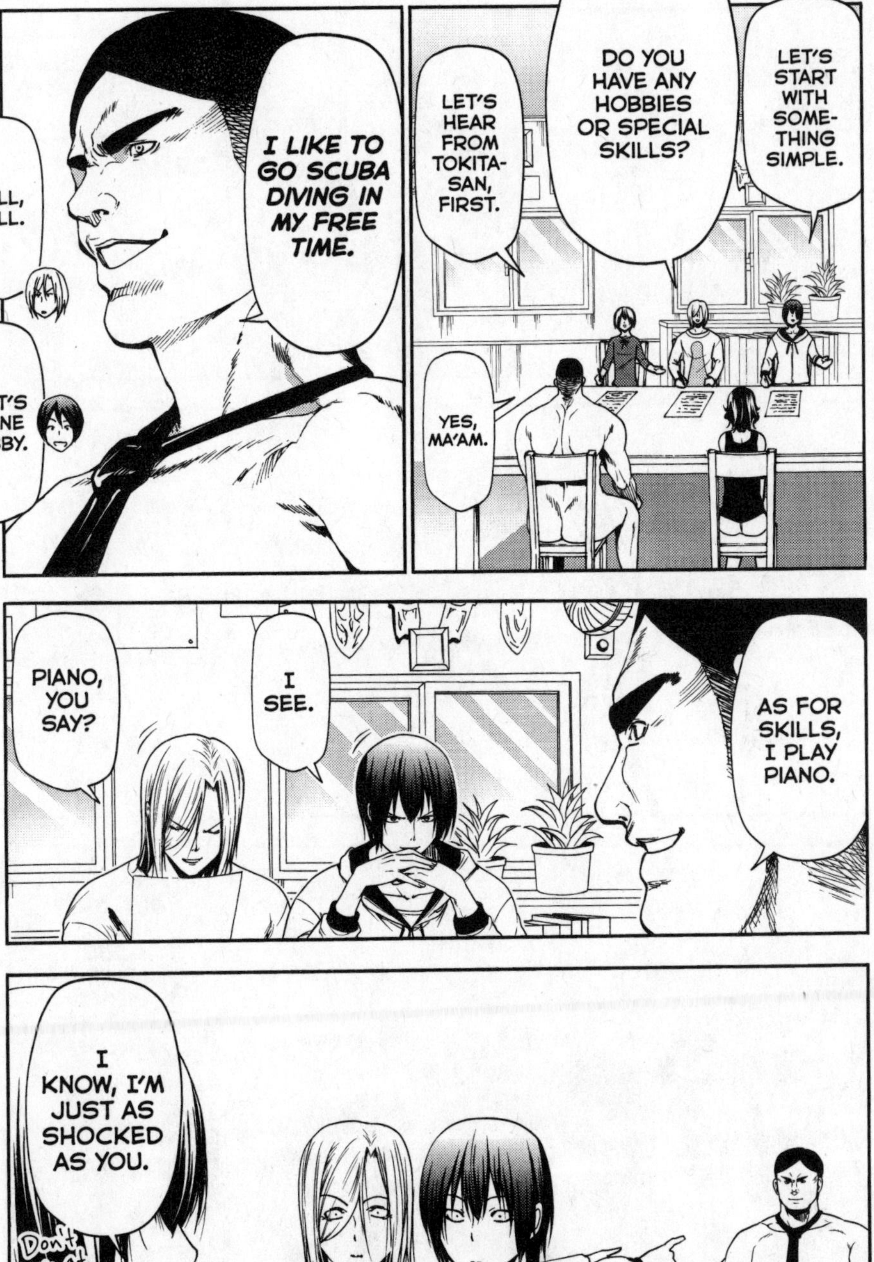
LET'S START WITH SOMETHING SIMPLE.
DO YOU HAVE ANY HOBBIES OR SPECIAL SKILLS?
LET'S HEAR FROM TOKITA-SAN, FIRST.
YES, MA'AM.
I LIKE TO GO SCUBA DIVING IN MY FREE TIME.
WELL, WELL.
THAT'S A FINE HOBBY.
AS FOR SKILLS, I PLAY PIANO.
I SEE.
PIANO, YOU SAY?
I KNOW, I'M JUST AS SHOCKED AS YOU.
Don't look at me like that.

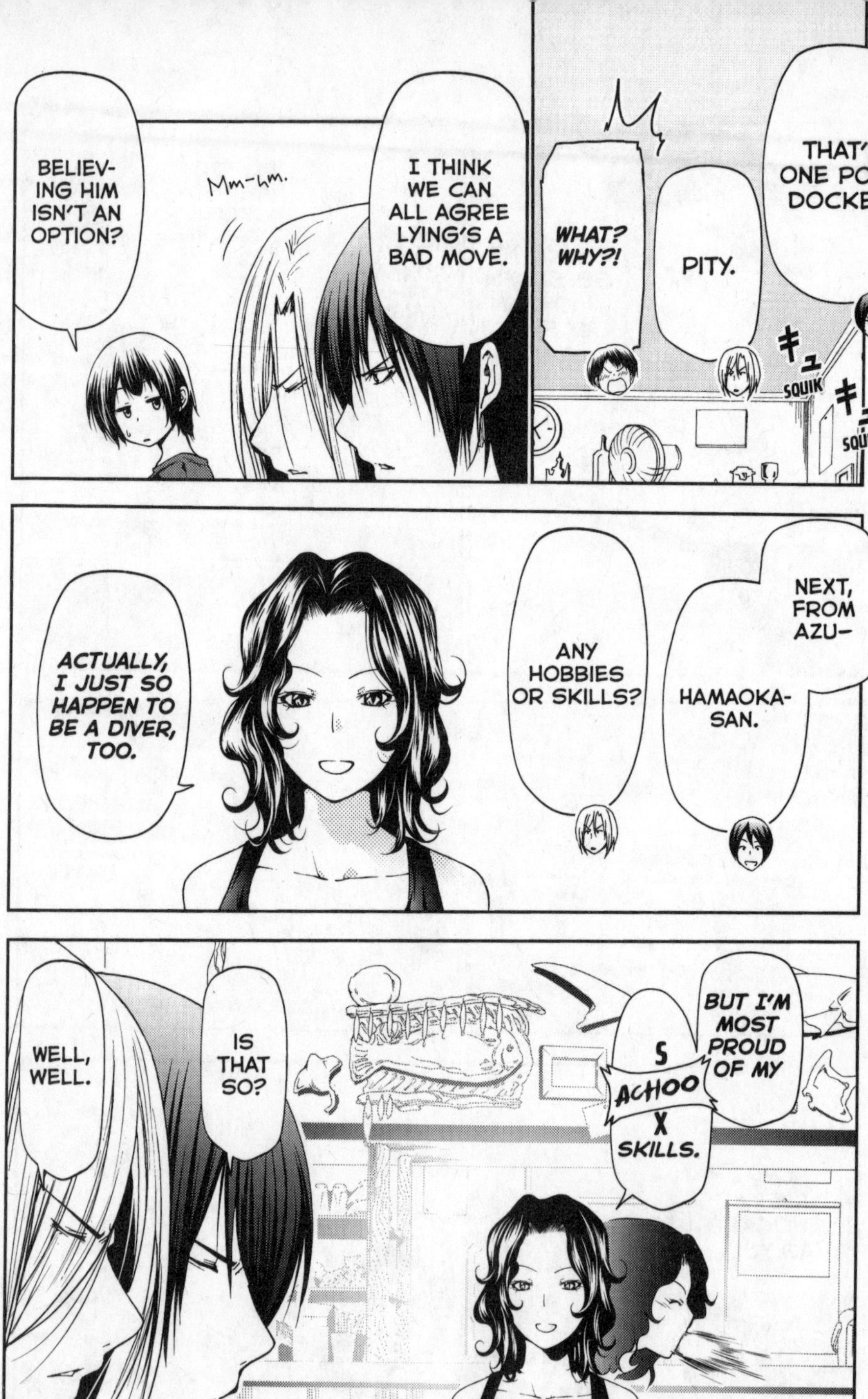
THAT'S ONE POINT DOCKED.
PITY.
WHAT? WHY?!
キュ SQUIK
キュ SQUIK
I THINK WE CAN ALL AGREE LYING'S A BAD MOVE.
Mm-hm.
BELIEV-ING HIM ISN'T AN OPTION?
NEXT, FROM AZU—
HAMAOKA-SAN.
ANY HOBBIES OR SKILLS?
ACTUALLY, I JUST SO HAPPEN TO BE A DIVER, TOO.
BUT I'M MOST PROUD OF MY
S
ACHOO
X
SKILLS.
IS THAT SO?
WELL, WELL.

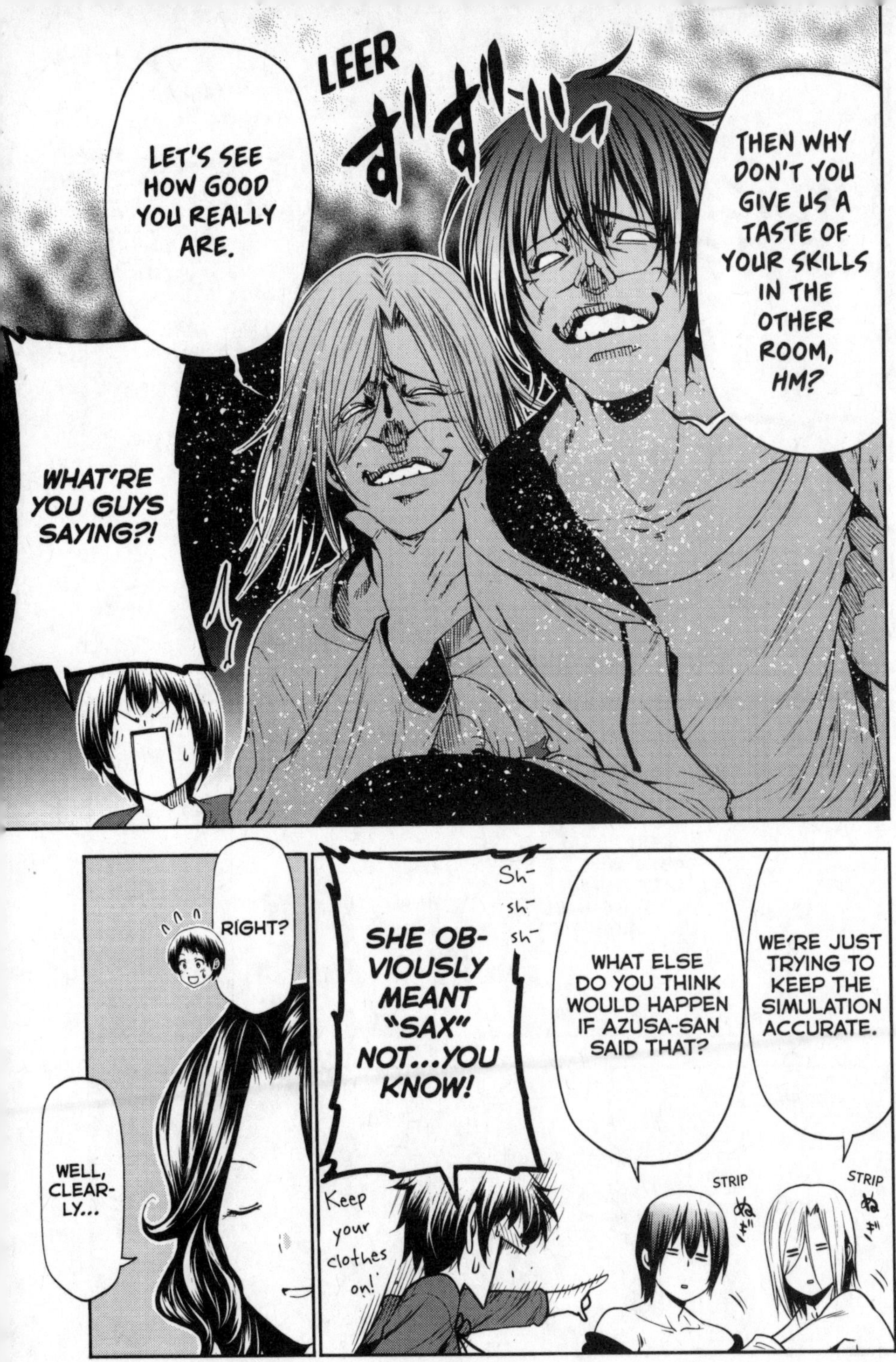
THEN WHY DON'T YOU GIVE US A TASTE OF YOUR SKILLS IN THE OTHER ROOM, HM?
LEER
LET'S SEE HOW GOOD YOU REALLY ARE.
WHAT'RE YOU GUYS SAYING?!
WE'RE JUST TRYING TO KEEP THE SIMULATION ACCURATE.
WHAT ELSE DO YOU THINK WOULD HAPPEN IF AZUSA-SAN SAID THAT?
STRIP ぬぎ
STRIP ぬぎ
Sh- sh- sh-
SHE OB-VIOUSLY MEANT "SAX" NOT...YOU KNOW!
Keep your clothes on!
RIGHT?
WELL, CLEAR-LY...

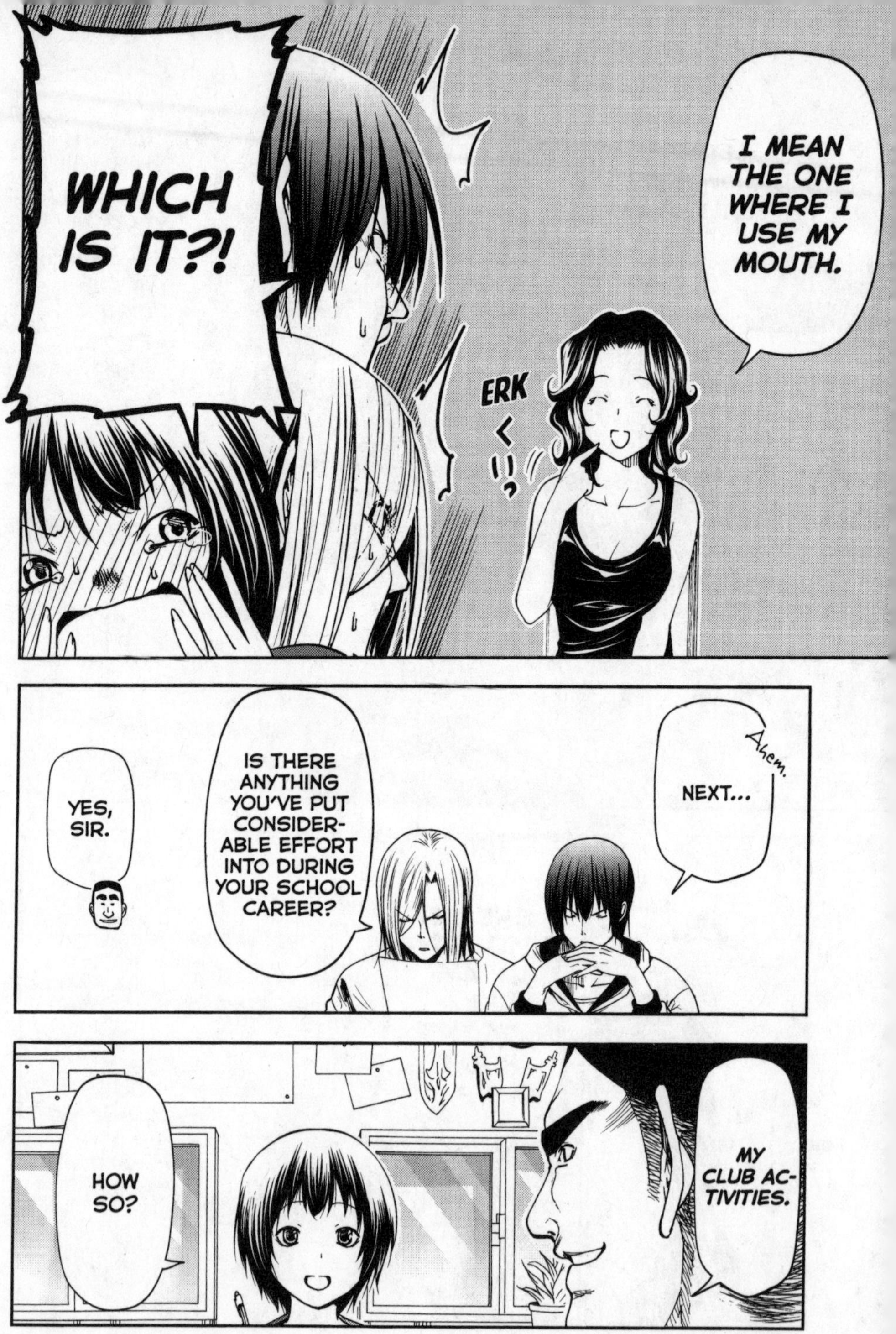
I MEAN THE ONE WHERE I USE MY MOUTH.
ERK
くッ
WHICH IS IT?!
Ahem.
NEXT...
IS THERE ANYTHING YOU'VE PUT CONSIDER-ABLE EFFORT INTO DURING YOUR SCHOOL CAREER?
YES, SIR.
MY CLUB AC-TIVITIES.
HOW SO?

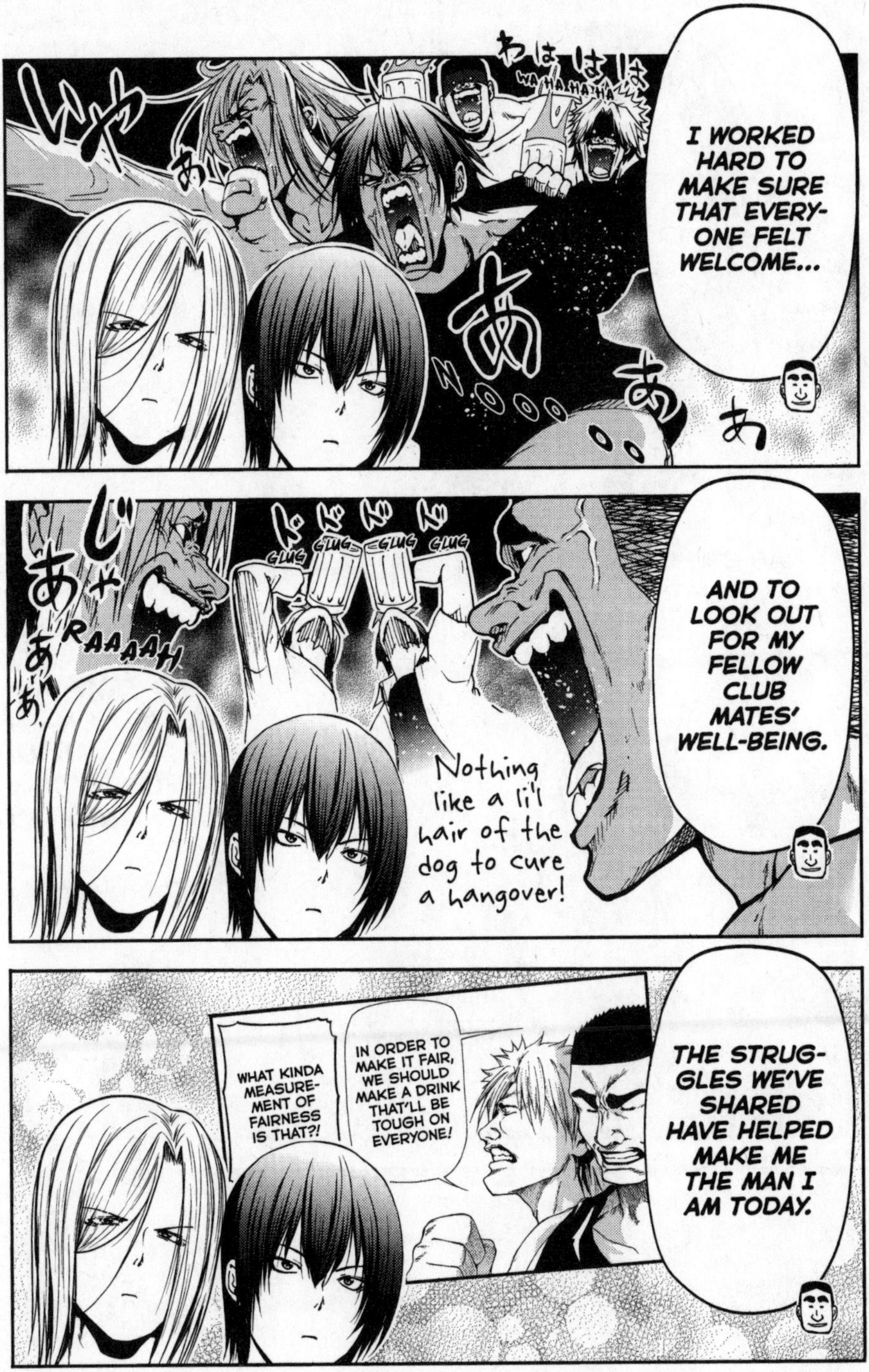
I WORKED HARD TO MAKE SURE THAT EVERY-ONE FELT WELCOME...
WA HA HA HA
NOOOO
AND TO LOOK OUT FOR MY FELLOW CLUB MATES' WELL-BEING.
GLUG GLUG GLUG GLUG
RAAAAH
Nothing like a li'l hair of the dog to cure a hangover!
THE STRUG-GLES WE'VE SHARED HAVE HELPED MAKE ME THE MAN I AM TODAY.
IN ORDER TO MAKE IT FAIR, WE SHOULD MAKE A DRINK THAT'LL BE TOUGH ON EVERYONE!
WHAT KINDA MEASURE-MENT OF FAIRNESS IS THAT?!

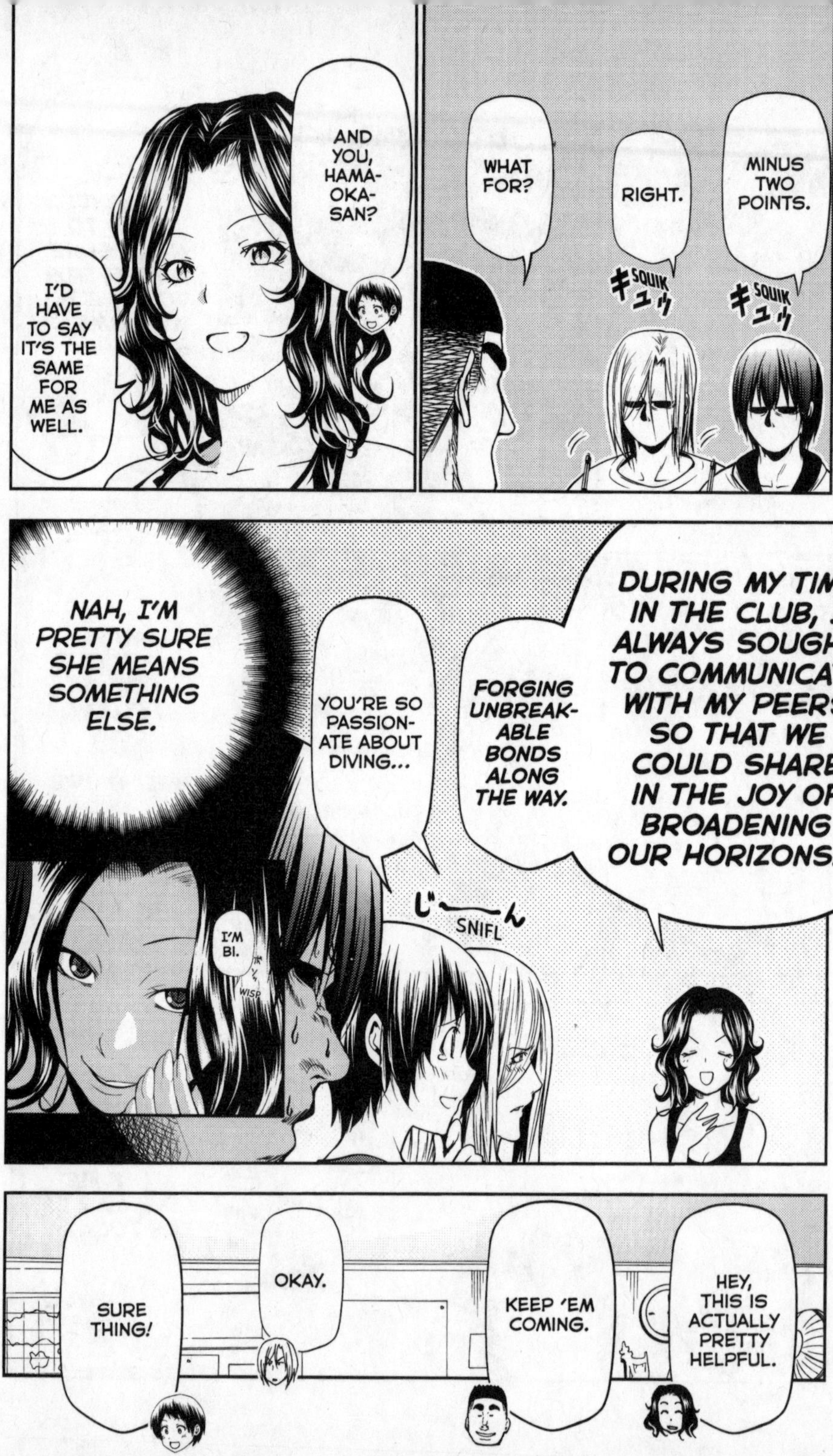
MINUS TWO POINTS.
キュッ SQUIK
RIGHT.
キュッ SQUIK
WHAT FOR?
AND YOU, HAMAOKA-SAN?
I'D HAVE TO SAY IT'S THE SAME FOR ME AS WELL.
DURING MY TIME IN THE CLUB, I ALWAYS SOUGHT TO COMMUNICATE WITH MY PEERS SO THAT WE COULD SHARE IN THE JOY OF BROADENING OUR HORIZONS...
FORGING UNBREAKABLE BONDS ALONG THE WAY.
YOU'RE SO PASSIONATE ABOUT DIVING...
じーん SNIFL
NAH, I'M PRETTY SURE SHE MEANS SOMETHING ELSE.
I'M BI.
WISP
HEY, THIS IS ACTUALLY PRETTY HELPFUL.
KEEP 'EM COMING.
OKAY.
SURE THING!

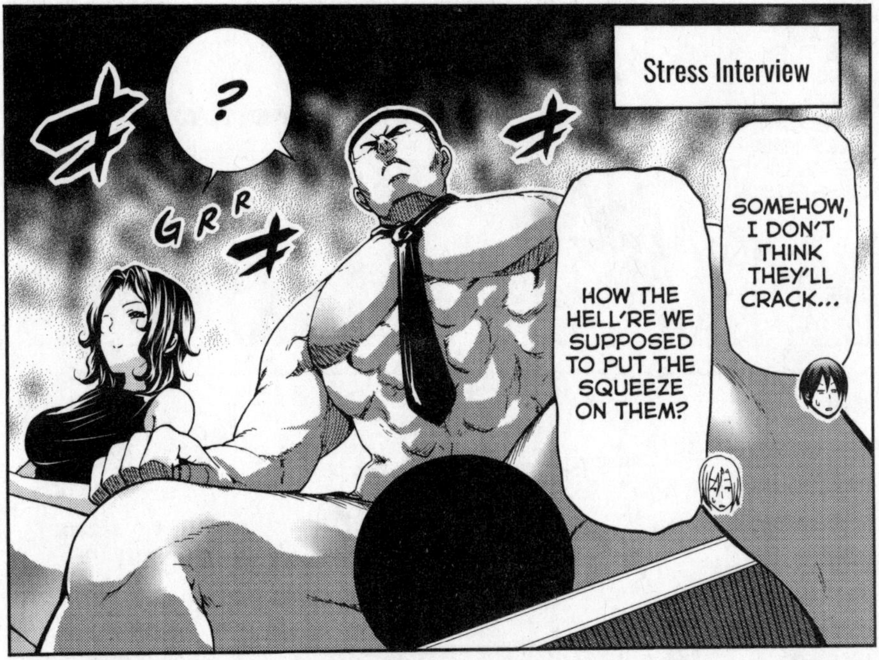
Stress Interview
SOMEHOW, I DON'T THINK THEY'LL CRACK...
HOW THE HELL'RE WE SUPPOSED TO PUT THE SQUEEZE ON THEM?
?
GRR

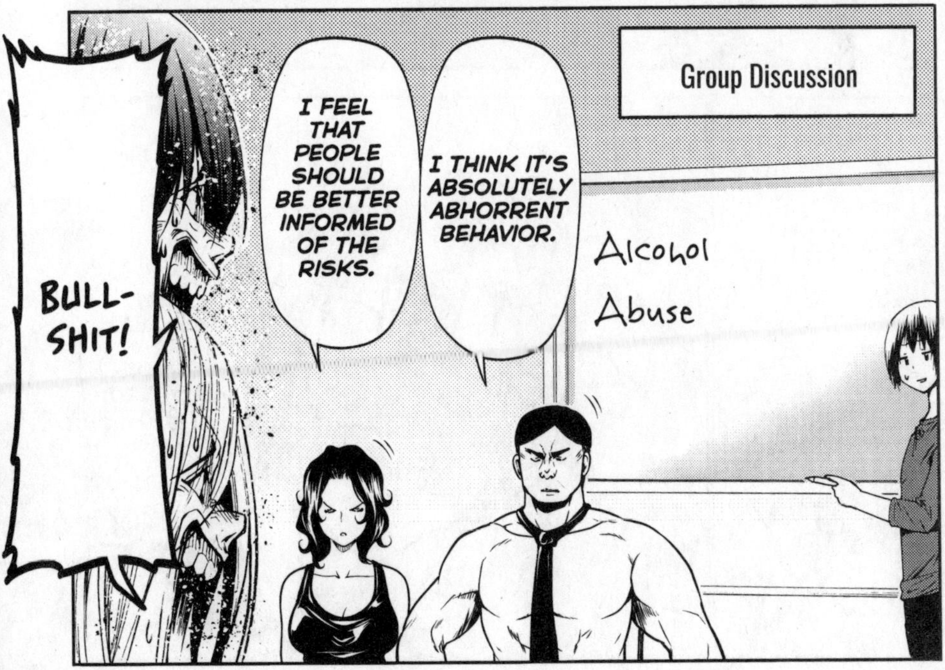
Group Discussion
Alcohol Abuse
I THINK IT'S ABSOLUTELY ABHORRENT BEHAVIOR.
I FEEL THAT PEOPLE SHOULD BE BETTER INFORMED OF THE RISKS.
BULL-SHIT!

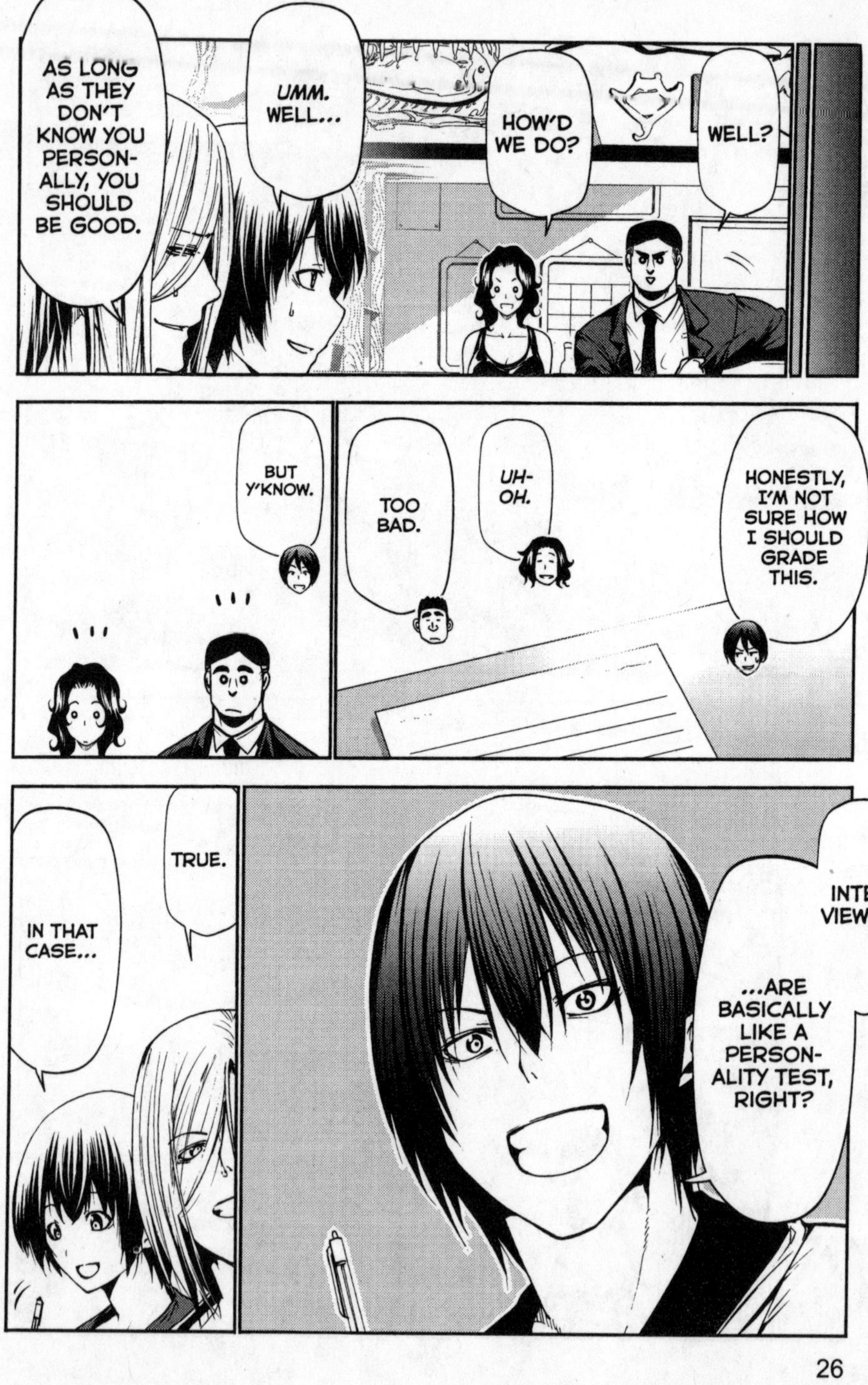
WELL?
HOW'D WE DO?
UMM. WELL...
AS LONG AS THEY DON'T KNOW YOU PERSONALLY, YOU SHOULD BE GOOD.
HONESTLY, I'M NOT SURE HOW I SHOULD GRADE THIS.
UH-OH.
TOO BAD.
BUT Y'KNOW.
INTERVIEWS...
...ARE BASICALLY LIKE A PERSONALITY TEST, RIGHT?
TRUE.
IN THAT CASE...

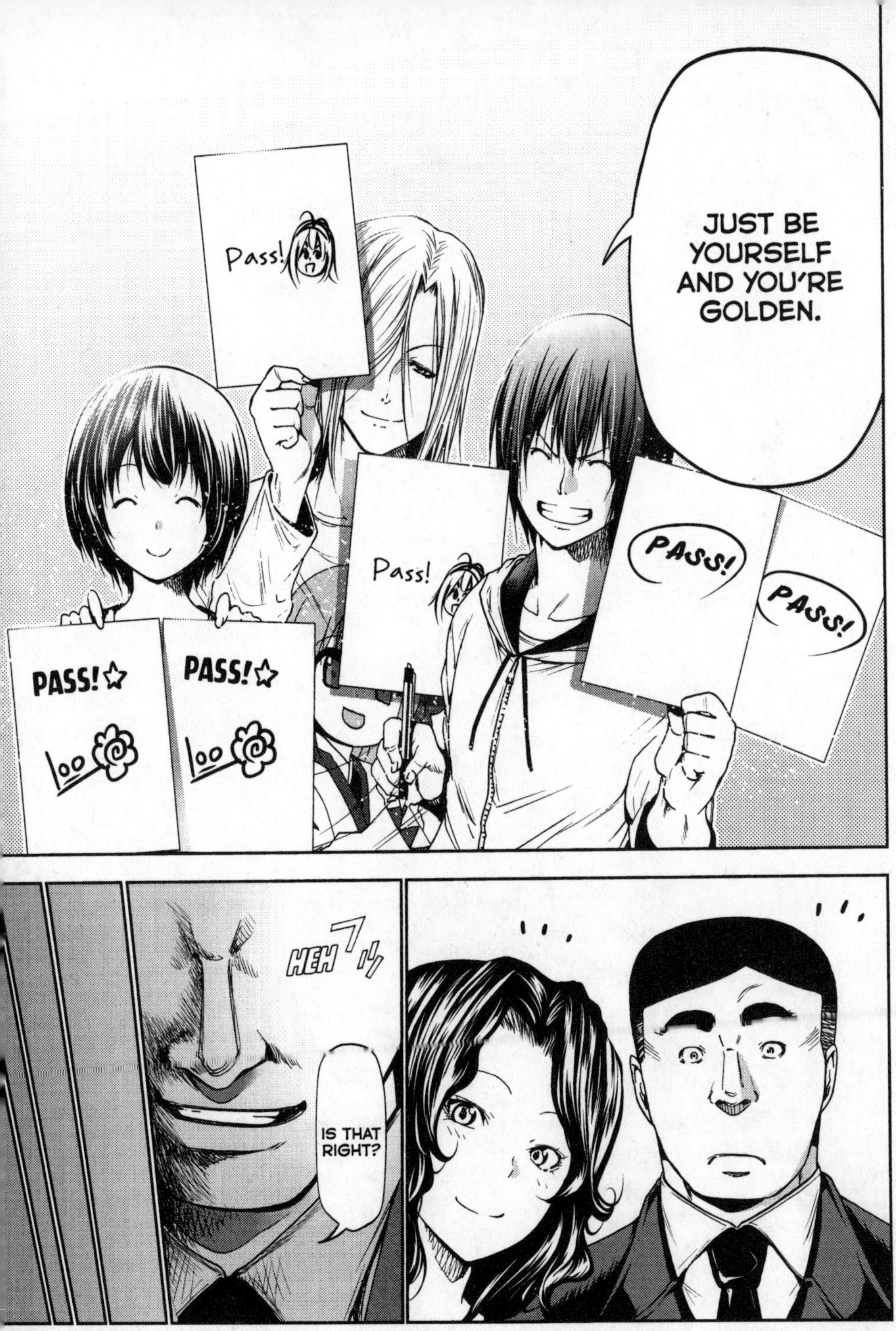
JUST BE YOURSELF AND YOU'RE GOLDEN.
PASS!
PASS!
Pass!
Pass!
PASS!☆
PASS!☆
HEH
IS THAT RIGHT?

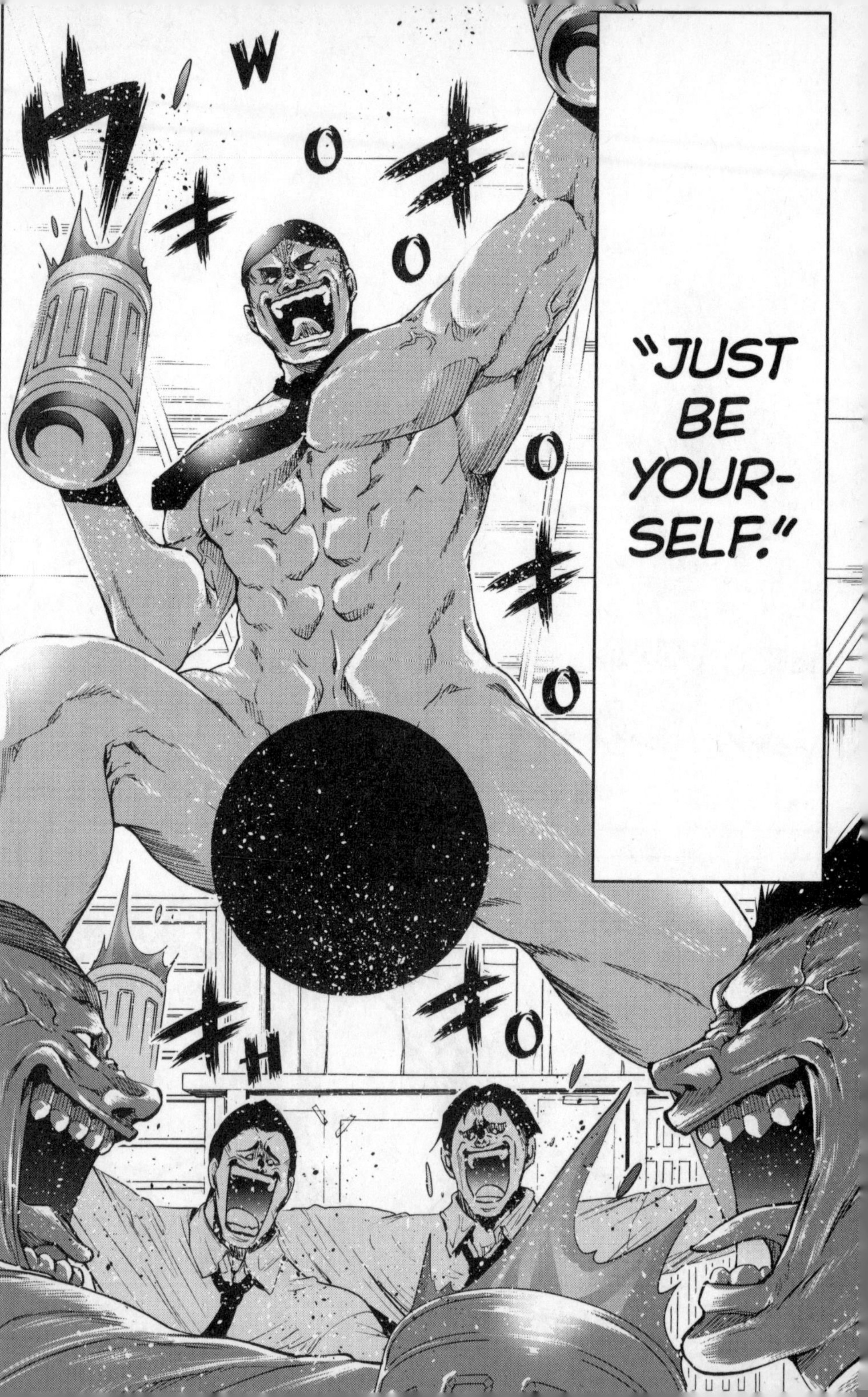
"JUST BE YOURSELF."
WOOOO
HO

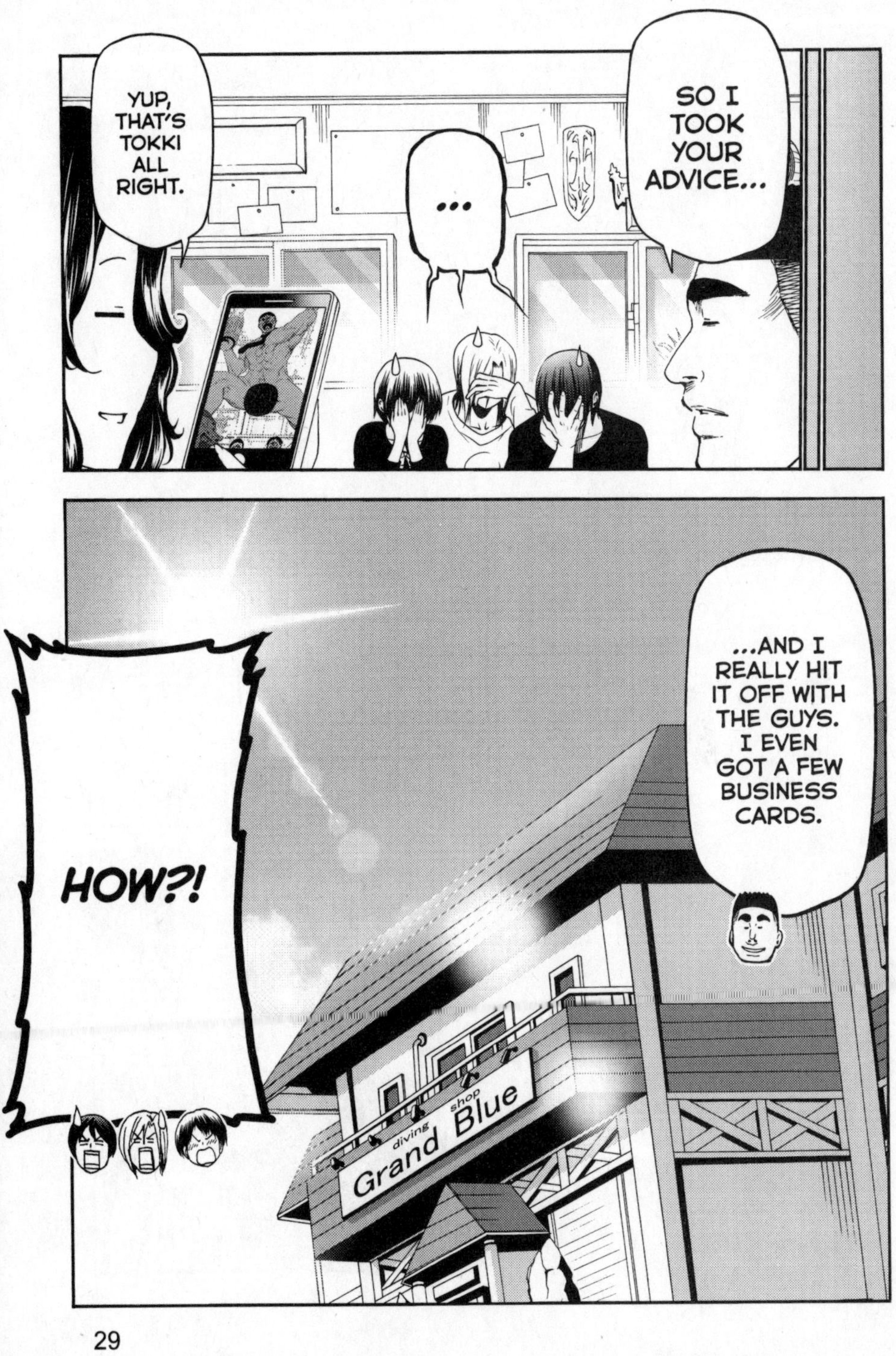
SO I TOOK YOUR ADVICE...
...
YUP, THAT'S TOKKI ALL RIGHT.
...AND I REALLY HIT IT OFF WITH THE GUYS. I EVEN GOT A FEW BUSINESS CARDS.
diving shop Grand Blue
HOW?!

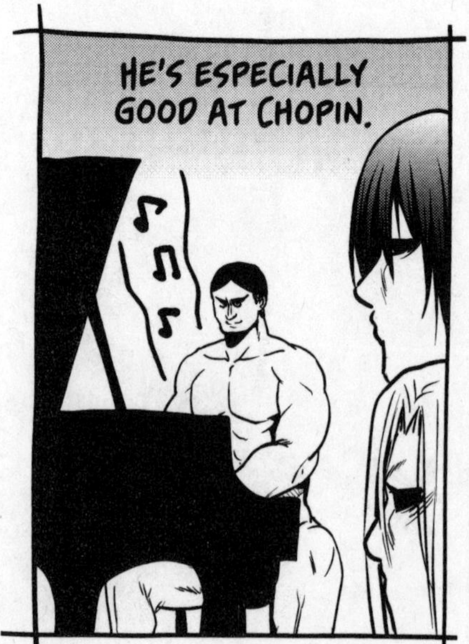
HE'S ESPECIALLY GOOD AT CHOPIN.

Ch. 59: Mixer-Round Two

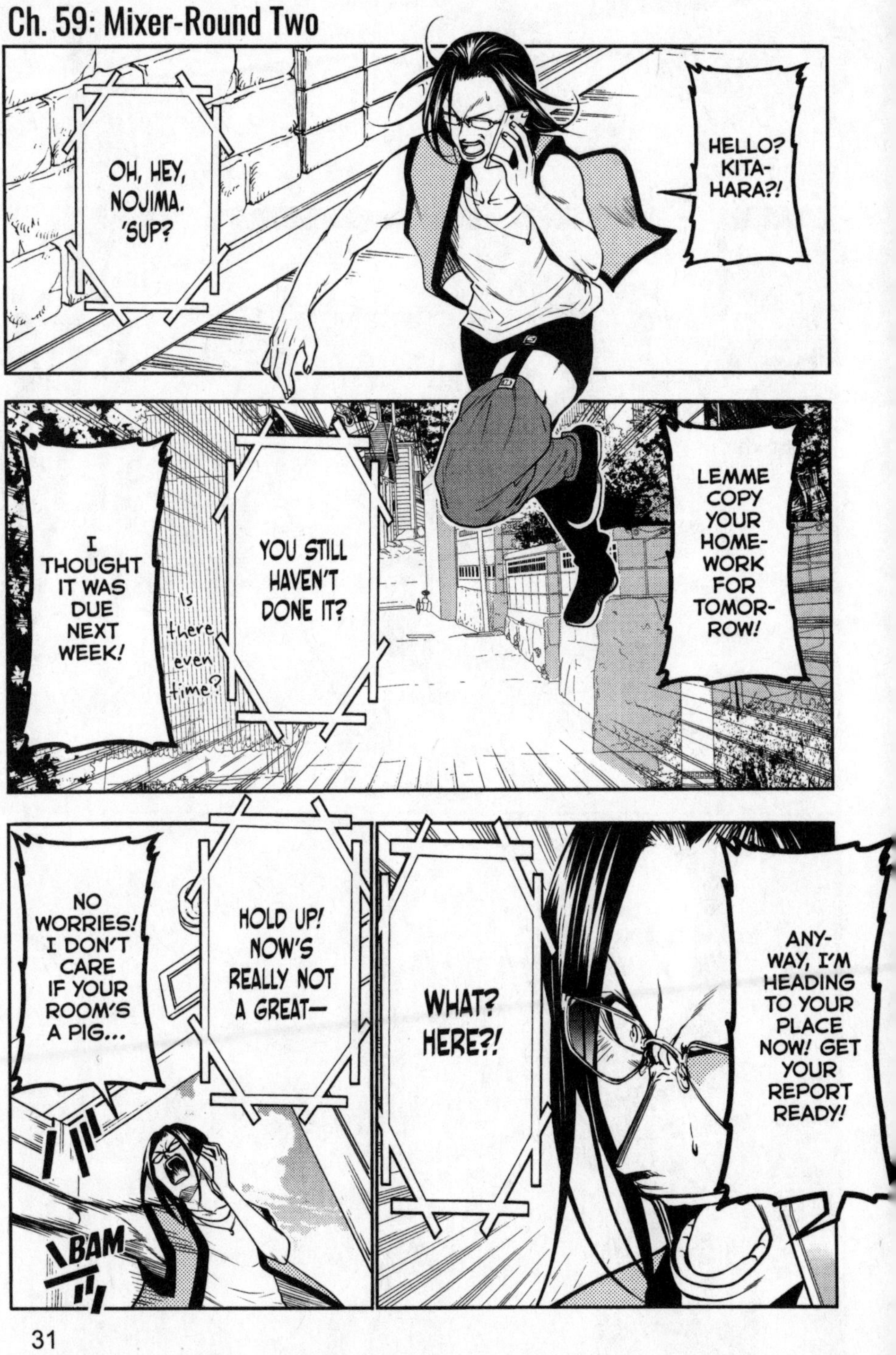
HELLO? KITA-HARA?!
OH, HEY, NOJIMA. 'SUP?
LEMME COPY YOUR HOMEWORK FOR TOMORROW!
YOU STILL HAVEN'T DONE IT?
Is there even time?
I THOUGHT IT WAS DUE NEXT WEEK!
ANYWAY, I'M HEADING TO YOUR PLACE NOW! GET YOUR REPORT READY!
WHAT? HERE?!
HOLD UP! NOW'S REALLY NOT A GREAT—
NO WORRIES! I DON'T CARE IF YOUR ROOM'S A PIG...
BAM

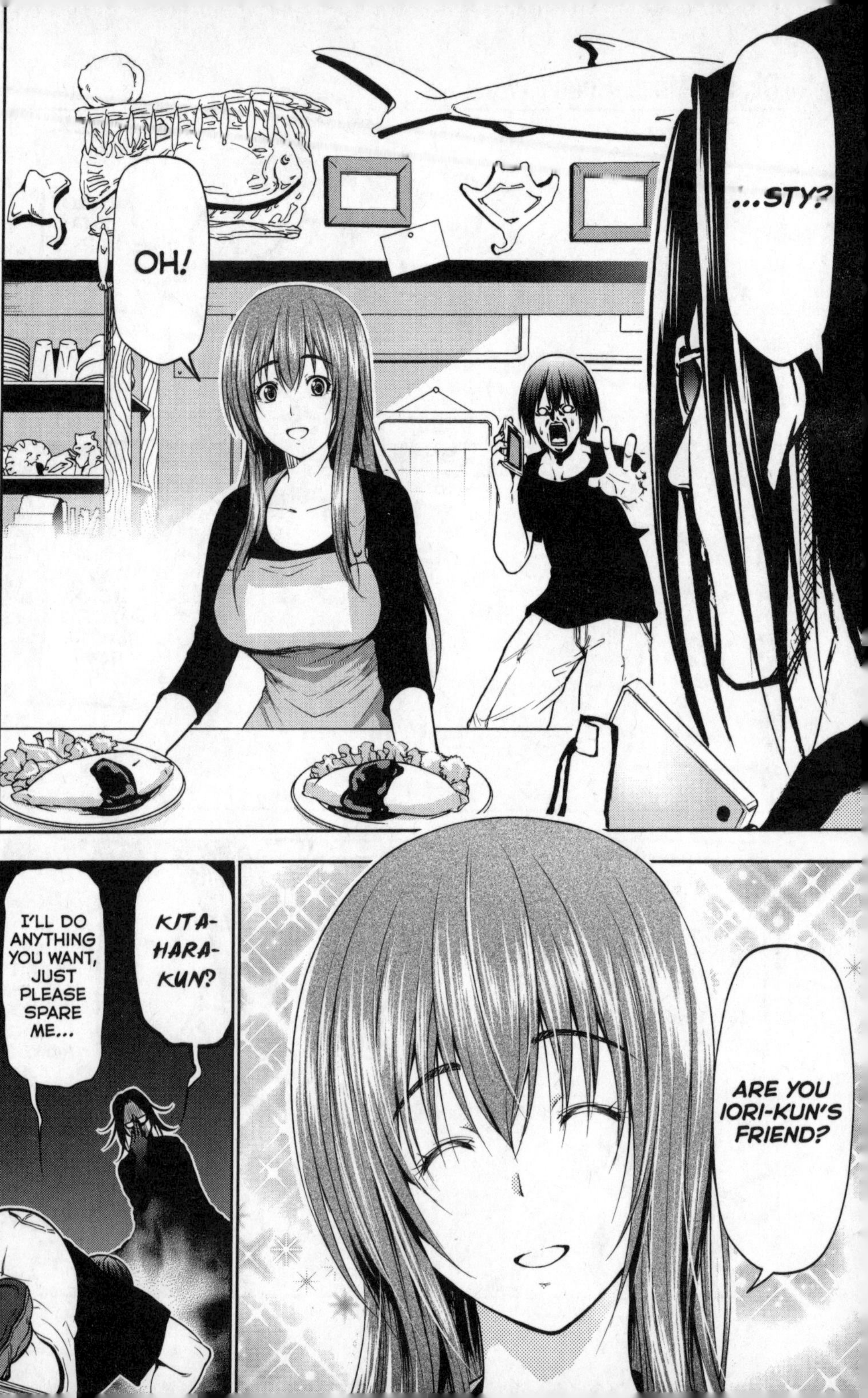
...STY?
OH!
ARE YOU IORI-KUN'S FRIEND?
KITA-HARA-KUN?
I'LL DO ANYTHING YOU WANT, JUST PLEASE SPARE ME...

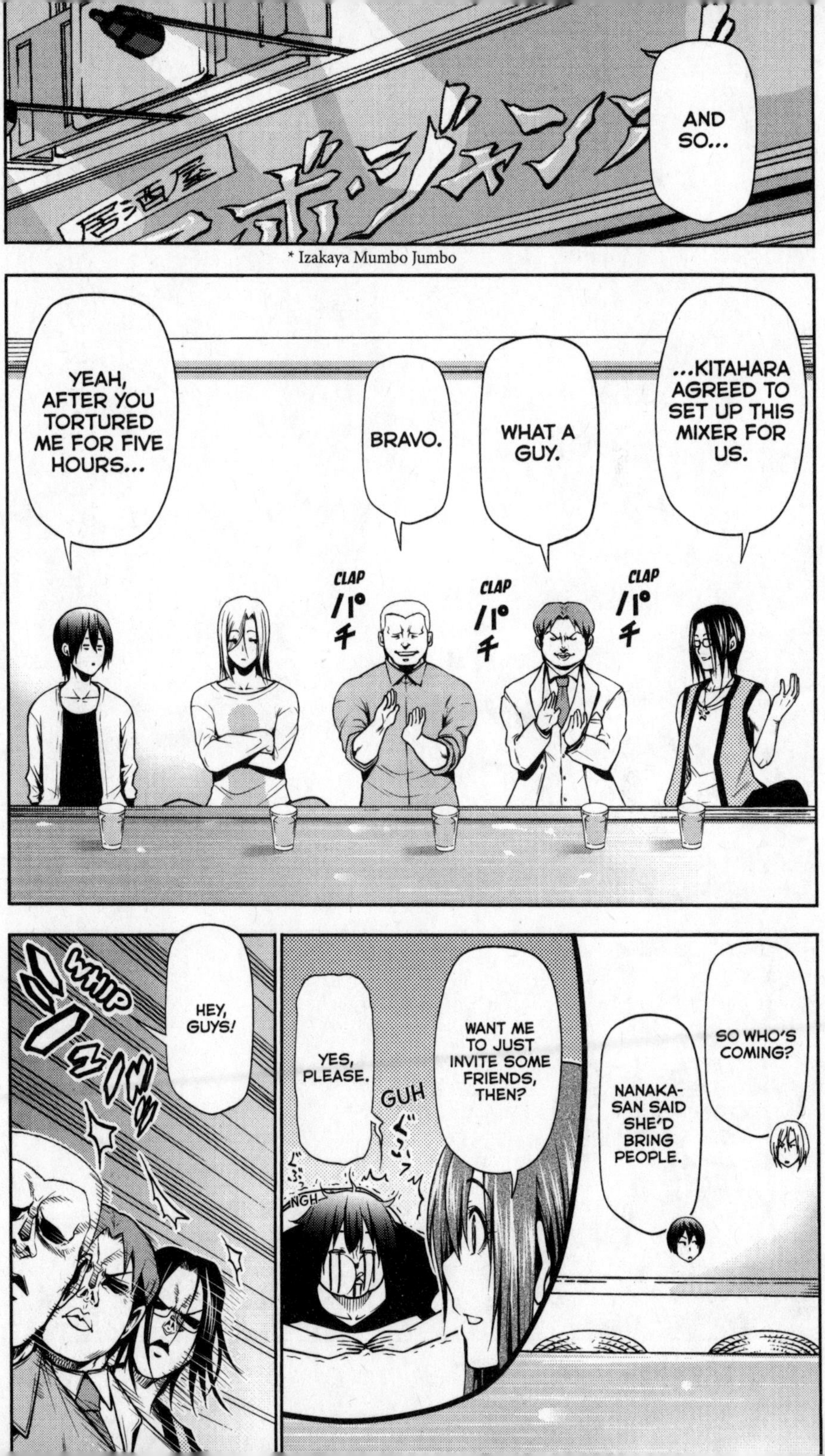
AND SO...
...KITAHARA AGREED TO SET UP THIS MIXER FOR US.
WHAT A GUY.
BRAVO.
YEAH, AFTER YOU TORTURED ME FOR FIVE HOURS...
CLAP
パチ
CLAP
パチ
CLAP
パチ
SO WHO'S COMING?
NANAKA-SAN SAID SHE'D BRING PEOPLE.
WANT ME TO JUST INVITE SOME FRIENDS, THEN?
YES, PLEASE.
GUH
NGH
HEY, GUYS!
WHIP

* Izakaya Mumbo Jumbo

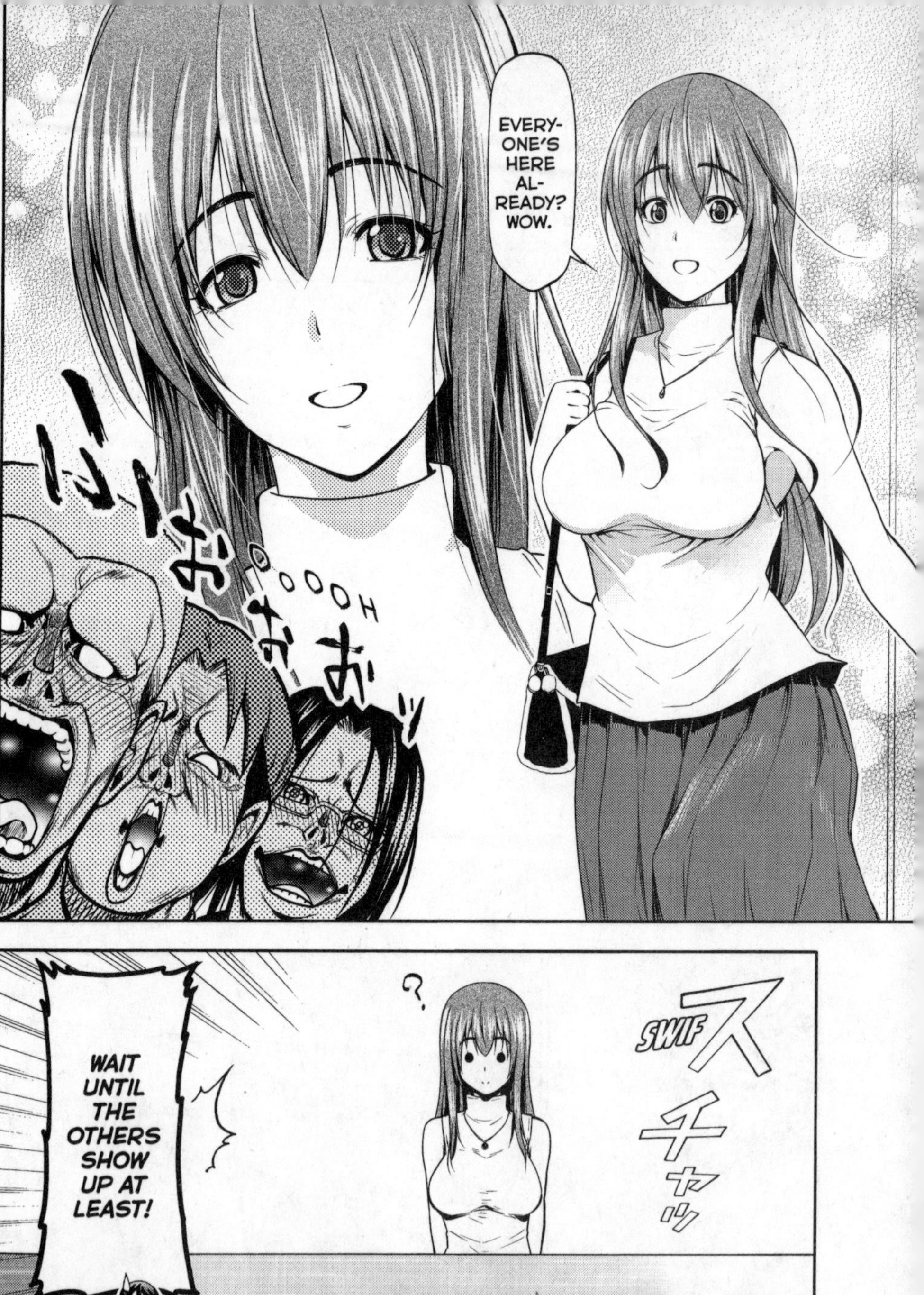
EVERY-ONE'S HERE AL-READY? WOW.
O...OOOH
?
SWIF
スチャッ
WAIT UNTIL THE OTHERS SHOW UP AT LEAST!

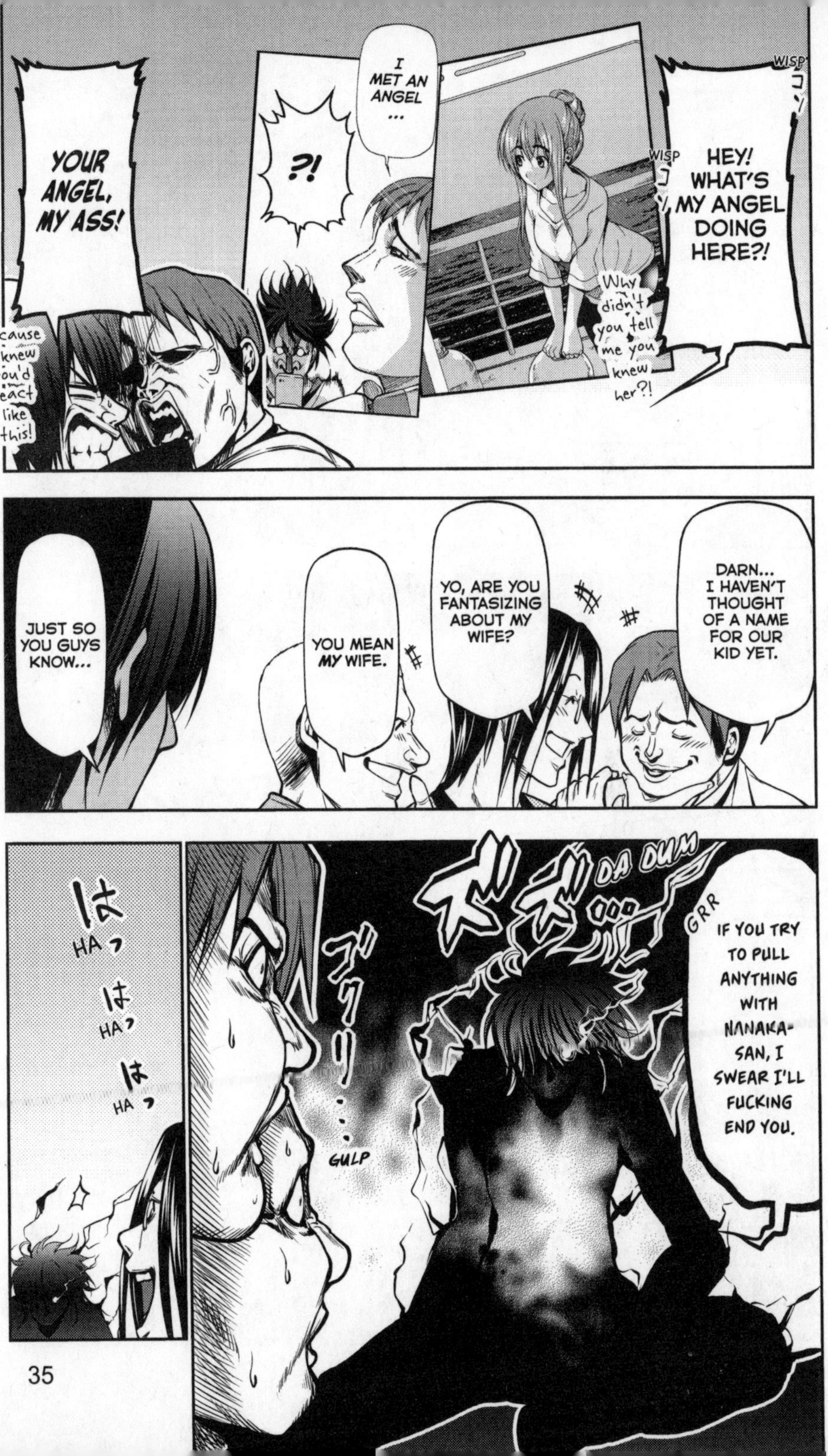

WISP
WISP
HEY! WHAT'S MY ANGEL DOING HERE?!
Why didn't you tell me you knew her?!
I MET AN ANGEL ...
?!
YOUR ANGEL, MY ASS!
Because I knew you'd react like this!
DARN... I HAVEN'T THOUGHT OF A NAME FOR OUR KID YET.
YO, ARE YOU FANTASIZING ABOUT MY WIFE?
YOU MEAN MY WIFE.
JUST SO YOU GUYS KNOW...
IF YOU TRY TO PULL ANYTHING WITH NANAKA-SAN, I SWEAR I'LL FUCKING END YOU.
GRR
DA DUM
GULP
HA
HA
HA

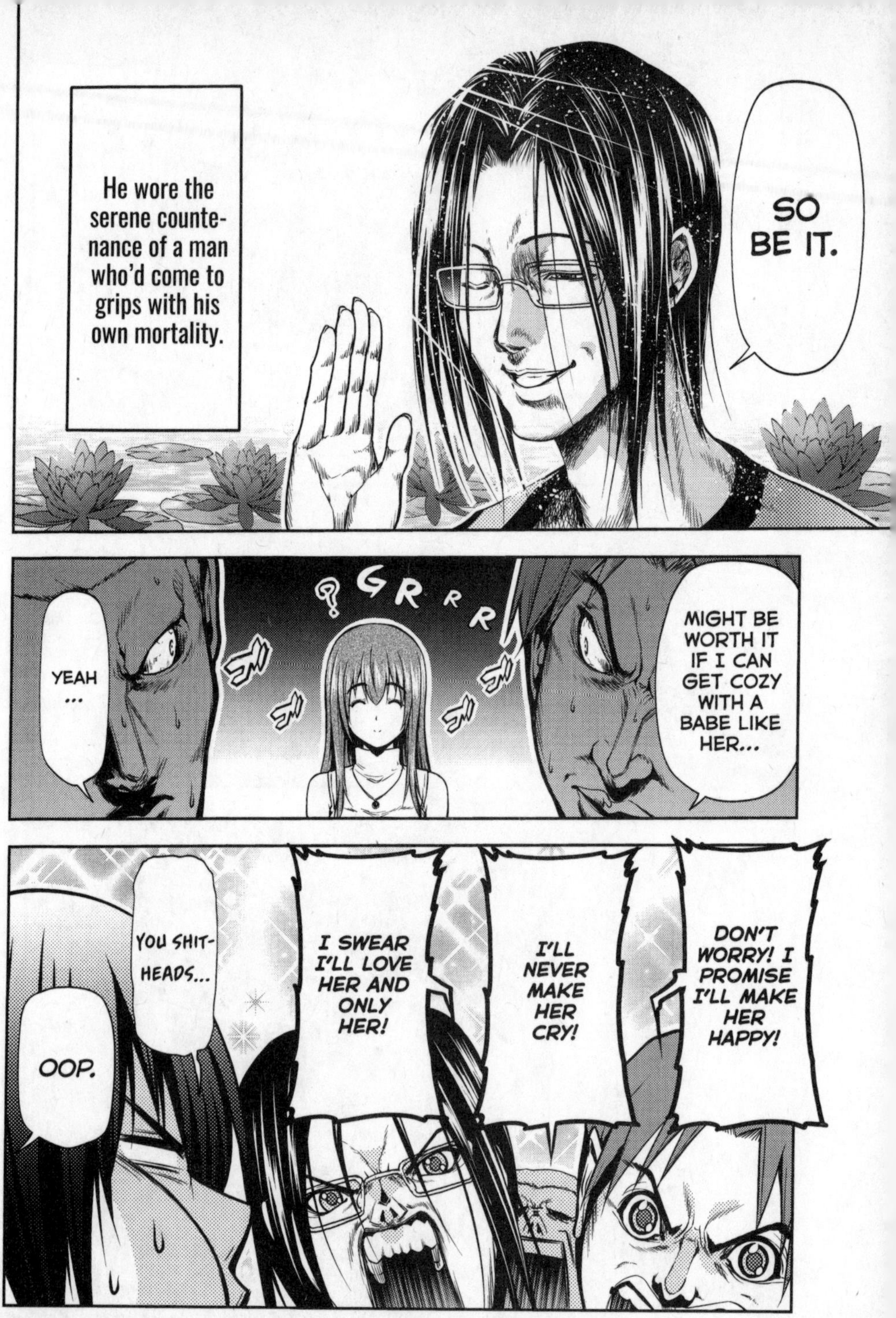
SO BE IT.
He wore the serene countenance of a man who'd come to grips with his own mortality.
MIGHT BE WORTH IT IF I CAN GET COZY WITH A BABE LIKE HER...
?
GRRR
YEAH ...
DON'T WORRY! I PROMISE I'LL MAKE HER HAPPY!
I'LL NEVER MAKE HER CRY!
I SWEAR I'LL LOVE HER AND ONLY HER!
YOU SHIT-HEADS...
OOP.

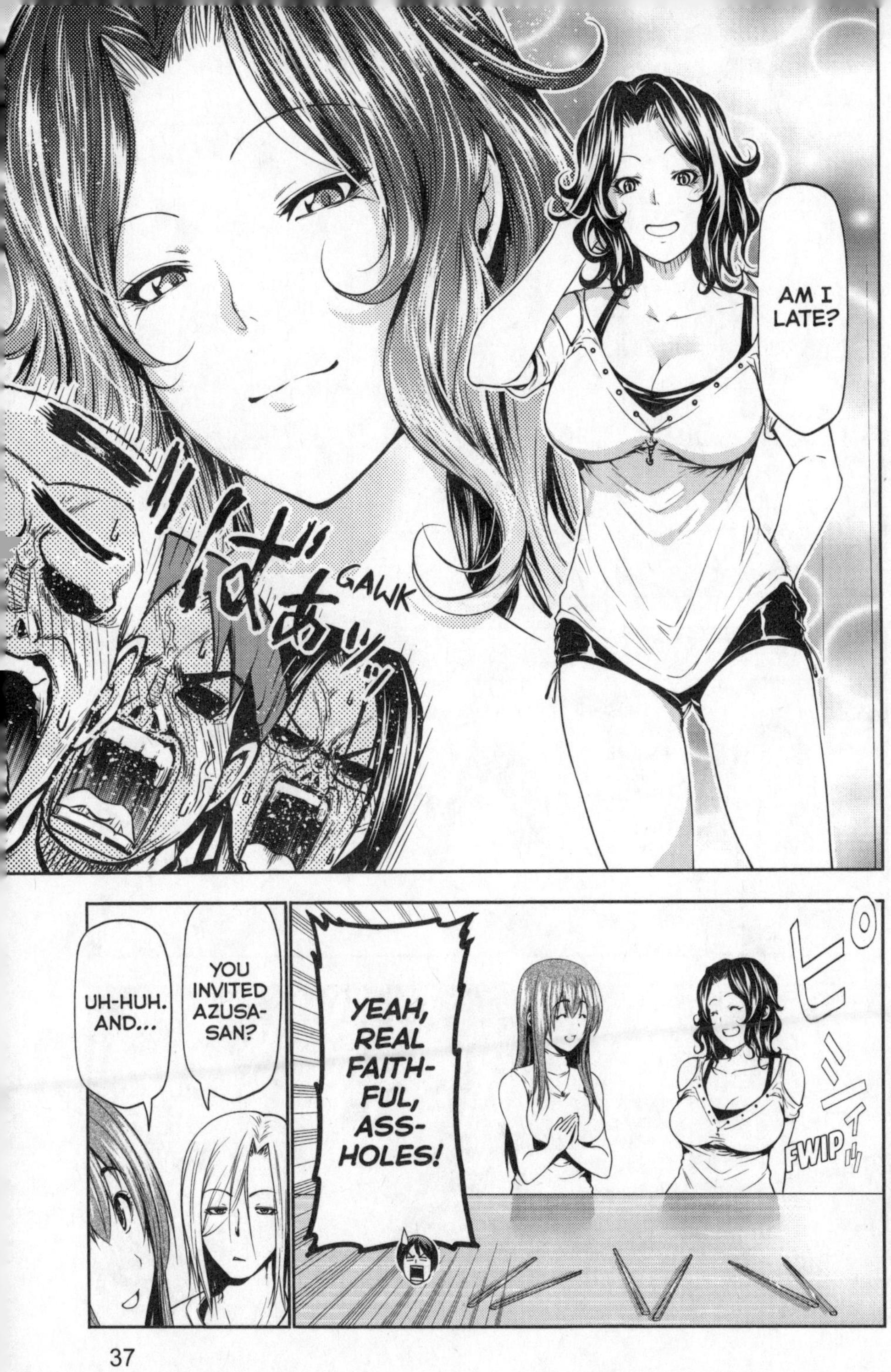
AM I LATE?
GAWK
FWIP
YEAH, REAL FAITH-FUL, ASS-HOLES!
YOU INVITED AZUSA-SAN?
UH-HUH. AND...

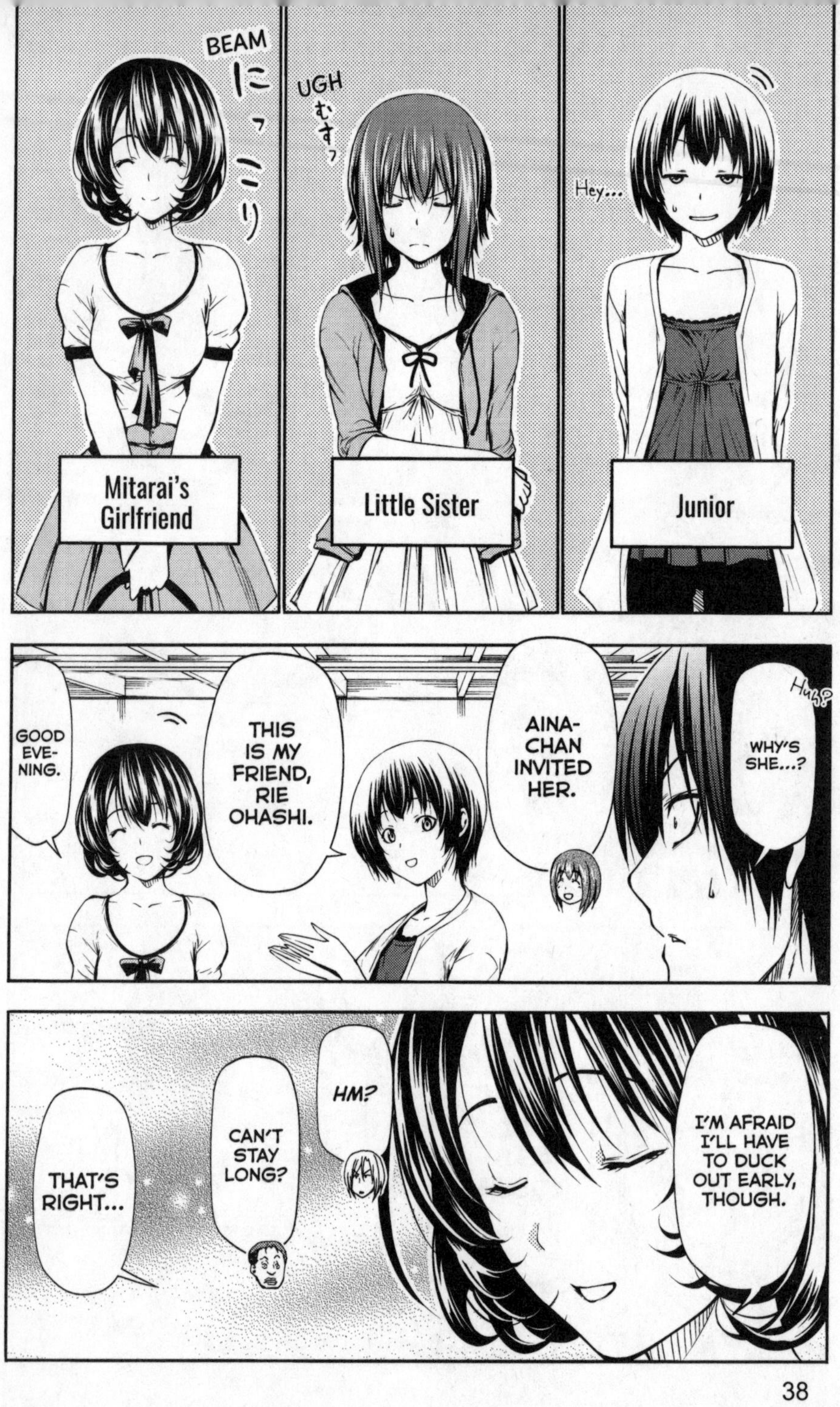
Hey...
Junior
UGH
むすっ
Little Sister
BEAM
にっこり
Mitarai's Girlfriend
Huh?
WHY'S SHE...?
AINA-CHAN INVITED HER.
THIS IS MY FRIEND, RIE OHASHI.
GOOD EVENING.
I'M AFRAID I'LL HAVE TO DUCK OUT EARLY, THOUGH.
HM?
CAN'T STAY LONG?
THAT'S RIGHT...

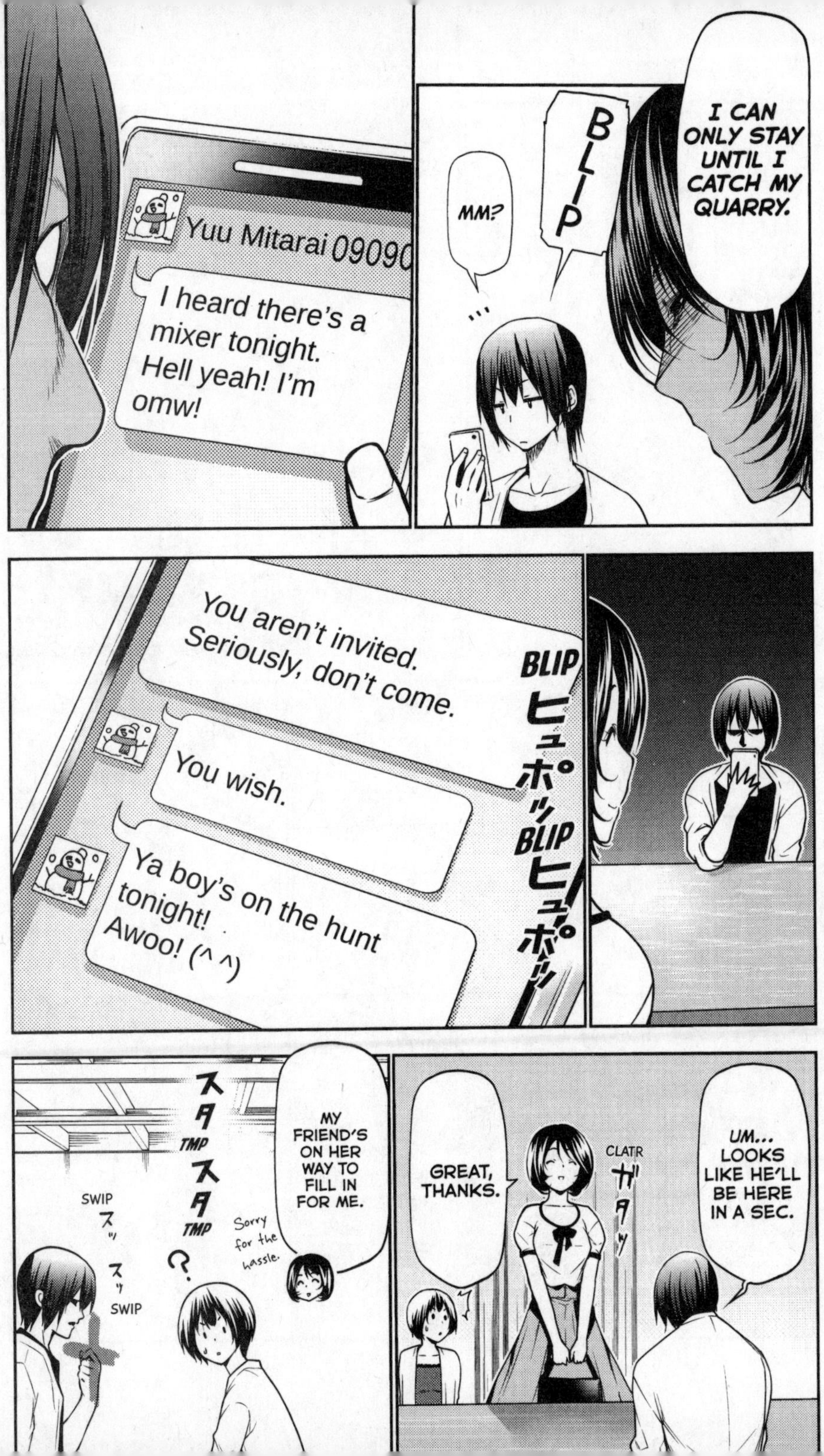
I CAN ONLY STAY UNTIL I CATCH MY QUARRY.
BLIP
MM?
...
Yuu Mitarai 09090
I heard there's a mixer tonight. Hell yeah! I'm omw!
BLIP
ヒュポッ
BLIP
ヒュポッ
You aren't invited. Seriously, don't come.
You wish.
Ya boy's on the hunt tonight! Awoo! (^ ^)
UM... LOOKS LIKE HE'LL BE HERE IN A SEC.
CLATR
ガタッ
GREAT, THANKS.
MY FRIEND'S ON HER WAY TO FILL IN FOR ME.
Sorry for the hassle.
スタ
TMP
スタ
TMP
?
SWIP
スッ
スッ
SWIP

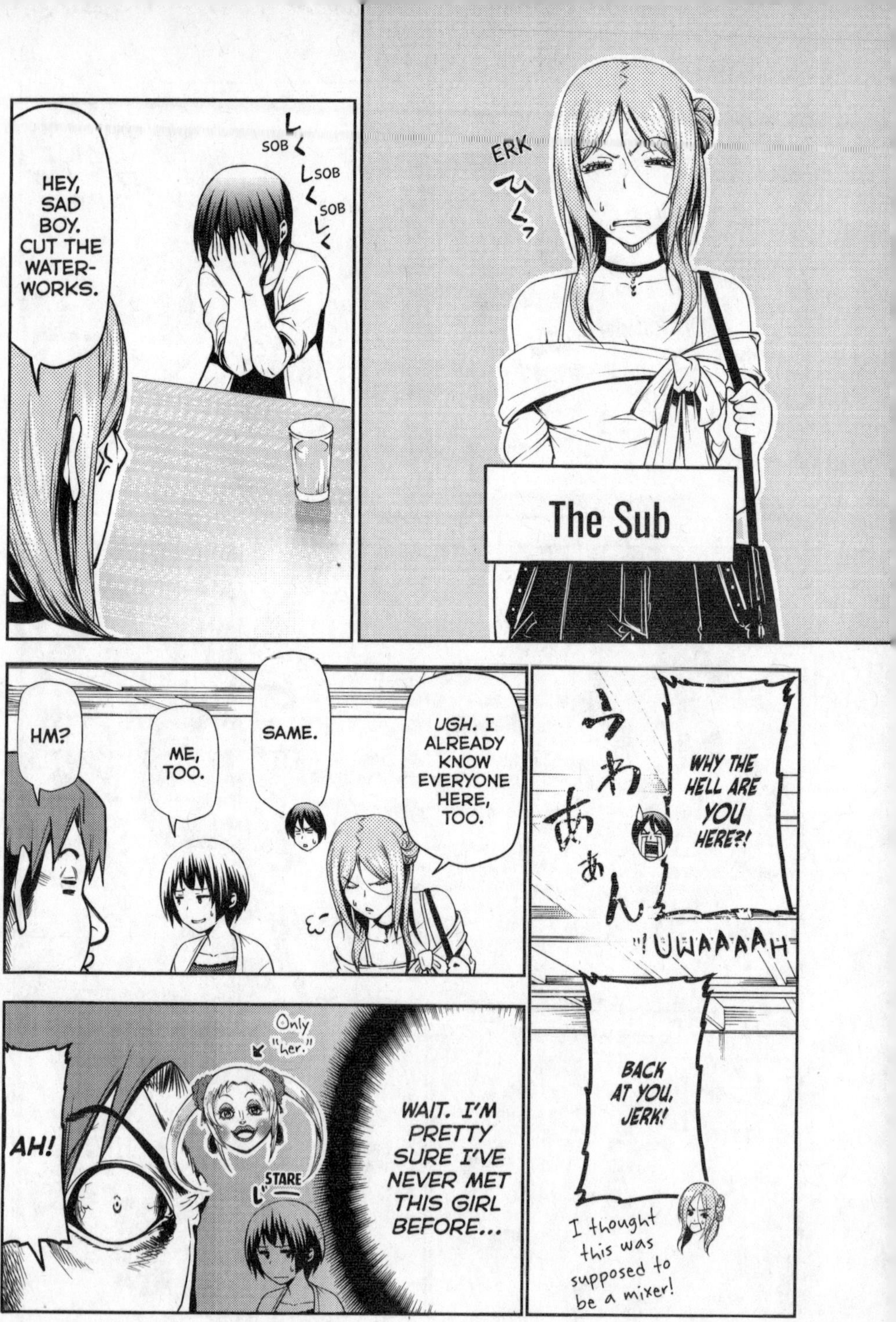
ERK
ひくっ
The Sub
SOB しく
SOB しく
SOB しく
HEY, SAD BOY. CUT THE WATER-WORKS.
うわぁあん
UWAAAAH!
WHY THE HELL ARE YOU HERE?!
BACK AT YOU, JERK!
I thought this was supposed to be a mixer!
UGH. I ALREADY KNOW EVERYONE HERE, TOO.
SAME.
ME, TOO.
HM?
WAIT. I'M PRETTY SURE I'VE NEVER MET THIS GIRL BEFORE...
Only "her."
STARE
AH!

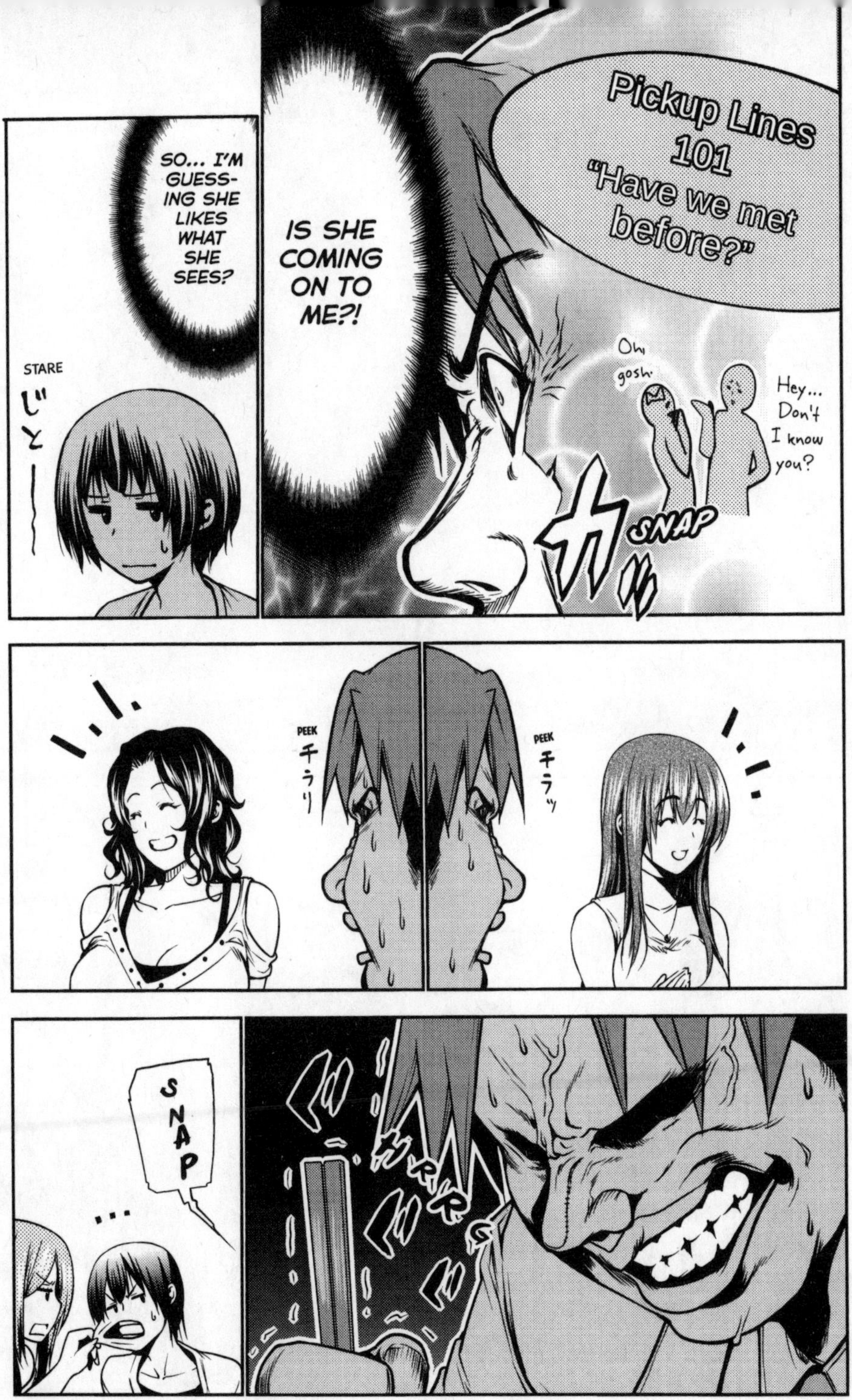
Pickup Lines 101 "Have we met before?"
IS SHE COMING ON TO ME?!
Hey... Don't I know you?
Oh gosh
SNAP
SO... I'M GUESSING SHE LIKES WHAT SHE SEES?
STARE
じとー
PEEK
チラッ
PEEK
チラリ
HRRRG
SNAP
...

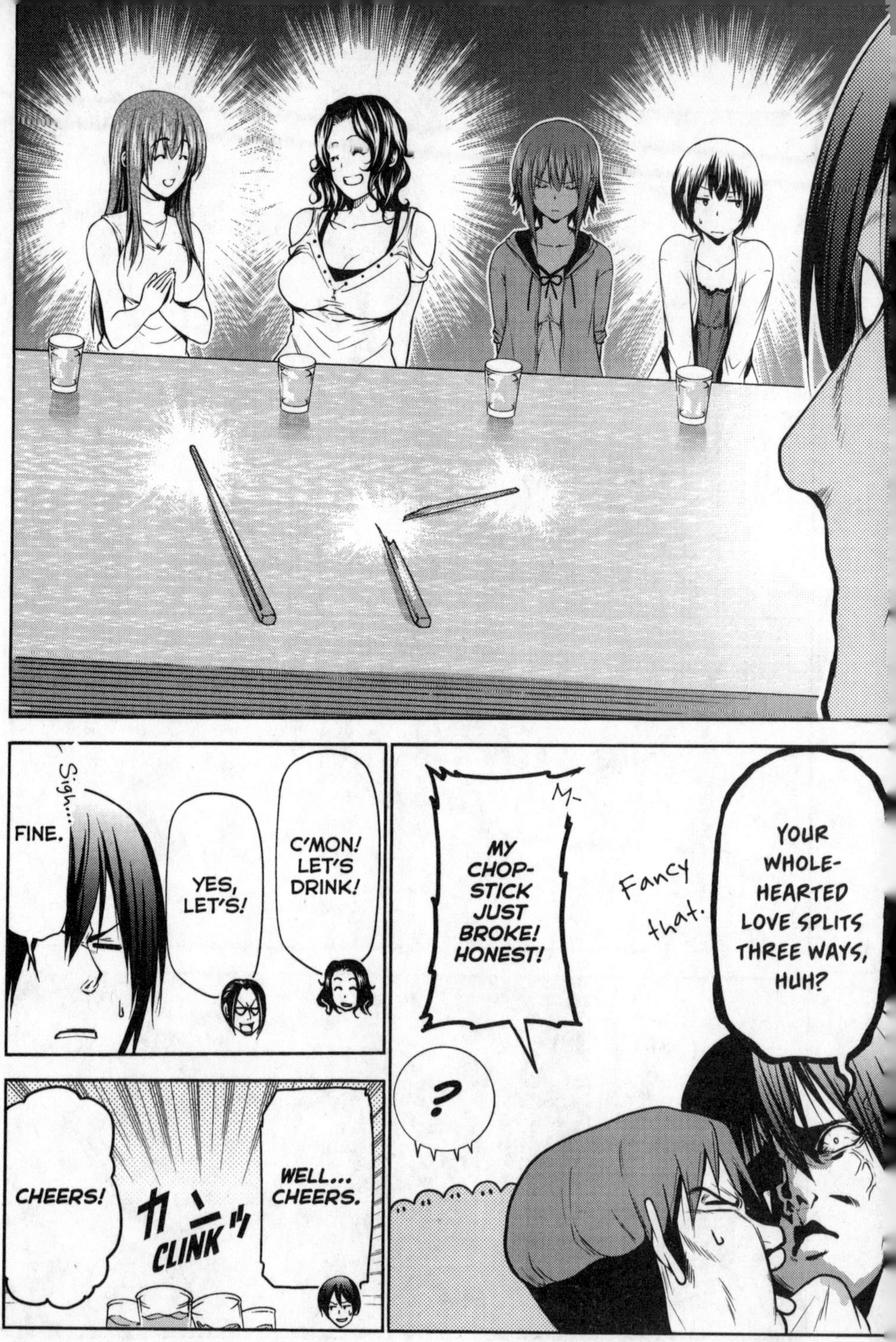
YOUR WHOLE-HEARTED LOVE SPLITS THREE WAYS, HUH?
Fancy that.
M- MY CHOP-STICK JUST BROKE! HONEST!
?
C'MON! LET'S DRINK!
YES, LET'S!
Sigh...
FINE.
WELL... CHEERS.
カーンッ
CLINK
CHEERS!

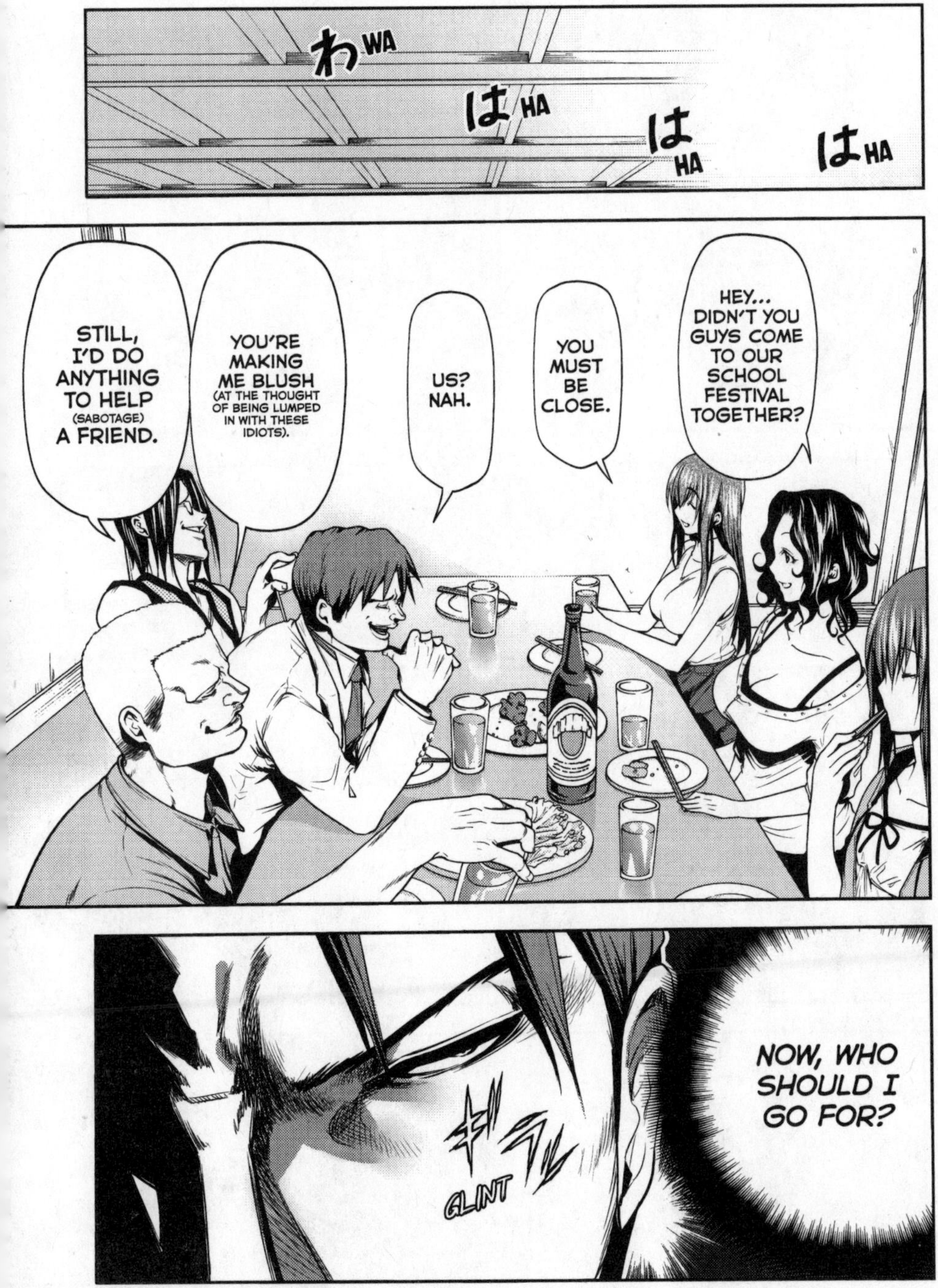
わ WA は HA は HA は HA
HEY... DIDN'T YOU GUYS COME TO OUR SCHOOL FESTIVAL TOGETHER?
YOU MUST BE CLOSE.
US? NAH.
YOU'RE MAKING ME BLUSH (AT THE THOUGHT OF BEING LUMPED IN WITH THESE IDIOTS).
STILL, I'D DO ANYTHING TO HELP (SABOTAGE) A FRIEND.
NOW, WHO SHOULD I GO FOR?
GLINT

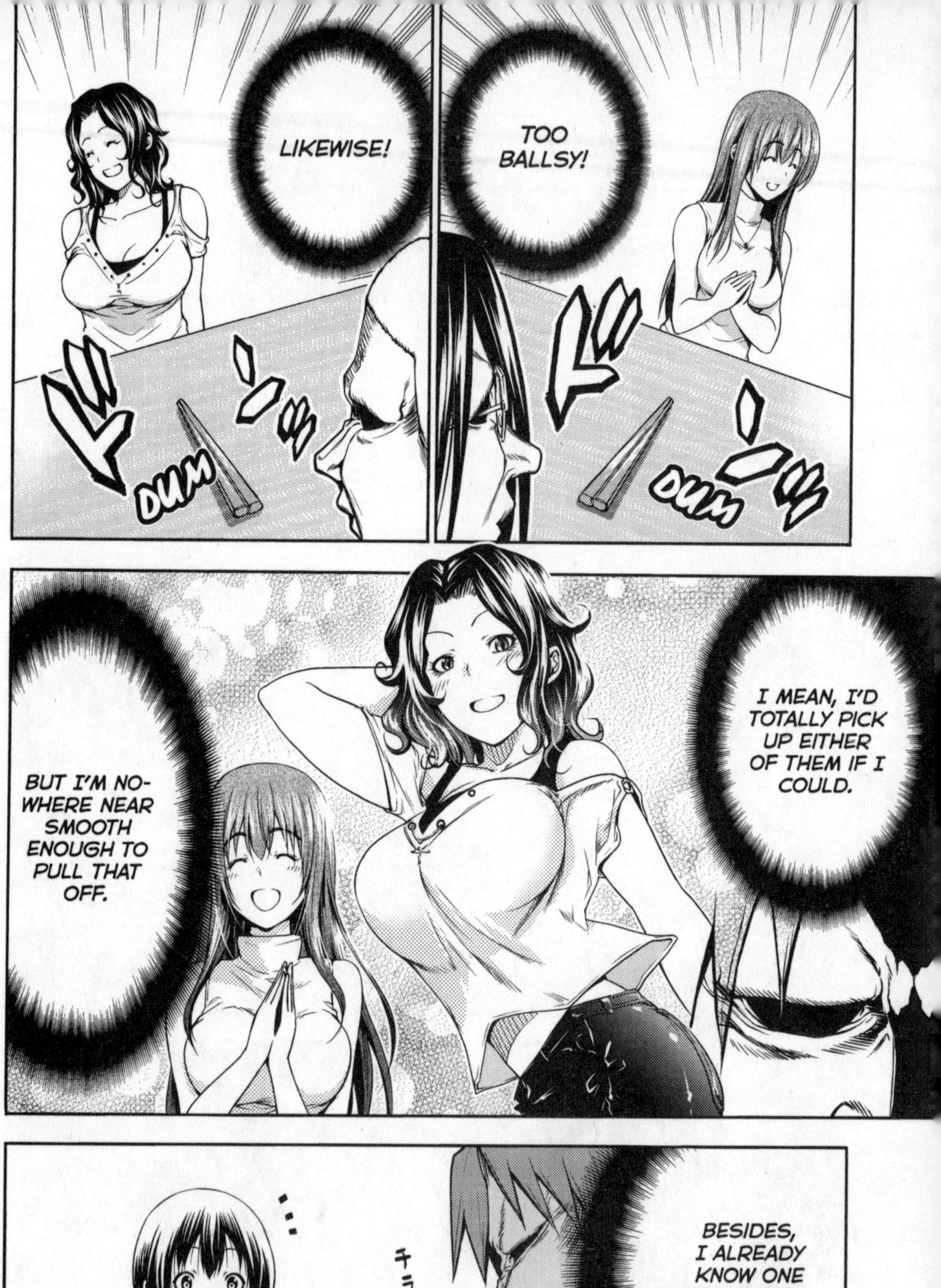
TOO BALLSY!
DUM
LIKEWISE!
DUM
I MEAN, I'D TOTALLY PICK UP EITHER OF THEM IF I COULD.
BUT I'M NO-WHERE NEAR SMOOTH ENOUGH TO PULL THAT OFF.
BESIDES, I ALREADY KNOW ONE GIRL'S INTO ME!
チラリ
PEEK
...

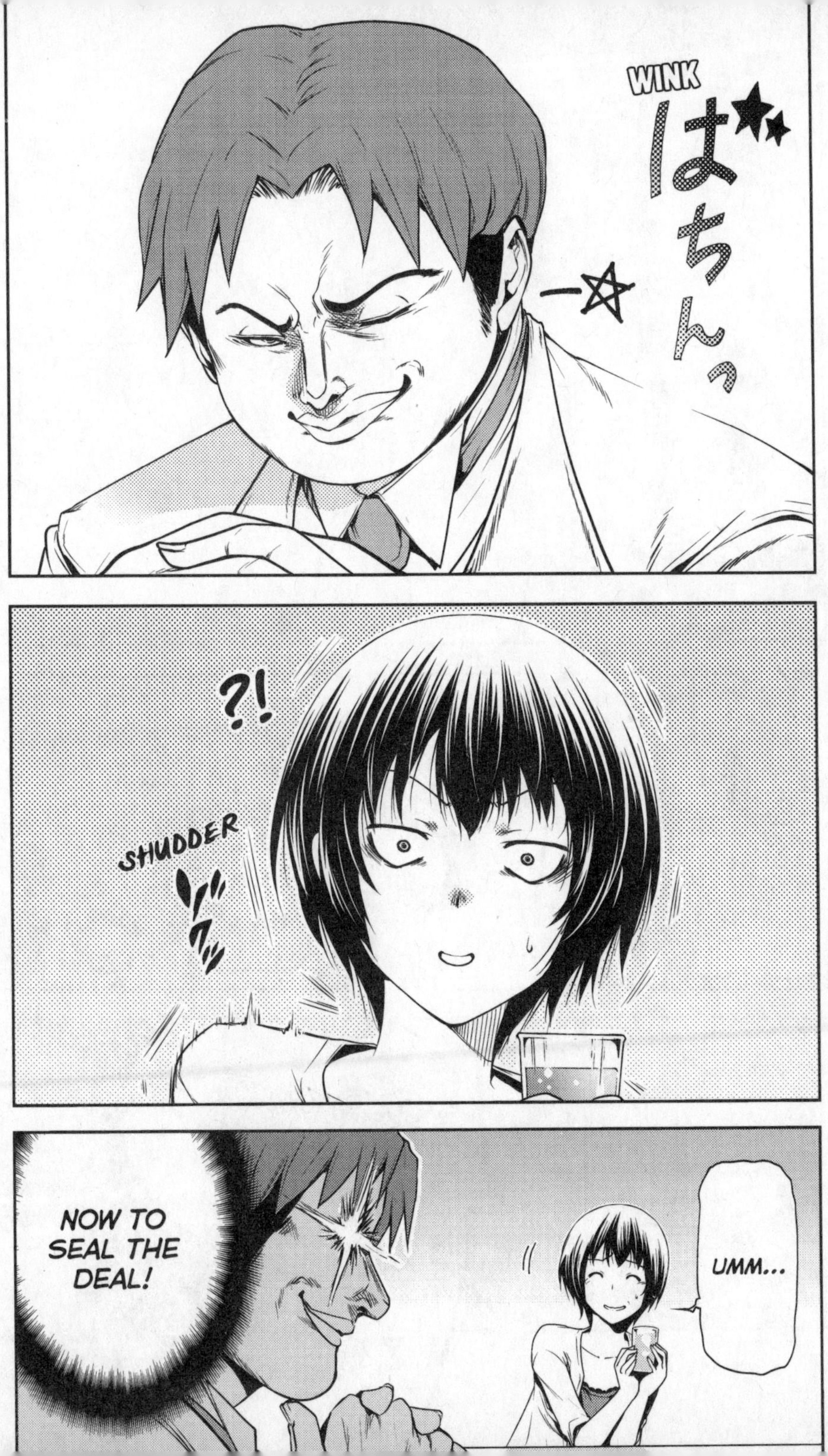
WINK
ぱちんっ
?!
SHUDDER
ゾクッ
NOW TO SEAL THE DEAL!
UMM...

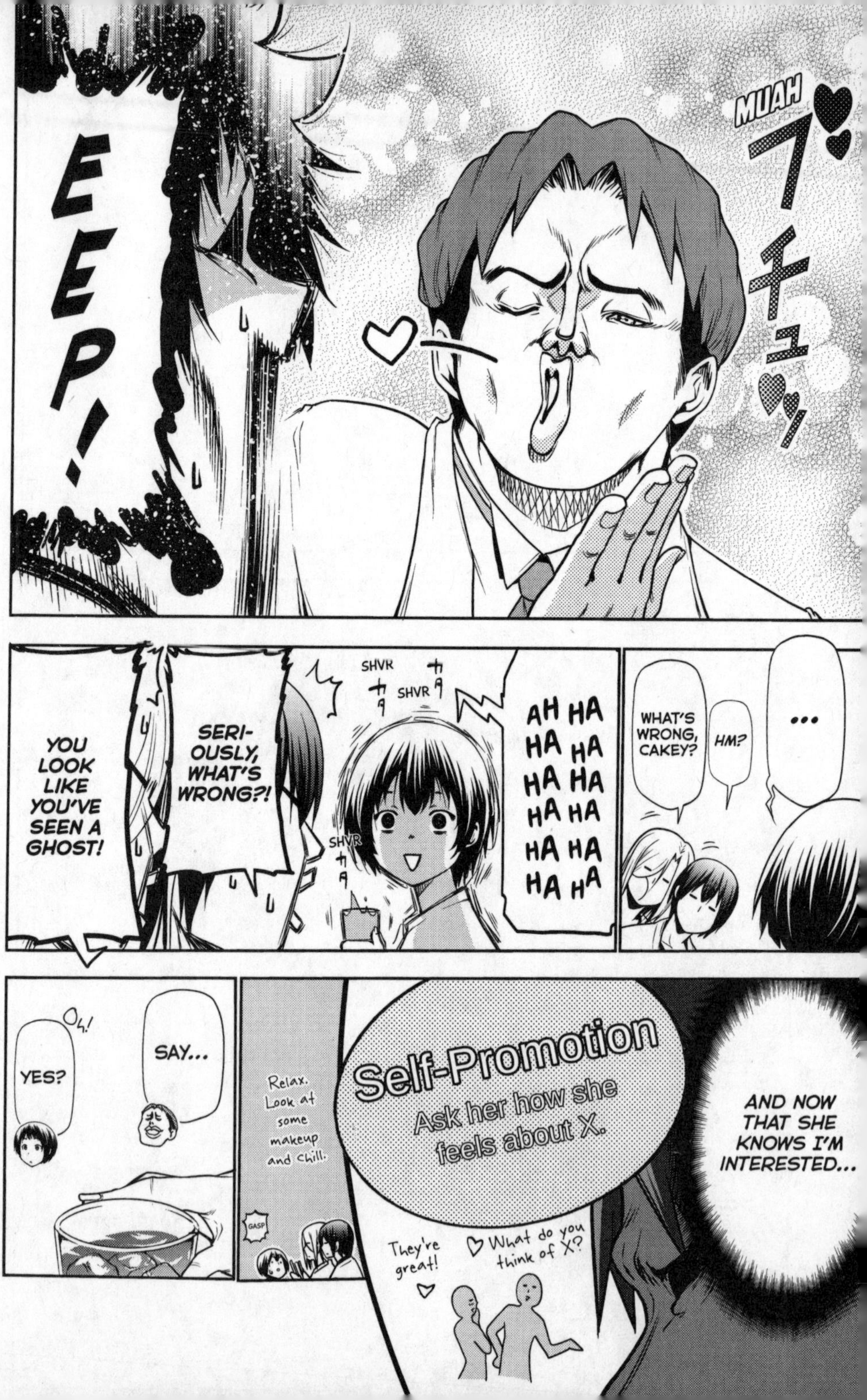
MUAH
EEP!!
...
HM?
WHAT'S WRONG, CAKEY?
AH HA HA HA HA HA HA HA HA HA HA HA
SHVR
SHVR
SHVR
SERIOUSLY, WHAT'S WRONG?!
YOU LOOK LIKE YOU'VE SEEN A GHOST!
AND NOW THAT SHE KNOWS I'M INTERESTED...
Self-Promotion
Ask her how she feels about X.
What do you think of X?
They're great!
Relax. Look at some makeup and chill.
GASP
SAY...
Oh!
YES?

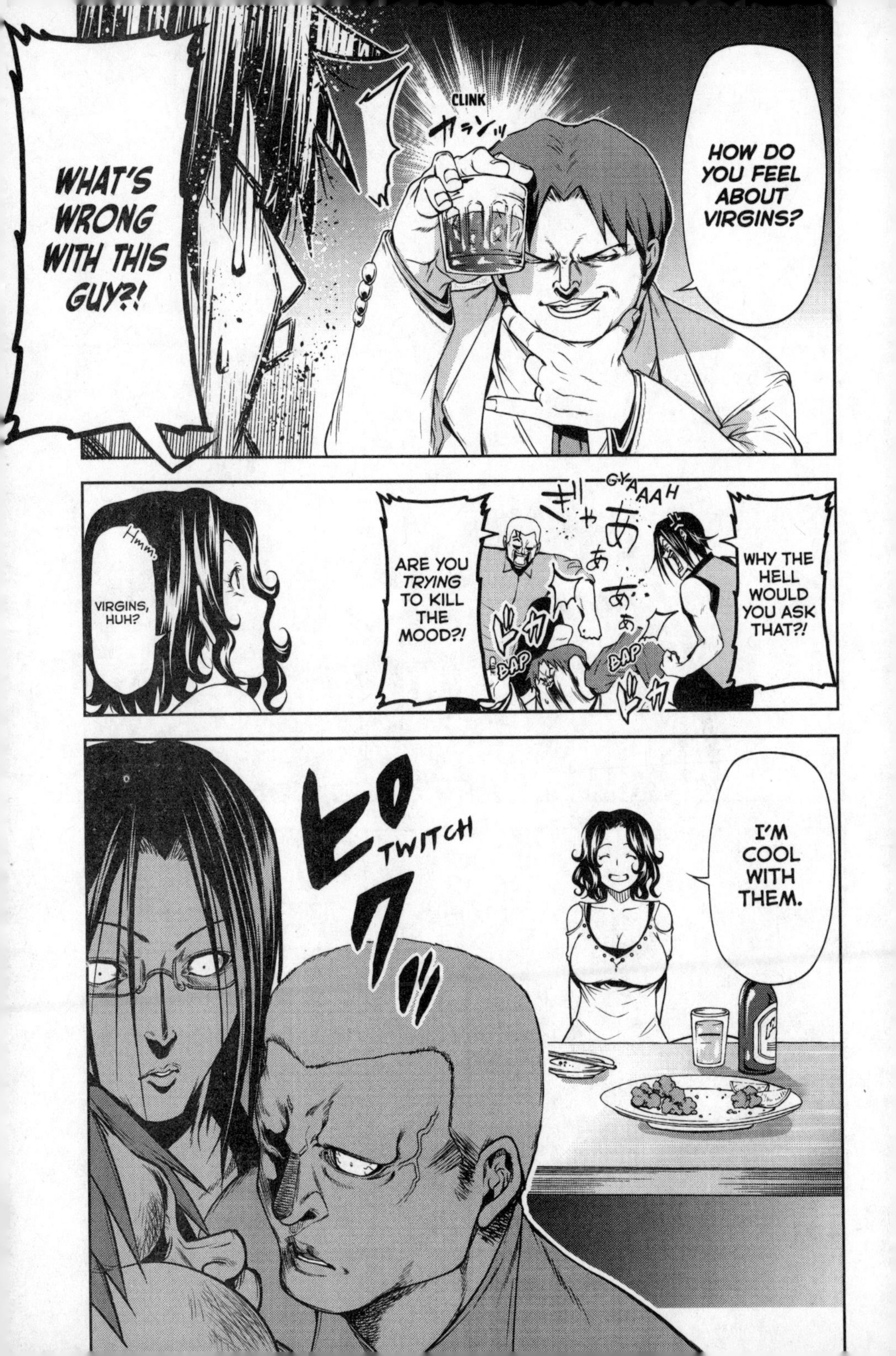
HOW DO YOU FEEL ABOUT VIRGINS?
CLINK
WHAT'S WRONG WITH THIS GUY?!
WHY THE HELL WOULD YOU ASK THAT?!
GYAAAH
ARE YOU TRYING TO KILL THE MOOD?!
BAP
BAP
Hmm.
VIRGINS, HUH?
I'M COOL WITH THEM.
TWITCH

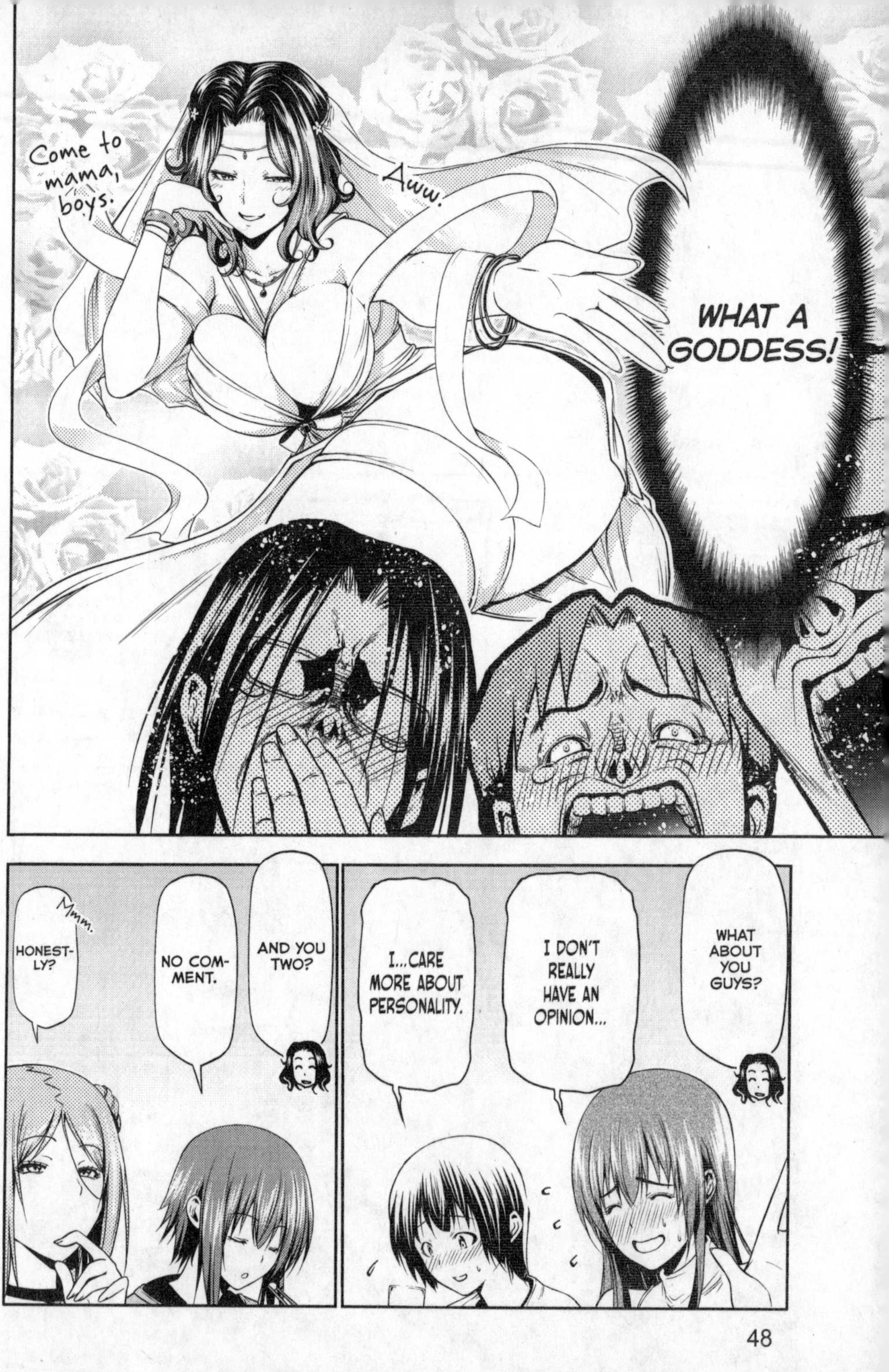

Come to mama, boys.
Aww.
WHAT A GODDESS!
WHAT ABOUT YOU GUYS?
I DON'T REALLY HAVE AN OPINION...
I...CARE MORE ABOUT PERSONALITY.
AND YOU TWO?
NO COMMENT.
Mmm.
HONESTLY?

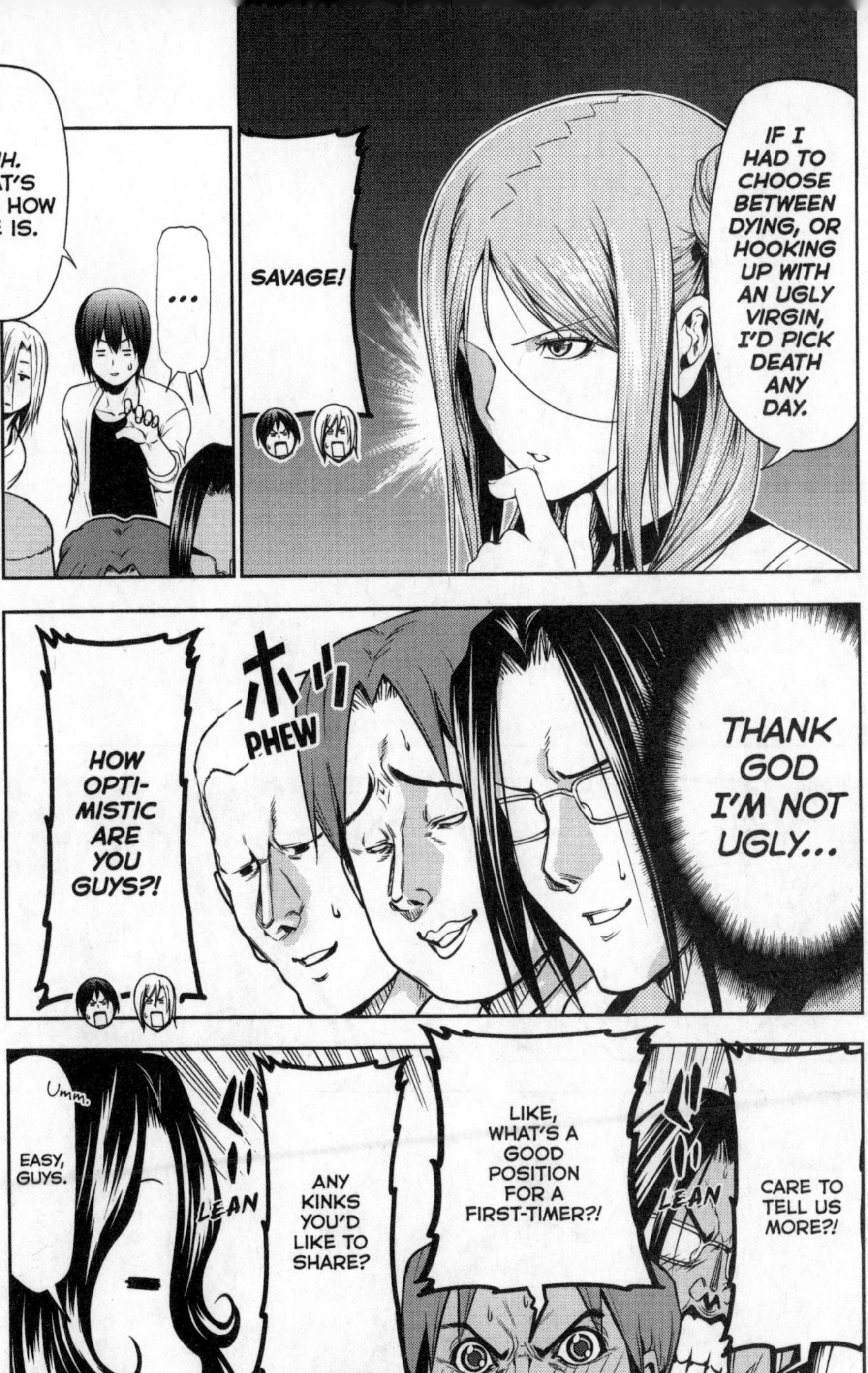
IF I HAD TO CHOOSE BETWEEN DYING, OR HOOKING UP WITH AN UGLY VIRGIN, I'D PICK DEATH ANY DAY.
SAVAGE!
...
UHH. THAT'S JUST HOW SHE IS.
THANK GOD I'M NOT UGLY...
ホッ
PHEW
HOW OPTI-MISTIC ARE YOU GUYS?!
CARE TO TELL US MORE?!
LEAN
LIKE, WHAT'S A GOOD POSITION FOR A FIRST-TIMER?!
ANY KINKS YOU'D LIKE TO SHARE?
LEAN
Umm.
EASY, GUYS.

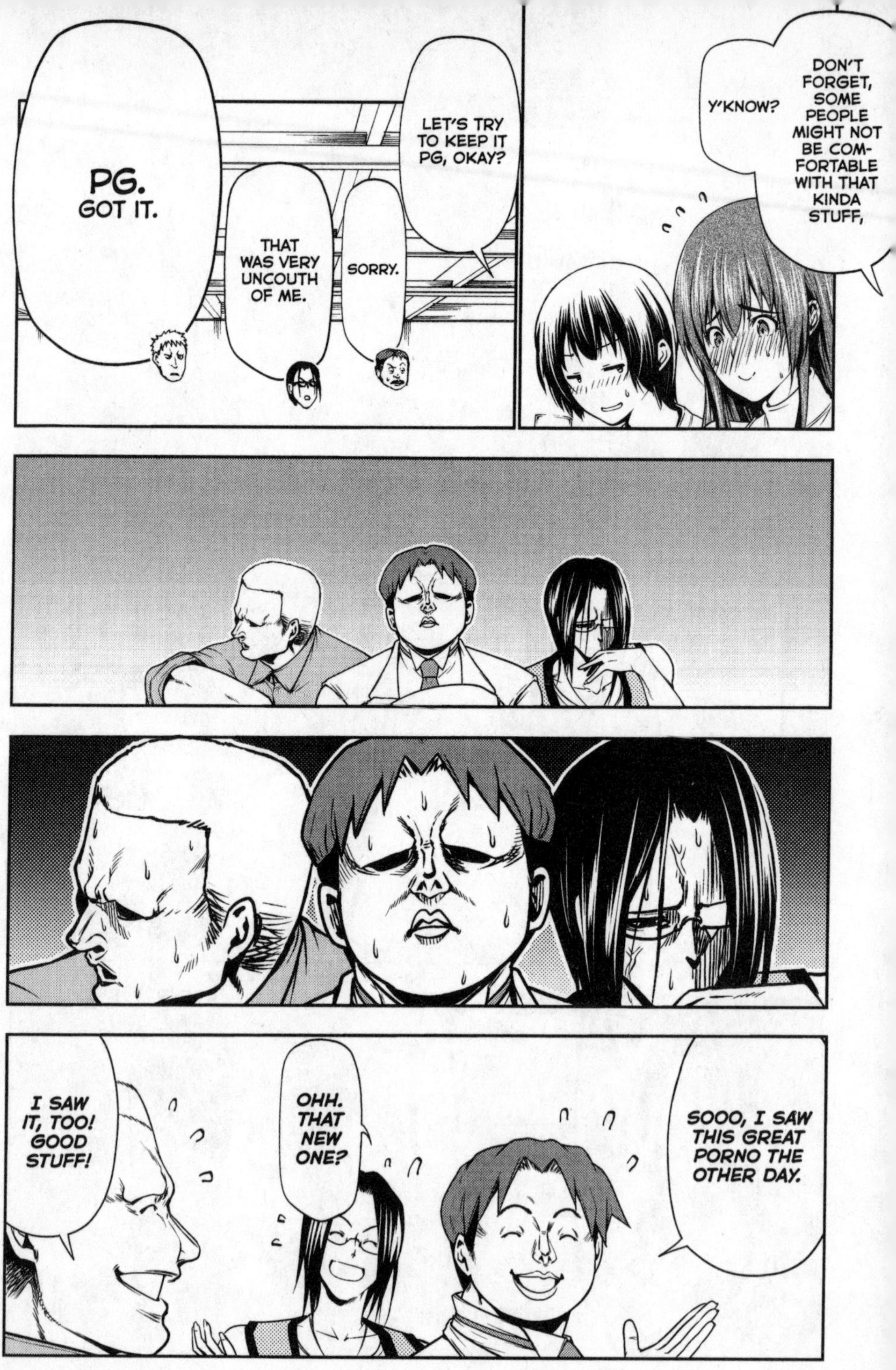
DON'T FORGET, SOME PEOPLE MIGHT NOT BE COMFORTABLE WITH THAT KINDA STUFF,
Y'KNOW?
LET'S TRY TO KEEP IT PG, OKAY?
SORRY.
THAT WAS VERY UNCOUTH OF ME.
PG. GOT IT.
SOOO, I SAW THIS GREAT PORNO THE OTHER DAY.
OHH. THAT NEW ONE?
I SAW IT, TOO! GOOD STUFF!

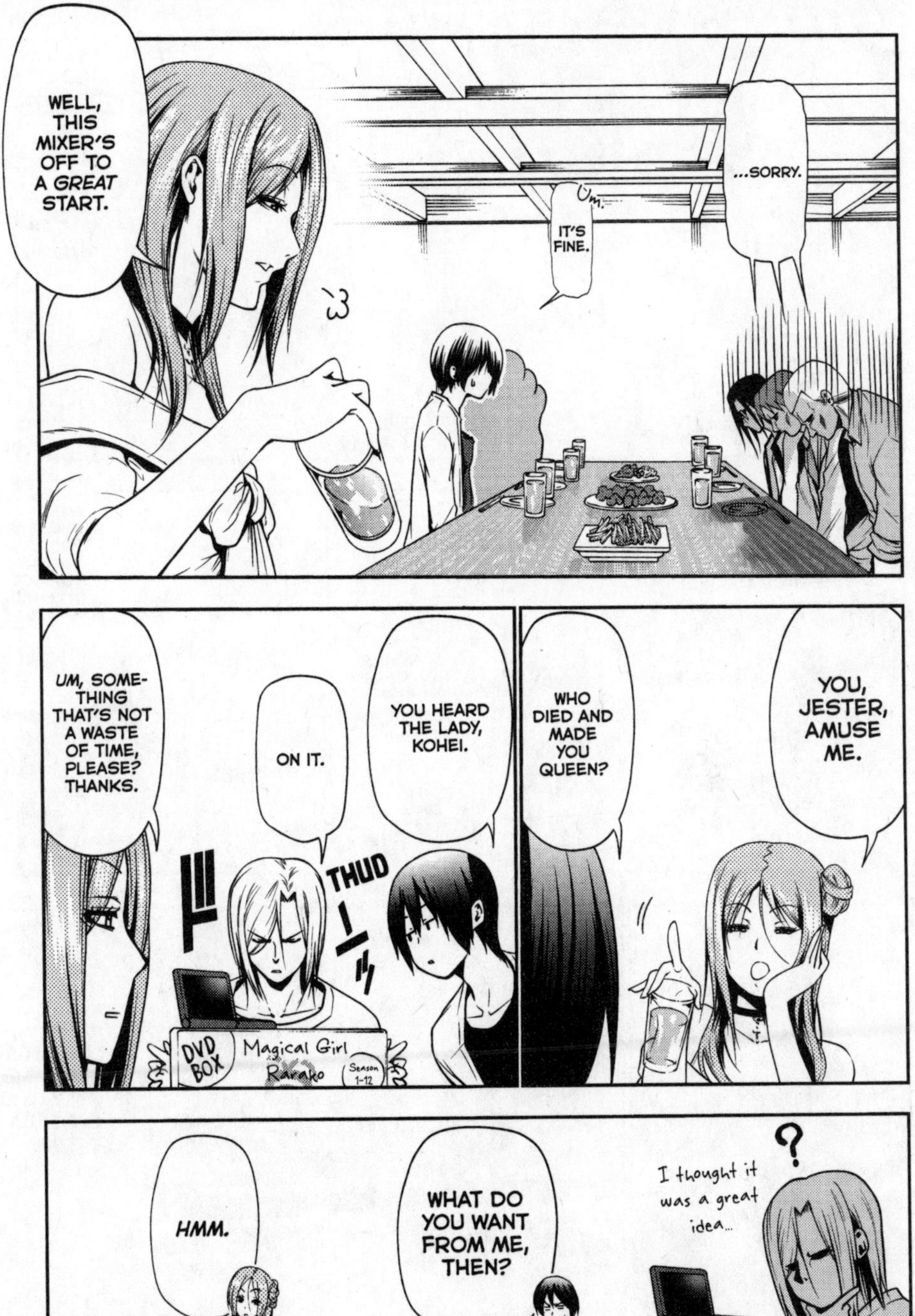
...SORRY.
Um.
IT'S FINE.
WELL, THIS MIXER'S OFF TO A *GREAT* START.
YOU, JESTER, AMUSE ME.
WHO DIED AND MADE YOU QUEEN?
YOU HEARD THE LADY, KOHEI.
THUD
ON IT.
UM, SOMETHING THAT'S NOT A WASTE OF TIME, PLEASE? THANKS.
DVD BOX
Magical Girl
Rarako
Season 1-12
?
I thought it was a great idea...
DVD
Magical Girl
WHAT DO YOU WANT FROM ME, THEN?
HMM.

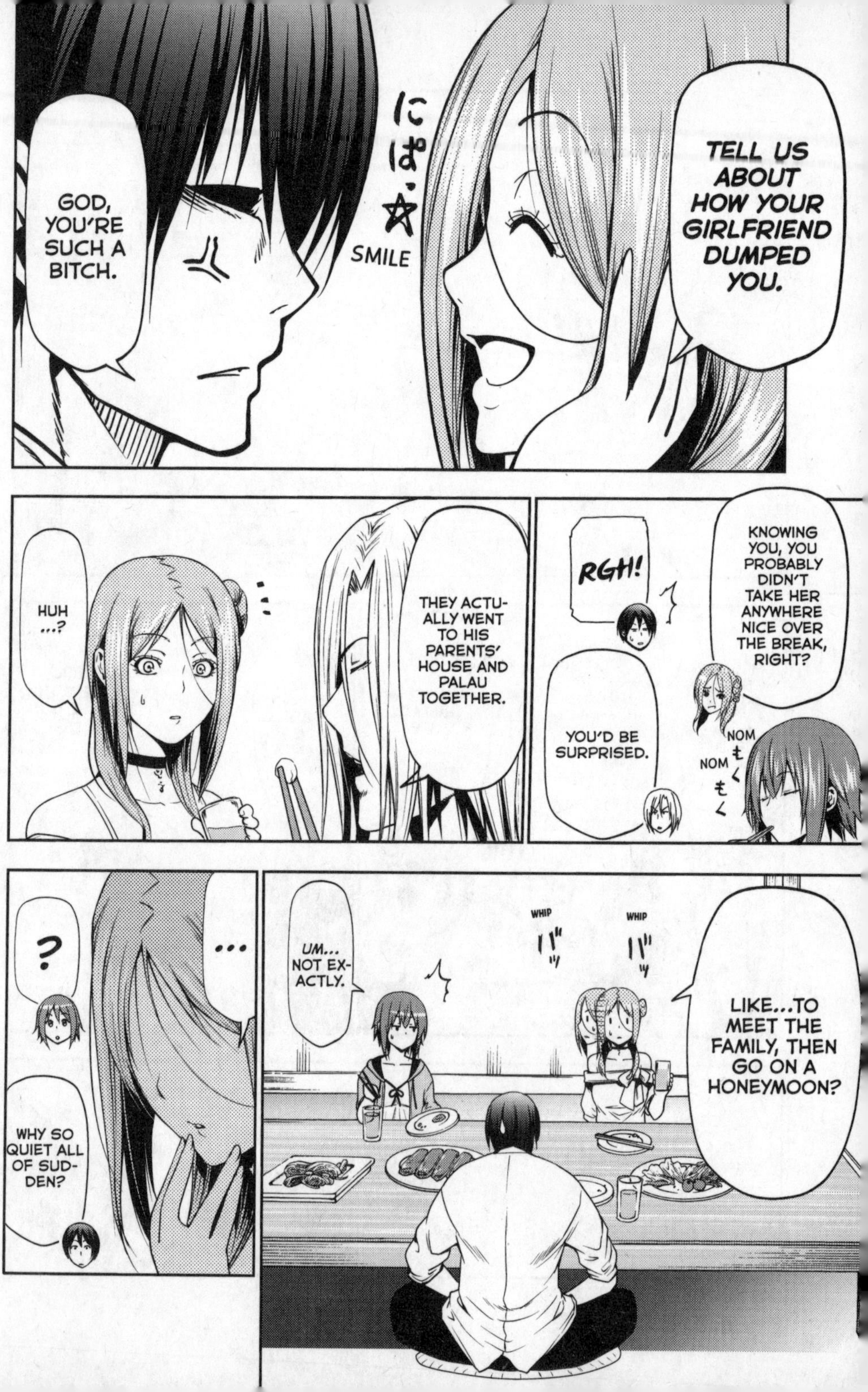
TELL US ABOUT HOW YOUR GIRLFRIEND DUMPED YOU.
にぱっ☆
SMILE
GOD, YOU'RE SUCH A BITCH.
KNOWING YOU, YOU PROBABLY DIDN'T TAKE HER ANYWHERE NICE OVER THE BREAK, RIGHT?
RGH!
NOM NOM
もくもく
YOU'D BE SURPRISED.
THEY ACTU-ALLY WENT TO HIS PARENTS' HOUSE AND PALAU TOGETHER.
HUH ...?
LIKE...TO MEET THE FAMILY, THEN GO ON A HONEYMOON?
WHIP
バッ
WHIP
バッ
UM... NOT EX-ACTLY.
...
?
WHY SO QUIET ALL OF SUD-DEN?

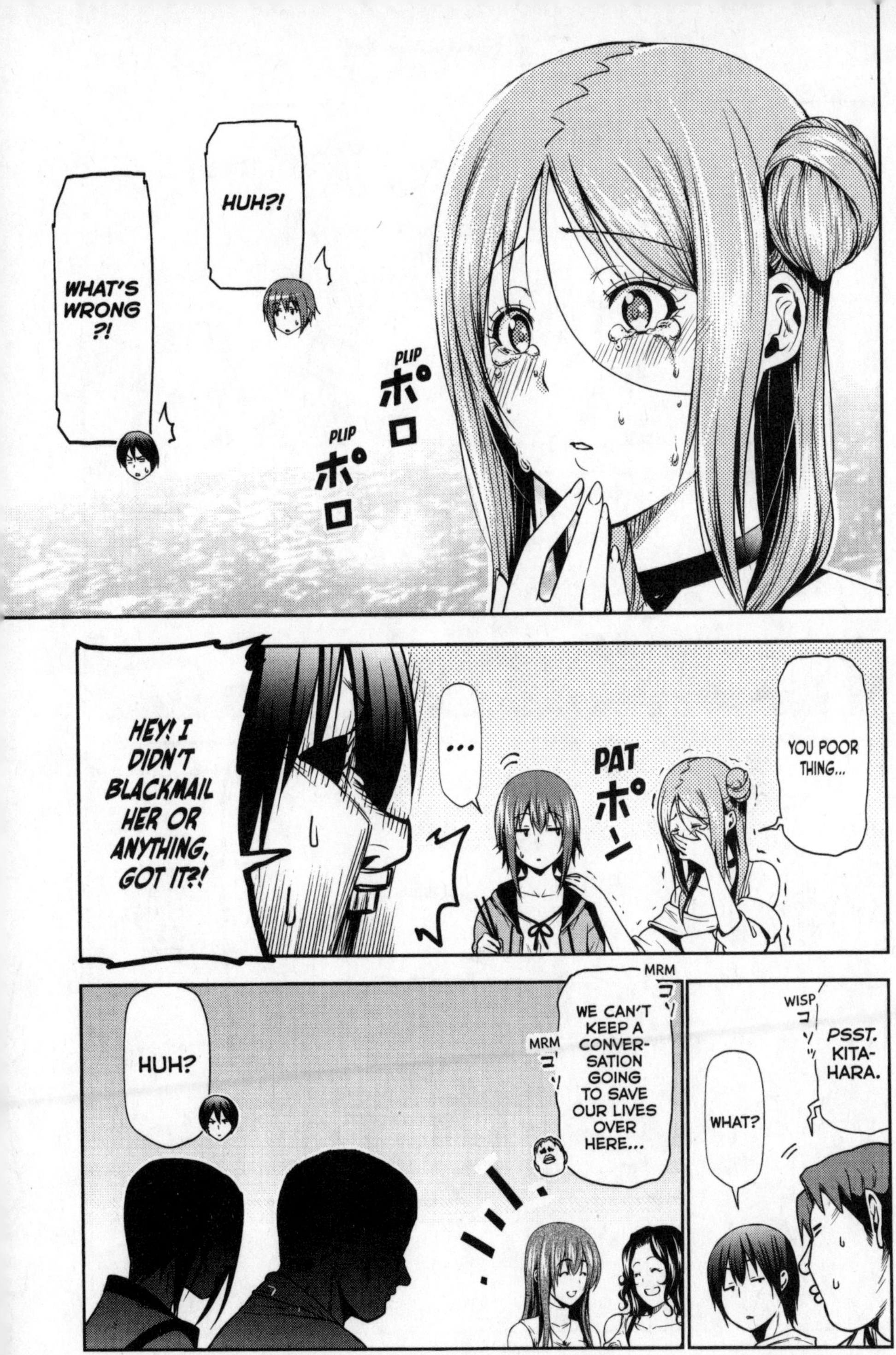
PLIP
ポロ
PLIP
ポロ
HUH?!
WHAT'S WRONG ?!
YOU POOR THING...
PAT
ポン
...
HEY! I DIDN'T BLACKMAIL HER OR ANYTHING, GOT IT?!
WISP
コソッ
PSST. KITA-HARA.
WHAT?
MRM
コソ
WE CAN'T KEEP A CONVER-SATION GOING TO SAVE OUR LIVES OVER HERE...
MRM
コソ
HUH?

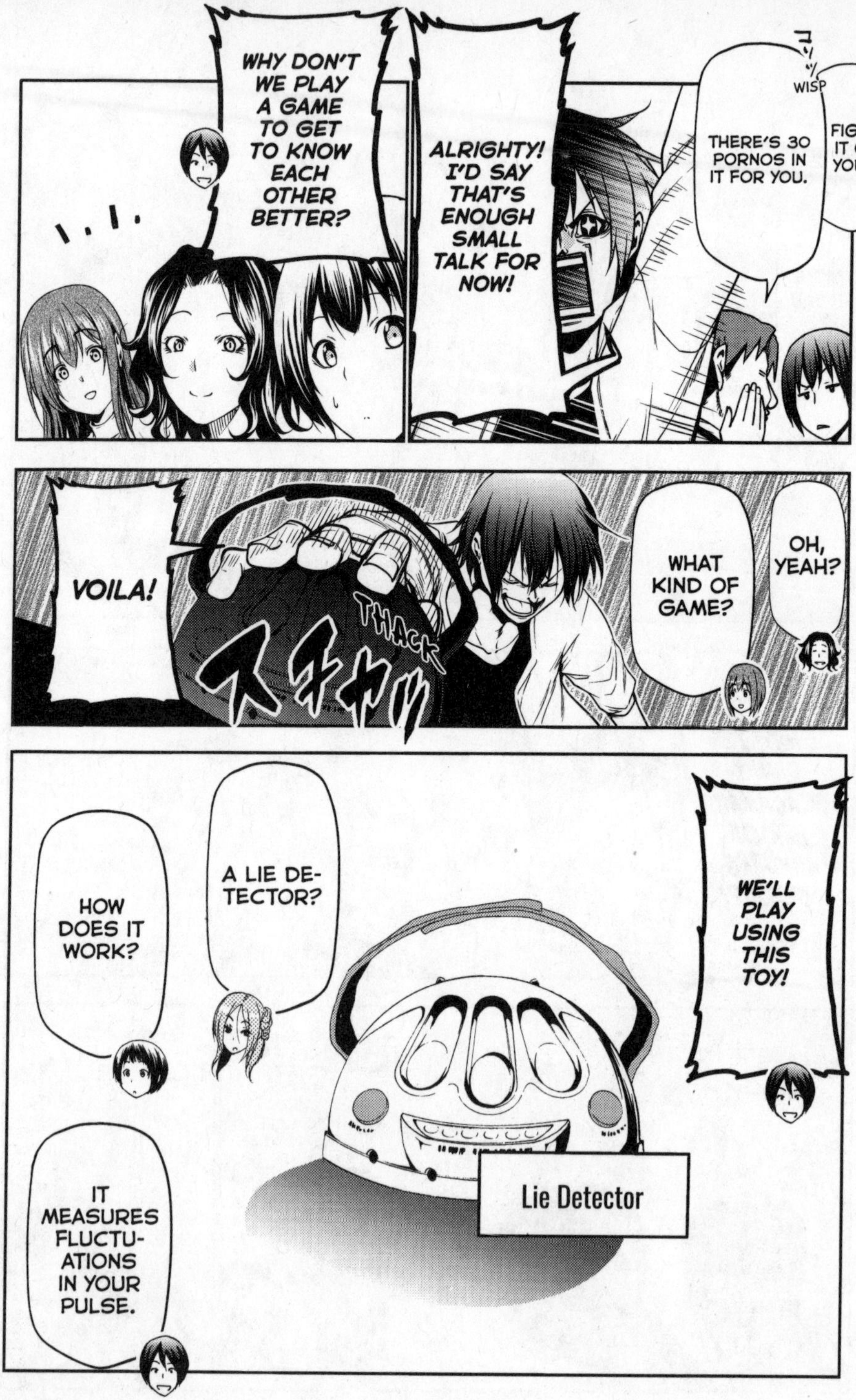
FIGURE IT OUT YOUR—
WISP
THERE'S 30 PORNOS IN IT FOR YOU.
ALRIGHTY! I'D SAY THAT'S ENOUGH SMALL TALK FOR NOW!
WHY DON'T WE PLAY A GAME TO GET TO KNOW EACH OTHER BETTER?
OH, YEAH?
WHAT KIND OF GAME?
THACK
VOILA!
WE'LL PLAY USING THIS TOY!
A LIE DE-TECTOR?
HOW DOES IT WORK?
Lie Detector
IT MEASURES FLUCTU-ATIONS IN YOUR PULSE.

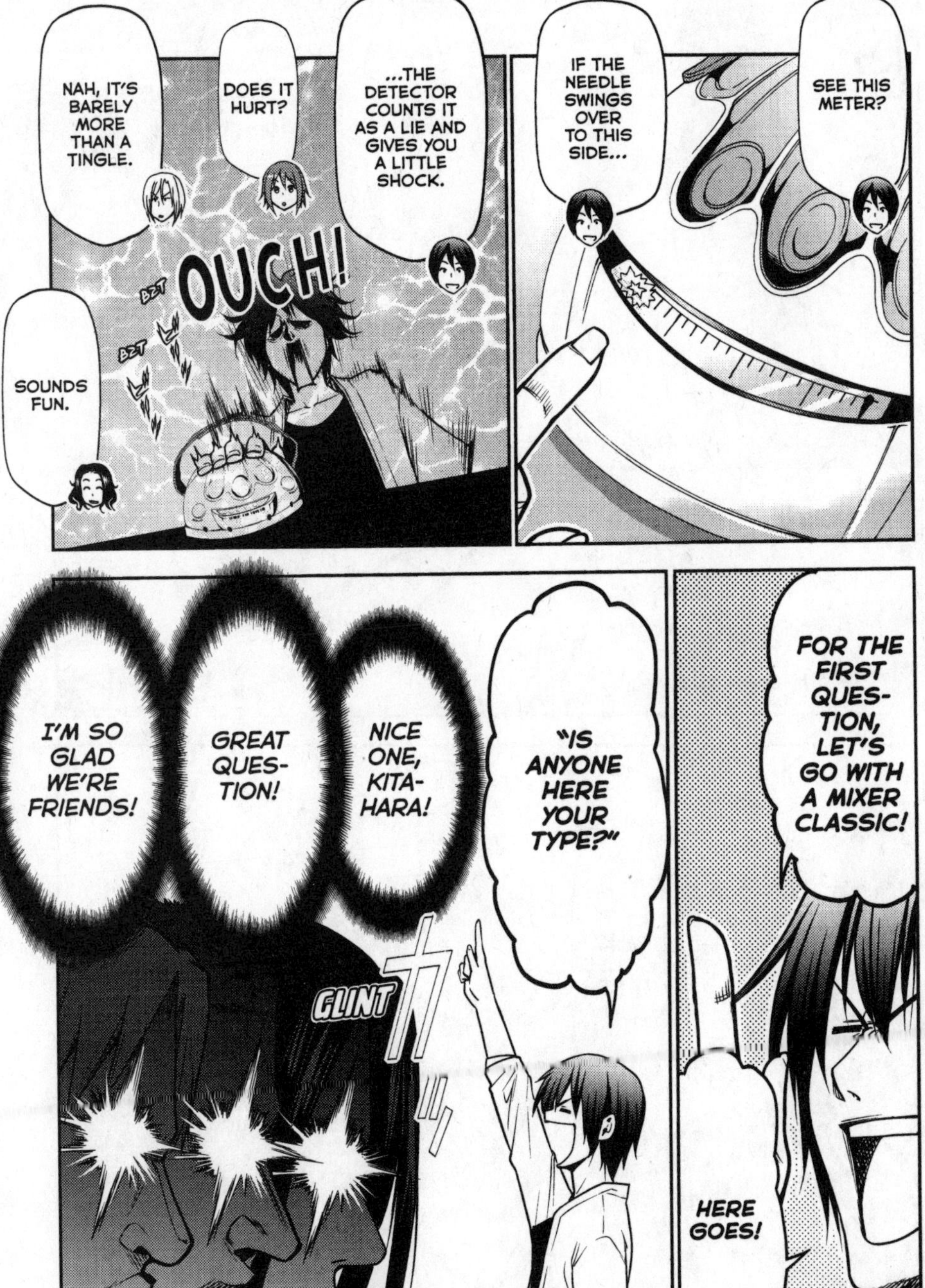
SEE THIS METER?
IF THE NEEDLE SWINGS OVER TO THIS SIDE...
...THE DETECTOR COUNTS IT AS A LIE AND GIVES YOU A LITTLE SHOCK.
DOES IT HURT?
NAH, IT'S BARELY MORE THAN A TINGLE.
OUCH!
BZT
BZT
SOUNDS FUN.
FOR THE FIRST QUESTION, LET'S GO WITH A MIXER CLASSIC!
HERE GOES!
"IS ANYONE HERE YOUR TYPE?"
NICE ONE, KITAHARA!
GREAT QUESTION!
I'M SO GLAD WE'RE FRIENDS!
GLINT

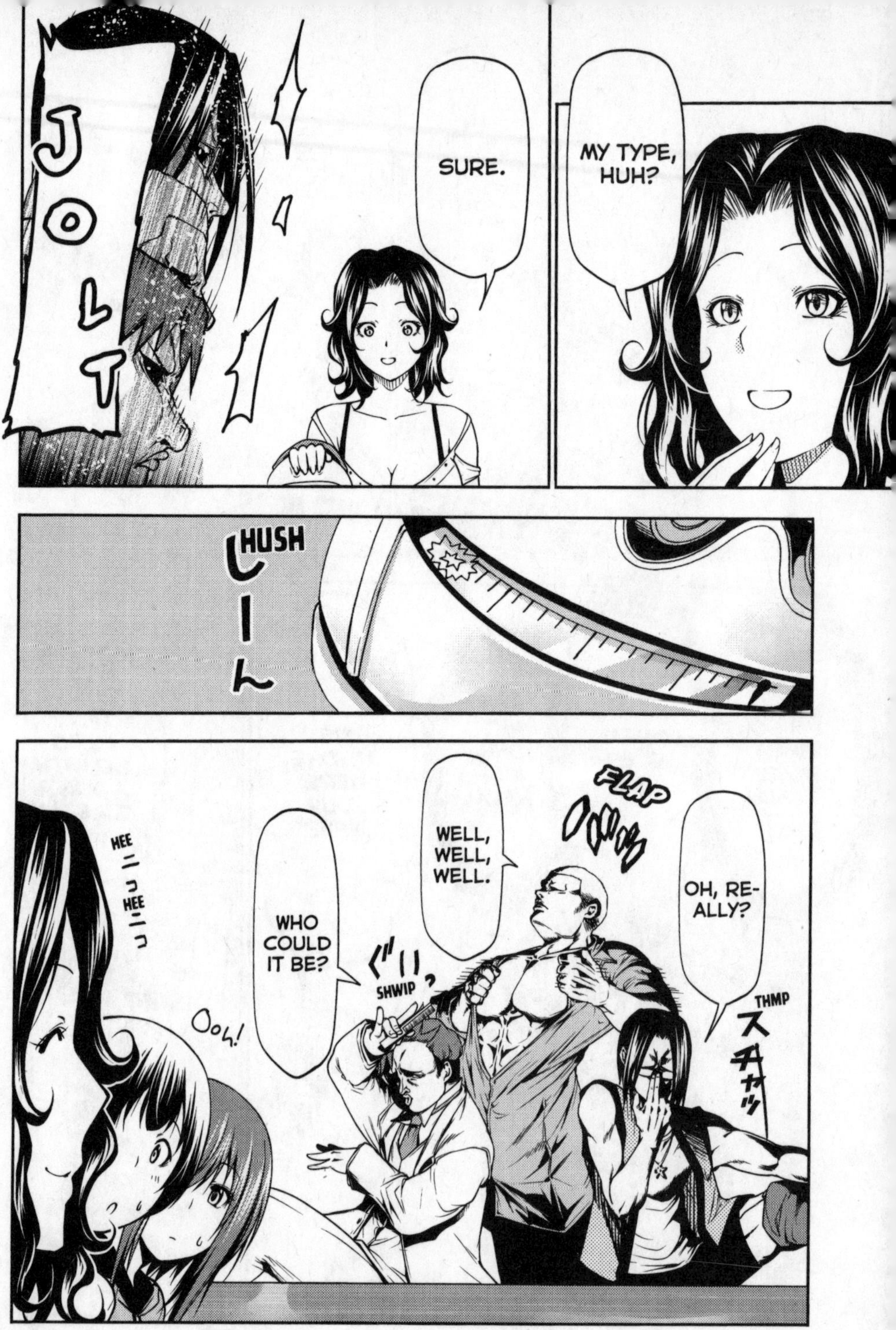
MY TYPE, HUH?
SURE.
JOLT
HUSH
しーん
OH, RE-ALLY?
THMP
スチャッ
FLAP
WELL, WELL, WELL.
SHWIP
ぐいっ
WHO COULD IT BE?
Ooh!
HEE
ニッ
HEE
ニッ

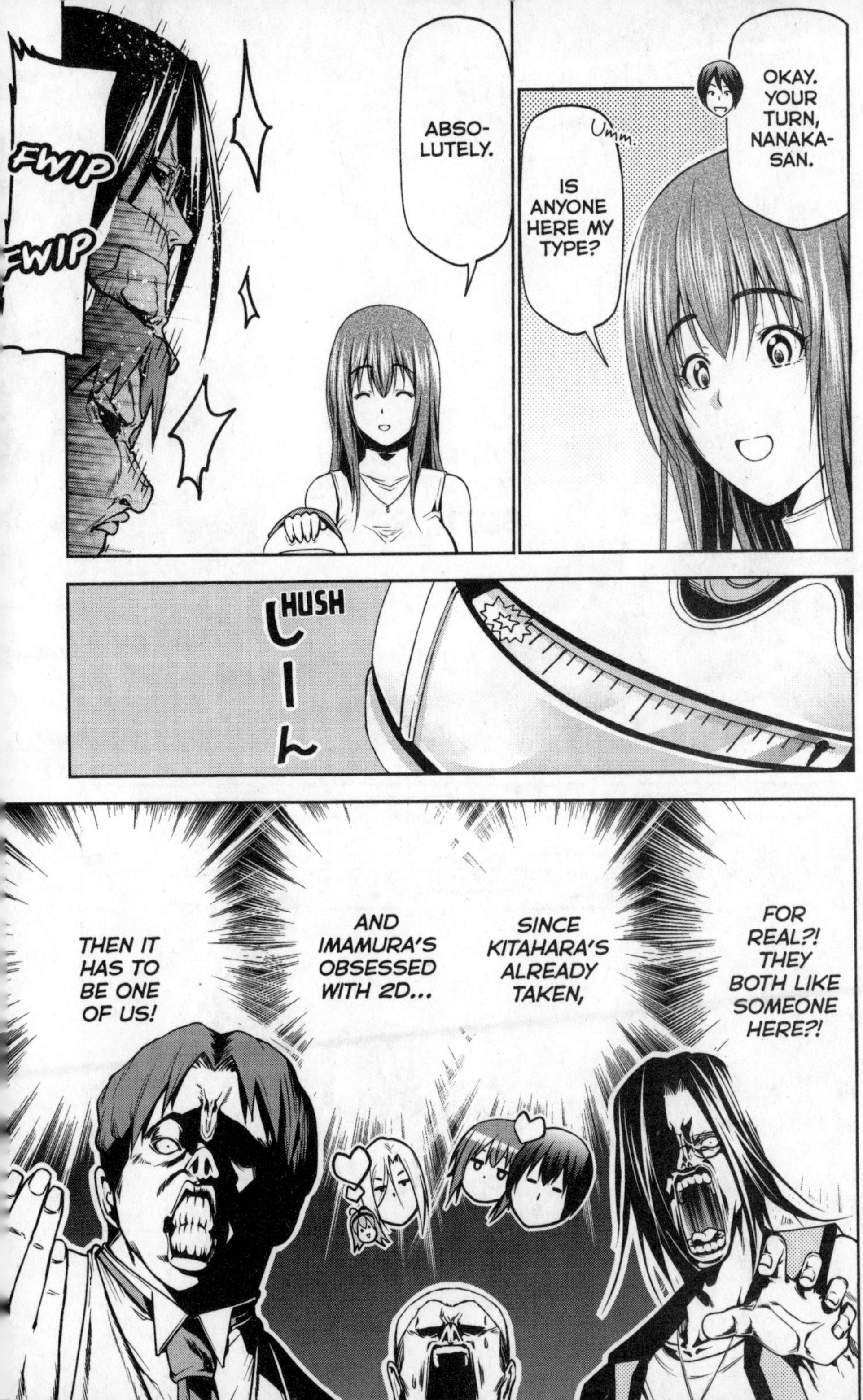
OKAY. YOUR TURN, NANAKA-SAN.
Umm.
IS ANYONE HERE MY TYPE?
ABSO-LUTELY.
FWIP
FWIP
HUSH
しーん
FOR REAL?! THEY BOTH LIKE SOMEONE HERE?!
SINCE KITAHARA'S ALREADY TAKEN,
AND IMAMURA'S OBSESSED WITH 2D...
THEN IT HAS TO BE ONE OF US!

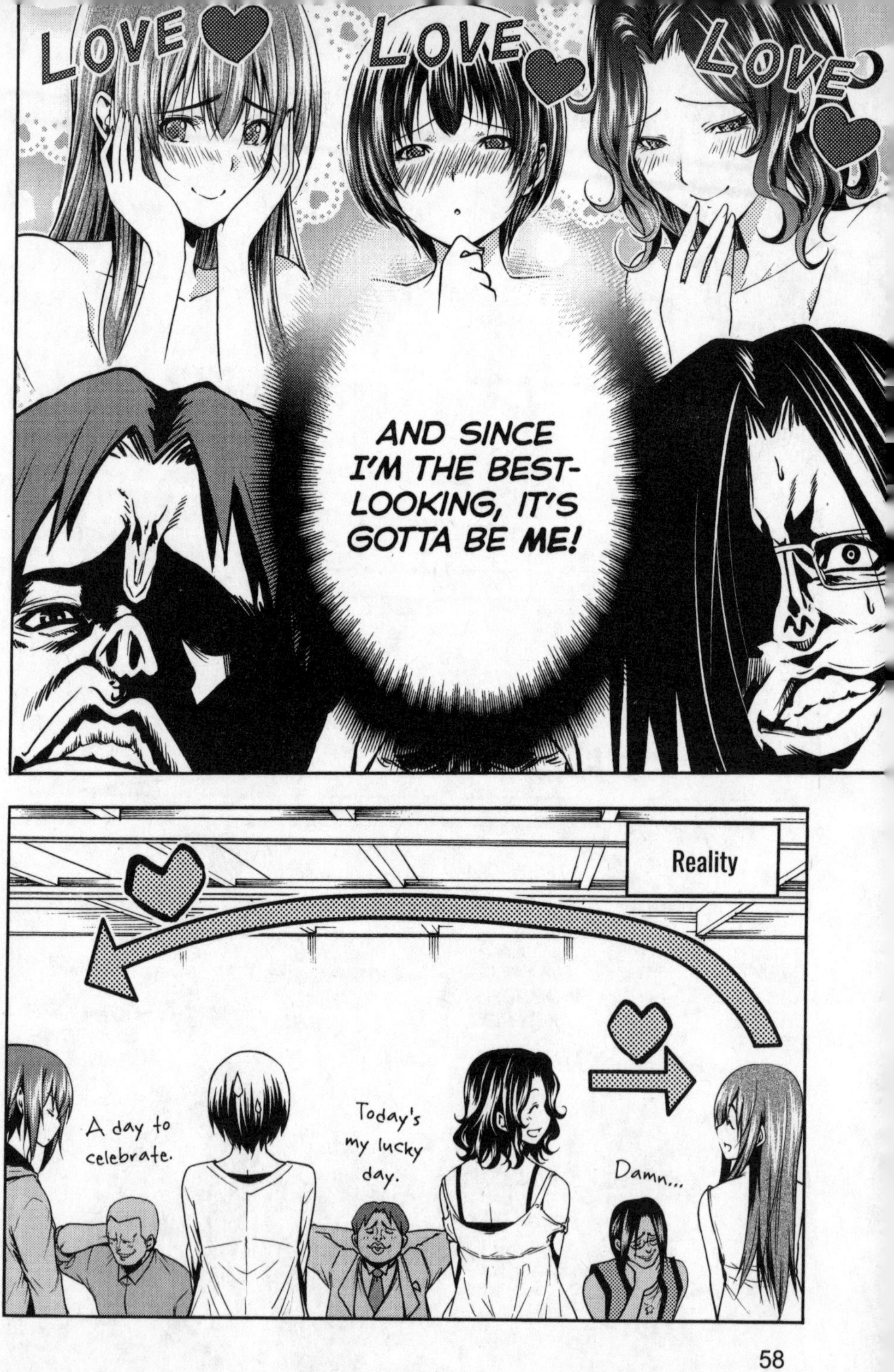
LOVE
LOVE
LOVE
AND SINCE I'M THE BEST-LOOKING, IT'S GOTTA BE ME!
Reality
Damn...
Today's my lucky day.
A day to celebrate.

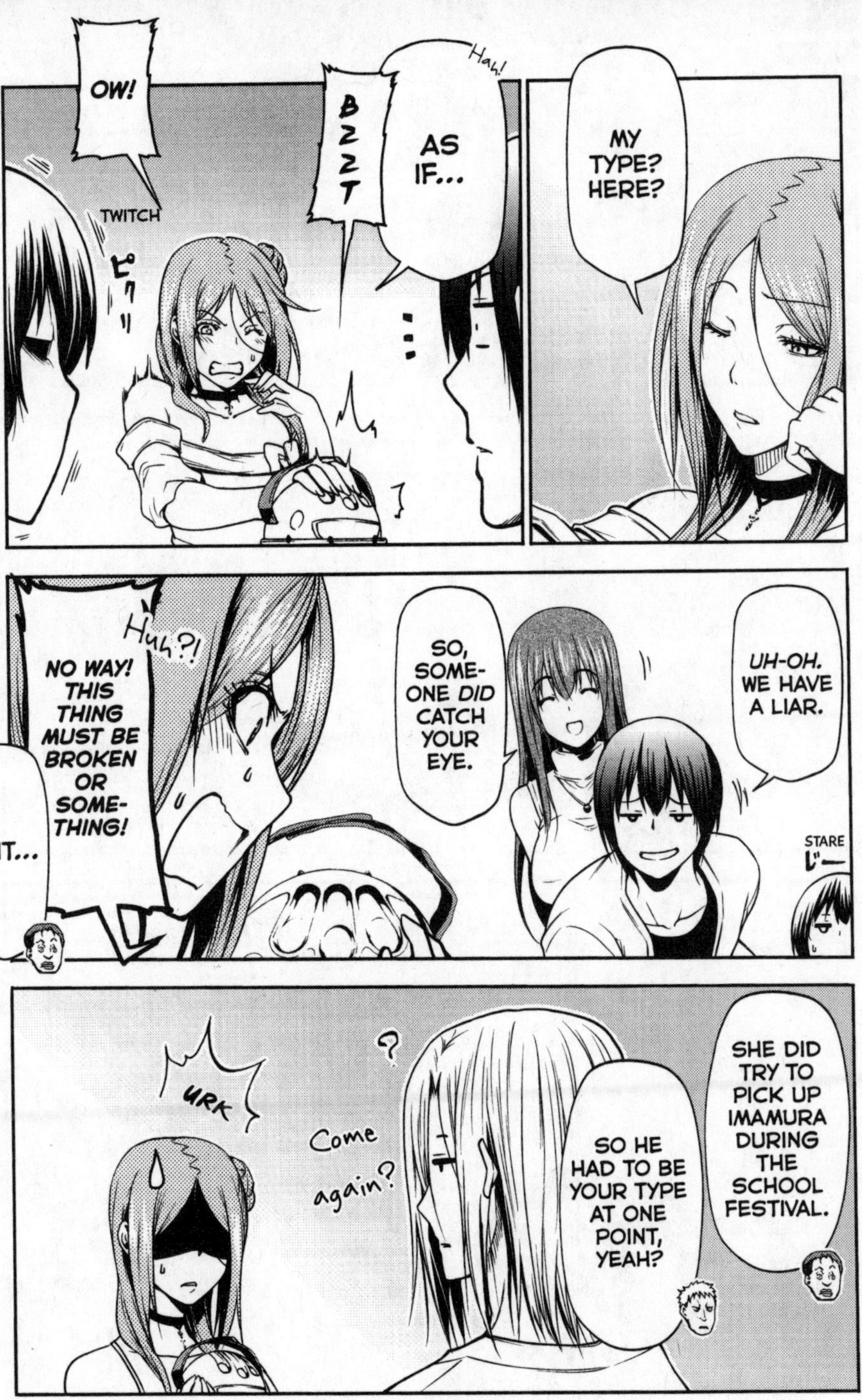
MY TYPE? HERE?
Hah!
AS IF...
BZZT
OW!
TWITCH
ピクリ
UH-OH. WE HAVE A LIAR.
STARE
ジー
SO, SOME-ONE *DID* CATCH YOUR EYE.
Huh?!
NO WAY! THIS THING MUST BE BROKEN OR SOME-THING!
WAIT...
SHE DID TRY TO PICK UP IMAMURA DURING THE SCHOOL FESTIVAL.
SO HE HAD TO BE YOUR TYPE AT ONE POINT, YEAH?
?
Come again?
URK

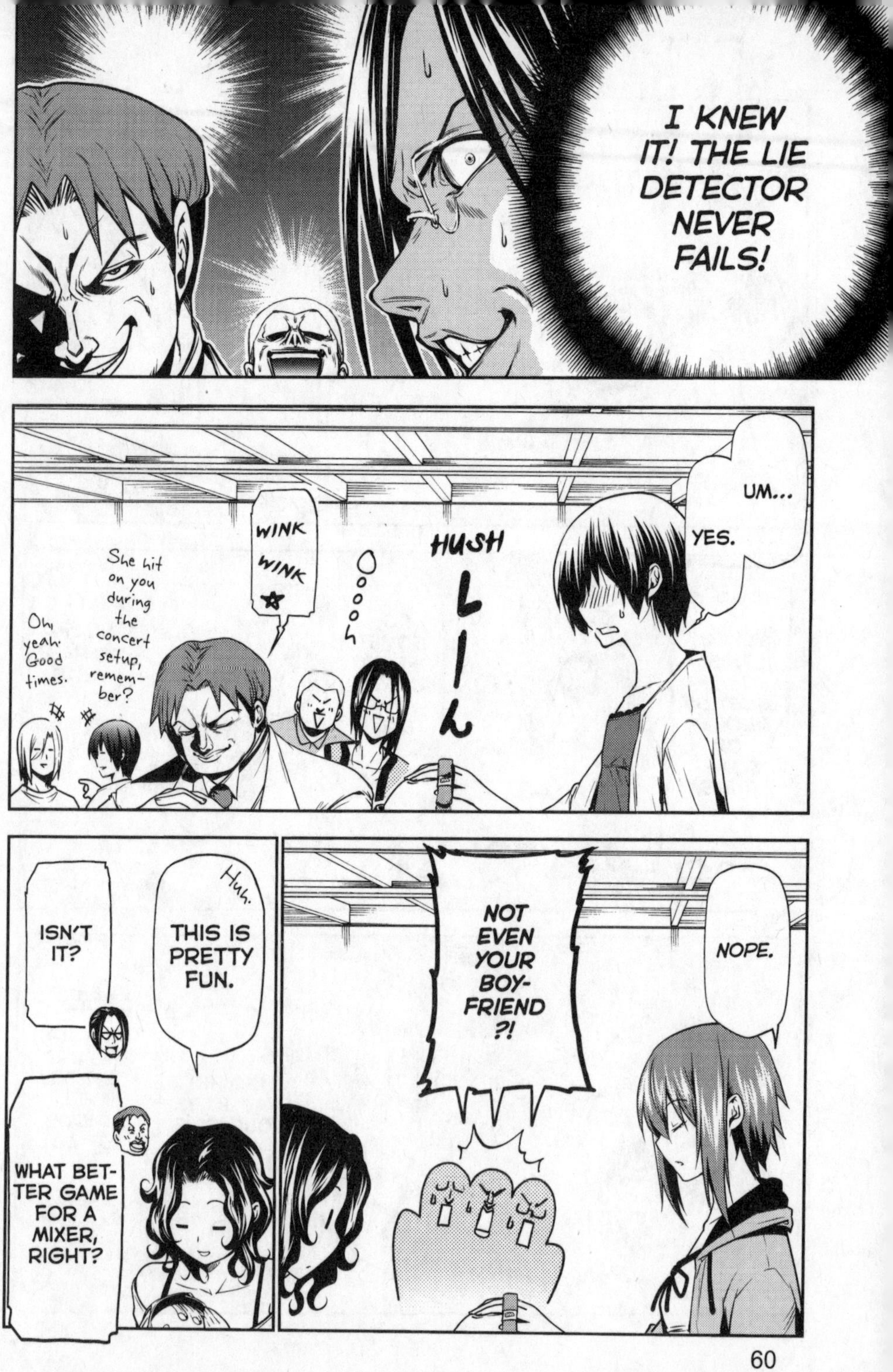
I KNEW IT! THE LIE DETECTOR NEVER FAILS!
UM... YES.
HUSH
しーん
Ooooh
WINK WINK ☆
She hit on you during the concert setup, remember?
Oh, yeah. Good times.
NOPE.
NOT EVEN YOUR BOYFRIEND?!
Huh.
THIS IS PRETTY FUN.
ISN'T IT?
WHAT BETTER GAME FOR A MIXER, RIGHT?

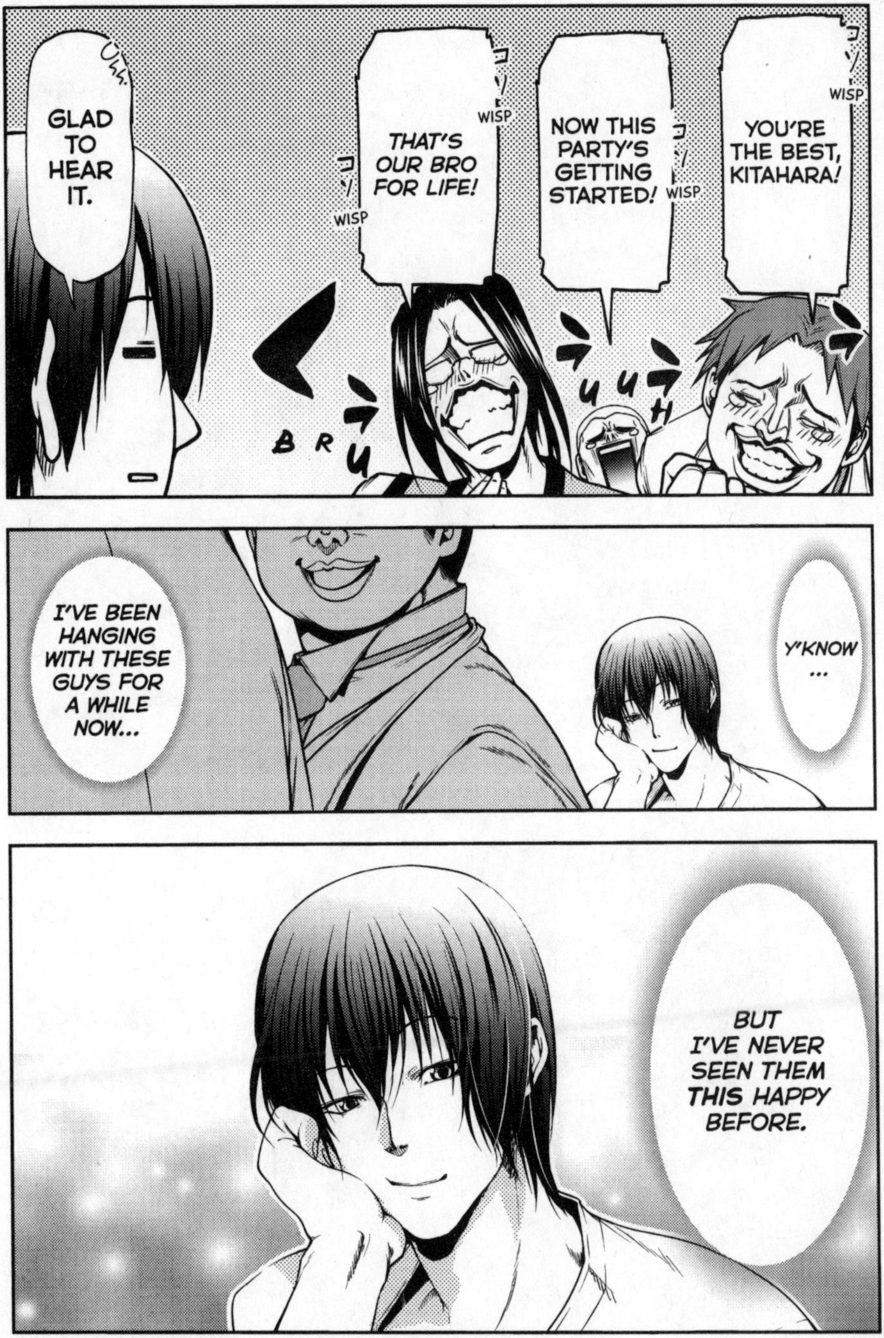
WISP
YOU'RE THE BEST, KITAHARA!
WISP
NOW THIS PARTY'S GETTING STARTED!
WISP
THAT'S OUR BRO FOR LIFE!
WISP
UUH
BRU
Uhh.
GLAD TO HEAR IT.
Y'KNOW ...
I'VE BEEN HANGING WITH THESE GUYS FOR A WHILE NOW...
BUT I'VE NEVER SEEN THEM THIS HAPPY BEFORE.

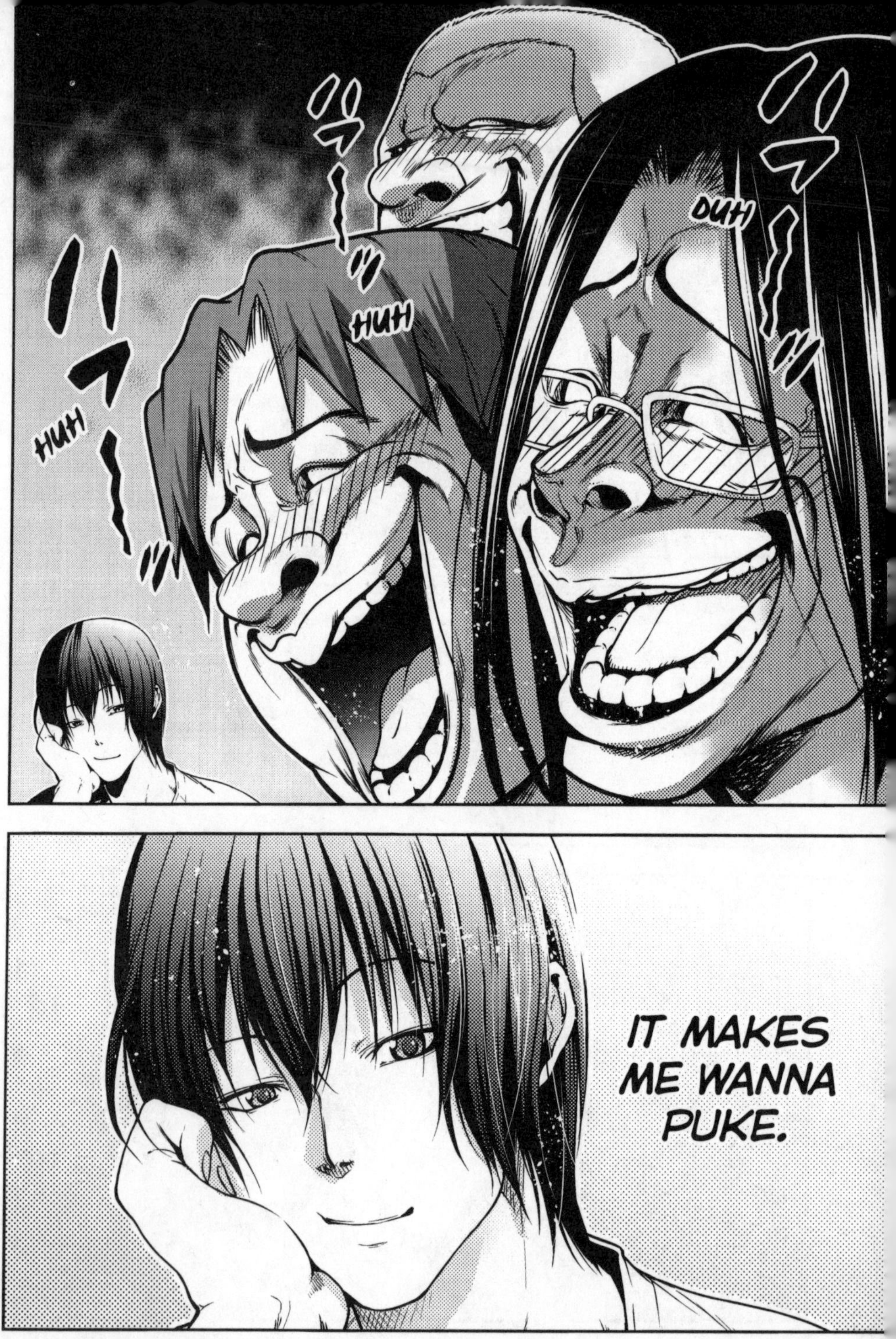
DUH
HUH
HUH
IT MAKES ME WANNA PUKE.

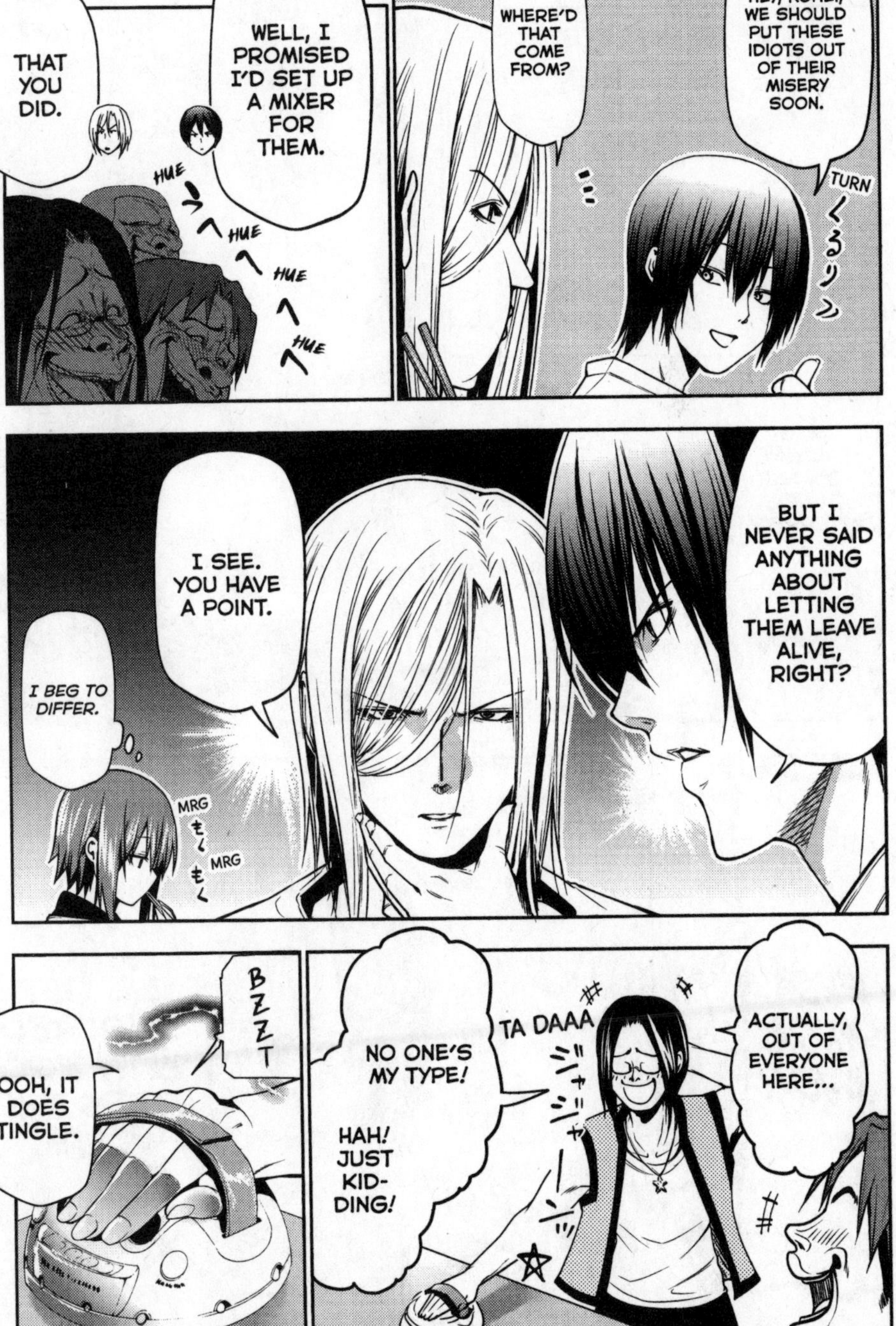
HEY, KOHEI, WE SHOULD PUT THESE IDIOTS OUT OF THEIR MISERY SOON.
TURN
くるり
WHERE'D THAT COME FROM?
WELL, I PROMISED I'D SET UP A MIXER FOR THEM.
THAT YOU DID.
HUE
HUE
HUE
HUE
BUT I NEVER SAID ANYTHING ABOUT LETTING THEM LEAVE ALIVE, RIGHT?
I SEE. YOU HAVE A POINT.
I BEG TO DIFFER.
MRG
もく
MRG
もく
ACTUALLY, OUT OF EVERYONE HERE...
TA DAAA
ジャジャーン
NO ONE'S MY TYPE!
HAH! JUST KID-DING!
BZZT
OOH, IT DOES TINGLE.

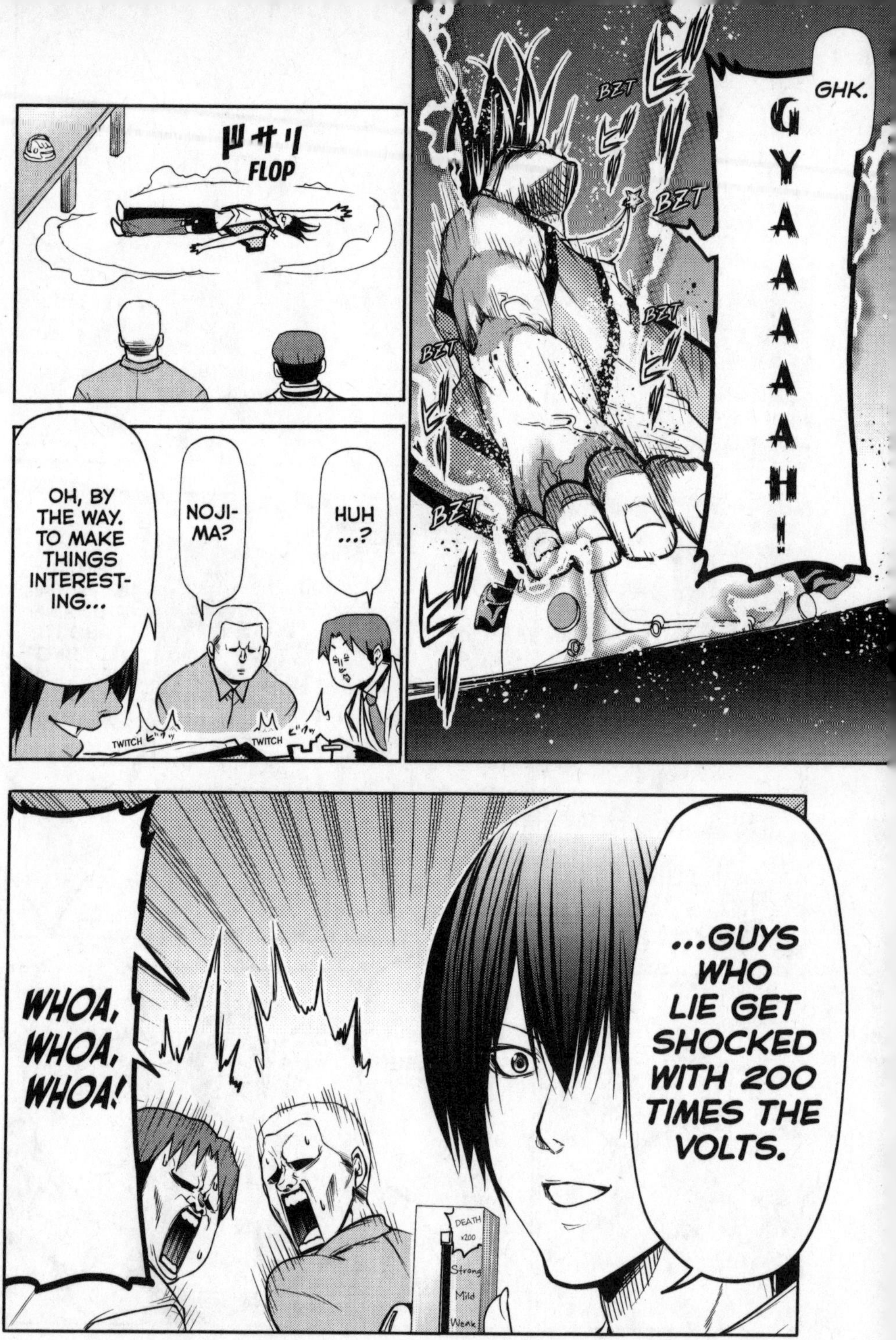
GHK.
GYAAAAAAH!
BZT
BZT
BZT
BZT
BZT
ドサリ
FLOP
HUH ...?
NOJI-MA?
OH, BY THE WAY. TO MAKE THINGS INTEREST-ING...
TWITCH ビクッ
TWITCH ビクッ
...GUYS WHO LIE GET SHOCKED WITH 200 TIMES THE VOLTS.
WHOA, WHOA, WHOA!
DEATH
x200
Strong
Mild
Weak

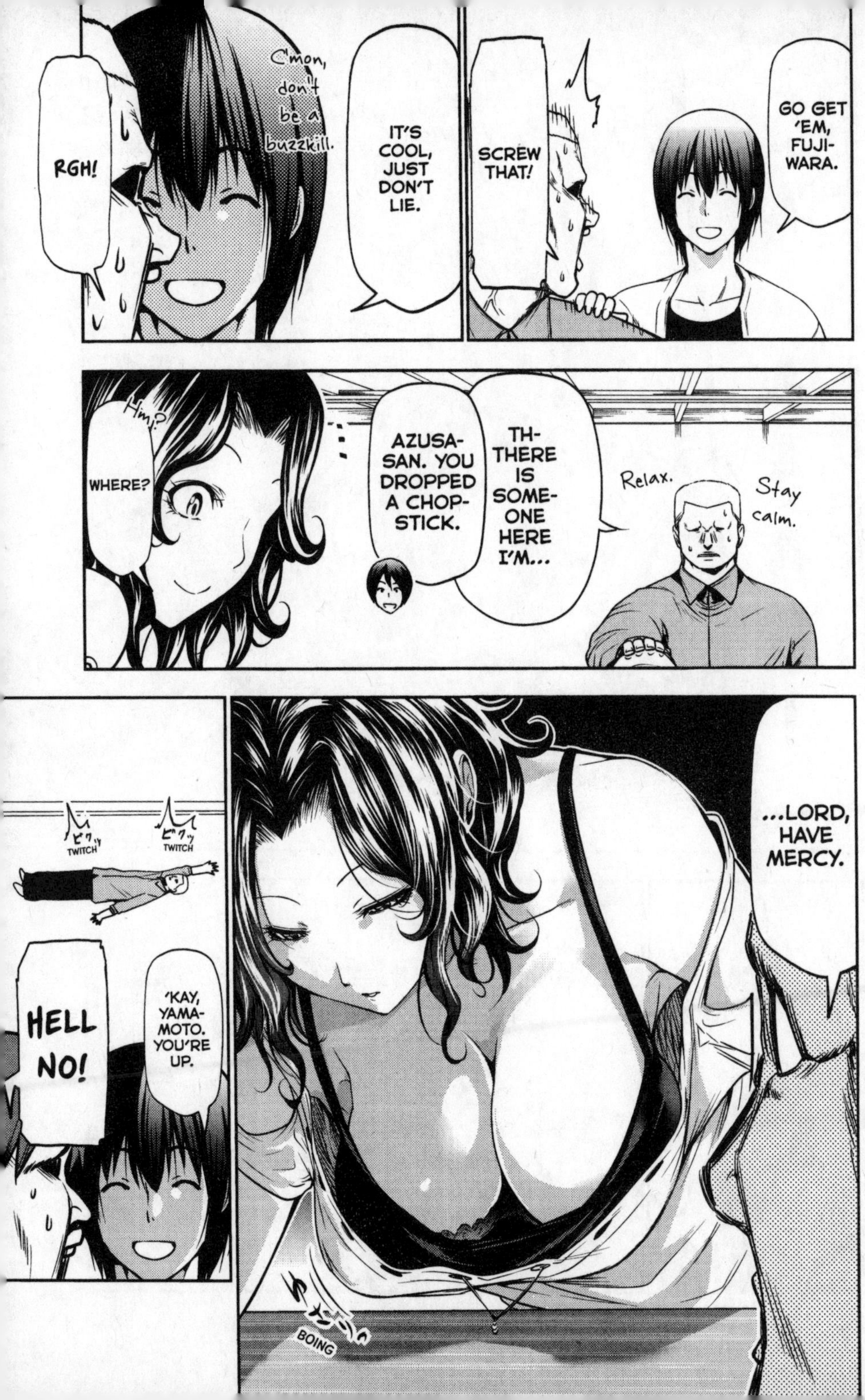
GO GET 'EM, FUJI-WARA.
SCREW THAT!
IT'S COOL, JUST DON'T LIE.
C'mon, don't be a buzzkill.
RGH!
Stay calm.
Relax.
TH-THERE IS SOME-ONE HERE I'M...
AZUSA-SAN. YOU DROPPED A CHOP-STICK.
Hm?
WHERE?
...LORD, HAVE MERCY.
BOING
TWITCH
TWITCH
'KAY, YAMA-MOTO. YOU'RE UP.
HELL NO!

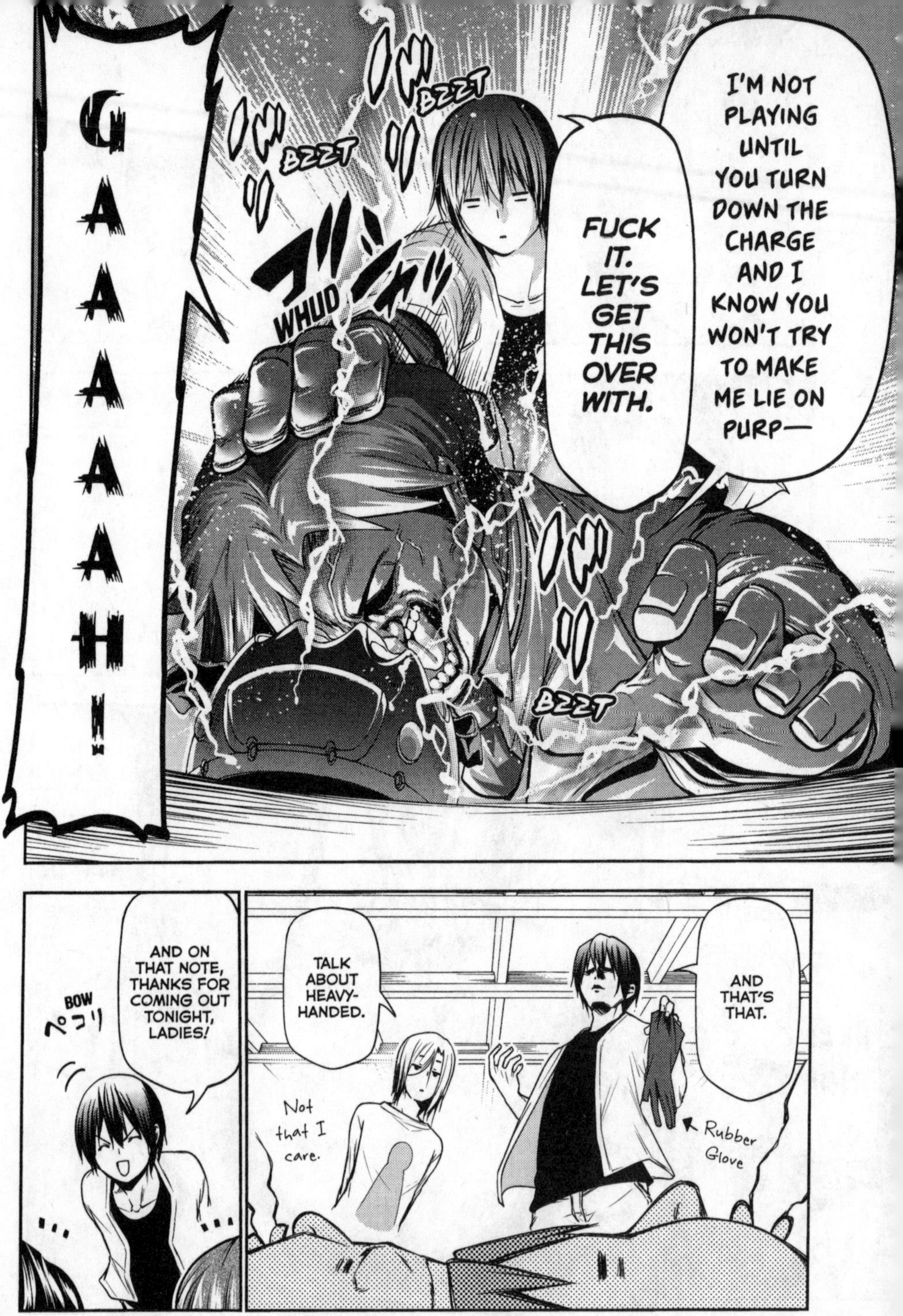
I'M NOT PLAYING UNTIL YOU TURN DOWN THE CHARGE AND I KNOW YOU WON'T TRY TO MAKE ME LIE ON PURP—
FUCK IT. LET'S GET THIS OVER WITH.
BZZT
BZZT
WHUD
BZZT
GAAAAAH!!
AND THAT'S THAT.
Rubber Glove
TALK ABOUT HEAVY-HANDED.
Not that I care.
AND ON THAT NOTE, THANKS FOR COMING OUT TONIGHT, LADIES!
BOW
...
...

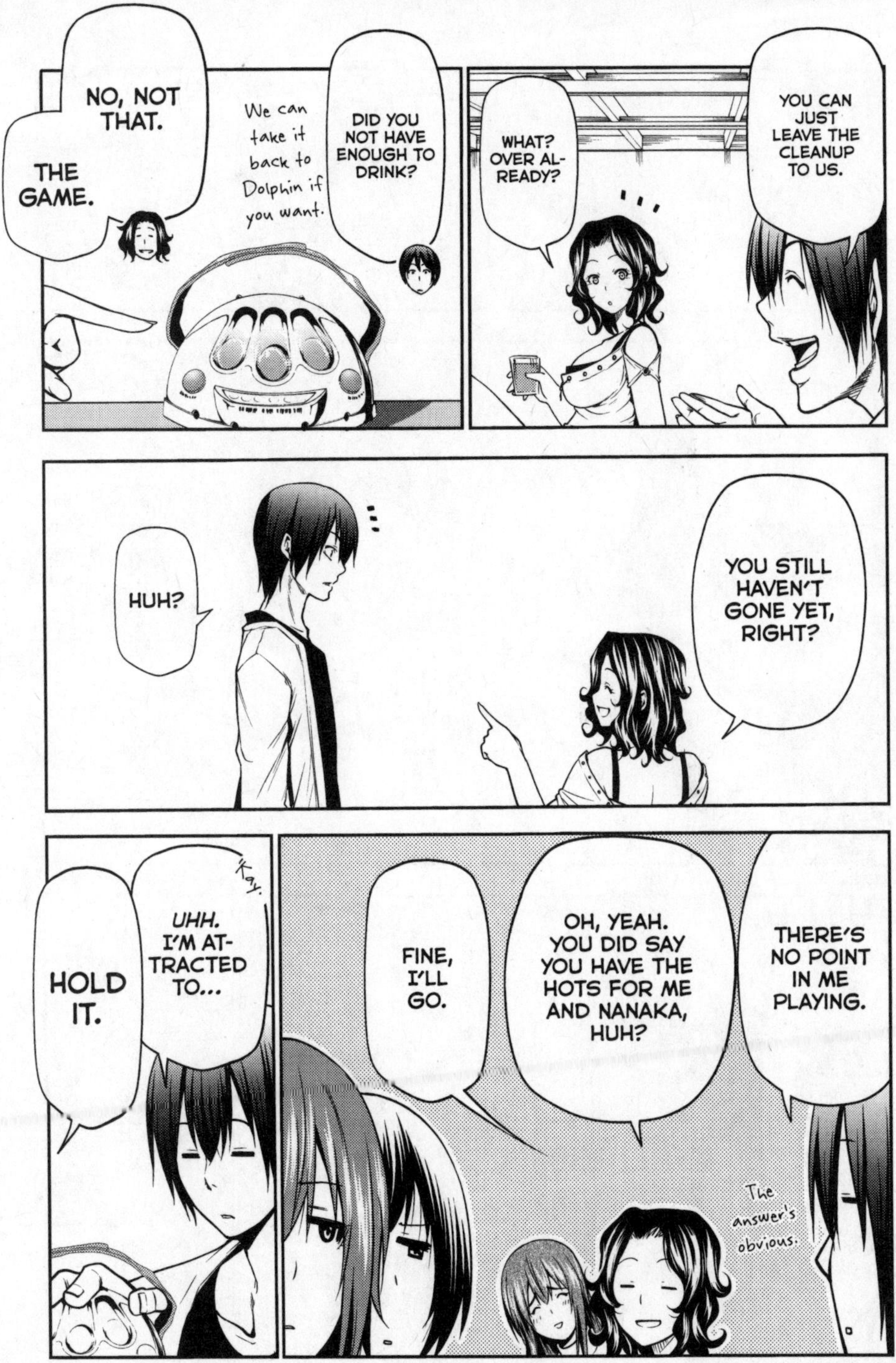
YOU CAN JUST LEAVE THE CLEANUP TO US.
WHAT? OVER AL-READY?
DID YOU NOT HAVE ENOUGH TO DRINK?
We can take it back to Dolphin if you want.
NO, NOT THAT.
THE GAME.
YOU STILL HAVEN'T GONE YET, RIGHT?
HUH?
THERE'S NO POINT IN ME PLAYING.
OH, YEAH. YOU DID SAY YOU HAVE THE HOTS FOR ME AND NANAKA, HUH?
FINE, I'LL GO.
The answer's obvious.
'Kay.
UHH. I'M AT-TRACTED TO...
HOLD IT.

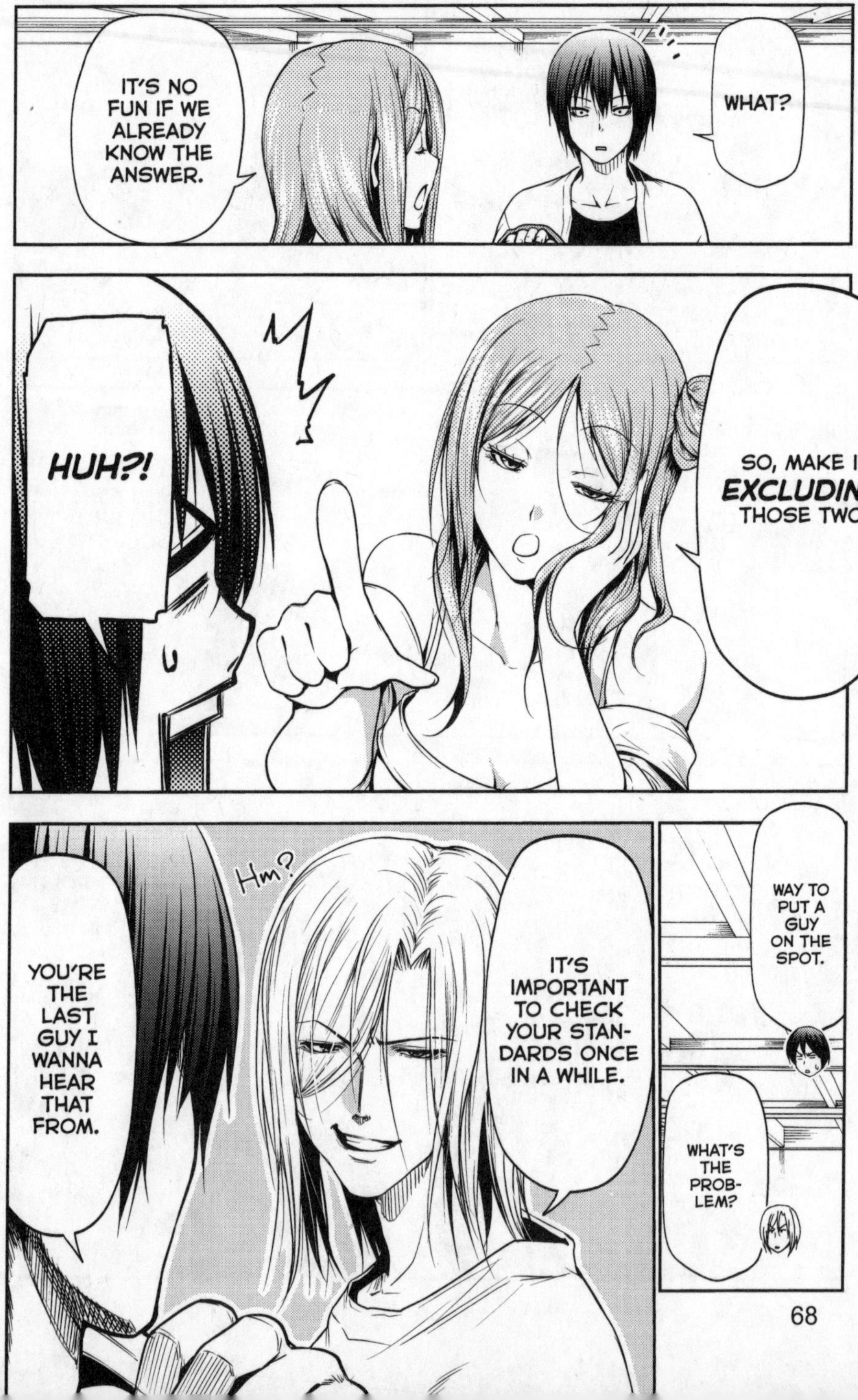
WHAT?
IT'S NO FUN IF WE ALREADY KNOW THE ANSWER.
SO, MAKE IT EXCLUDING THOSE TWO.
HUH?!
WAY TO PUT A GUY ON THE SPOT.
WHAT'S THE PROB-LEM?
Hm?
IT'S IMPORTANT TO CHECK YOUR STAN-DARDS ONCE IN A WHILE.
YOU'RE THE LAST GUY I WANNA HEAR THAT FROM.

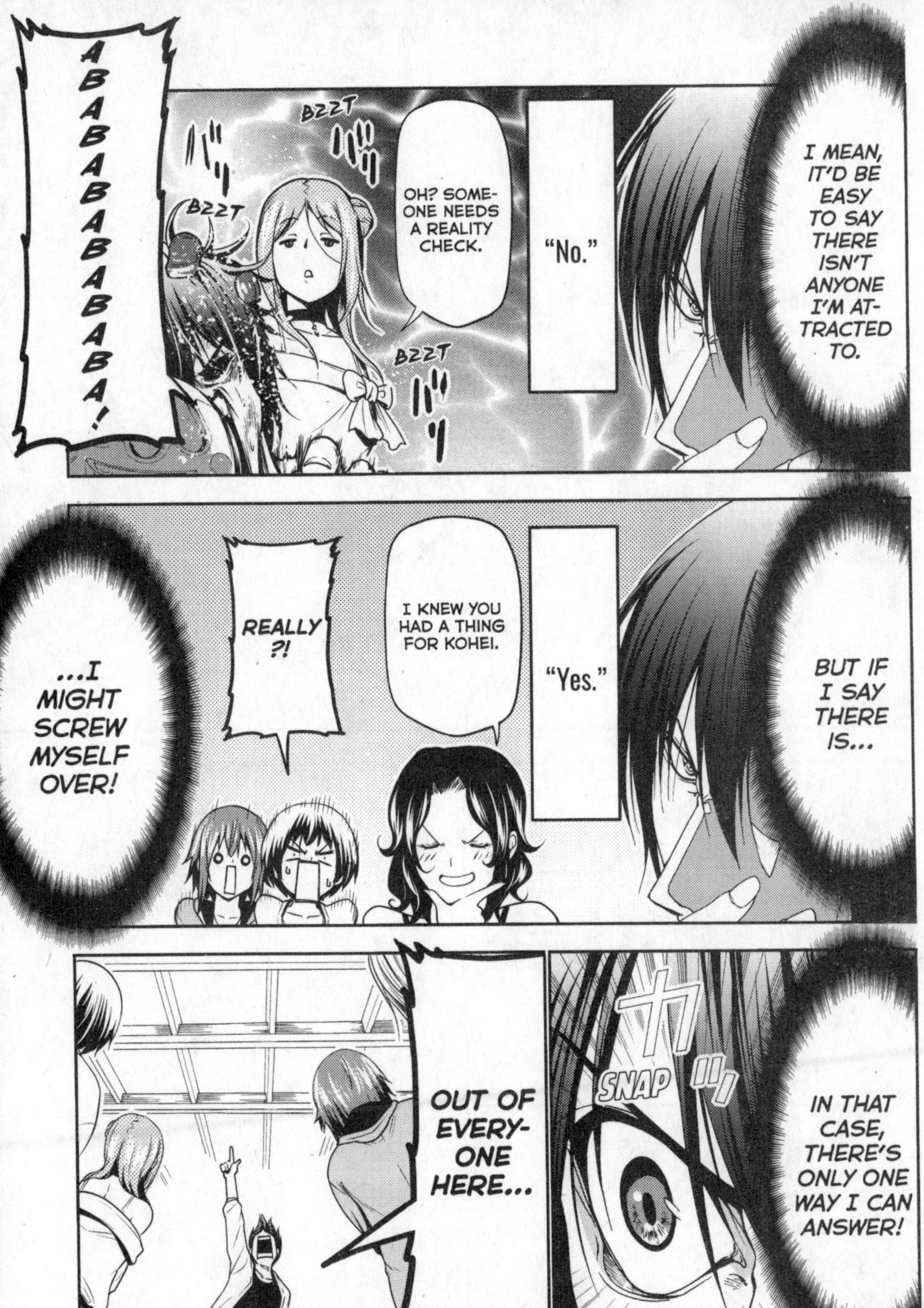
I MEAN, IT'D BE EASY TO SAY THERE ISN'T ANYONE I'M AT-TRACTED TO.
"No."
OH? SOME-ONE NEEDS A REALITY CHECK.
BZZT
BZZT
BZZT
ABABABABABABABA!
BUT IF I SAY THERE IS...
"Yes."
I KNEW YOU HAD A THING FOR KOHEI.
REALLY?!
...I MIGHT SCREW MYSELF OVER!
IN THAT CASE, THERE'S ONLY ONE WAY I CAN ANSWER!
SNAP
OUT OF EVERY-ONE HERE...

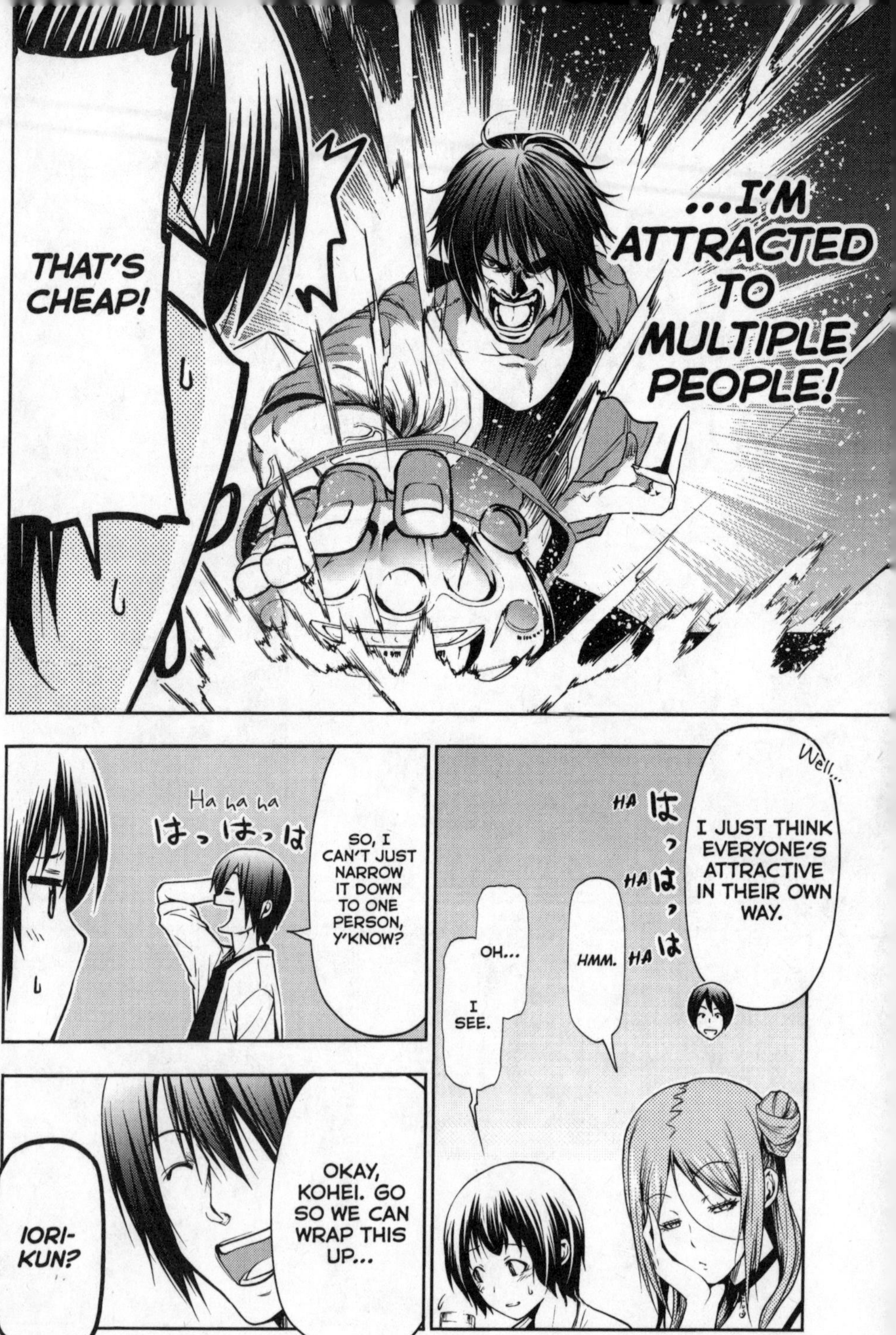
...I'M ATTRACTED TO MULTIPLE PEOPLE!
THAT'S CHEAP!
Well...
I JUST THINK EVERYONE'S ATTRACTIVE IN THEIR OWN WAY.
HA は っ HA は っ HA は
HMM.
OH... I SEE.
Ha ha ha
はっはっは
SO, I CAN'T JUST NARROW IT DOWN TO ONE PERSON, Y'KNOW?
OKAY, KOHEI. GO SO WE CAN WRAP THIS UP...
IORI-KUN?

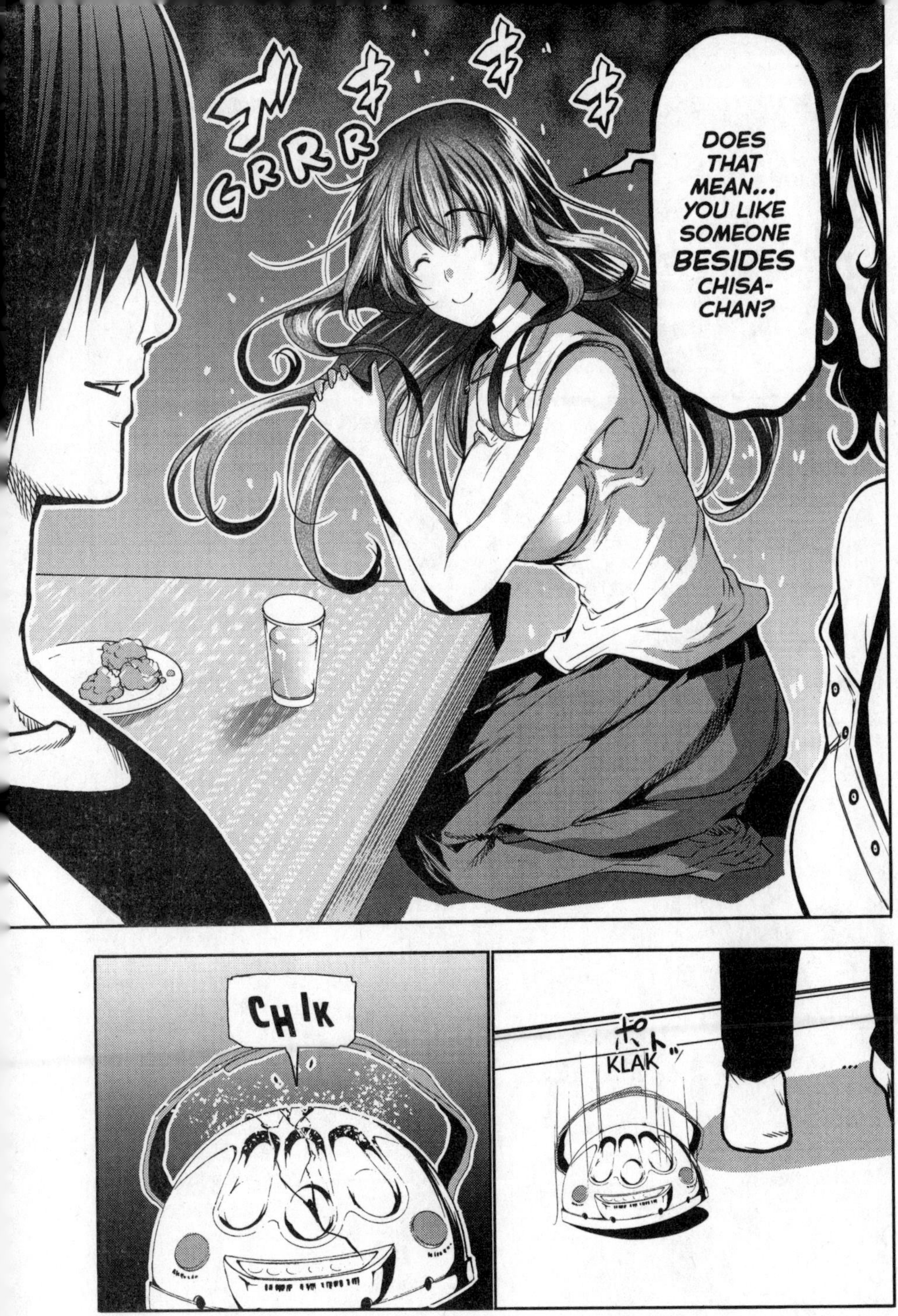
DOES THAT MEAN... YOU LIKE SOMEONE BESIDES CHISA-CHAN?
GRRR
KLAK
...
CHIK

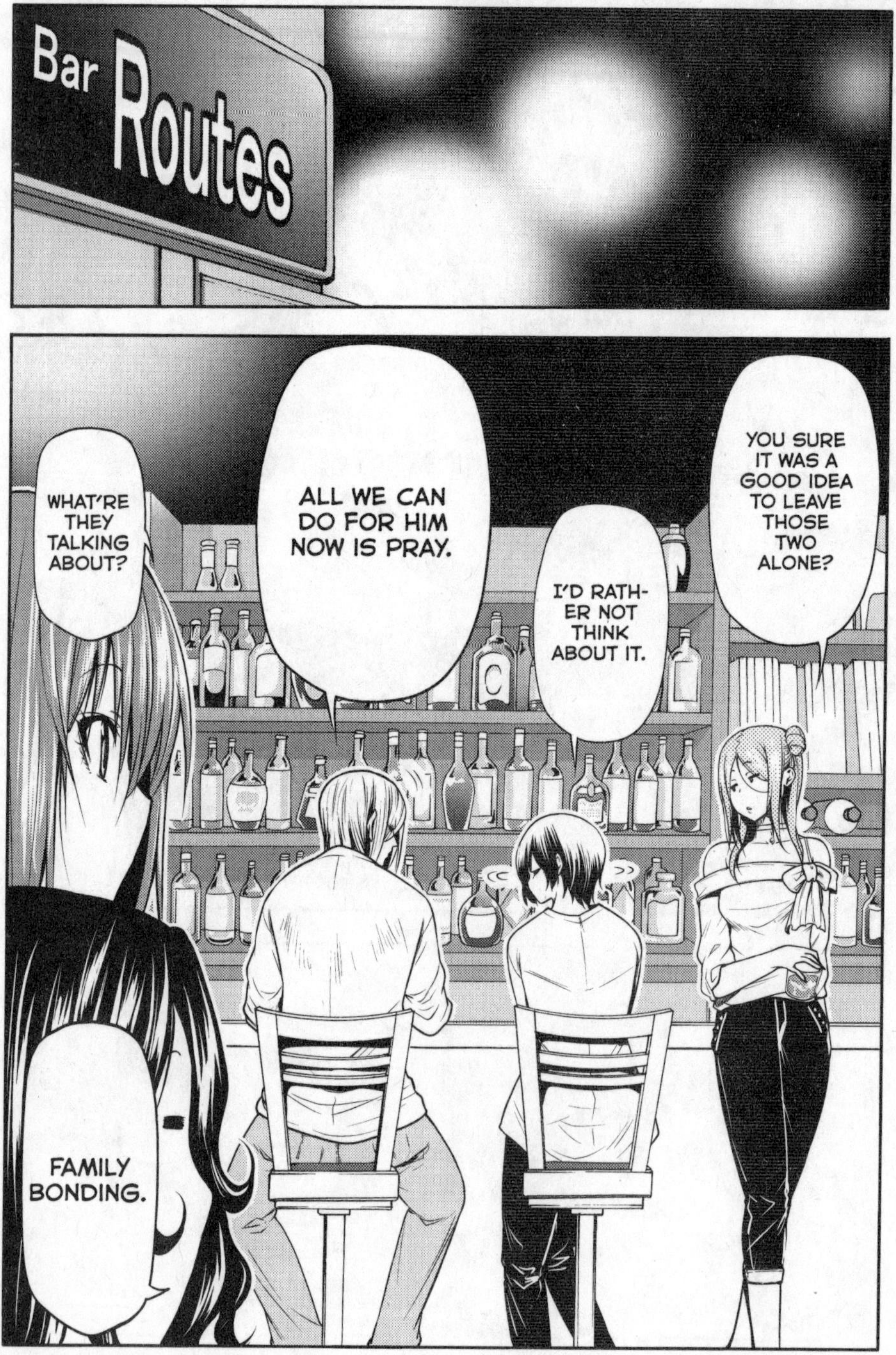
Bar Routes
YOU SURE IT WAS A GOOD IDEA TO LEAVE THOSE TWO ALONE?
I'D RATHER NOT THINK ABOUT IT.
ALL WE CAN DO FOR HIM NOW IS PRAY.
WHAT'RE THEY TALKING ABOUT?
FAMILY BONDING.

THEY GET ALONG
SURPRISINGLY WELL.

...Is that
blood?

Morning, Sakurako.
Thanks for trading
shifts with me
yesterday.

Grand Blue Dreaming

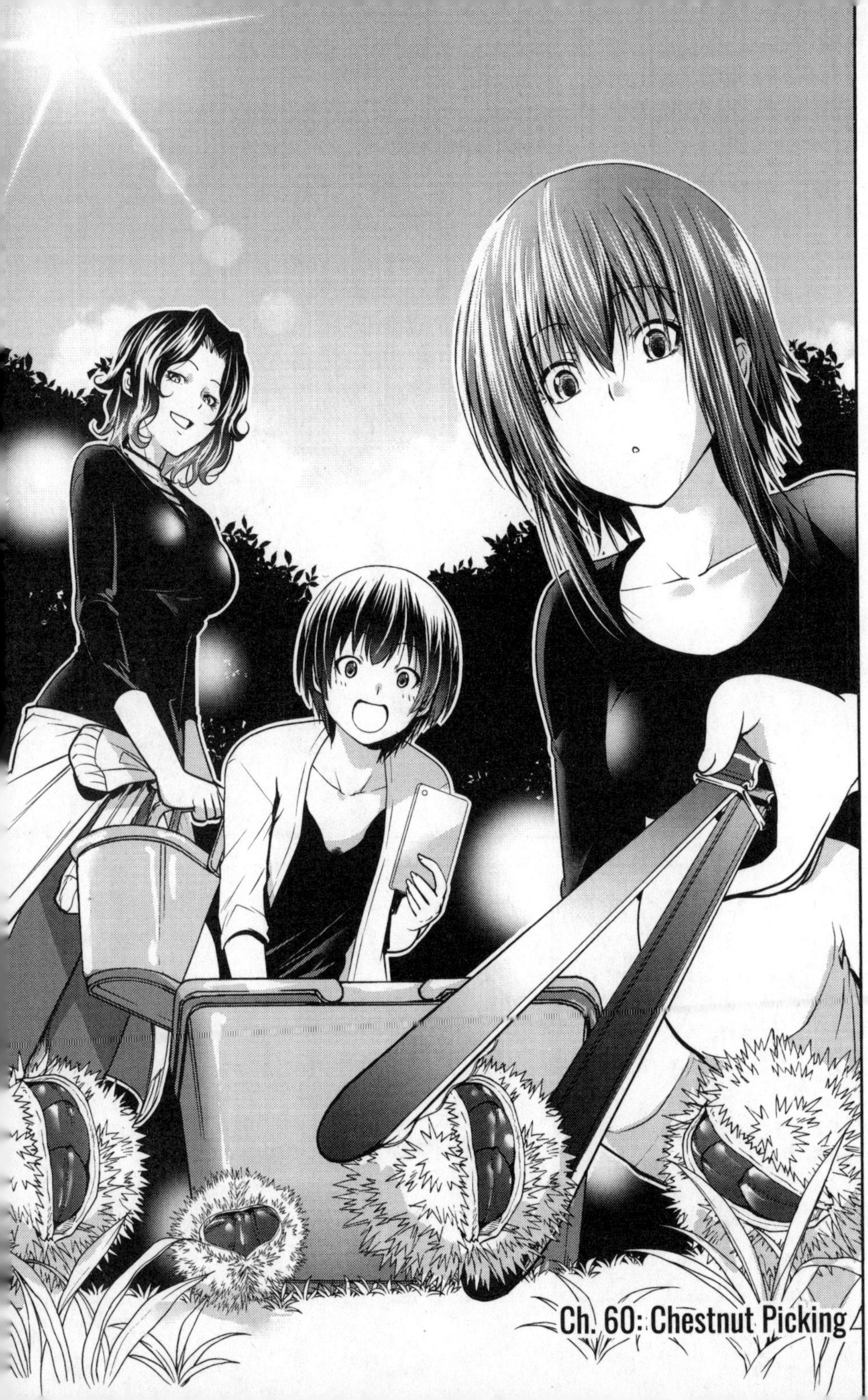
Ch. 60: Chestnut Picking

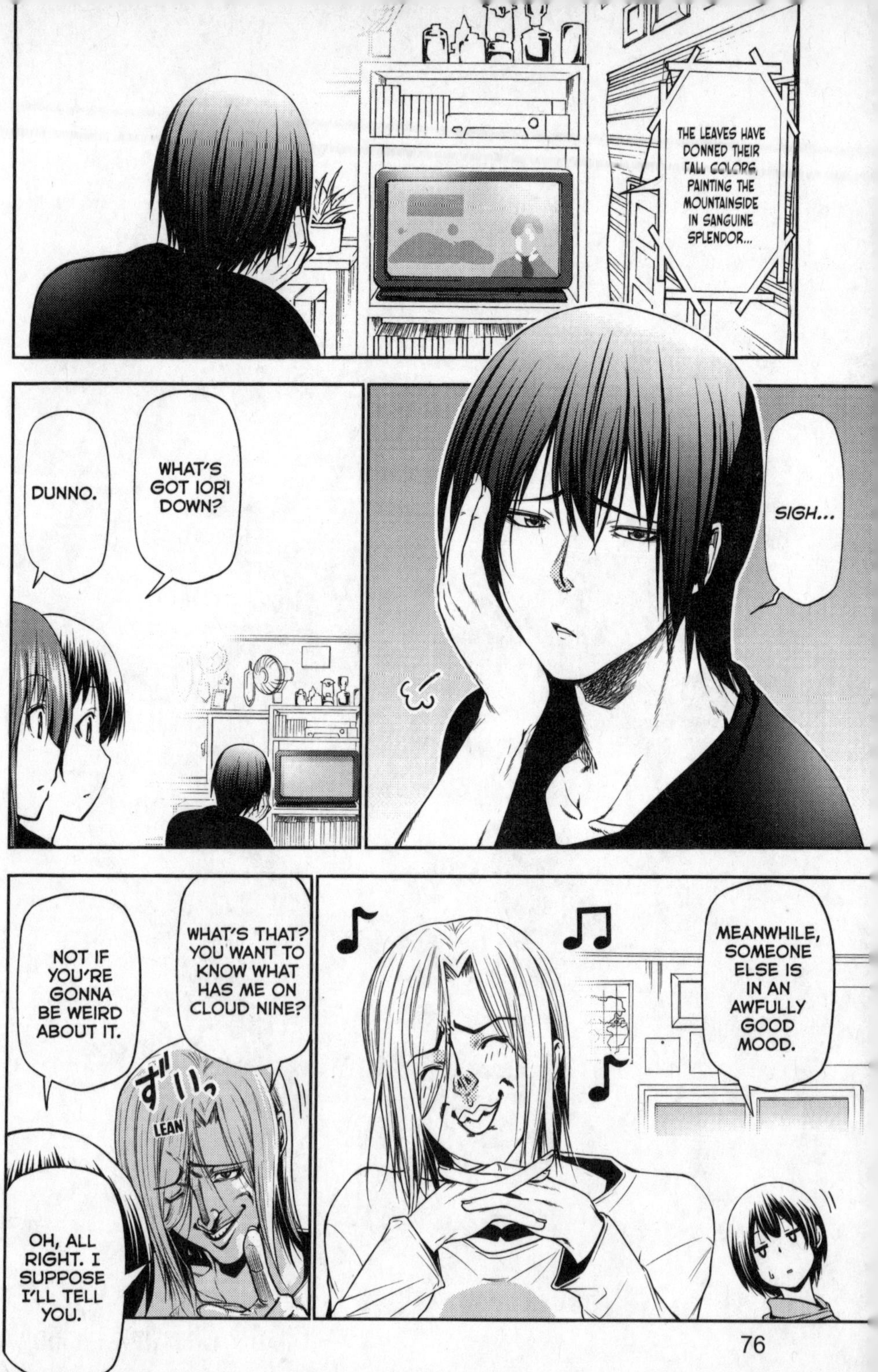
THE LEAVES HAVE DONNED THEIR FALL COLORS, PAINTING THE MOUNTAINSIDE IN SANGUINE SPLENDOR...
SIGH...
WHAT'S GOT IORI DOWN?
DUNNO.
MEANWHILE, SOMEONE ELSE IS IN AN AWFULLY GOOD MOOD.
WHAT'S THAT? YOU WANT TO KNOW WHAT HAS ME ON CLOUD NINE?
NOT IF YOU'RE GONNA BE WEIRD ABOUT IT.
ずい
LEAN
OH, ALL RIGHT. I SUPPOSE I'LL TELL YOU.

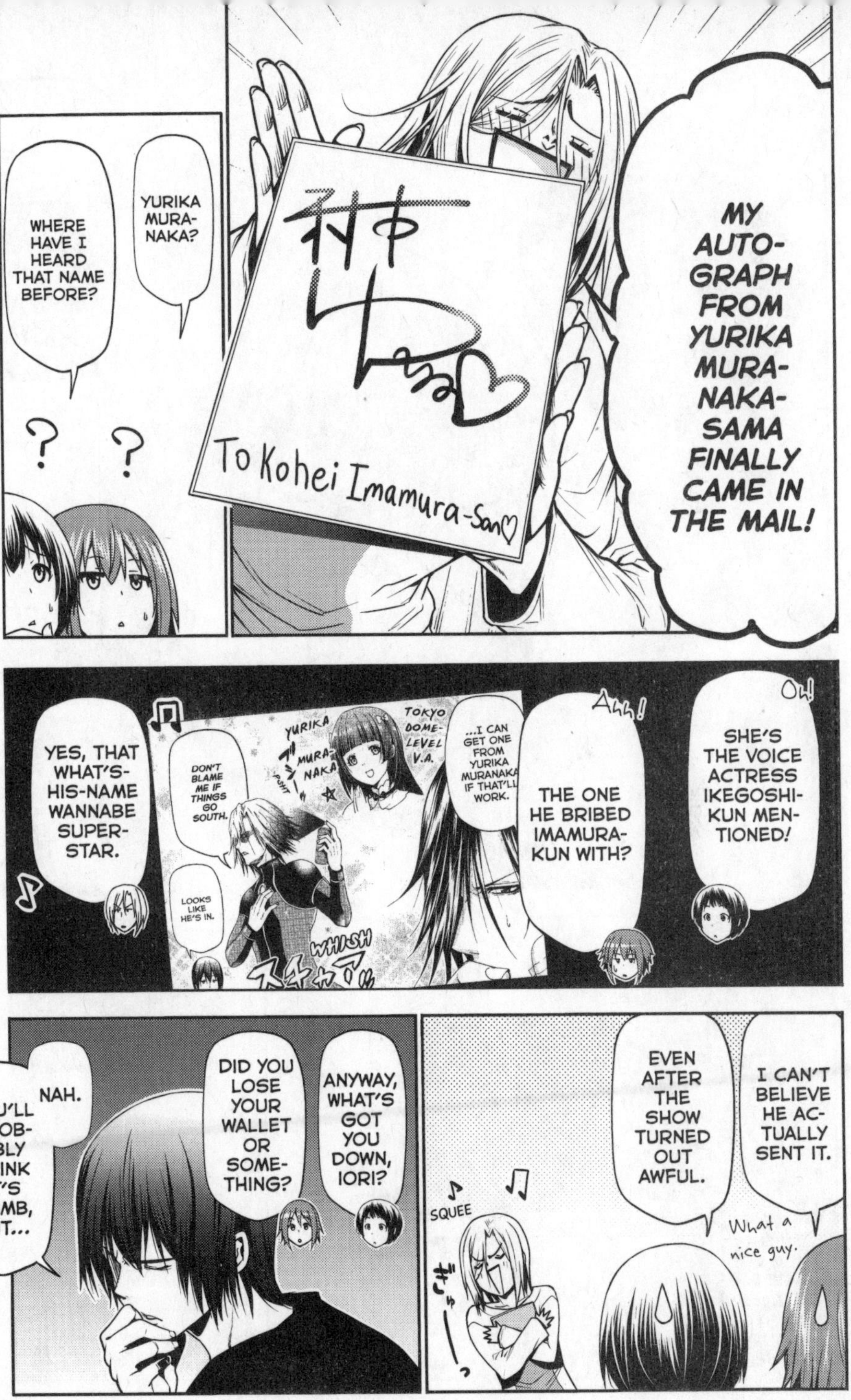
MY AUTO-GRAPH FROM YURIKA MURA-NAKA-SAMA FINALLY CAME IN THE MAIL!
To Kohei Imamura-San♡
YURIKA MURA-NAKA?
WHERE HAVE I HEARD THAT NAME BEFORE?
? ?
Oh!
SHE'S THE VOICE ACTRESS IKEGOSHI-KUN MEN-TIONED!
Ahh!
THE ONE HE BRIBED IMAMURA-KUN WITH?
...I CAN GET ONE FROM YURIKA MURANAKA IF THAT'LL WORK.
TOKYO DOME-LEVEL V.A.
YURIKA MURA-NAKA
DON'T BLAME ME IF THINGS GO SOUTH.
LOOKS LIKE HE'S IN.
WHISH
YES, THAT WHAT'S-HIS-NAME WANNABE SUPER-STAR.
I CAN'T BELIEVE HE AC-TUALLY SENT IT.
EVEN AFTER THE SHOW TURNED OUT AWFUL.
What a nice guy.
SQUEE
ANYWAY, WHAT'S GOT YOU DOWN, IORI?
DID YOU LOSE YOUR WALLET OR SOME-THING?
NAH.
YOU'LL PROB-ABLY THINK IT'S DUMB, BUT...

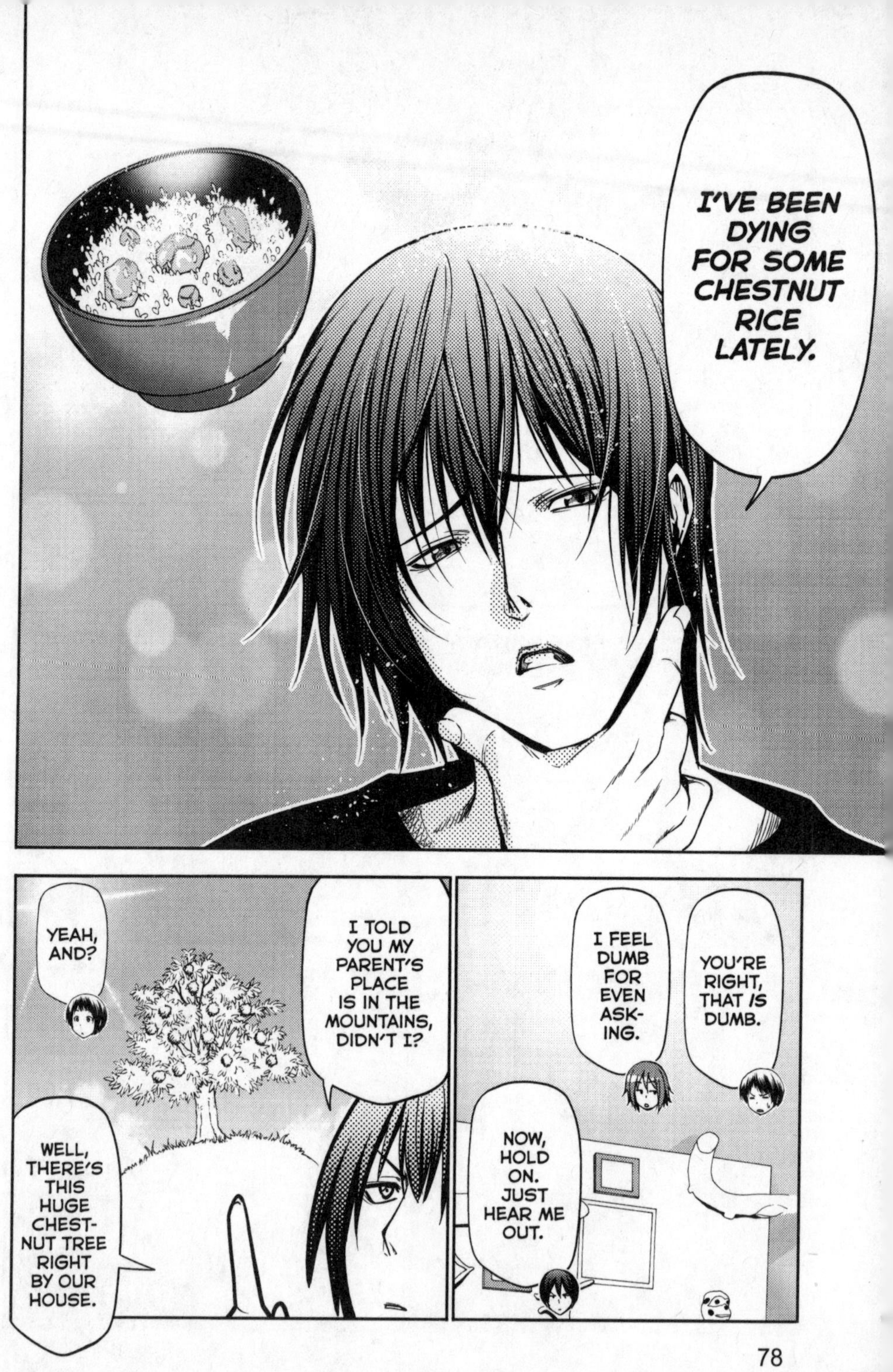
I'VE BEEN DYING FOR SOME CHESTNUT RICE LATELY.
YOU'RE RIGHT, THAT *IS* DUMB.
I FEEL DUMB FOR EVEN ASKING.
NOW, HOLD ON. JUST HEAR ME OUT.
I TOLD YOU MY PARENT'S PLACE IS IN THE MOUNTAINS, DIDN'T I?
YEAH, AND?
WELL, THERE'S THIS HUGE CHEST-NUT TREE RIGHT BY OUR HOUSE.

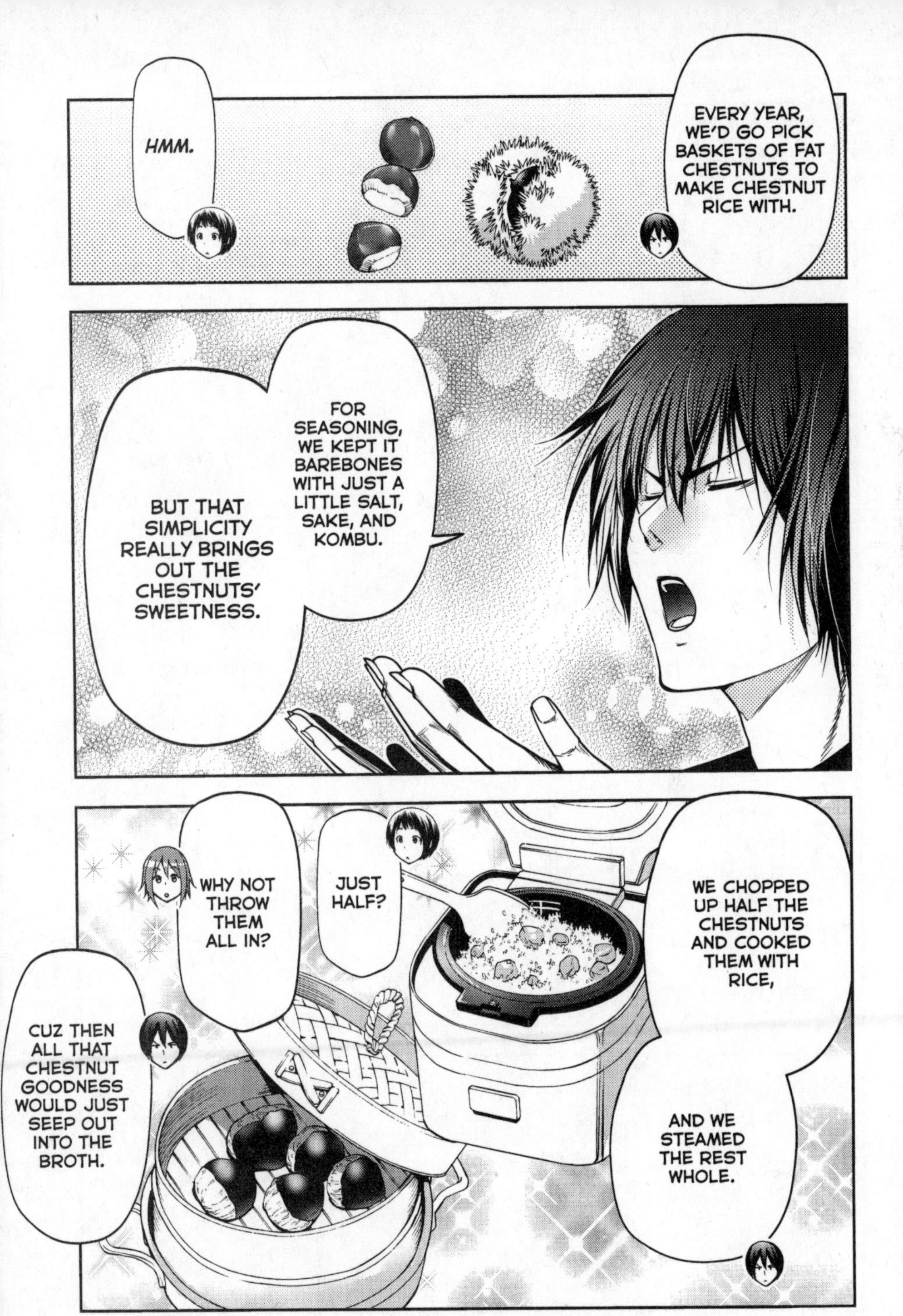
EVERY YEAR, WE'D GO PICK BASKETS OF FAT CHESTNUTS TO MAKE CHESTNUT RICE WITH.
HMM.
FOR SEASONING, WE KEPT IT BAREBONES WITH JUST A LITTLE SALT, SAKE, AND KOMBU.
BUT THAT SIMPLICITY REALLY BRINGS OUT THE CHESTNUTS' SWEETNESS.
WE CHOPPED UP HALF THE CHESTNUTS AND COOKED THEM WITH RICE,
AND WE STEAMED THE REST WHOLE.
JUST HALF?
WHY NOT THROW THEM ALL IN?
CUZ THEN ALL THAT CHESTNUT GOODNESS WOULD JUST SEEP OUT INTO THE BROTH.

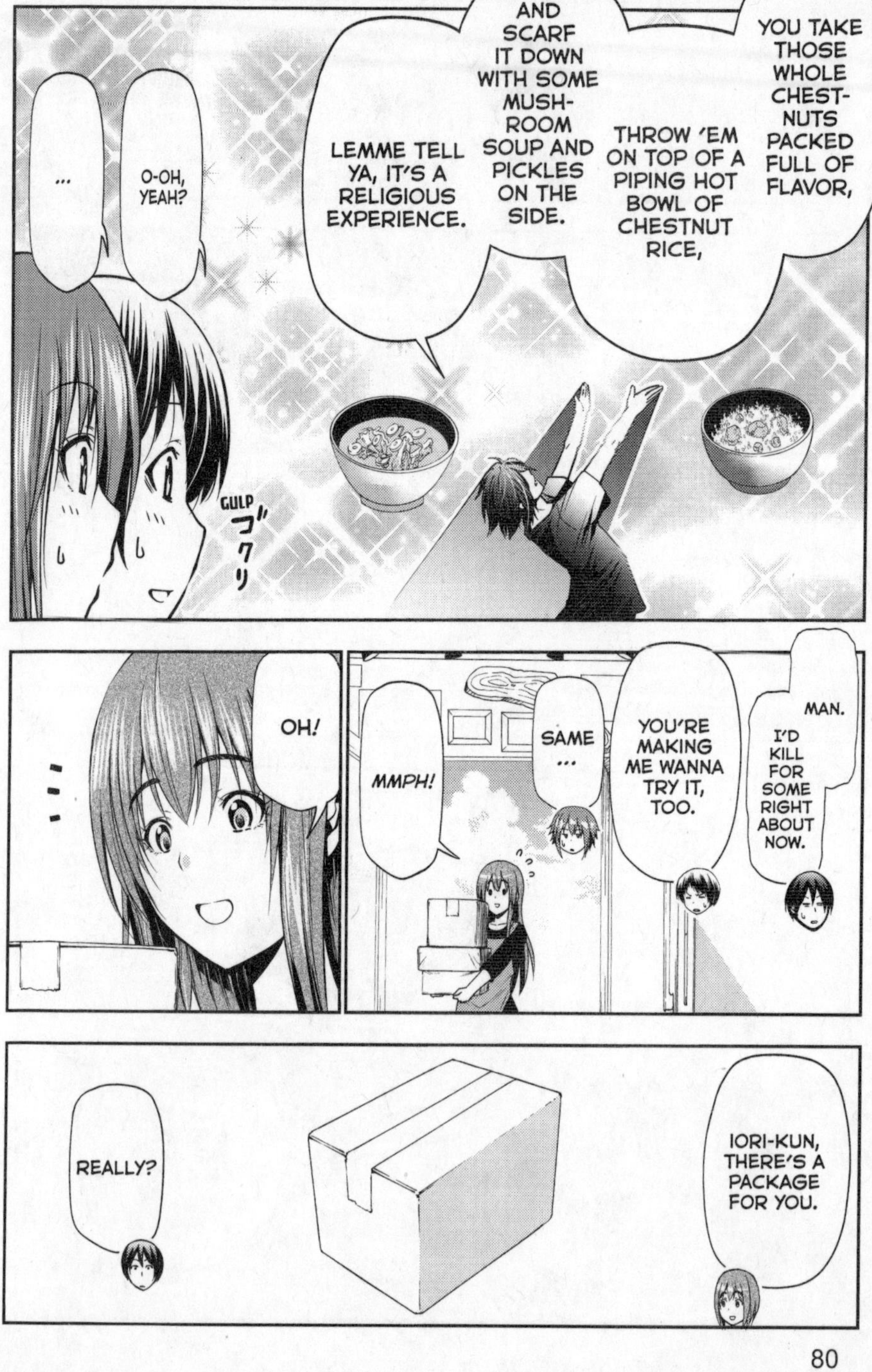
YOU TAKE THOSE WHOLE CHEST-NUTS PACKED FULL OF FLAVOR,
THROW 'EM ON TOP OF A PIPING HOT BOWL OF CHESTNUT RICE,
AND SCARF IT DOWN WITH SOME MUSH-ROOM SOUP AND PICKLES ON THE SIDE.
LEMME TELL YA, IT'S A RELIGIOUS EXPERIENCE.
O-OH, YEAH?
...
GULP
ゴクリ
MAN.
I'D KILL FOR SOME RIGHT ABOUT NOW.
YOU'RE MAKING ME WANNA TRY IT, TOO.
SAME...
MMPH!
OH!
IORI-KUN, THERE'S A PACKAGE FOR YOU.
REALLY?

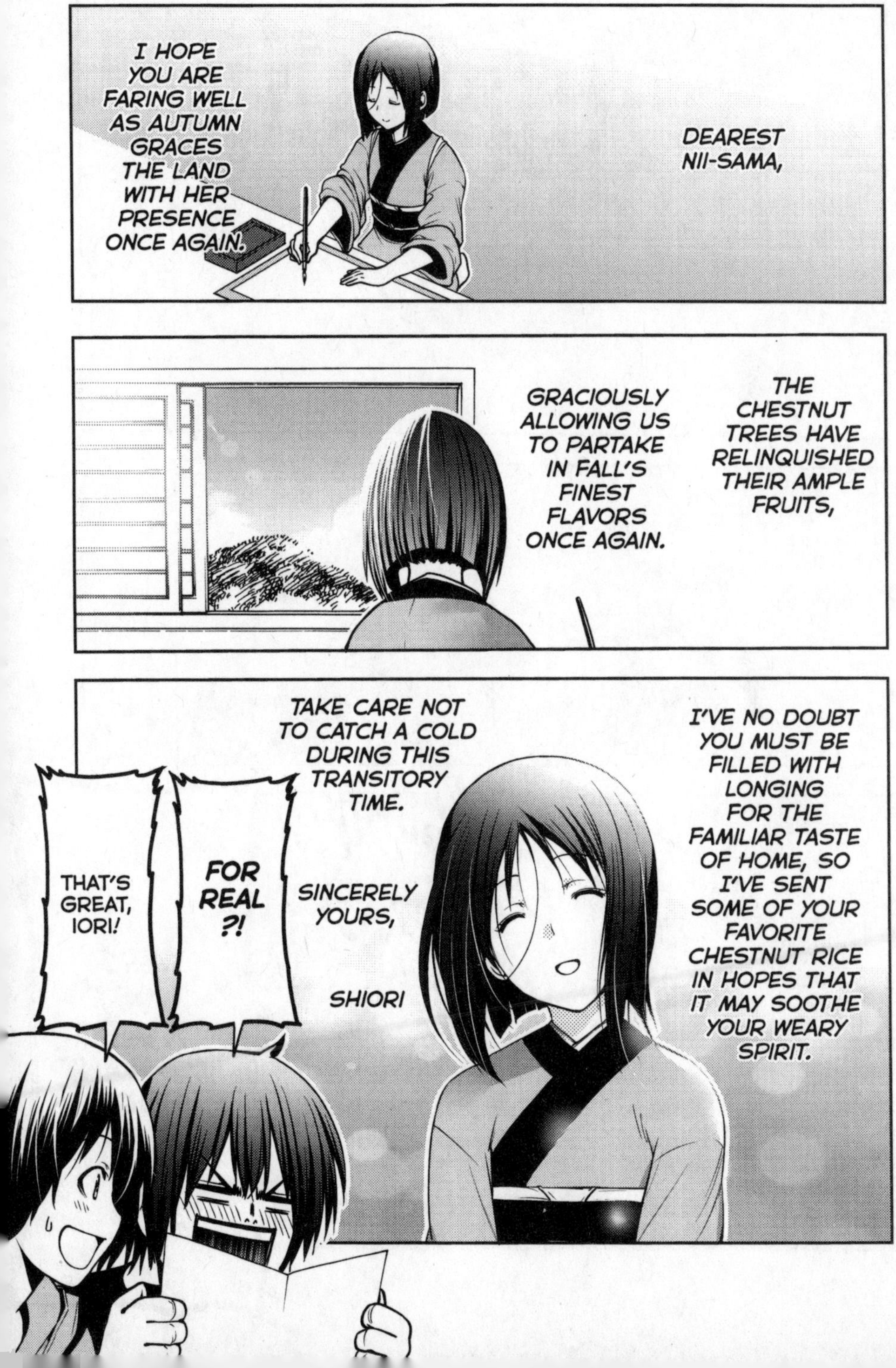
DEAREST NII-SAMA,
I HOPE YOU ARE FARING WELL AS AUTUMN GRACES THE LAND WITH HER PRESENCE ONCE AGAIN.
THE CHESTNUT TREES HAVE RELINQUISHED THEIR AMPLE FRUITS,
GRACIOUSLY ALLOWING US TO PARTAKE IN FALL'S FINEST FLAVORS ONCE AGAIN.
I'VE NO DOUBT YOU MUST BE FILLED WITH LONGING FOR THE FAMILIAR TASTE OF HOME, SO I'VE SENT SOME OF YOUR FAVORITE CHESTNUT RICE IN HOPES THAT IT MAY SOOTHE YOUR WEARY SPIRIT.
TAKE CARE NOT TO CATCH A COLD DURING THIS TRANSITORY TIME.
SINCERELY YOURS,
SHIORI
FOR REAL?!
THAT'S GREAT, IORI!

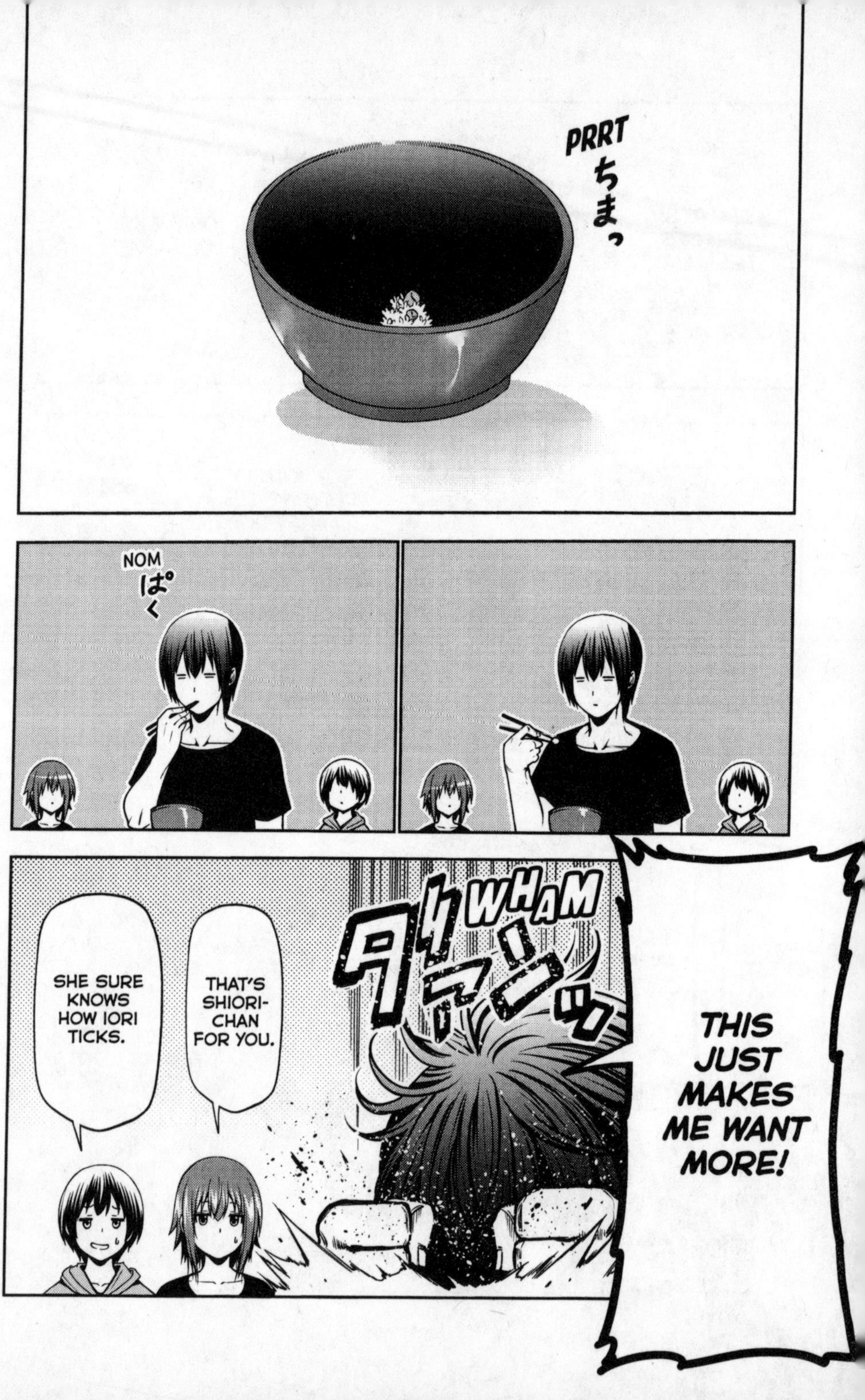

PRRT
ちまっ
NOM
ぱく
THIS JUST MAKES ME WANT MORE!
WHAM
THAT'S SHIORI-CHAN FOR YOU.
SHE SURE KNOWS HOW IORI TICKS.

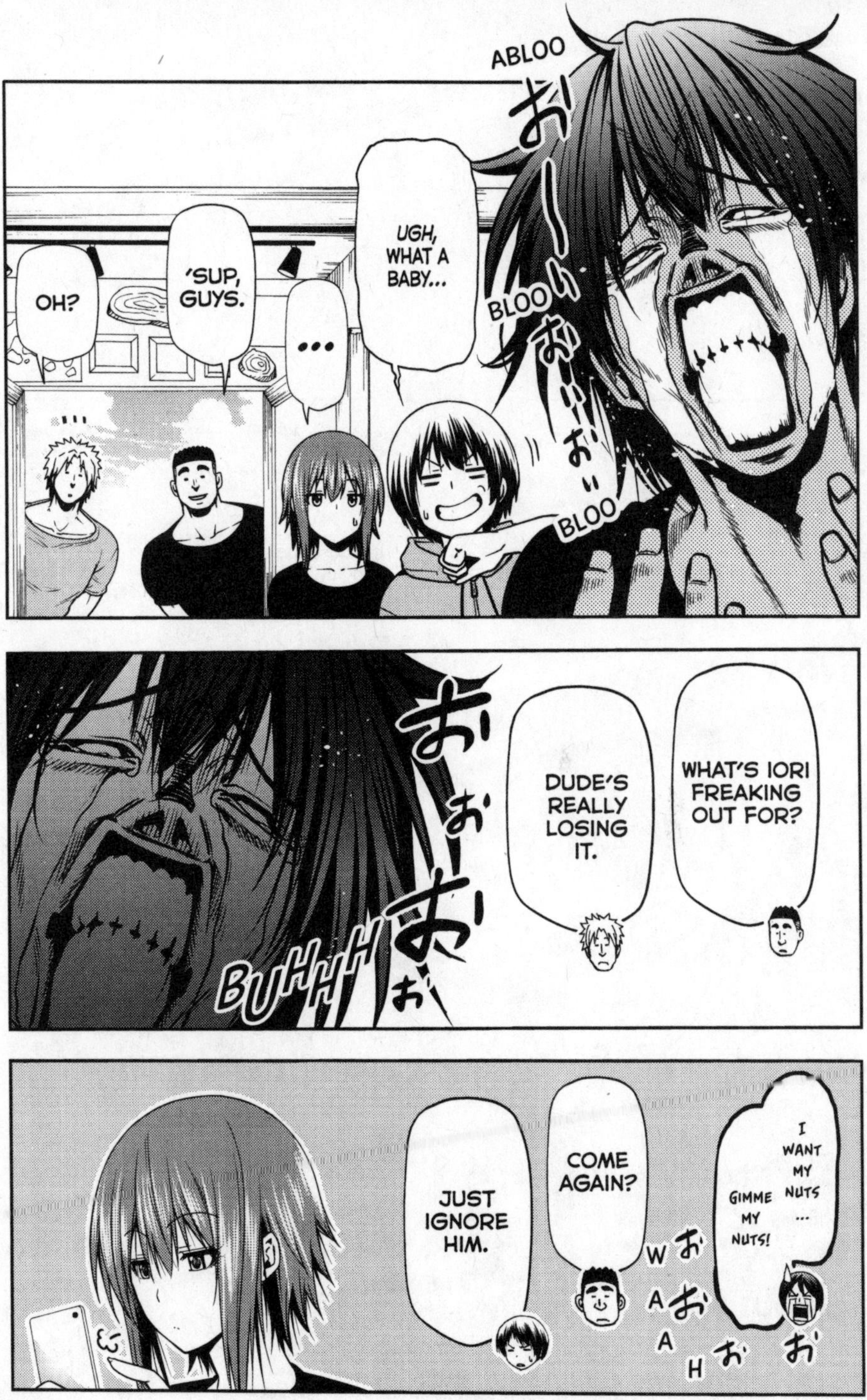
ABLOO
BLOO
BLOO
UGH, WHAT A BABY...
...
'SUP, GUYS.
OH?
WHAT'S IORI FREAKING OUT FOR?
DUDE'S REALLY LOSING IT.
BUHHH
I WANT MY NUTS...
GIMME MY NUTS!
WAAH
COME AGAIN?
JUST IGNORE HIM.

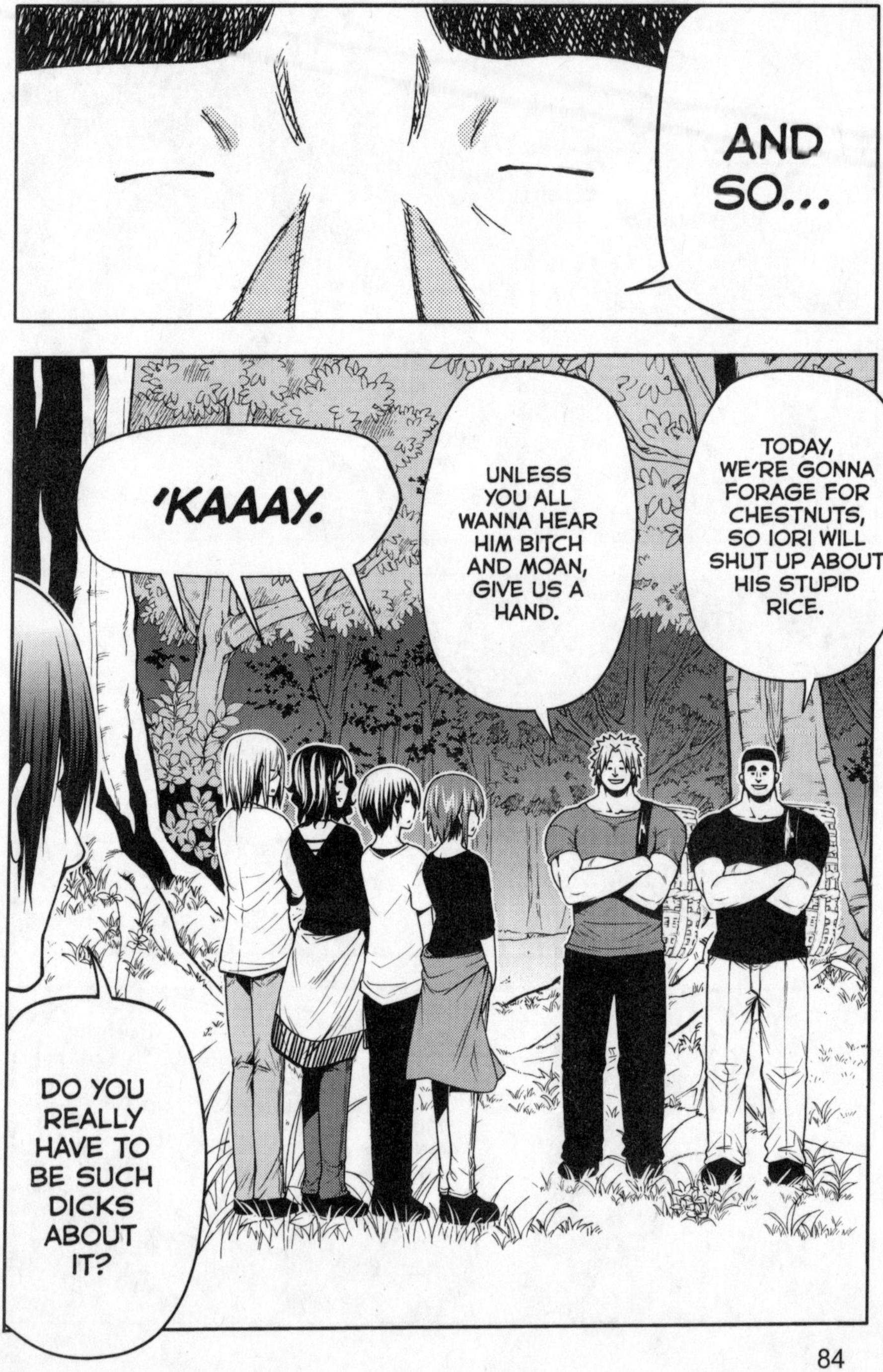
AND SO...
TODAY, WE'RE GONNA FORAGE FOR CHESTNUTS, SO IORI WILL SHUT UP ABOUT HIS STUPID RICE.
UNLESS YOU ALL WANNA HEAR HIM BITCH AND MOAN, GIVE US A HAND.
'KAAAY.
DO YOU REALLY HAVE TO BE SUCH DICKS ABOUT IT?

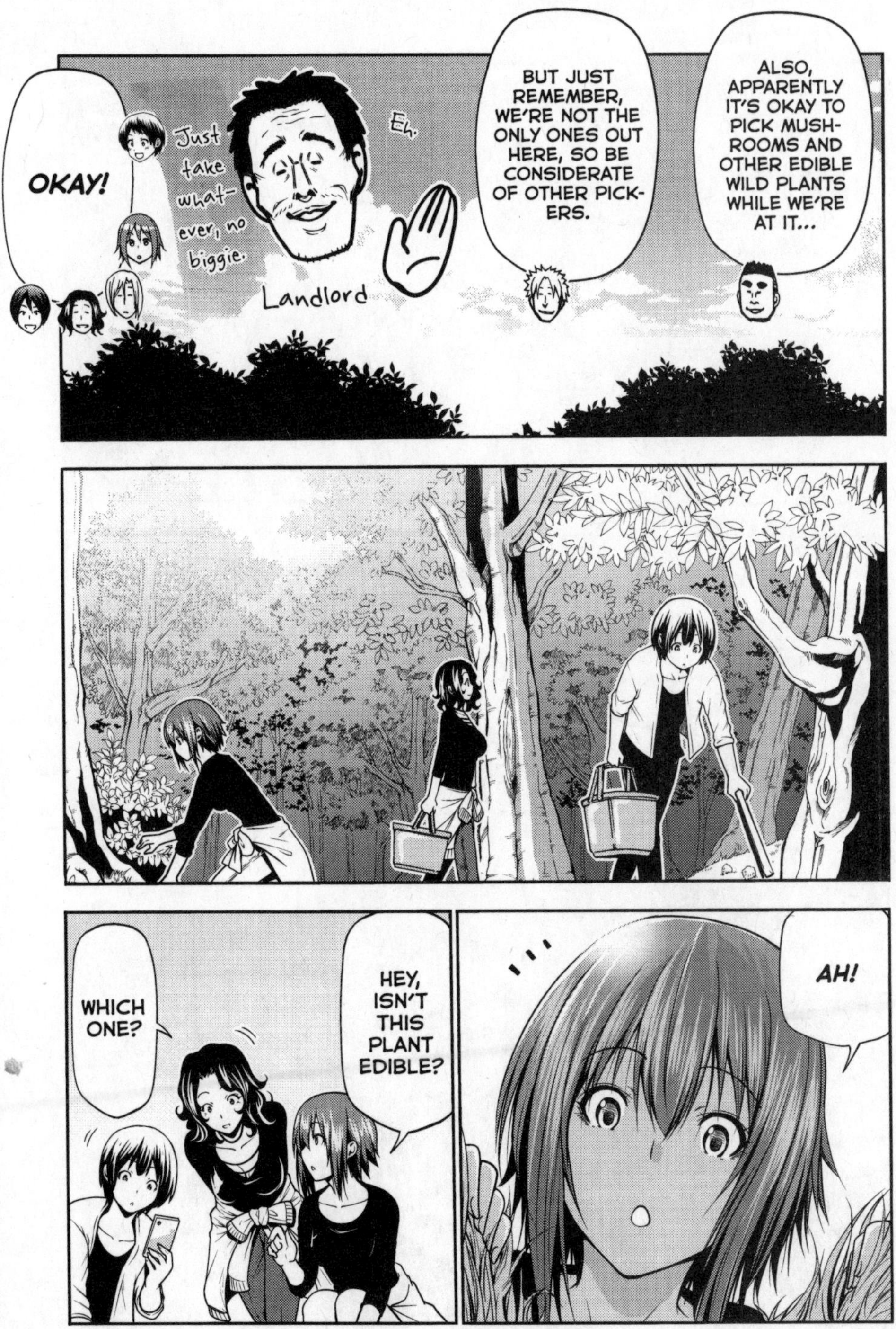
ALSO, APPARENTLY IT'S OKAY TO PICK MUSH-ROOMS AND OTHER EDIBLE WILD PLANTS WHILE WE'RE AT IT...
BUT JUST REMEMBER, WE'RE NOT THE ONLY ONES OUT HERE, SO BE CONSIDERATE OF OTHER PICK-ERS.
Eh.
Just take what-ever, no biggie.
Landlord
OKAY!
AH!
HEY, ISN'T THIS PLANT EDIBLE?
WHICH ONE?

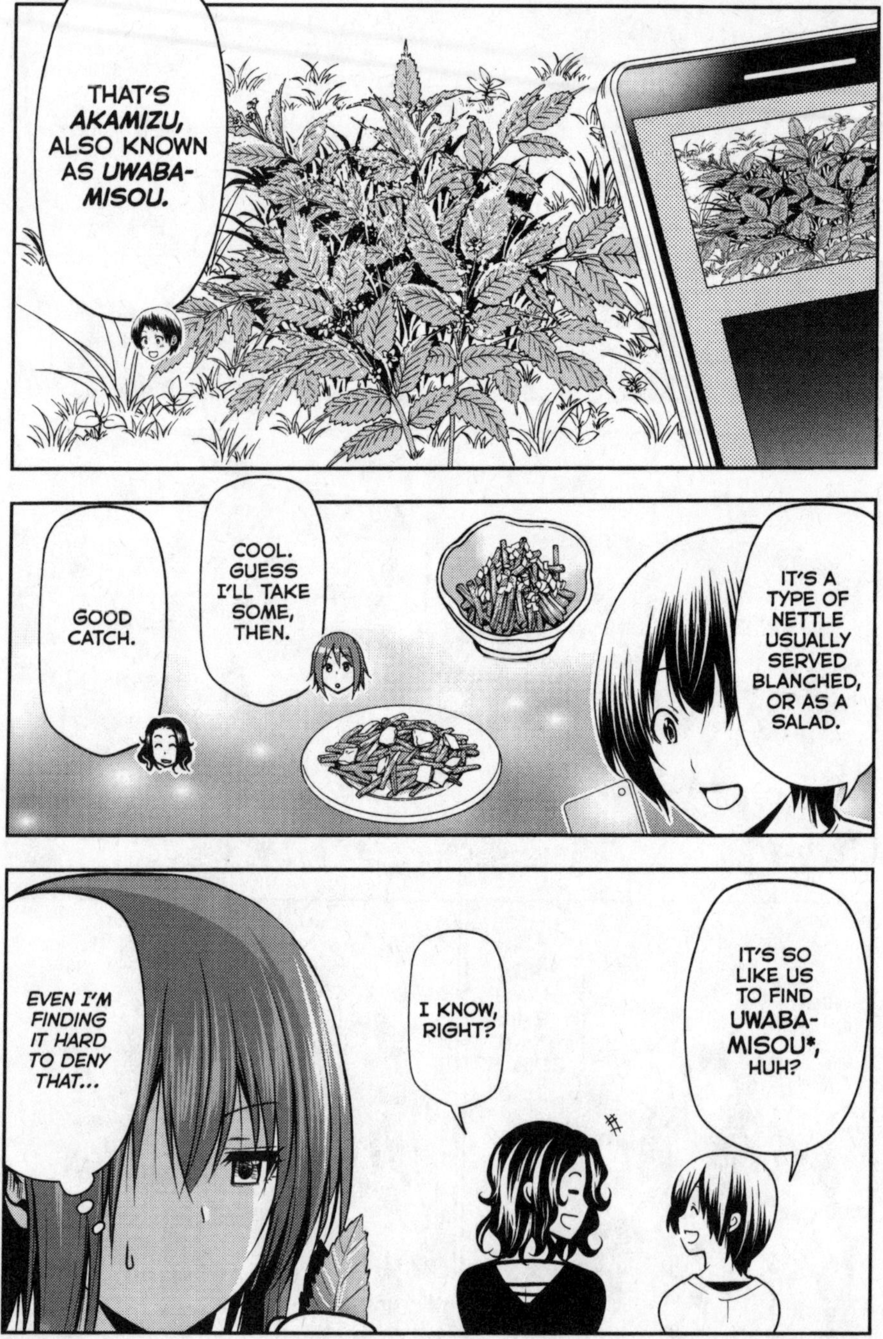
THAT'S AKAMIZU, ALSO KNOWN AS UWABA-MISOU.
IT'S A TYPE OF NETTLE USUALLY SERVED BLANCHED, OR AS A SALAD.
COOL. GUESS I'LL TAKE SOME, THEN.
GOOD CATCH.
IT'S SO LIKE US TO FIND UWABA-MISOU*, HUH?
I KNOW, RIGHT?
EVEN I'M FINDING IT HARD TO DENY THAT...

*Uwabami: A heavy drinker.

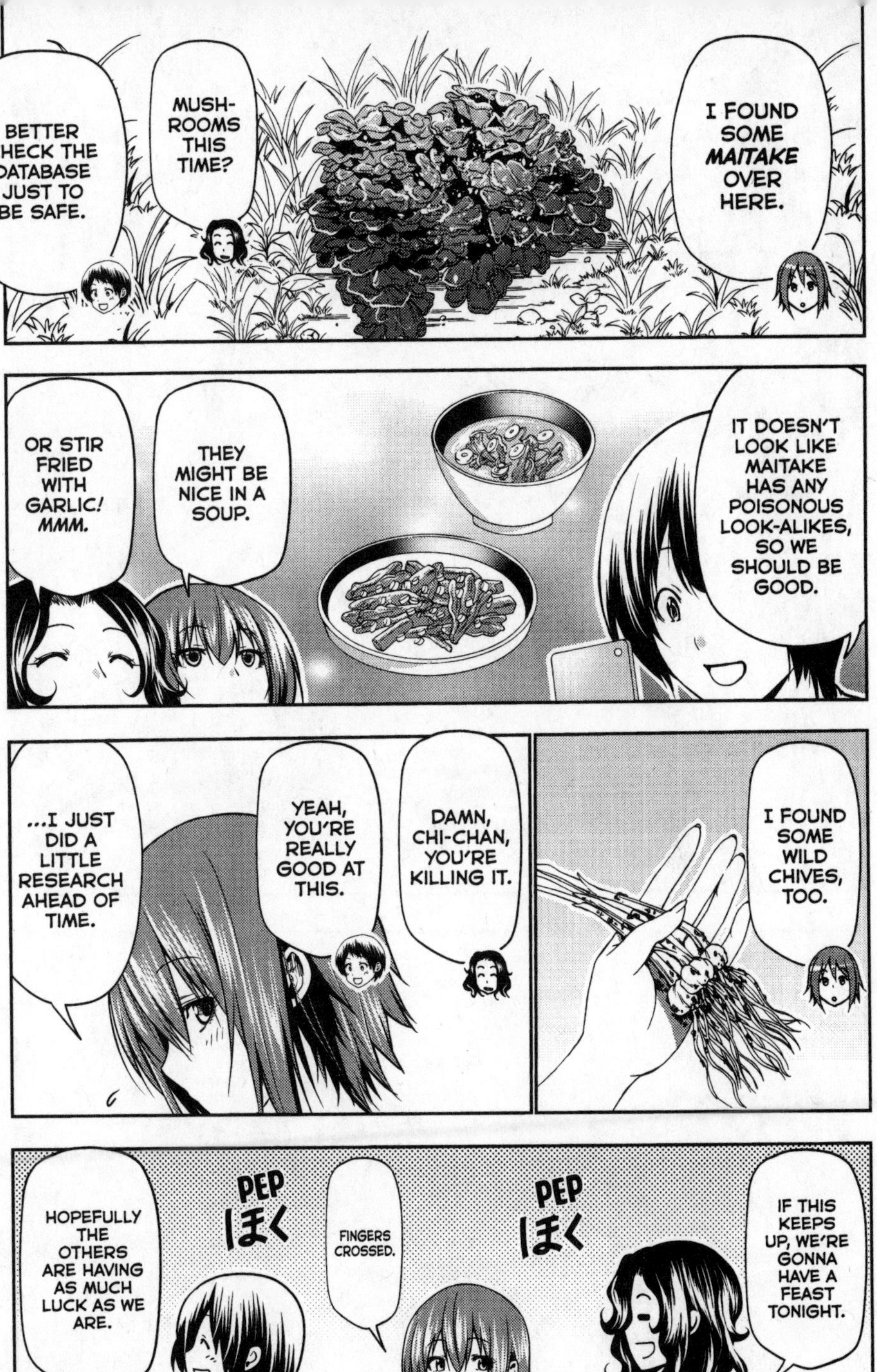

I FOUND SOME *MAITAKE* OVER HERE.
MUSH-ROOMS THIS TIME?
BETTER CHECK THE DATABASE JUST TO BE SAFE.
IT DOESN'T LOOK LIKE MAITAKE HAS ANY POISONOUS LOOK-ALIKES, SO WE SHOULD BE GOOD.
THEY MIGHT BE NICE IN A SOUP.
OR STIR FRIED WITH GARLIC! *MMM.*
I FOUND SOME WILD CHIVES, TOO.
DAMN, CHI-CHAN, YOU'RE KILLING IT.
YEAH, YOU'RE REALLY GOOD AT THIS.
...I JUST DID A LITTLE RESEARCH AHEAD OF TIME.
IF THIS KEEPS UP, WE'RE GONNA HAVE A FEAST TONIGHT.
PEP ほく
FINGERS CROSSED.
PEP ほく
HOPEFULLY THE OTHERS ARE HAVING AS MUCH LUCK AS WE ARE.

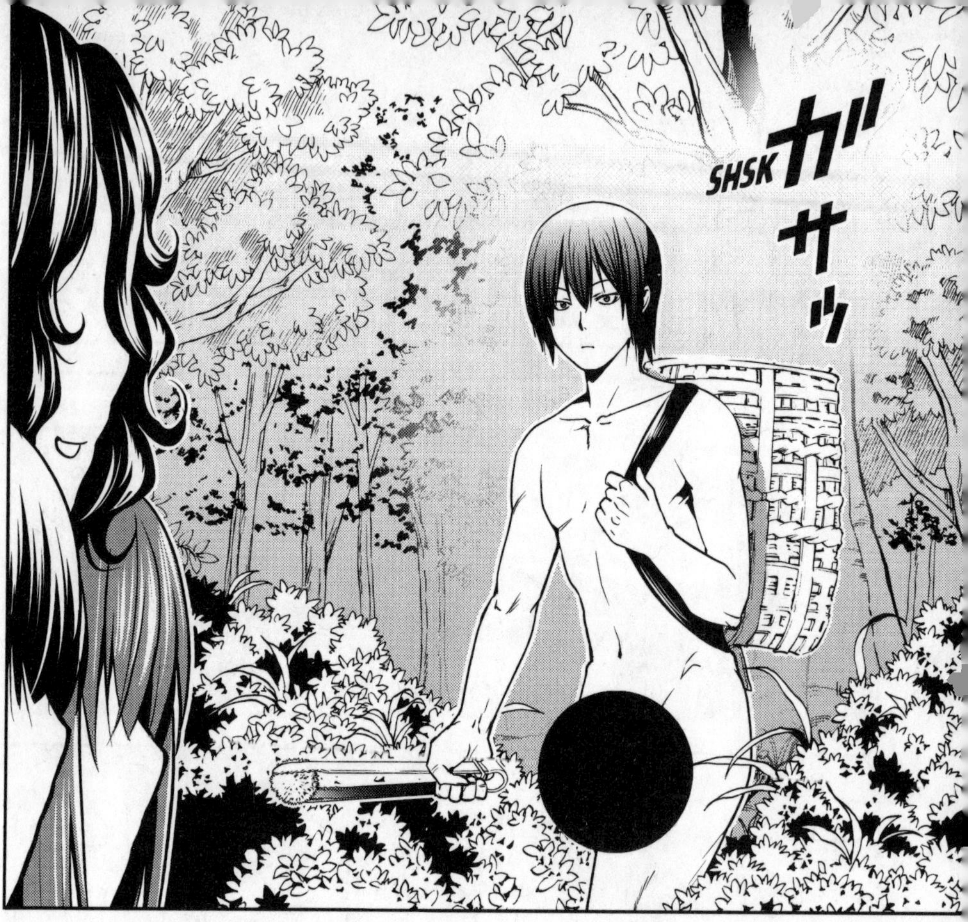
SHSK カサッ

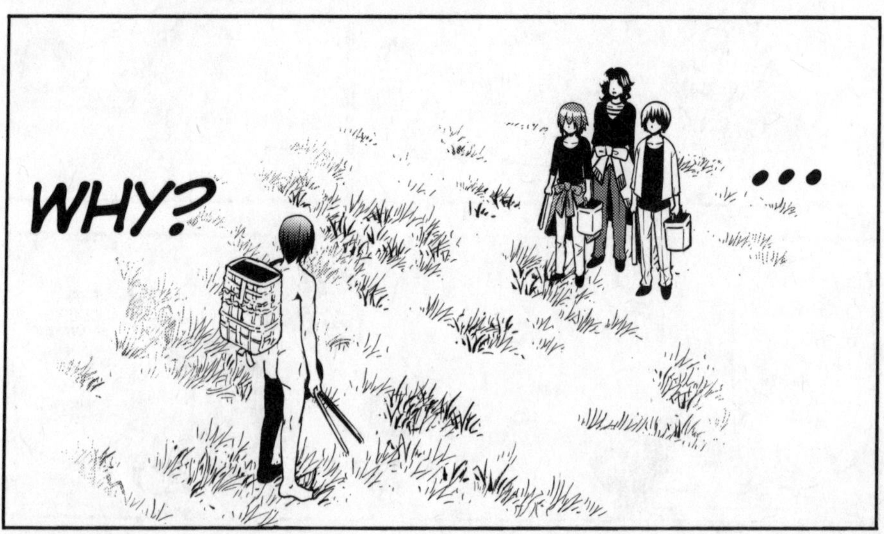
...
WHY?

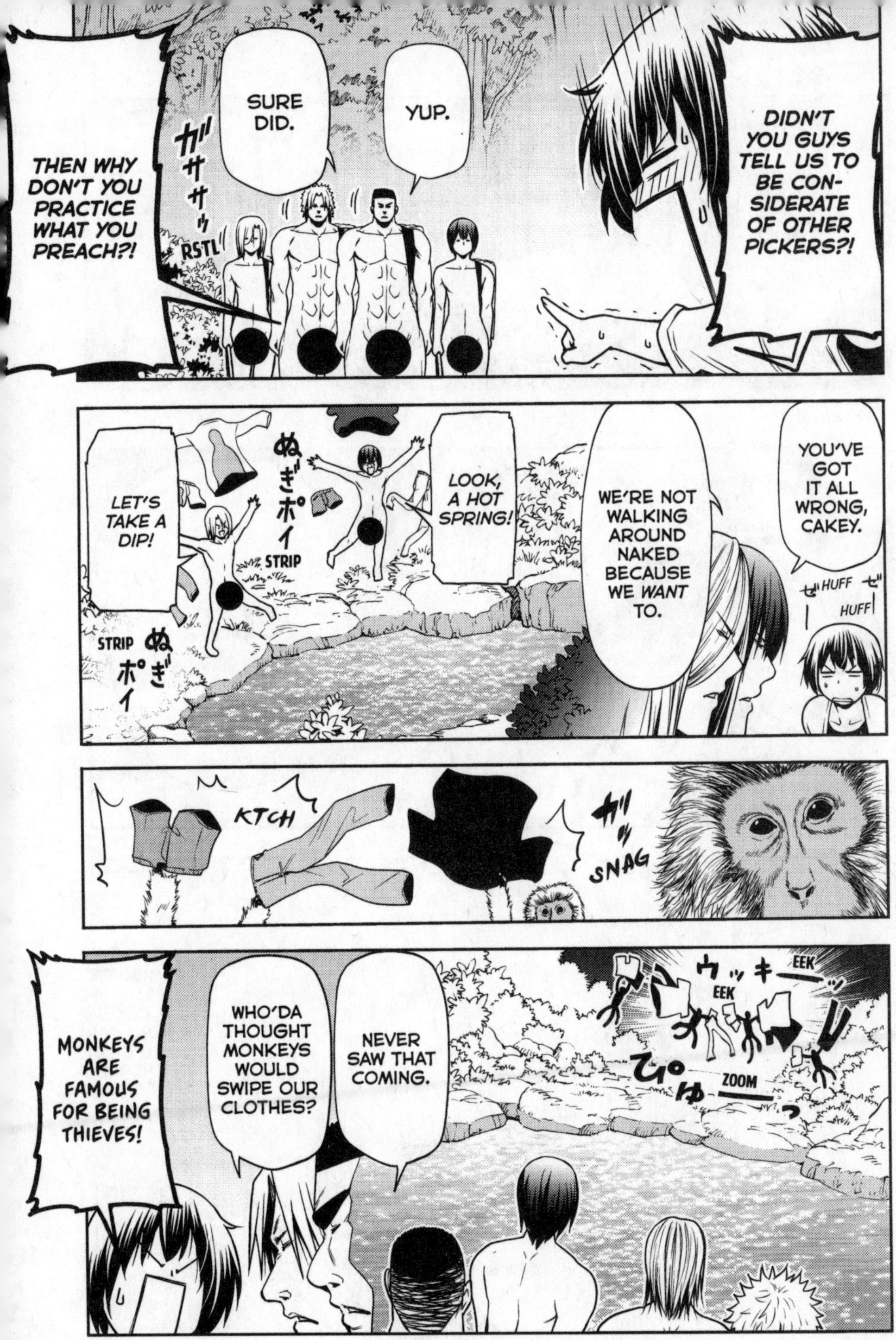
DIDN'T YOU GUYS TELL US TO BE CON-SIDERATE OF OTHER PICKERS?!
YUP.
SURE DID.
ガサササッ RSTL
THEN WHY DON'T YOU PRACTICE WHAT YOU PREACH?!
YOU'VE GOT IT ALL WRONG, CAKEY.
HUFF HUFF
WE'RE NOT WALKING AROUND NAKED BECAUSE WE *WANT* TO.
LOOK, A HOT SPRING!
ぬぎポイ STRIP
LET'S TAKE A DIP!
ぬぎポイ STRIP
ガッ SNAG
KTCH
ウッキー EEK
EEK
ぴゅ～っ ZOOM
NEVER SAW THAT COMING.
WHO'DA THOUGHT MONKEYS WOULD SWIPE OUR CLOTHES?
MONKEYS ARE FAMOUS FOR BEING THIEVES!

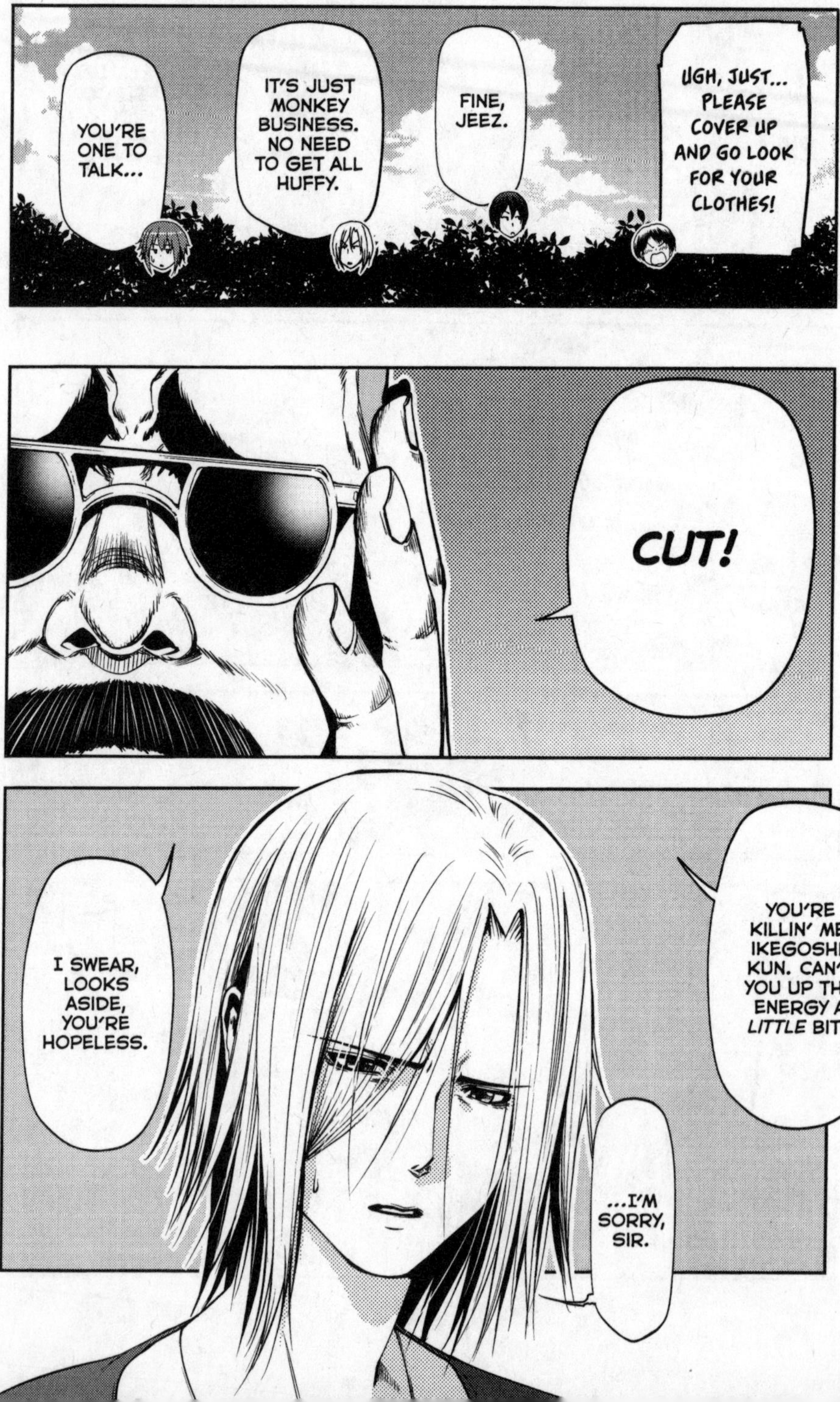
UGH, JUST... PLEASE COVER UP AND GO LOOK FOR YOUR CLOTHES!
FINE, JEEZ.
IT'S JUST MONKEY BUSINESS. NO NEED TO GET ALL HUFFY.
YOU'RE ONE TO TALK...
CUT!
YOU'RE KILLIN' ME, IKEGOSHI-KUN. CAN'T YOU UP THE ENERGY A *LITTLE* BIT?
...I'M SORRY, SIR.
I SWEAR, LOOKS ASIDE, YOU'RE HOPELESS.

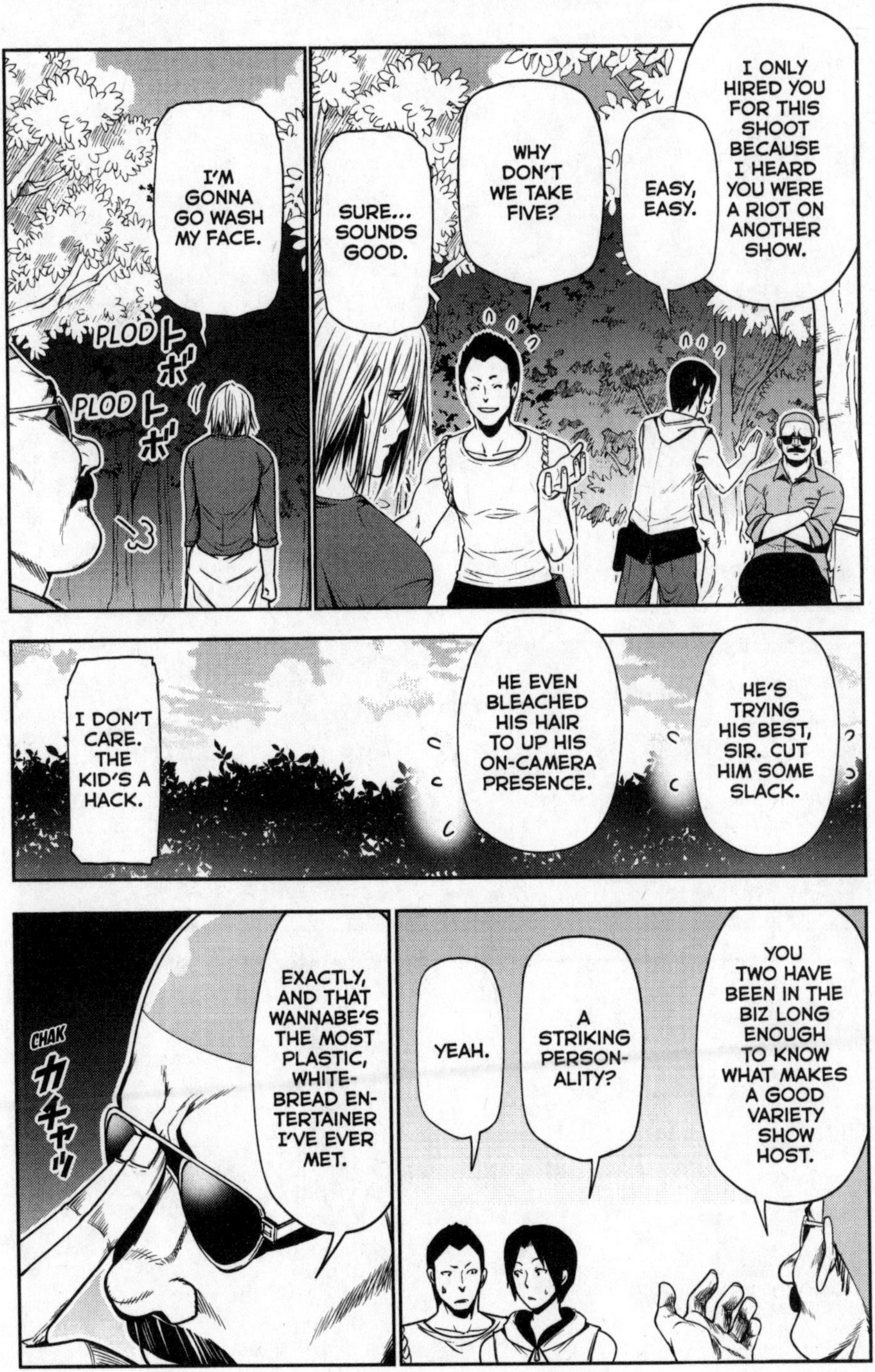

I ONLY HIRED YOU FOR THIS SHOOT BECAUSE I HEARD YOU WERE A RIOT ON ANOTHER SHOW.
EASY, EASY.
WHY DON'T WE TAKE FIVE?
SURE... SOUNDS GOOD.
I'M GONNA GO WASH MY FACE.
PLOD トボ
PLOD トボ
HE'S TRYING HIS BEST, SIR. CUT HIM SOME SLACK.
HE EVEN BLEACHED HIS HAIR TO UP HIS ON-CAMERA PRESENCE.
I DON'T CARE. THE KID'S A HACK.
YOU TWO HAVE BEEN IN THE BIZ LONG ENOUGH TO KNOW WHAT MAKES A GOOD VARIETY SHOW HOST.
A STRIKING PERSON-ALITY?
YEAH.
EXACTLY, AND THAT WANNABE'S THE MOST PLASTIC, WHITE-BREAD EN-TERTAINER I'VE EVER MET.
CHAK
カチャッ

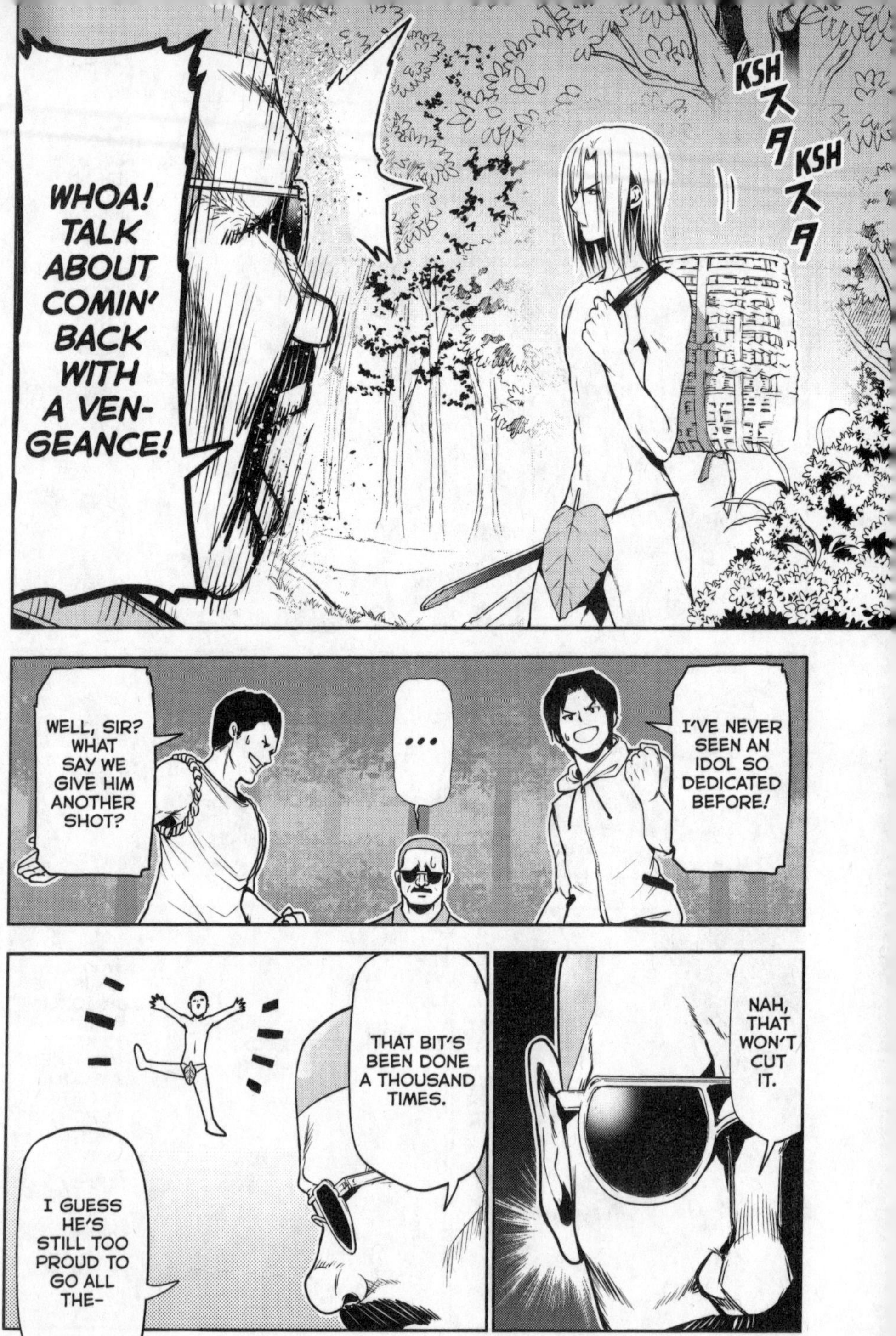
KSH スタ
KSH スタ
WHOA! TALK ABOUT COMIN' BACK WITH A VEN-GEANCE!
I'VE NEVER SEEN AN IDOL SO DEDICATED BEFORE!
...
WELL, SIR? WHAT SAY WE GIVE HIM ANOTHER SHOT?
NAH, THAT WON'T CUT IT.
THAT BIT'S BEEN DONE A THOUSAND TIMES.
I GUESS HE'S STILL TOO PROUD TO GO ALL THE-

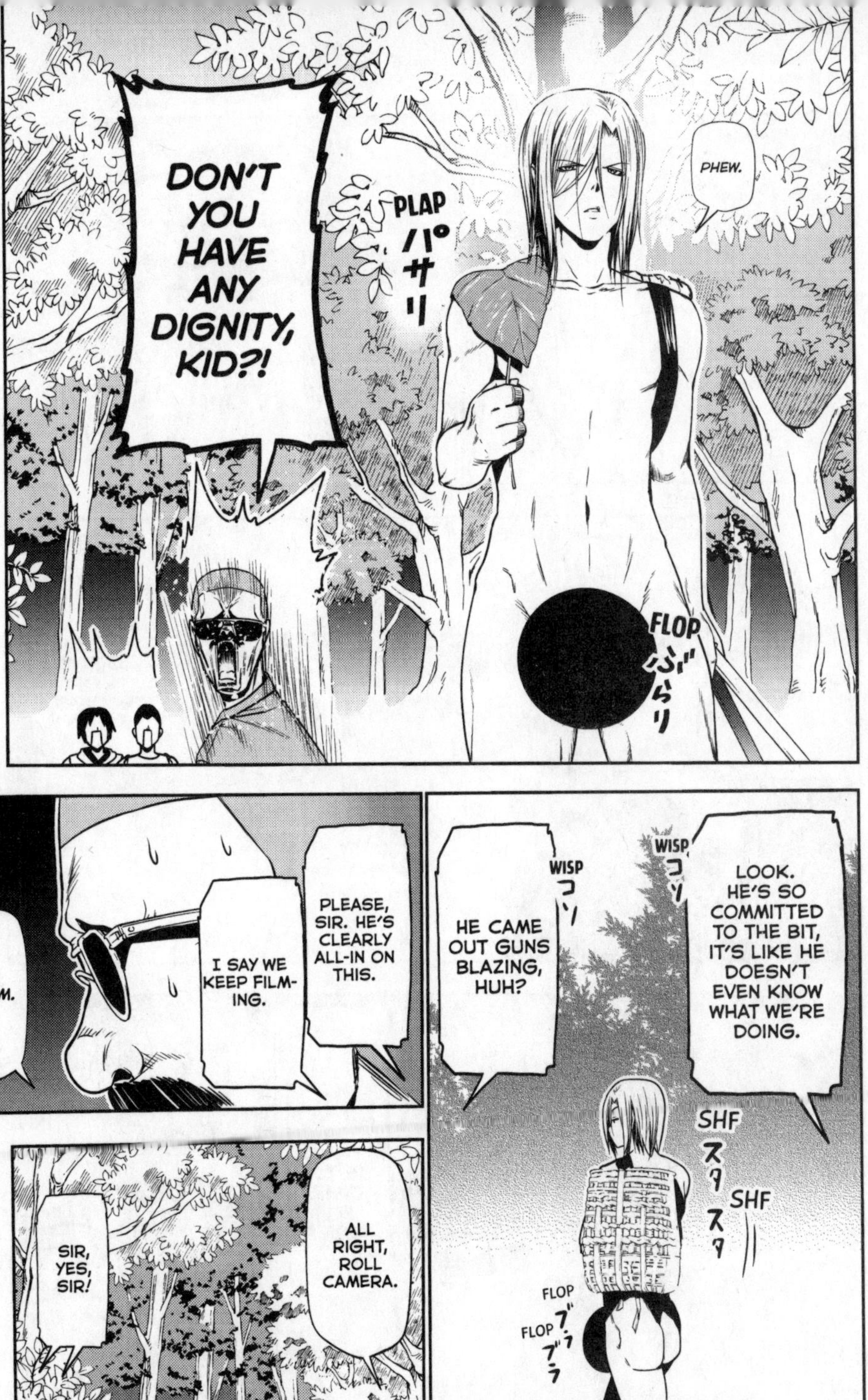
PHEW.
PLAP パサリ
DON'T YOU HAVE ANY DIGNITY, KID?!
FLOP ぶらり
WISP コソ
LOOK. HE'S SO COMMITTED TO THE BIT, IT'S LIKE HE DOESN'T EVEN KNOW WHAT WE'RE DOING.
WISP コソ
HE CAME OUT GUNS BLAZING, HUH?
SHF スタ
SHF スタ
FLOP ブラ
FLOP ブラ
PLEASE, SIR. HE'S CLEARLY ALL-IN ON THIS.
I SAY WE KEEP FILMING.
HRM.
ALL RIGHT, ROLL CAMERA.
SIR, YES, SIR!

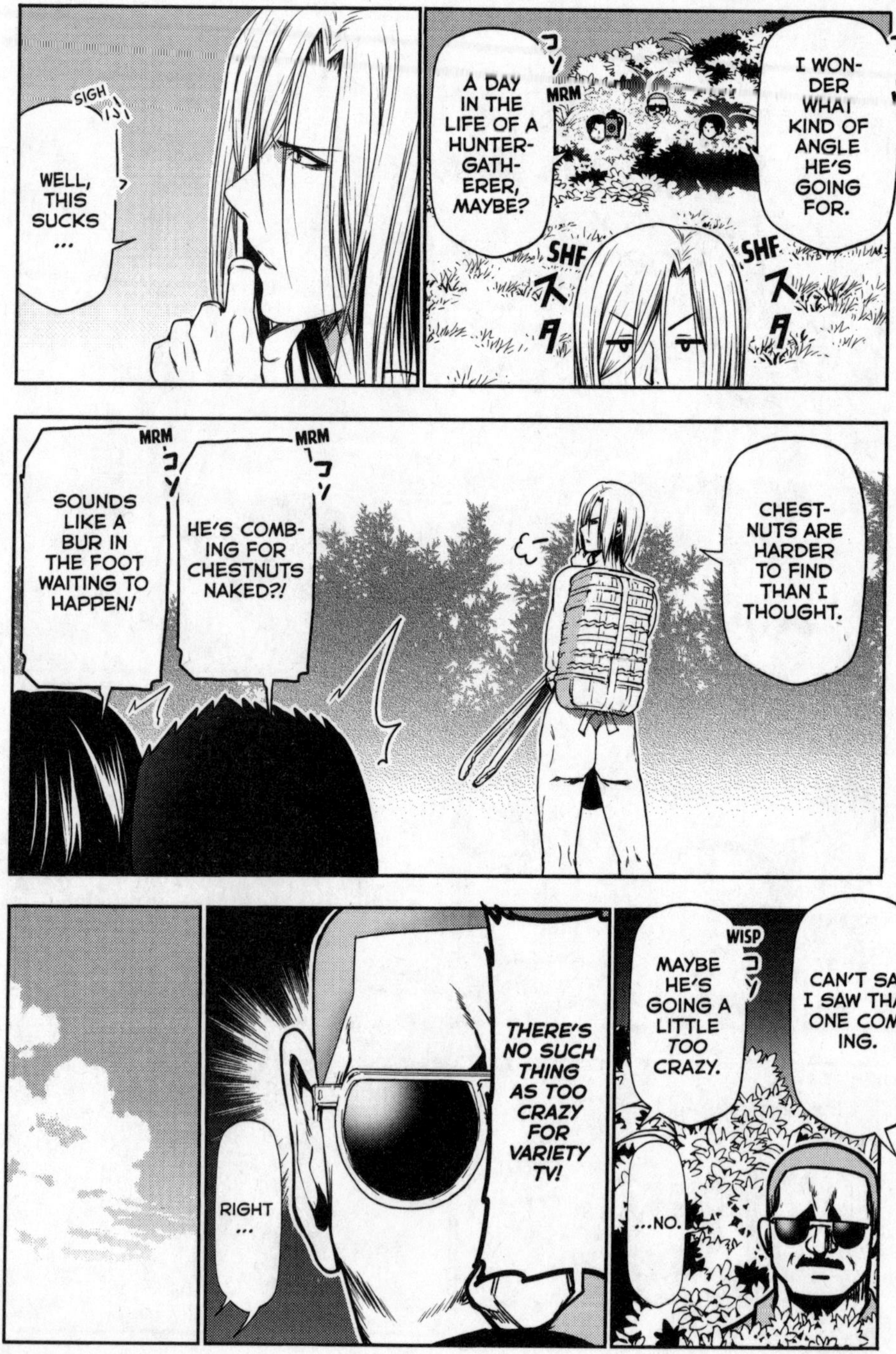
コソ MRM
I WONDER WHAT KIND OF ANGLE HE'S GOING FOR.
コソ MRM
A DAY IN THE LIFE OF A HUNTER-GATHERER, MAYBE?
SHF スタ
SHF スタ
SIGH
WELL, THIS SUCKS ...
CHESTNUTS ARE HARDER TO FIND THAN I THOUGHT.
MRM コソ
HE'S COMBING FOR CHESTNUTS NAKED?!
MRM コソ
SOUNDS LIKE A BUR IN THE FOOT WAITING TO HAPPEN!
WISP コソ
CAN'T SAY I SAW THAT ONE COMING.
WISP コソ
MAYBE HE'S GOING A LITTLE *TOO* CRAZY.
...NO.
THERE'S NO SUCH THING AS TOO CRAZY FOR VARIETY TV!
RIGHT ...

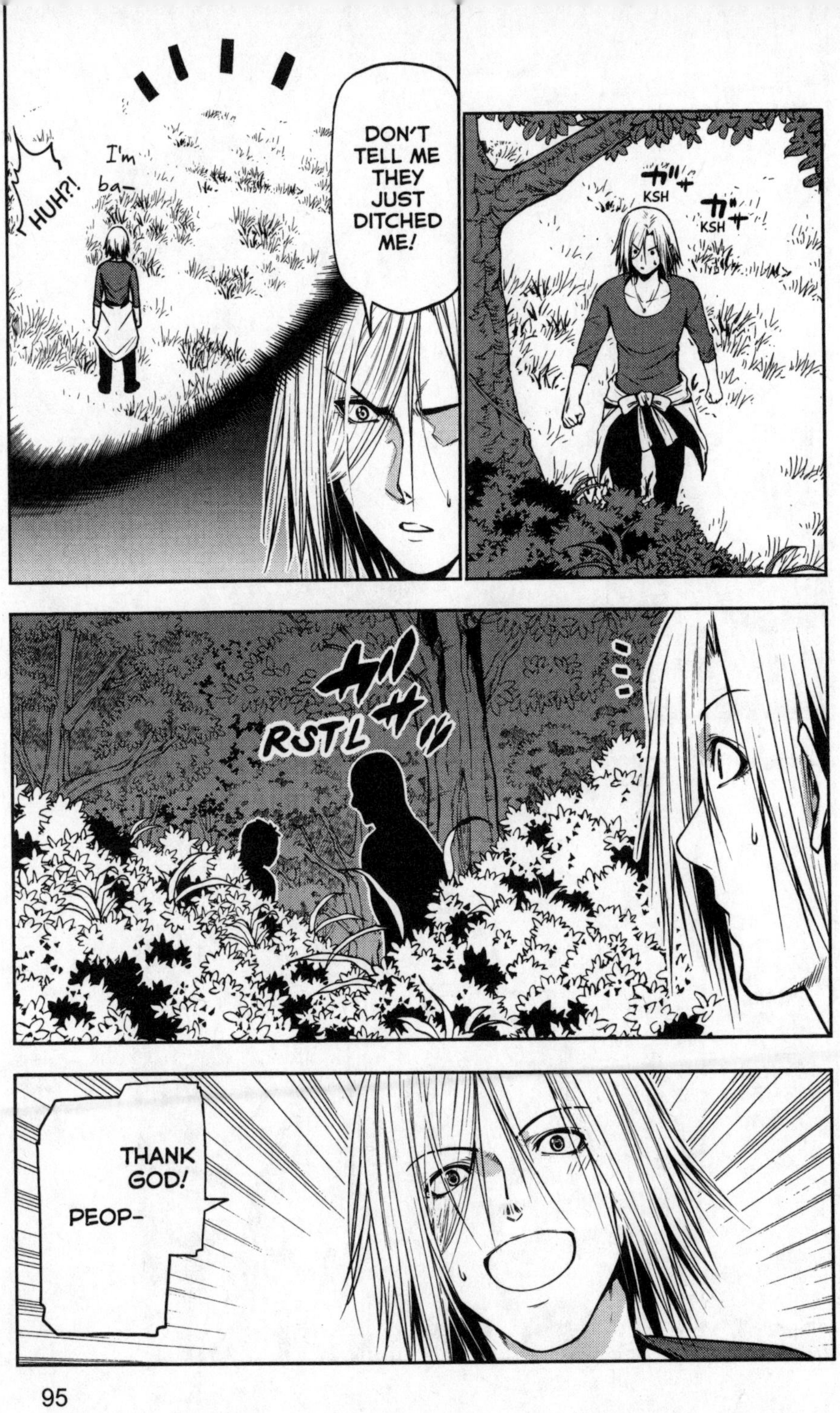
KSH
KSH
DON'T TELL ME THEY JUST DITCHED ME!
I'm ba–
HUH?!
...
RSTL
THANK GOD!
PEOP–

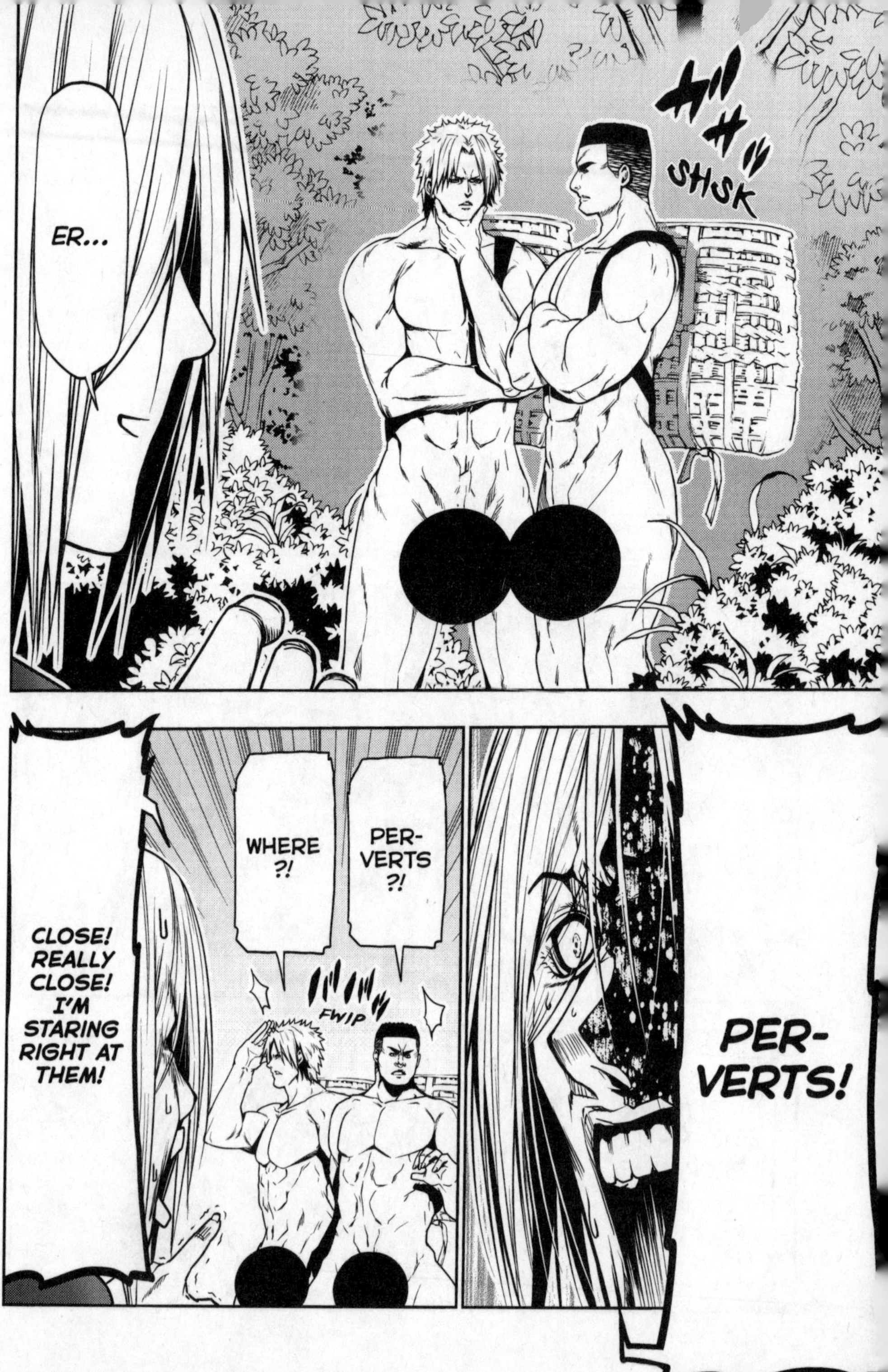
SHSK
ER...
PER-VERTS!
PER-VERTS?!
WHERE?!
FWIP
CLOSE! REALLY CLOSE! I'M STARING RIGHT AT THEM!

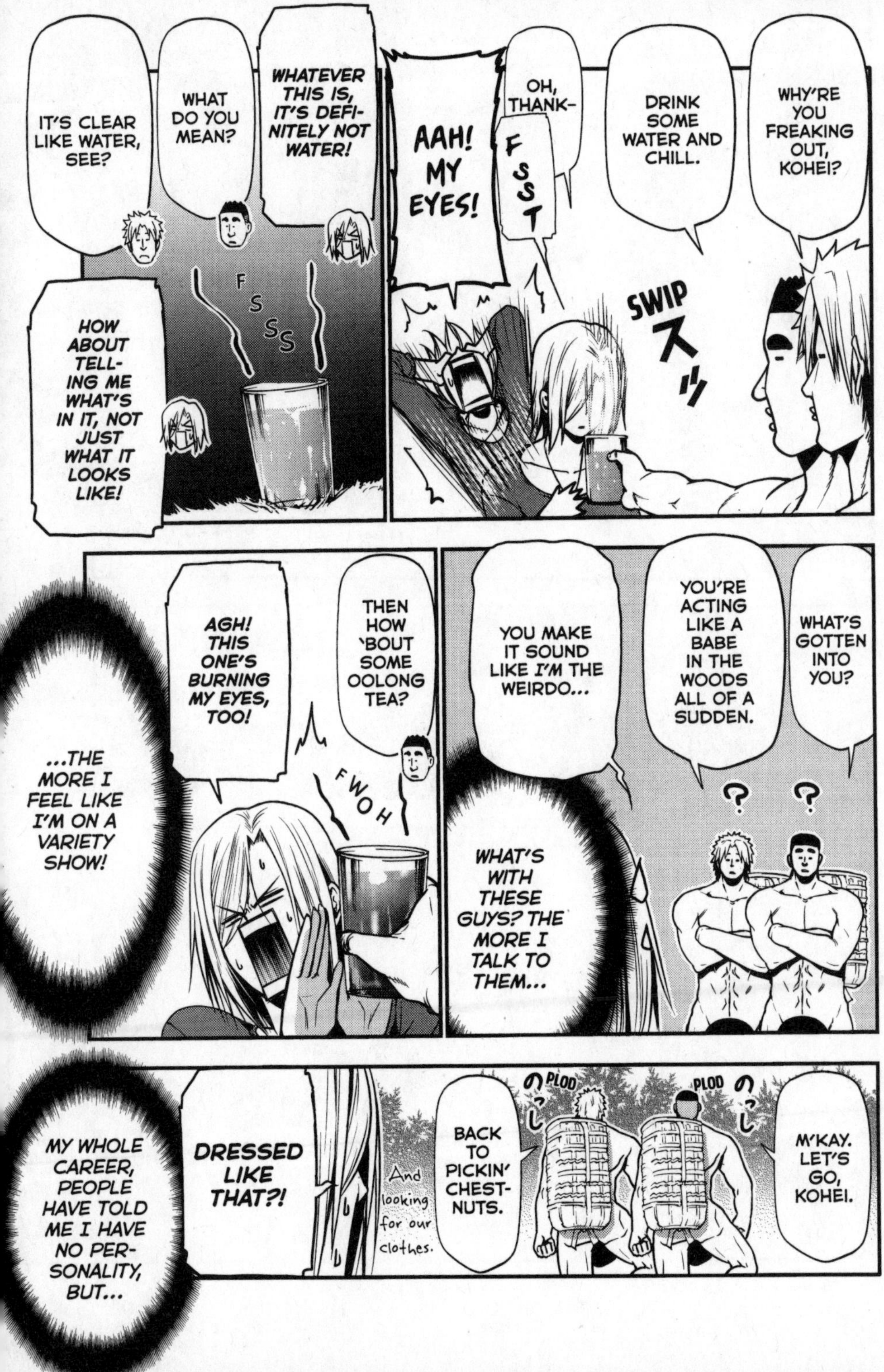

WHY'RE YOU FREAKING OUT, KOHEI?
DRINK SOME WATER AND CHILL.
OH, THANK-
FSST
AAH! MY EYES!
SWIP
スッ
WHATEVER THIS IS, IT'S DEFINITELY NOT WATER!
WHAT DO YOU MEAN?
IT'S CLEAR LIKE WATER, SEE?
FSSS
HOW ABOUT TELLING ME WHAT'S IN IT, NOT JUST WHAT IT LOOKS LIKE!
WHAT'S GOTTEN INTO YOU?
YOU'RE ACTING LIKE A BABE IN THE WOODS ALL OF A SUDDEN.
YOU MAKE IT SOUND LIKE I'M THE WEIRDO...
? ?
WHAT'S WITH THESE GUYS? THE MORE I TALK TO THEM...
THEN HOW 'BOUT SOME OOLONG TEA?
FWOH
AGH! THIS ONE'S BURNING MY EYES, TOO!
...THE MORE I FEEL LIKE I'M ON A VARIETY SHOW!
M'KAY. LET'S GO, KOHEI.
PLOD のっし
PLOD のっし
BACK TO PICKIN' CHESTNUTS.
And looking for our clothes.
DRESSED LIKE THAT?!
MY WHOLE CAREER, PEOPLE HAVE TOLD ME I HAVE NO PERSONALITY, BUT...

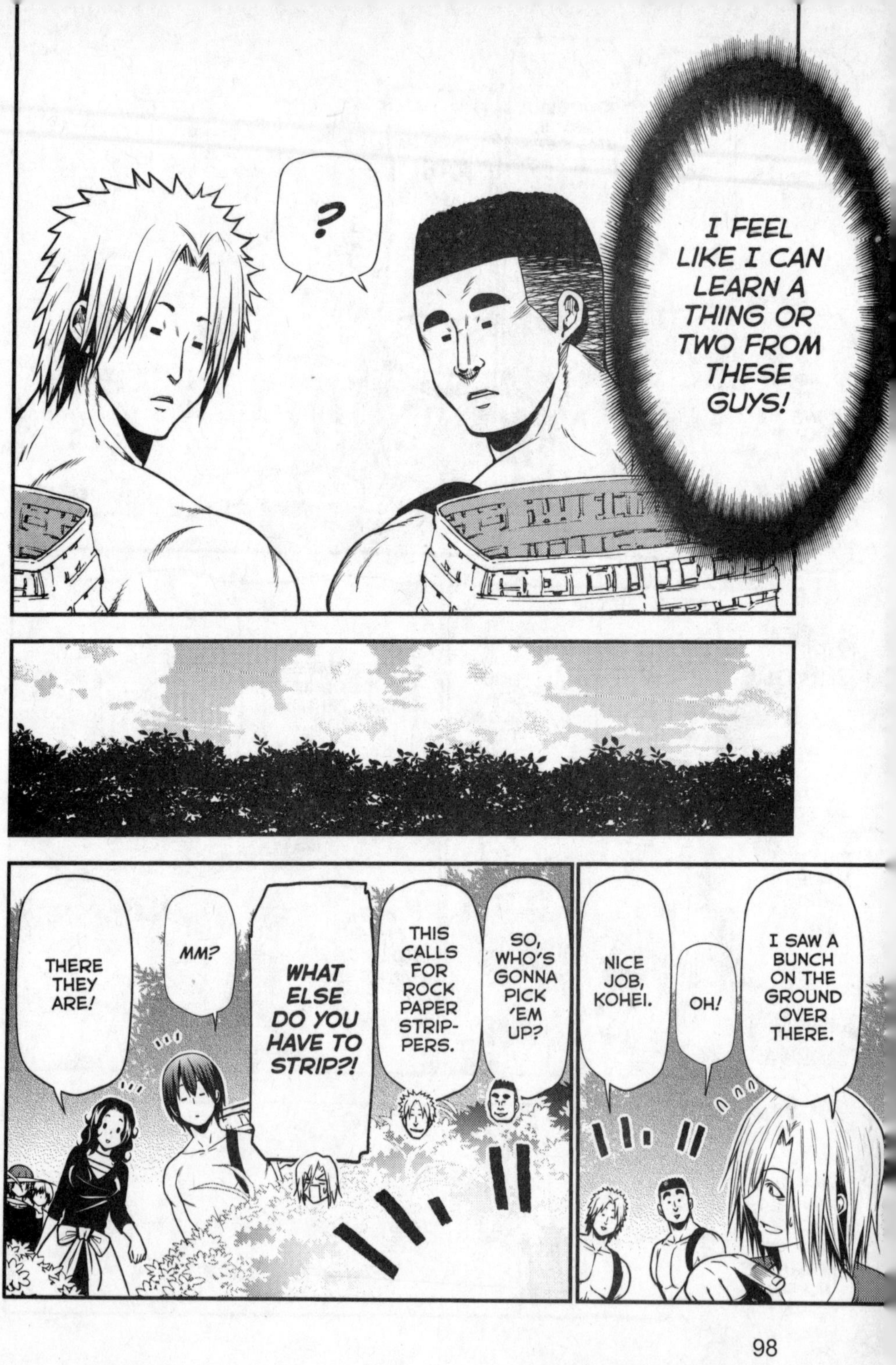
I FEEL LIKE I CAN LEARN A THING OR TWO FROM THESE GUYS!
?
I SAW A BUNCH ON THE GROUND OVER THERE.
OH!
NICE JOB, KOHEI.
SO, WHO'S GONNA PICK 'EM UP?
THIS CALLS FOR ROCK PAPER STRIP-PERS.
WHAT ELSE DO YOU HAVE TO STRIP?!
MM?
THERE THEY ARE!

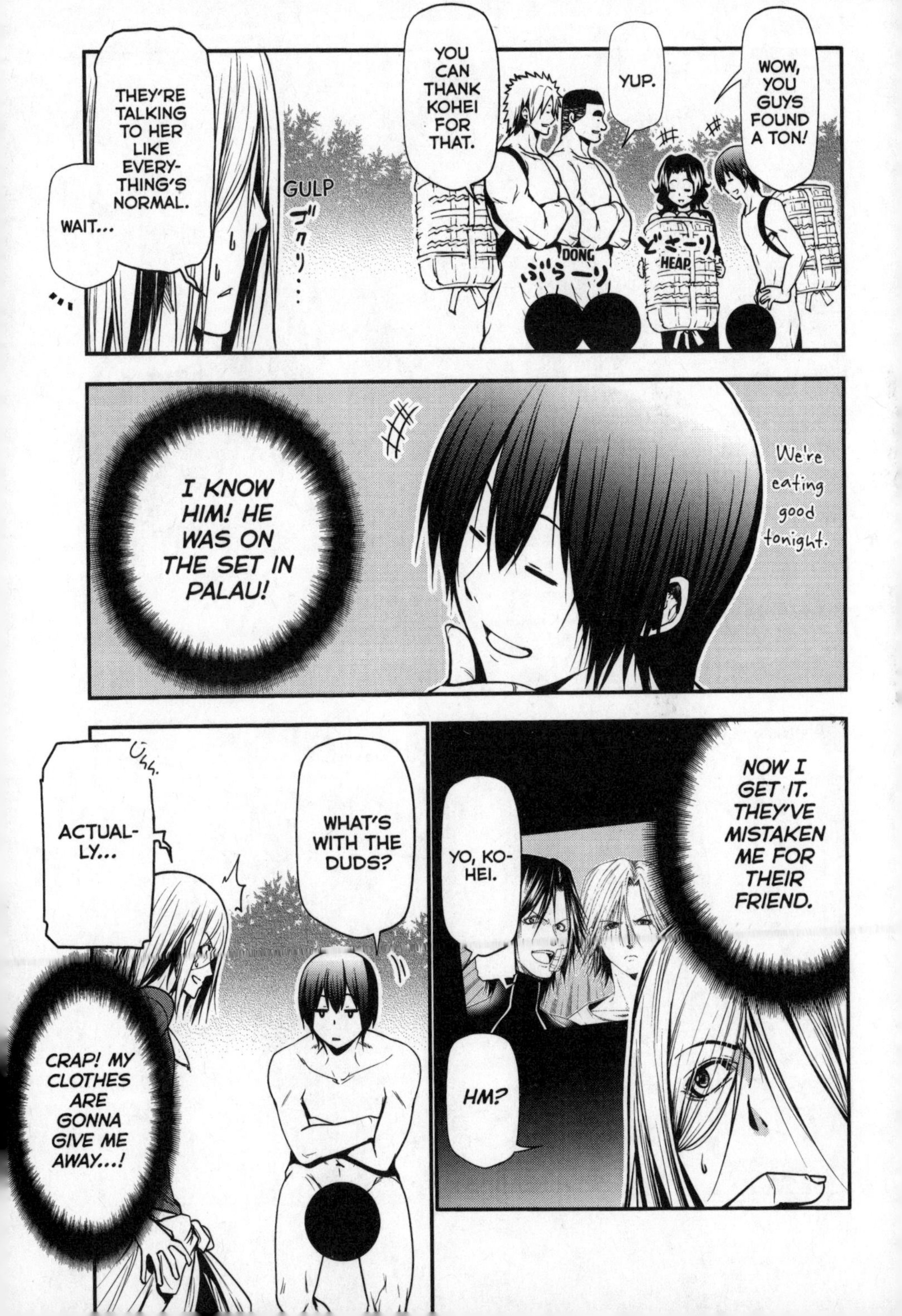
WOW, YOU GUYS FOUND A TON!
YUP.
YOU CAN THANK KOHEI FOR THAT.
HEAP
どさーり
DONG
ぶらーり
GULP
ゴクリ…
THEY'RE TALKING TO HER LIKE EVERY-THING'S NORMAL.
WAIT...
We're eating good tonight.
I KNOW HIM! HE WAS ON THE SET IN PALAU!
NOW I GET IT. THEY'VE MISTAKEN ME FOR THEIR FRIEND.
YO, KO-HEI.
HM?
WHAT'S WITH THE DUDS?
ACTUAL-LY...
CRAP! MY CLOTHES ARE GONNA GIVE ME AWAY...!

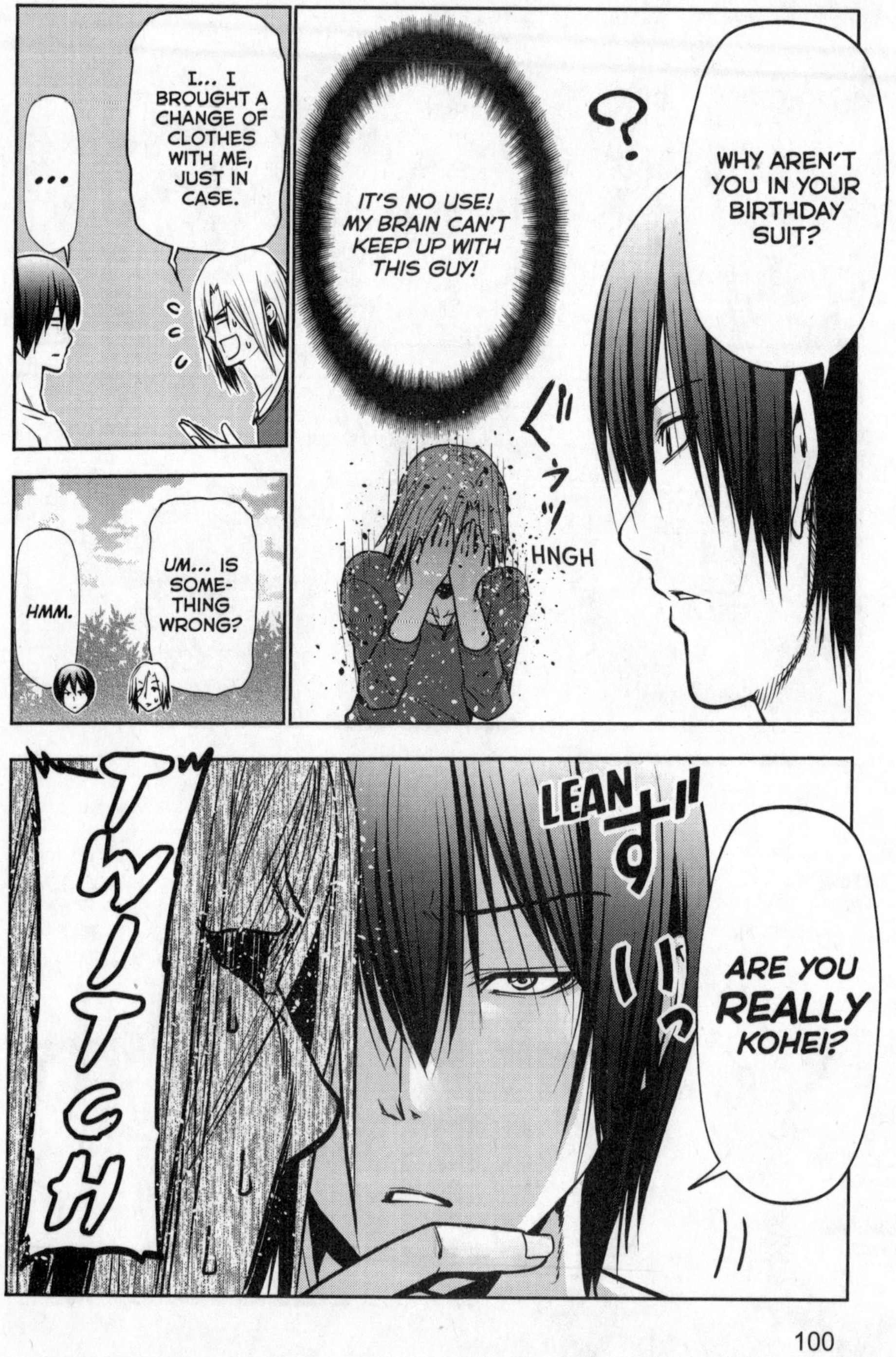
WHY AREN'T YOU IN YOUR BIRTHDAY SUIT?
?
IT'S NO USE! MY BRAIN CAN'T KEEP UP WITH THIS GUY!
HNGH
I... I BROUGHT A CHANGE OF CLOTHES WITH ME, JUST IN CASE.
...
UM... IS SOME-THING WRONG?
HMM.
ARE YOU REALLY KOHEI?
LEAN
TWITCH

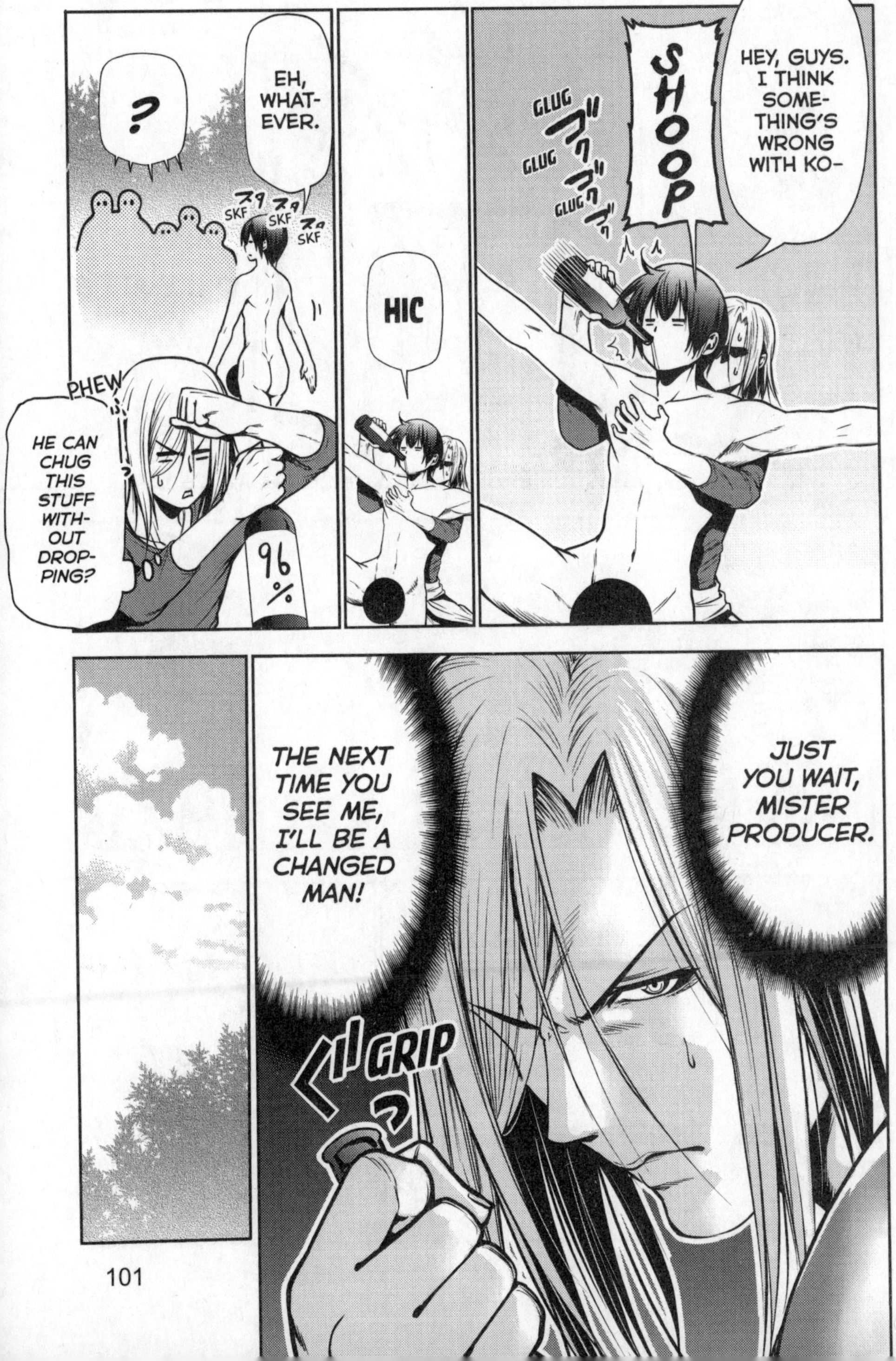
HEY, GUYS. I THINK SOME-THING'S WRONG WITH KO-
SHOOP
GLUG
GLUG
GLUG
HIC
EH, WHAT-EVER.
?
SKF
SKF
SKF
PHEW
HE CAN CHUG THIS STUFF WITH-OUT DROP-PING?
96%
JUST YOU WAIT, MISTER PRODUCER.
THE NEXT TIME YOU SEE ME, I'LL BE A CHANGED MAN!
GRIP

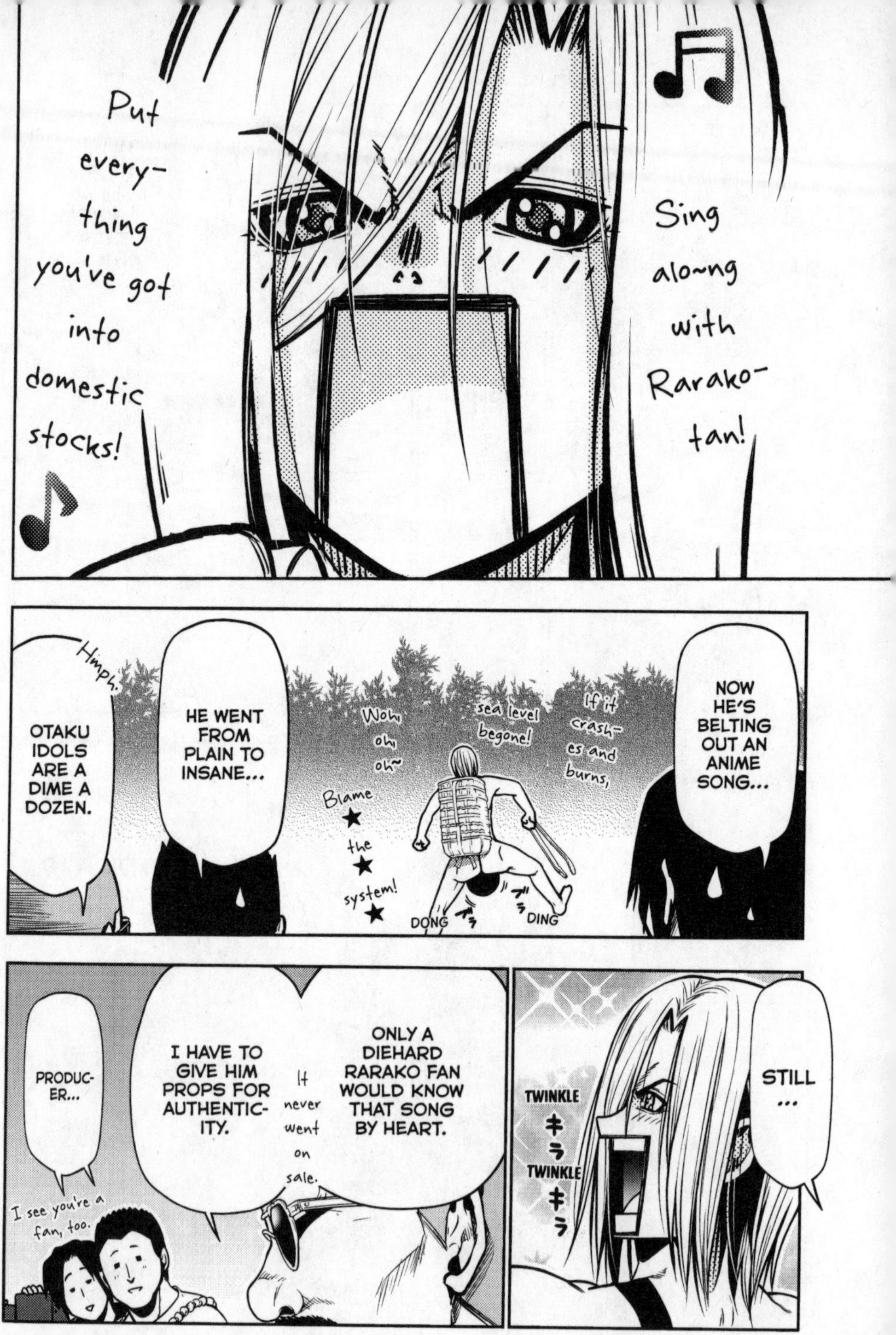

Sing alo~ng with Rarako-tan!
Put every-thing you've got into domestic stocks!
NOW HE'S BELTING OUT AN ANIME SONG...
If it crash-es and burns,
sea level begone!
Woh oh oh~
Blame ★ the ★ system! ★
DING
DONG
HE WENT FROM PLAIN TO INSANE...
Hmph.
OTAKU IDOLS ARE A DIME A DOZEN.
STILL ...
TWINKLE
キラ
TWINKLE
キラ
ONLY A DIEHARD RARAKO FAN WOULD KNOW THAT SONG BY HEART.
It never went on sale.
I HAVE TO GIVE HIM PROPS FOR AUTHENTIC-ITY.
PRODUC-ER...
I see you're a fan, too.

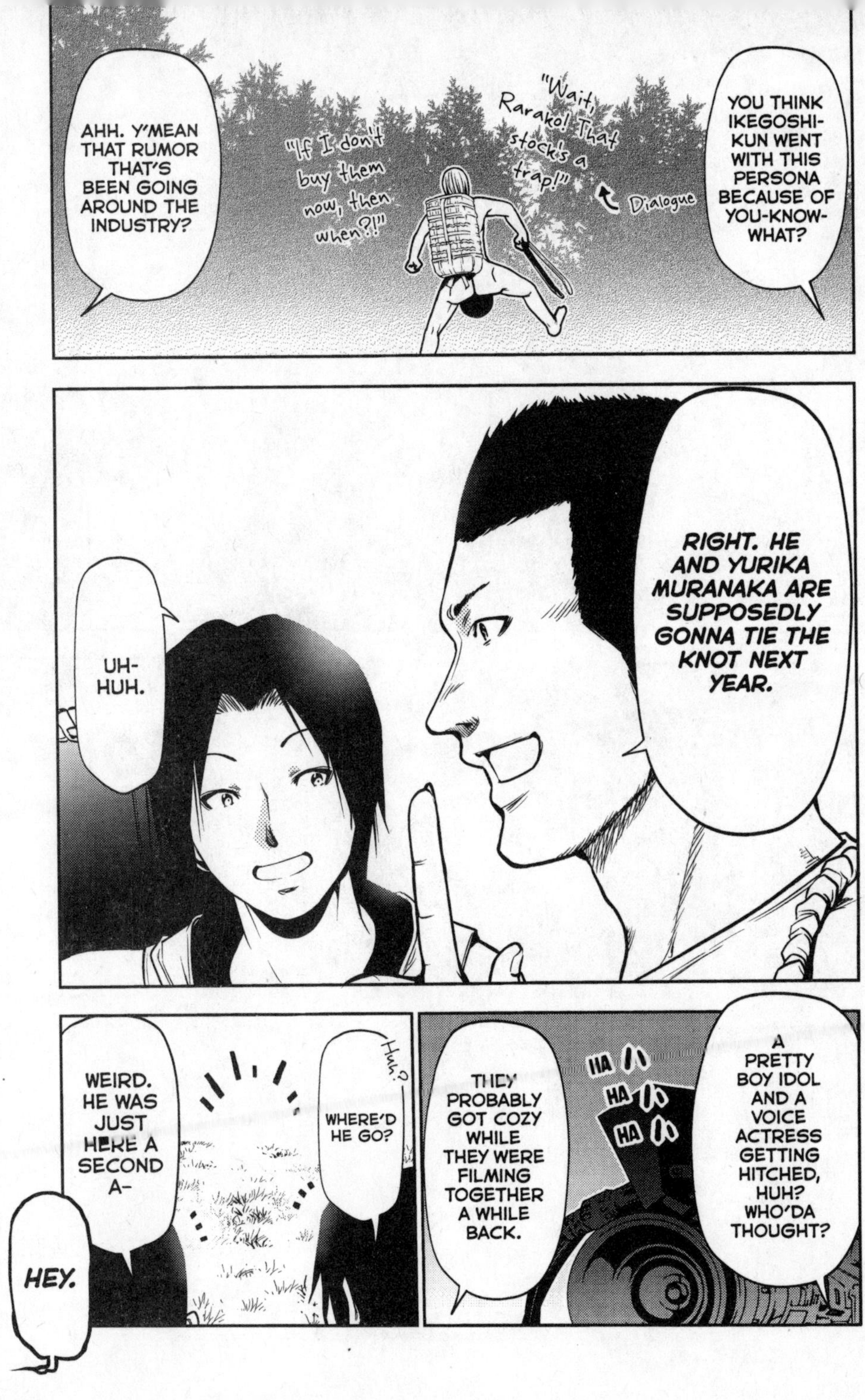
YOU THINK IKEGOSHI-KUN WENT WITH THIS PERSONA BECAUSE OF YOU-KNOW-WHAT?
"Wait, Rarako! That stock's a trap!"
Dialogue
"If I don't buy them now, then when?!"
AHH. Y'MEAN THAT RUMOR THAT'S BEEN GOING AROUND THE INDUSTRY?
RIGHT. HE AND YURIKA MURANAKA ARE SUPPOSEDLY GONNA TIE THE KNOT NEXT YEAR.
UH-HUH.
A PRETTY BOY IDOL AND A VOICE ACTRESS GETTING HITCHED, HUH? WHO'DA THOUGHT?
HA HA HA
THEY PROBABLY GOT COZY WHILE THEY WERE FILMING TOGETHER A WHILE BACK.
Huh?
WHERE'D HE GO?
WEIRD. HE WAS JUST HERE A SECOND A–
HEY.

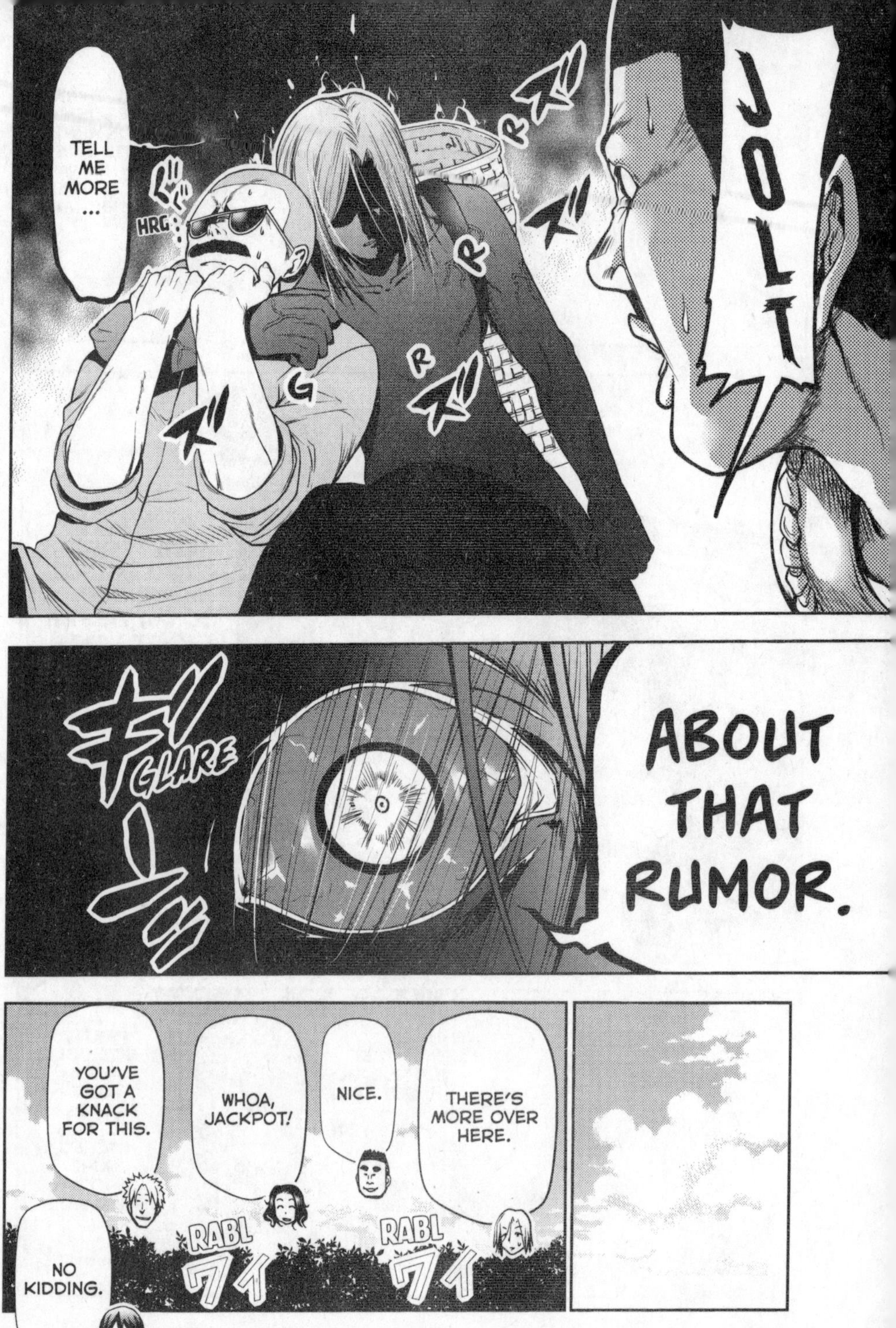
JOLT
TELL ME MORE ...
HRG
R
G
ABOUT THAT RUMOR.
GLARE
THERE'S MORE OVER HERE.
NICE.
WHOA, JACKPOT!
YOU'VE GOT A KNACK FOR THIS.
RABL
RABL
NO KIDDING.

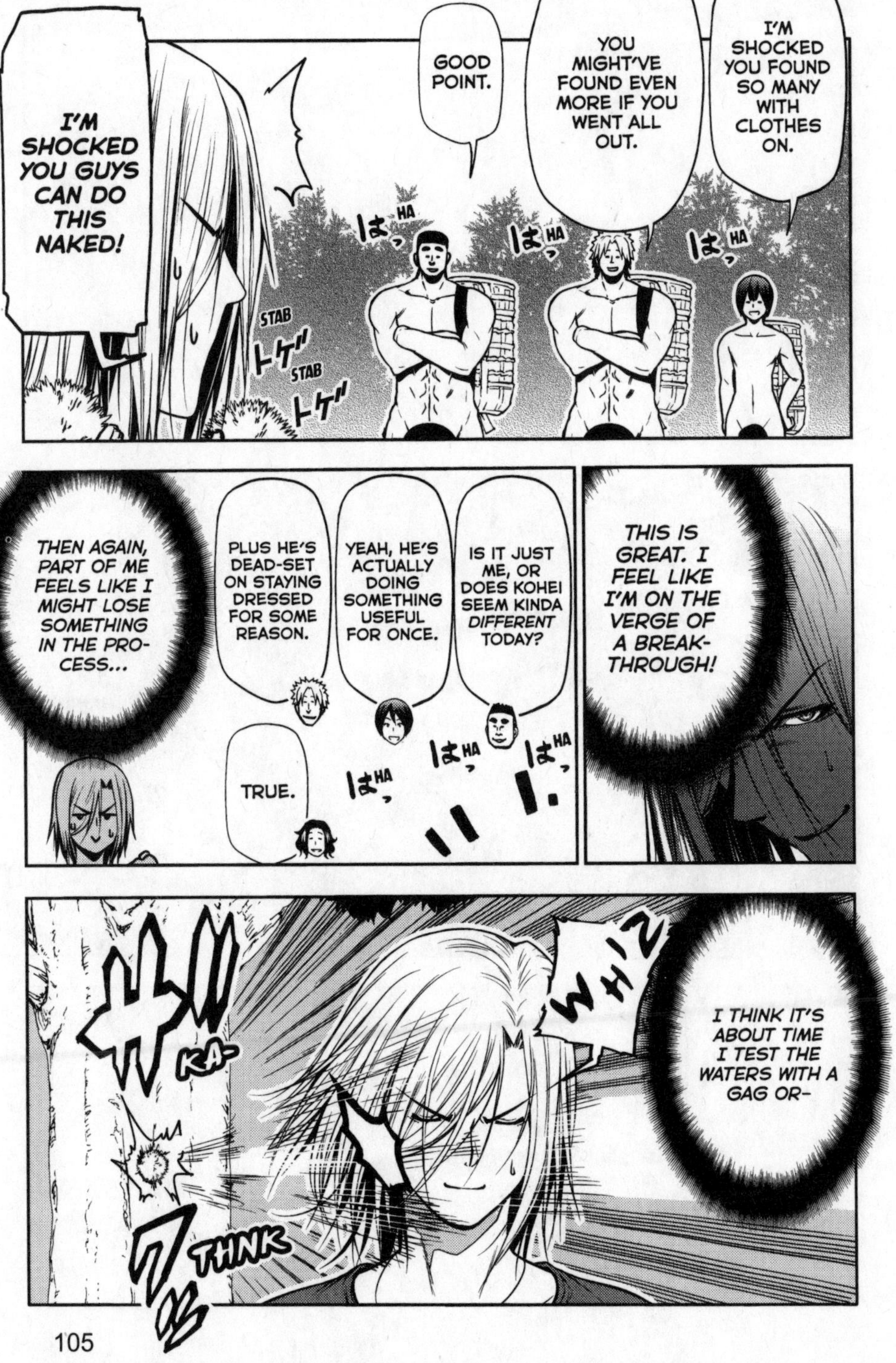
I'M SHOCKED YOU FOUND SO MANY WITH CLOTHES ON.
YOU MIGHT'VE FOUND EVEN MORE IF YOU WENT ALL OUT.
GOOD POINT.
は HA
は HA
は HA
I'M SHOCKED YOU GUYS CAN DO THIS NAKED!
STAB トゲ
STAB トゲ
THIS IS GREAT. I FEEL LIKE I'M ON THE VERGE OF A BREAK-THROUGH!
IS IT JUST ME, OR DOES KOHEI SEEM KINDA *DIFFERENT* TODAY?
YEAH, HE'S ACTUALLY DOING SOMETHING USEFUL FOR ONCE.
PLUS HE'S DEAD-SET ON STAYING DRESSED FOR SOME REASON.
は HA
は HA
は HA
TRUE.
THEN AGAIN, PART OF ME FEELS LIKE I MIGHT LOSE SOMETHING IN THE PRO-CESS...
I THINK IT'S ABOUT TIME I TEST THE WATERS WITH A GAG OR-
WHIZ
KA-
THNK

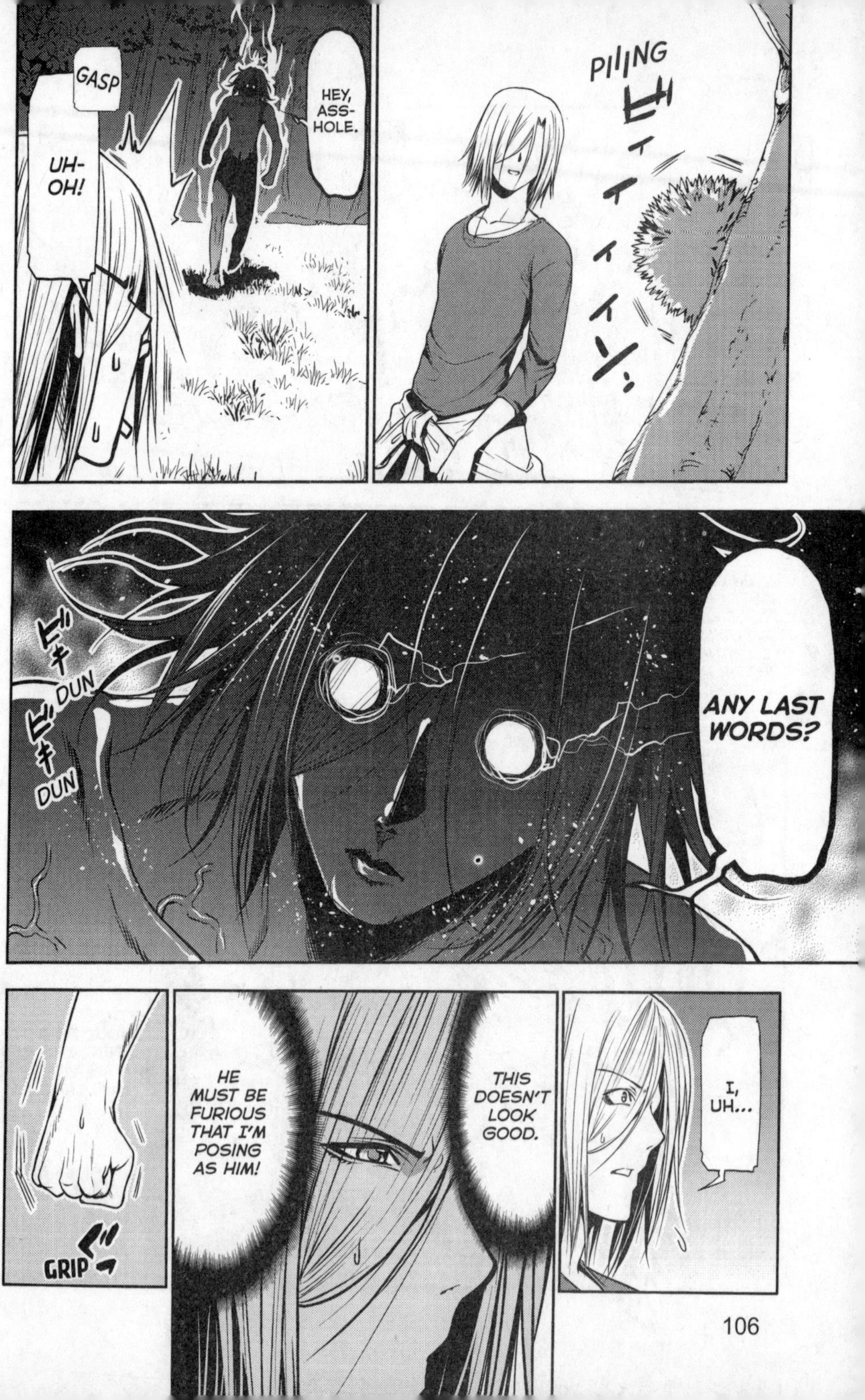

PIIING
ビィィィィン
HEY, ASSHOLE.
GASP
UH-OH!
ANY LAST WORDS?
ビキ
DUN
ビキ
DUN
I, UH...
THIS DOESN'T LOOK GOOD.
HE MUST BE FURIOUS THAT I'M POSING AS HIM!
ぐっ
GRIP

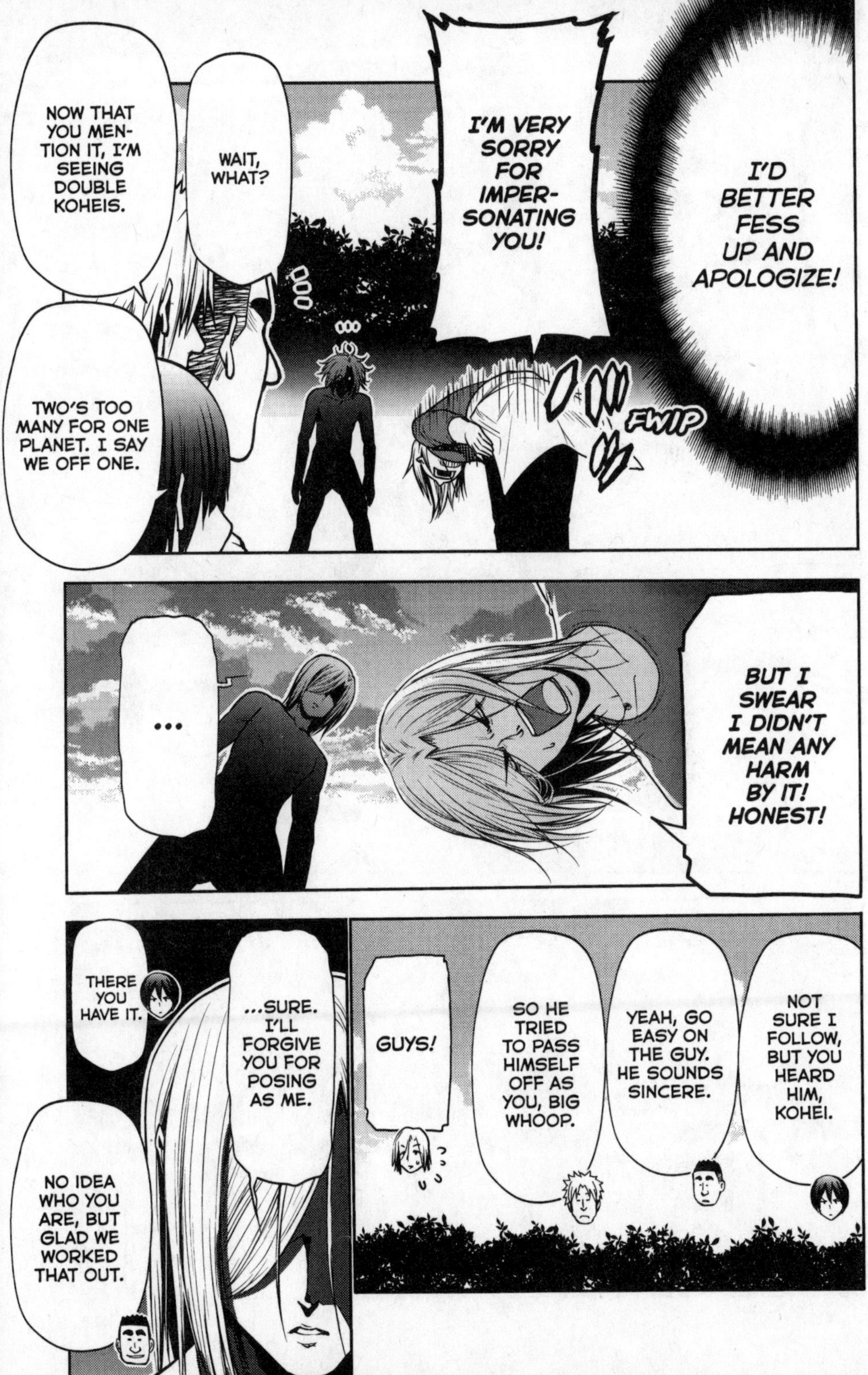
I'D BETTER FESS UP AND APOLOGIZE!
I'M VERY SORRY FOR IMPERSONATING YOU!
FWIP
WAIT, WHAT?
NOW THAT YOU MENTION IT, I'M SEEING DOUBLE KOHEIS.
TWO'S TOO MANY FOR ONE PLANET. I SAY WE OFF ONE.
BUT I SWEAR I DIDN'T MEAN ANY HARM BY IT! HONEST!
...
NOT SURE I FOLLOW, BUT YOU HEARD HIM, KOHEI.
YEAH, GO EASY ON THE GUY. HE SOUNDS SINCERE.
SO HE TRIED TO PASS HIMSELF OFF AS YOU, BIG WHOOP.
GUYS!
...SURE. I'LL FORGIVE YOU FOR POSING AS ME.
THERE YOU HAVE IT.
NO IDEA WHO YOU ARE, BUT GLAD WE WORKED THAT OUT.

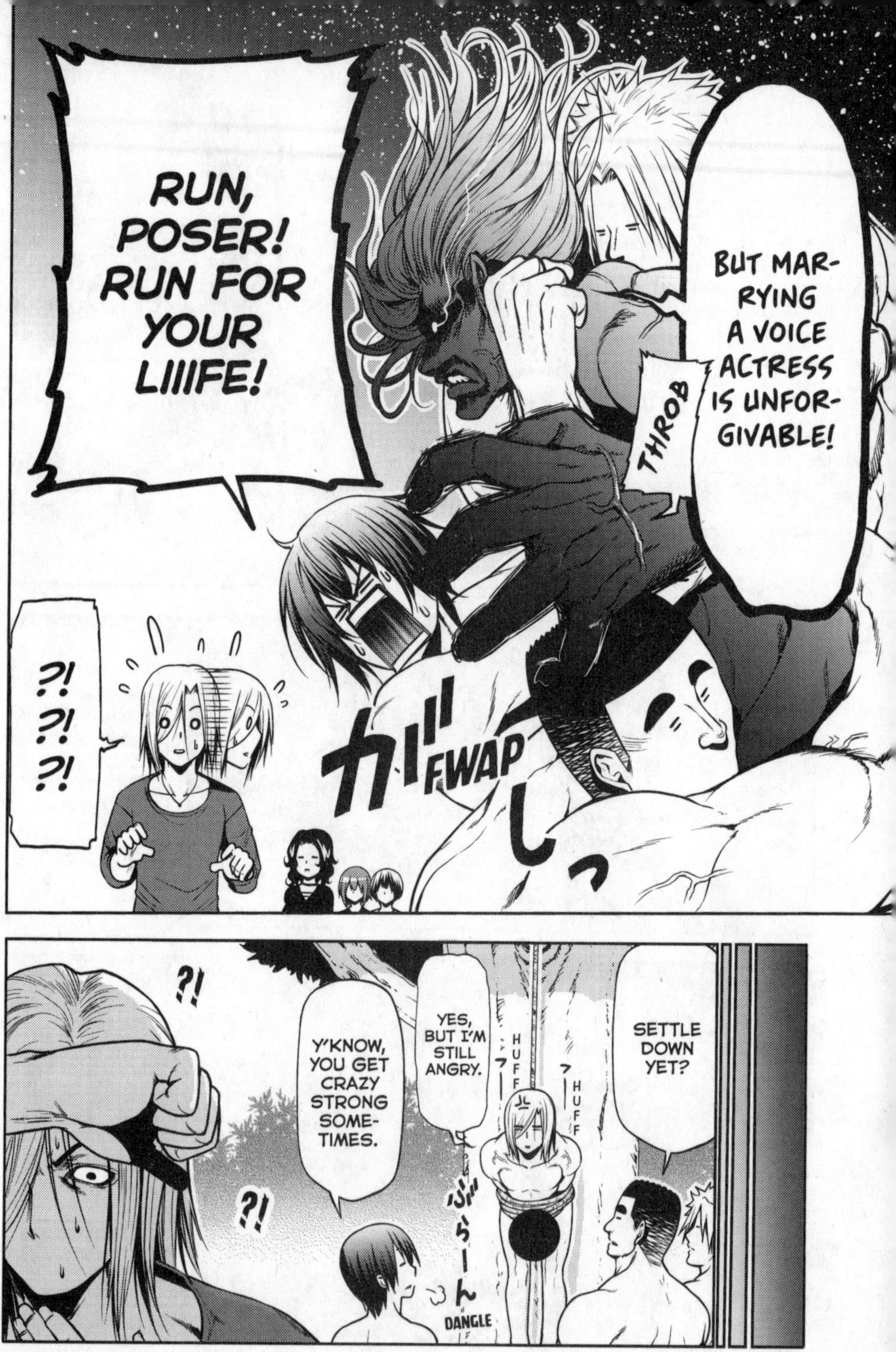

BUT MAR-
RYING
A VOICE
ACTRESS
IS UNFOR-
GIVABLE!
THROB
RUN,
POSER!
RUN FOR
YOUR
LIIIFE!
FWAP
?!
?!
?!
SETTLE
DOWN
YET?
HUFF
HUFF
YES,
BUT I'M
STILL
ANGRY.
Y'KNOW,
YOU GET
CRAZY
STRONG
SOME-
TIMES.
DANGLE
?!
?!

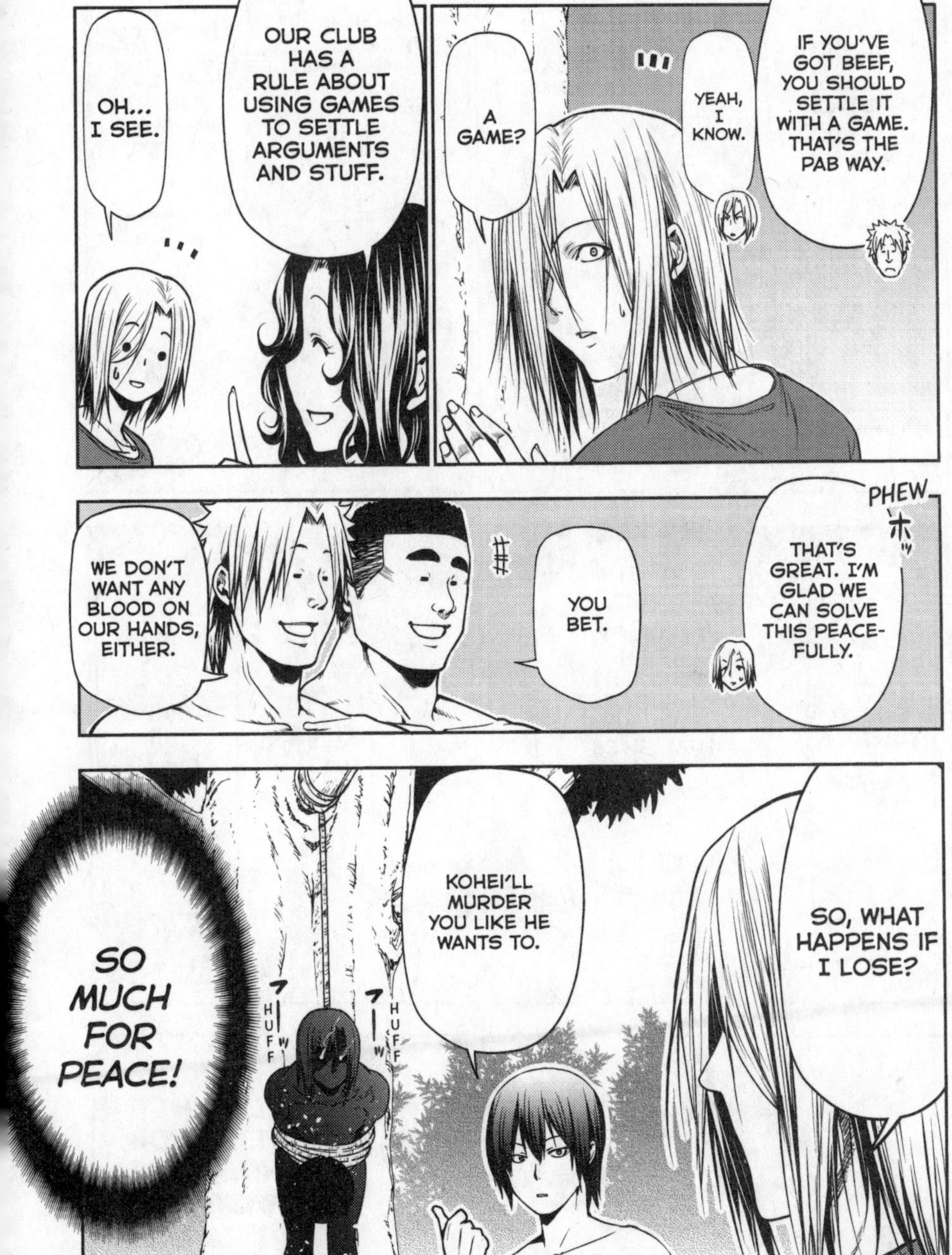
IF YOU'VE GOT BEEF, YOU SHOULD SETTLE IT WITH A GAME. THAT'S THE PAB WAY.
YEAH, I KNOW.
A GAME?
OUR CLUB HAS A RULE ABOUT USING GAMES TO SETTLE ARGUMENTS AND STUFF.
OH... I SEE.
...
PHEW
THAT'S GREAT. I'M GLAD WE CAN SOLVE THIS PEACE-FULLY.
YOU BET.
WE DON'T WANT ANY BLOOD ON OUR HANDS, EITHER.
SO, WHAT HAPPENS IF I LOSE?
KOHEI'LL MURDER YOU LIKE HE WANTS TO.
HUFF
HUFF
SO MUCH FOR PEACE!

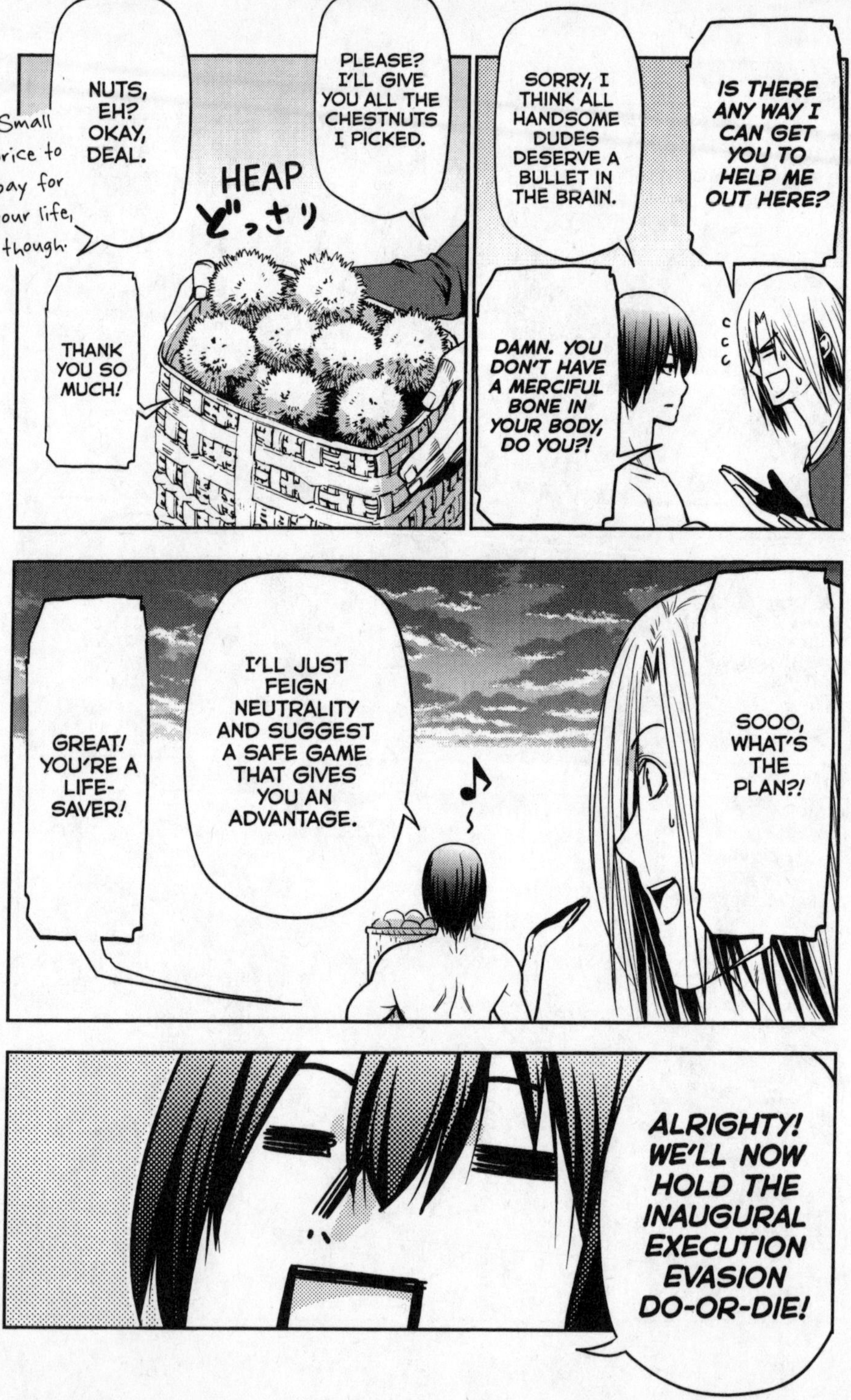
IS THERE ANY WAY I CAN GET YOU TO HELP ME OUT HERE?
SORRY, I THINK ALL HANDSOME DUDES DESERVE A BULLET IN THE BRAIN.
DAMN. YOU DON'T HAVE A MERCIFUL BONE IN YOUR BODY, DO YOU?!
PLEASE? I'LL GIVE YOU ALL THE CHESTNUTS I PICKED.
HEAP
どっさり
NUTS, EH? OKAY, DEAL.
Small price to pay for your life, though.
THANK YOU SO MUCH!
SOOO, WHAT'S THE PLAN?!
I'LL JUST FEIGN NEUTRALITY AND SUGGEST A SAFE GAME THAT GIVES YOU AN ADVANTAGE.
GREAT! YOU'RE A LIFE-SAVER!
ALRIGHTY! WE'LL NOW HOLD THE INAUGURAL EXECUTION EVASION DO-OR-DIE!

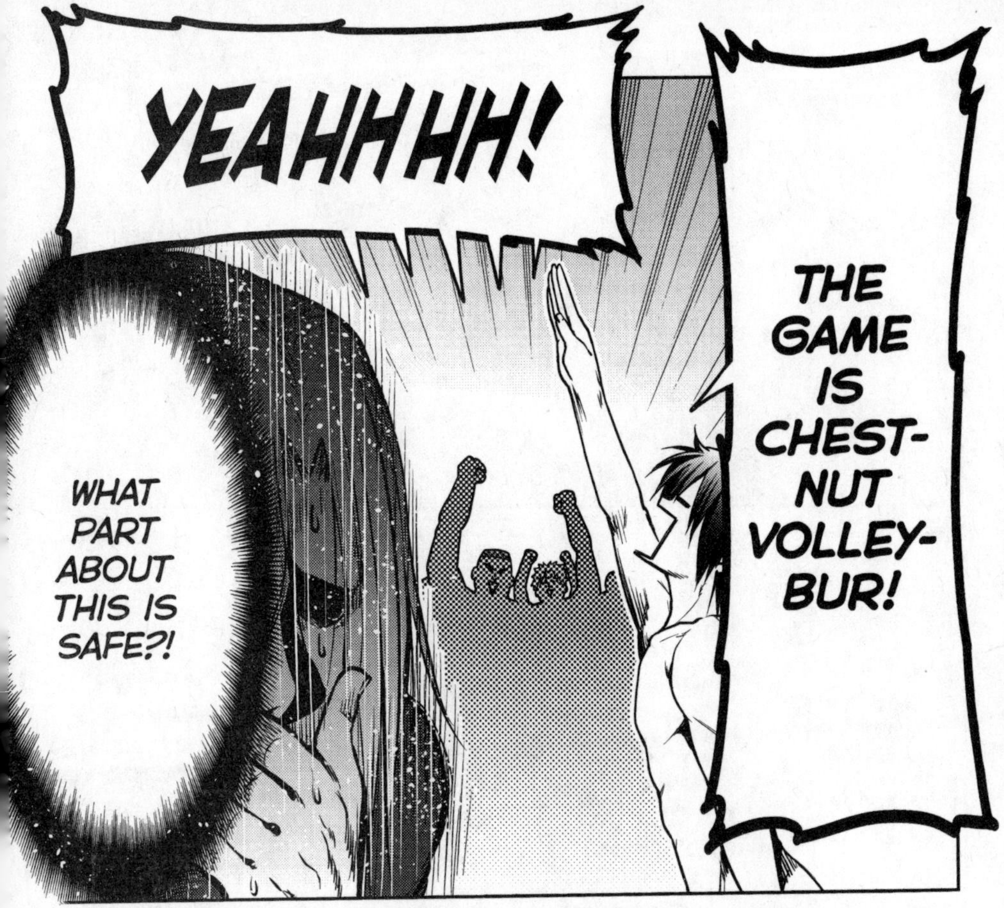
THE GAME IS CHEST-NUT VOLLEY-BUR!
YEAHHHH!
WHAT PART ABOUT THIS IS SAFE?!

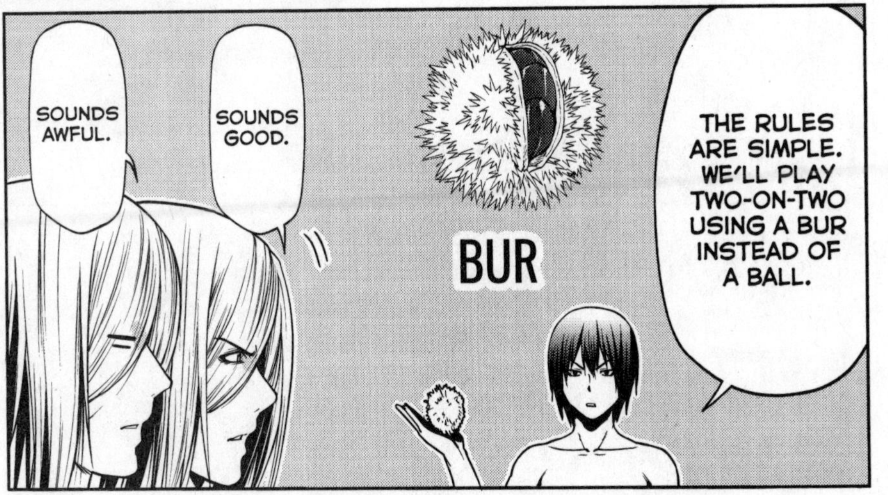
THE RULES ARE SIMPLE. WE'LL PLAY TWO-ON-TWO USING A BUR INSTEAD OF A BALL.
BUR
SOUNDS GOOD.
SOUNDS AWFUL.

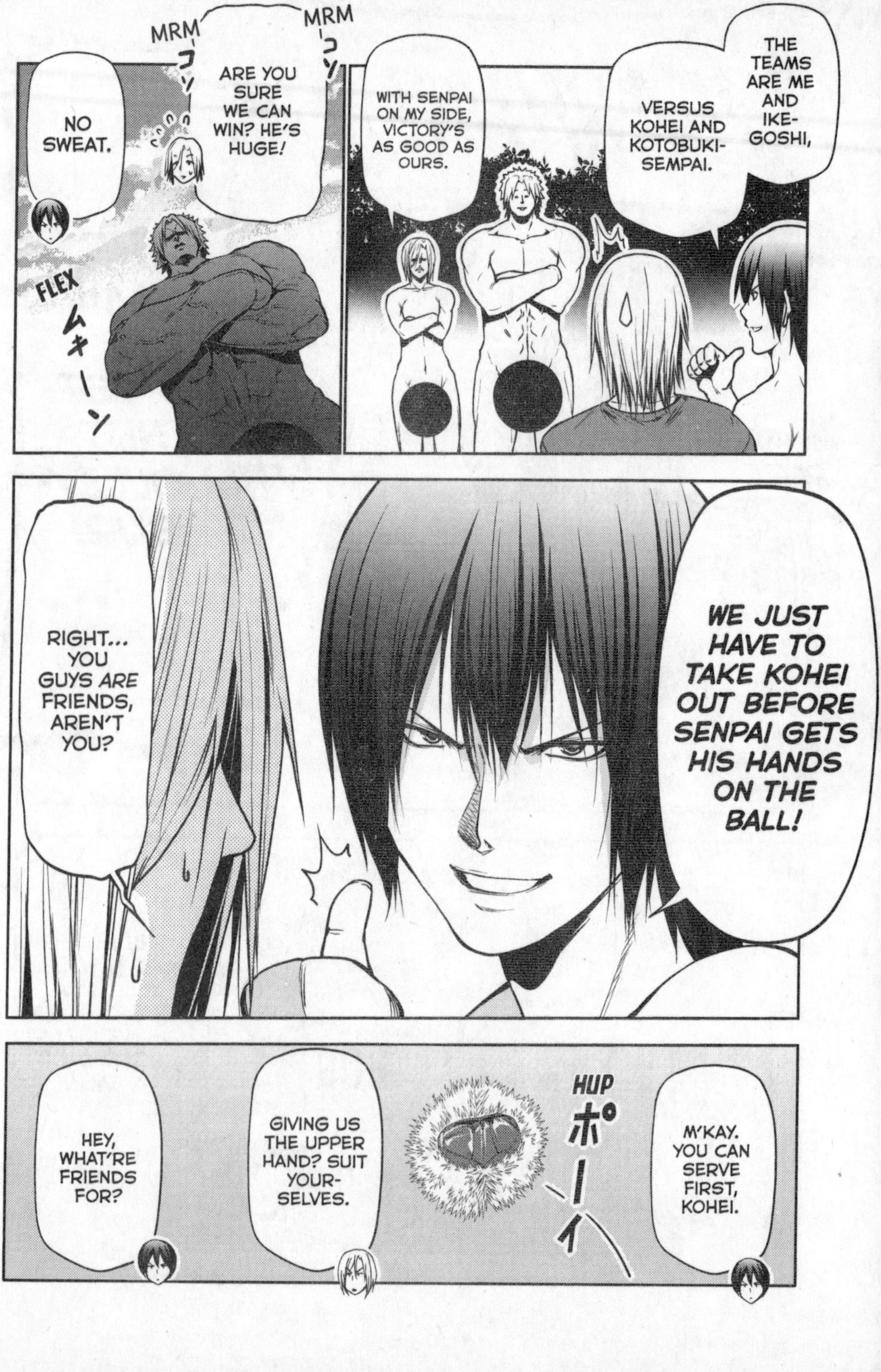
THE TEAMS ARE ME AND IKE-GOSHI,
VERSUS KOHEI AND KOTOBUKI-SEMPAI.
M
WITH SENPAI ON MY SIDE, VICTORY'S AS GOOD AS OURS.
MRM コソ
ARE YOU SURE WE CAN WIN? HE'S HUGE!
MRM コソ
NO SWEAT.
FLEX ムキーン
WE JUST HAVE TO TAKE KOHEI OUT BEFORE SENPAI GETS HIS HANDS ON THE BALL!
RIGHT... YOU GUYS *ARE* FRIENDS, AREN'T YOU?
M'KAY. YOU CAN SERVE FIRST, KOHEI.
HUP ポーイ
GIVING US THE UPPER HAND? SUIT YOUR-SELVES.
HEY, WHAT'RE FRIENDS FOR?

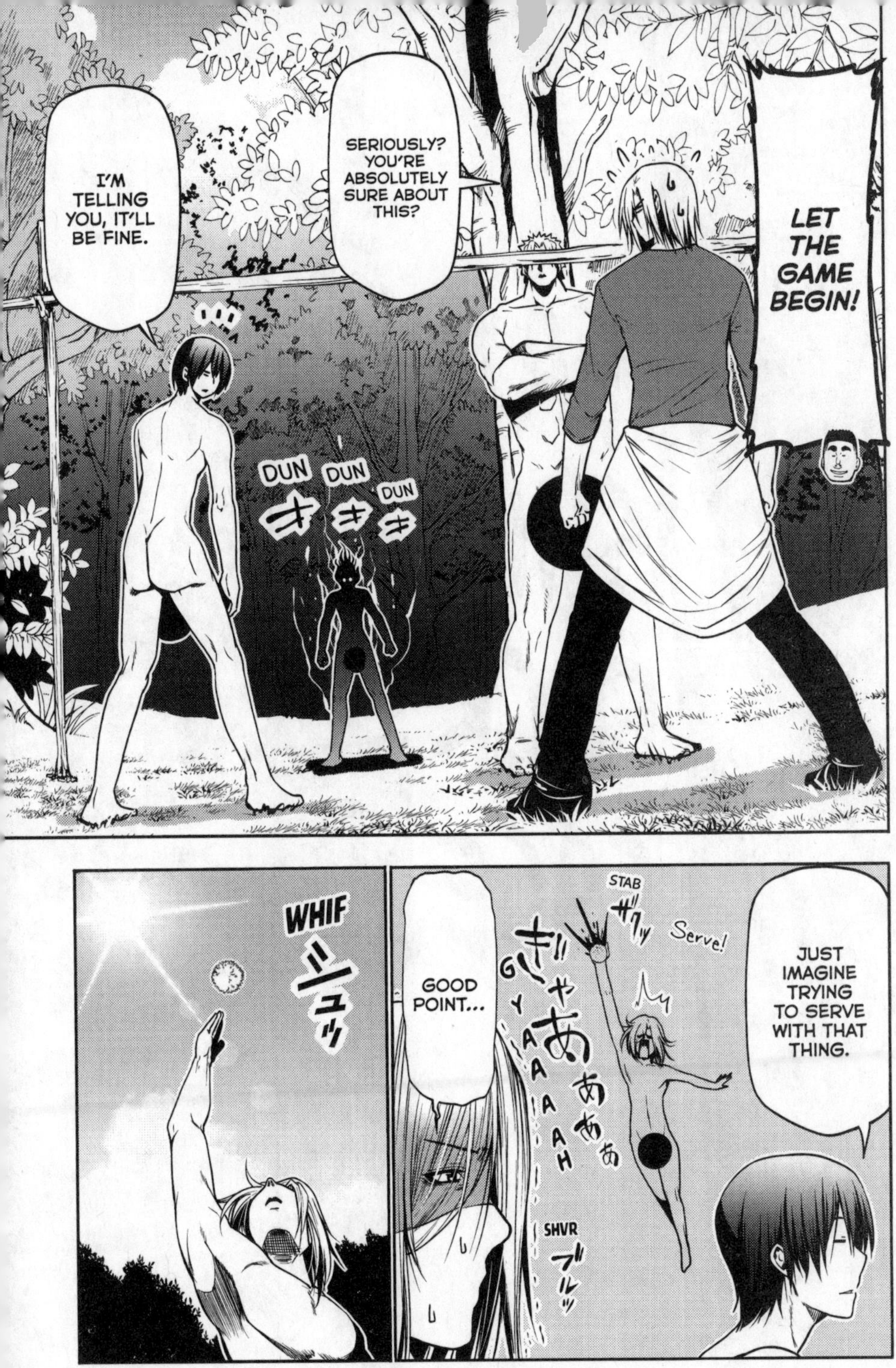
LET THE GAME BEGIN!
SERIOUSLY? YOU'RE ABSOLUTELY SURE ABOUT THIS?
I'M TELLING YOU, IT'LL BE FINE.
DUN
DUN
DUN
JUST IMAGINE TRYING TO SERVE WITH THAT THING.
Serve!
STAB
GYAAAAAH
SHVR
GOOD POINT...
WHIF

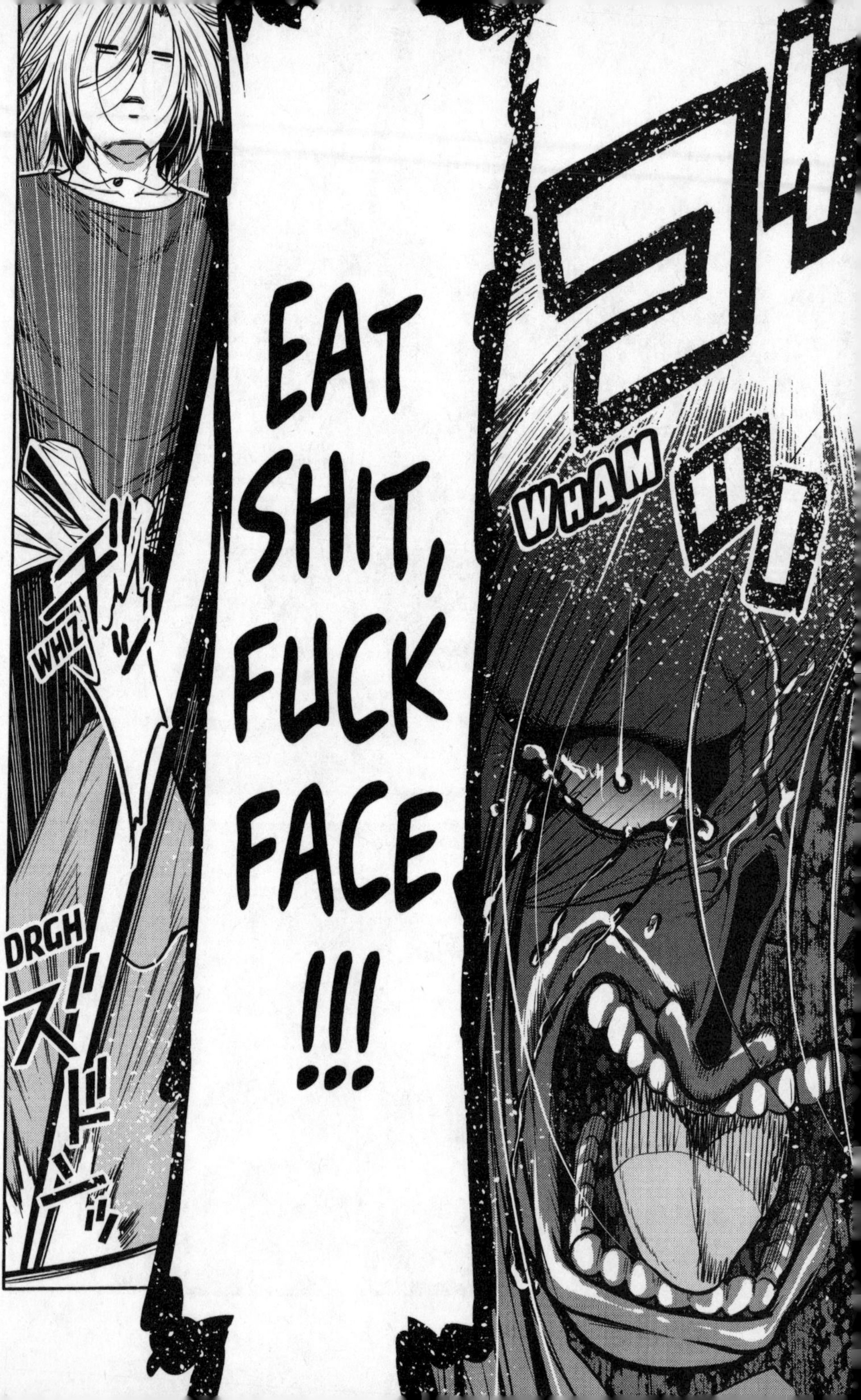
WHAM
EAT SHIT, FUCK FACE!!!
WHIZ
DRGH

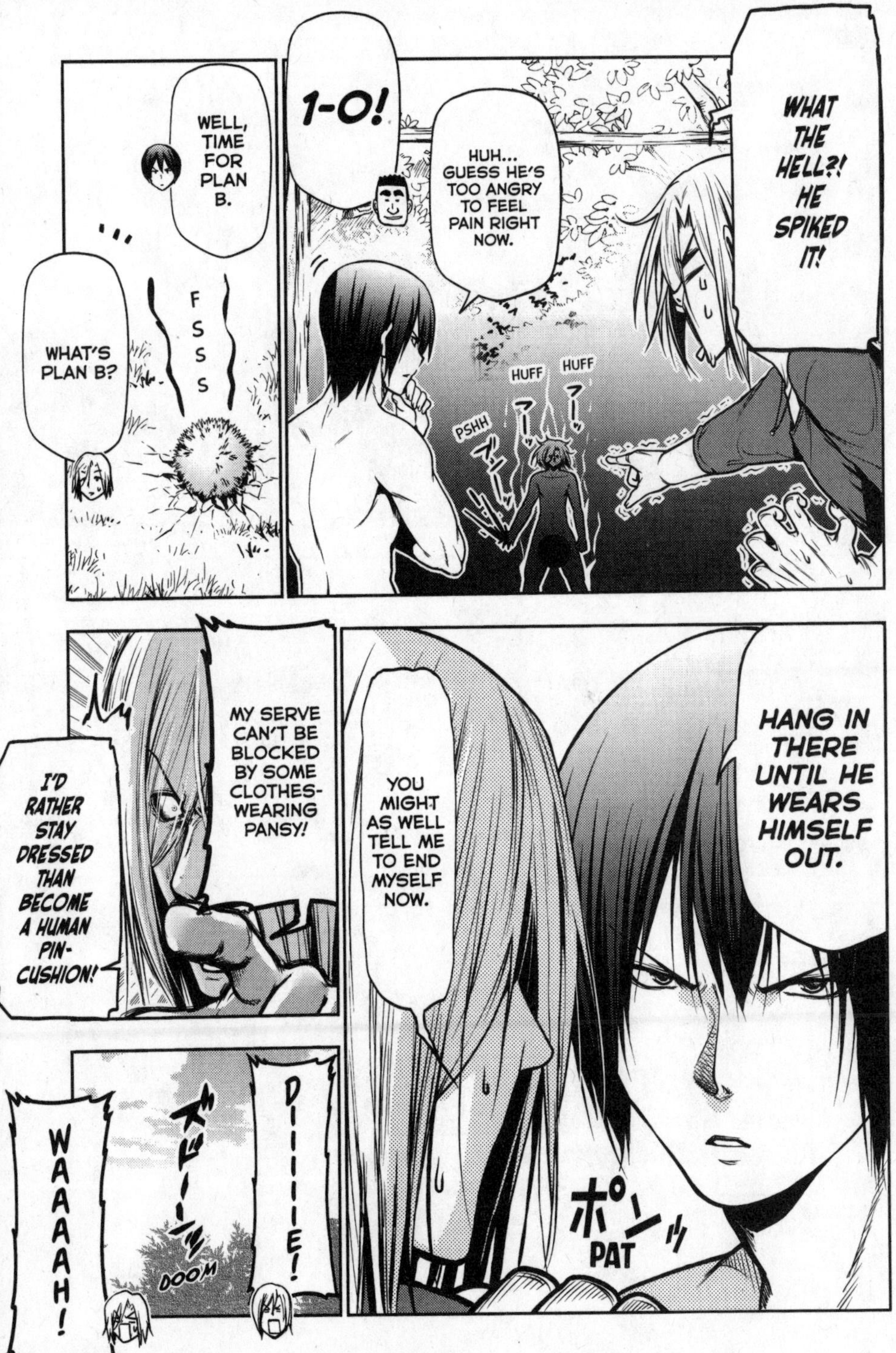
WHAT THE HELL?! HE SPIKED IT!
1-0!
HUH... GUESS HE'S TOO ANGRY TO FEEL PAIN RIGHT NOW.
HUFF HUFF
PSHH
WELL, TIME FOR PLAN B.
...
FSSS
WHAT'S PLAN B?
HANG IN THERE UNTIL HE WEARS HIMSELF OUT.
YOU MIGHT AS WELL TELL ME TO END MYSELF NOW.
PAT
MY SERVE CAN'T BE BLOCKED BY SOME CLOTHES-WEARING PANSY!
I'D RATHER STAY DRESSED THAN BECOME A HUMAN PIN-CUSHION!
DIIIIE!
DOOM
WAAAAAH!

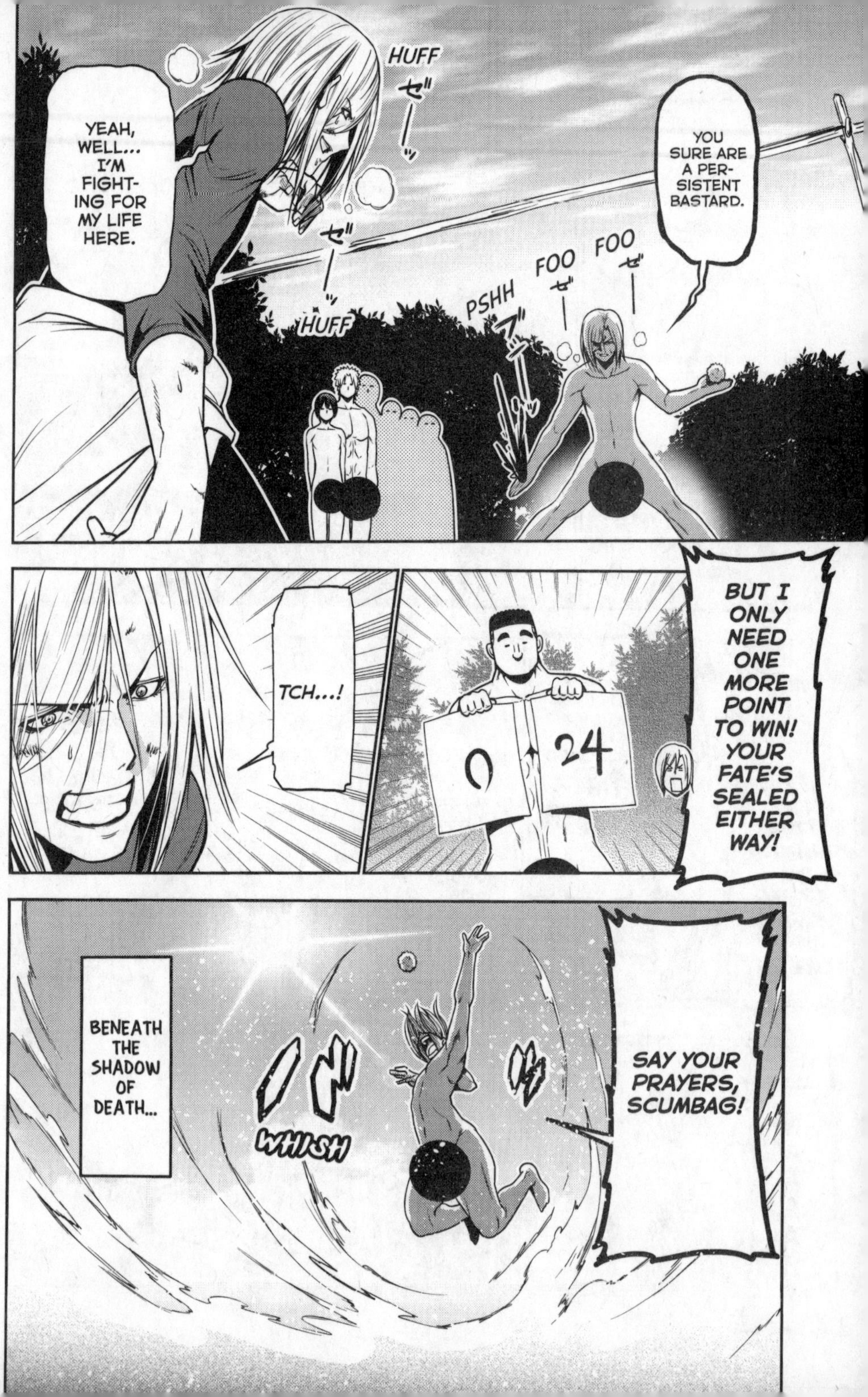
YOU SURE ARE A PERSISTENT BASTARD.
HUFF
YEAH, WELL... I'M FIGHTING FOR MY LIFE HERE.
FOO FOO
PSHH
HUFF
BUT I ONLY NEED ONE MORE POINT TO WIN! YOUR FATE'S SEALED EITHER WAY!
0 24
TCH...!
SAY YOUR PRAYERS, SCUMBAG!
WHISH
BENEATH THE SHADOW OF DEATH...

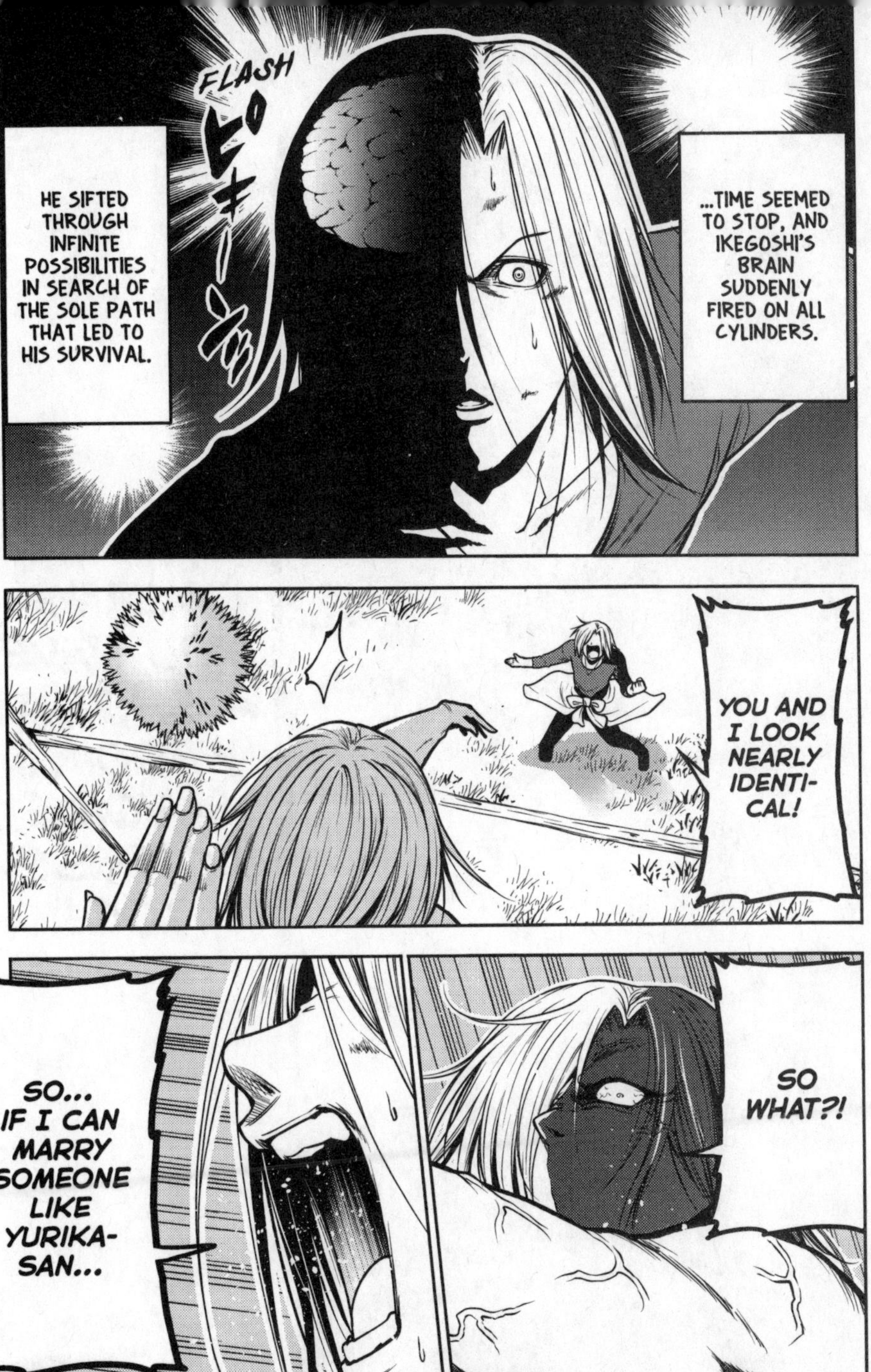
...TIME SEEMED TO STOP, AND IKEGOSHI'S BRAIN SUDDENLY FIRED ON ALL CYLINDERS.
FLASH
HE SIFTED THROUGH INFINITE POSSIBILITIES IN SEARCH OF THE SOLE PATH THAT LED TO HIS SURVIVAL.
YOU AND I LOOK NEARLY IDENTI-CAL!
SO WHAT?!
SO... IF I CAN MARRY SOMEONE LIKE YURIKA-SAN...

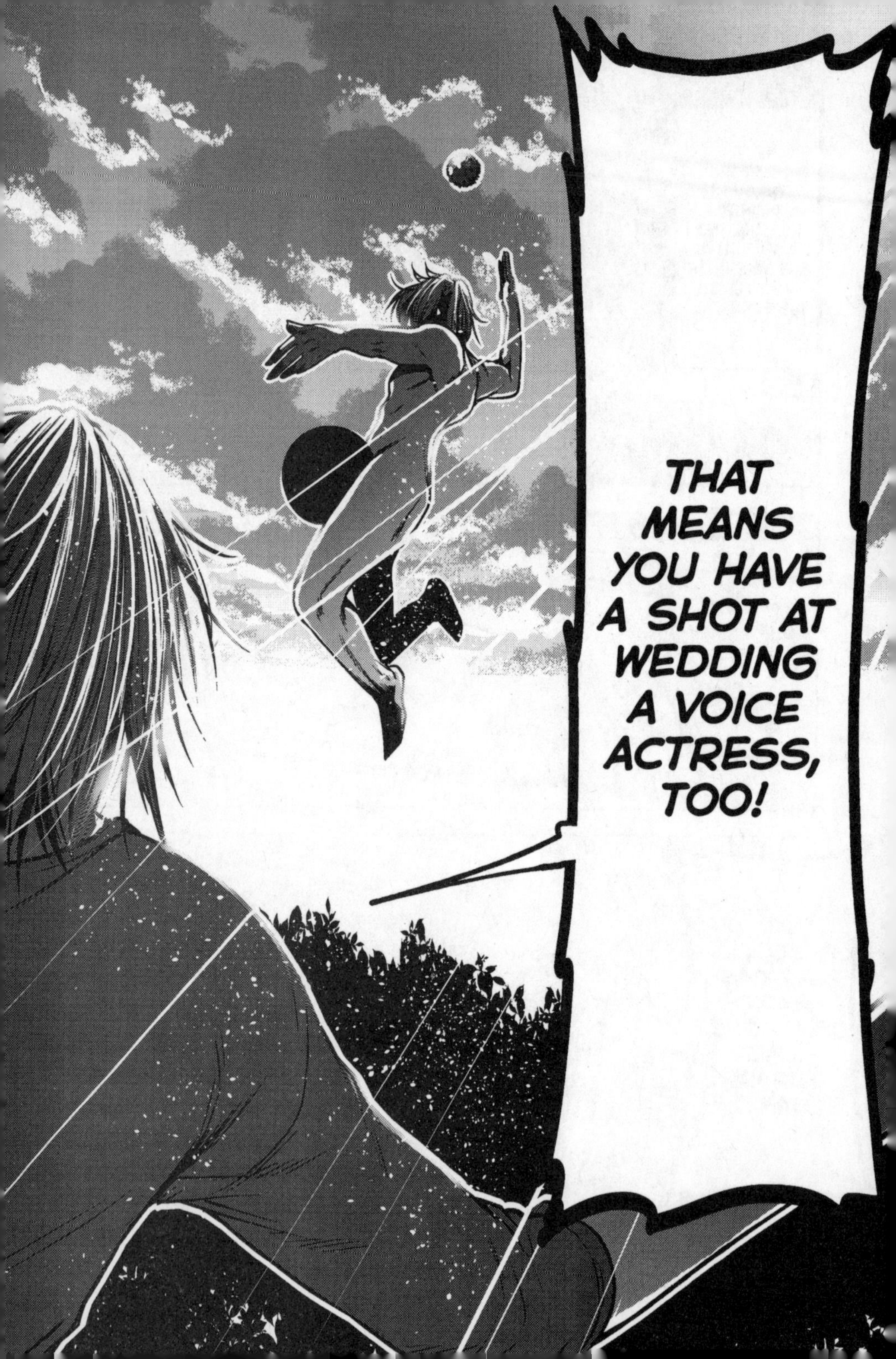
THAT MEANS YOU HAVE A SHOT AT WEDDING A VOICE ACTRESS, TOO!

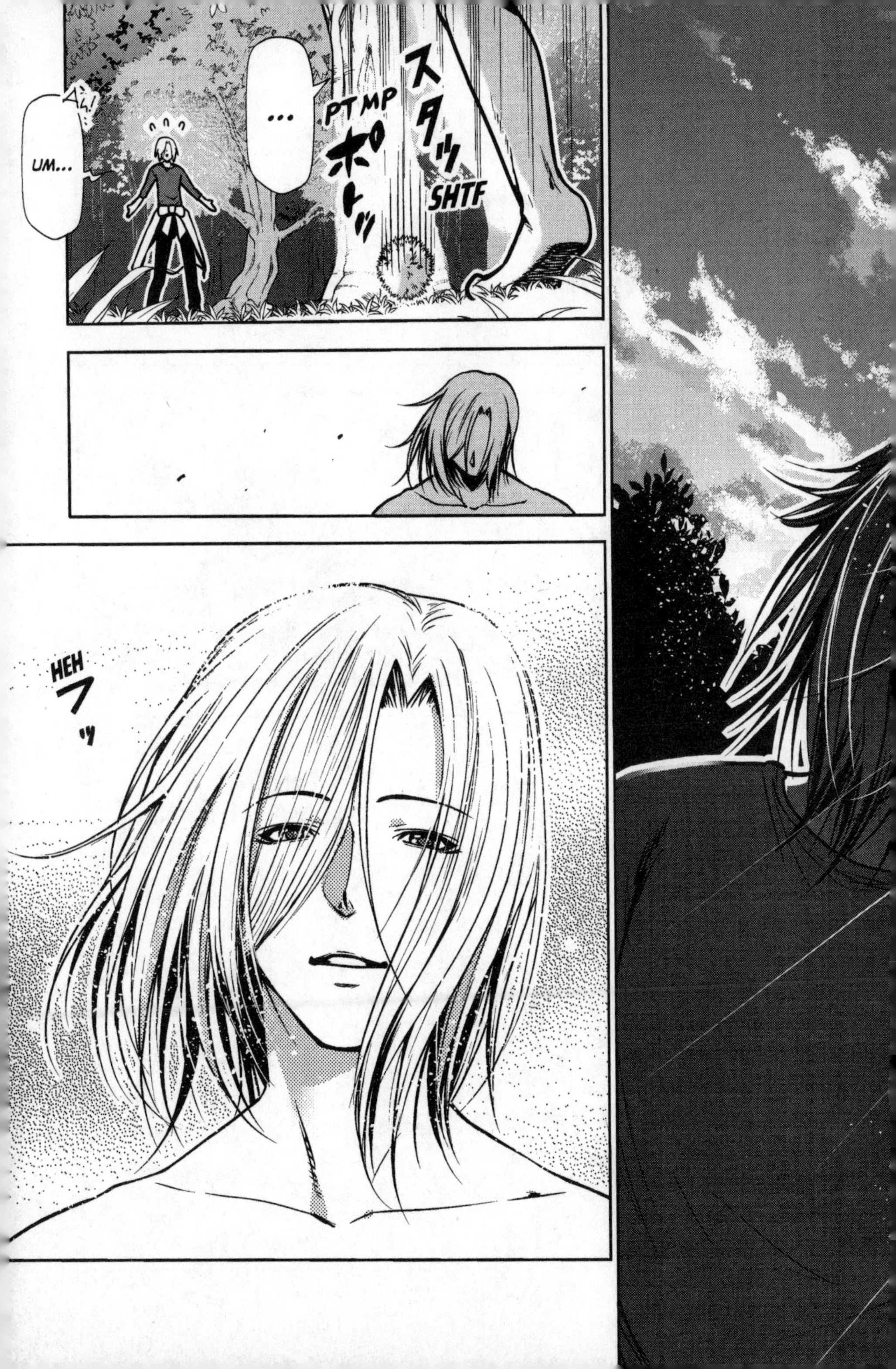
スタッ
SHTF
PTMP
ポトッ
...
AH!
UM...
HEH
フッ

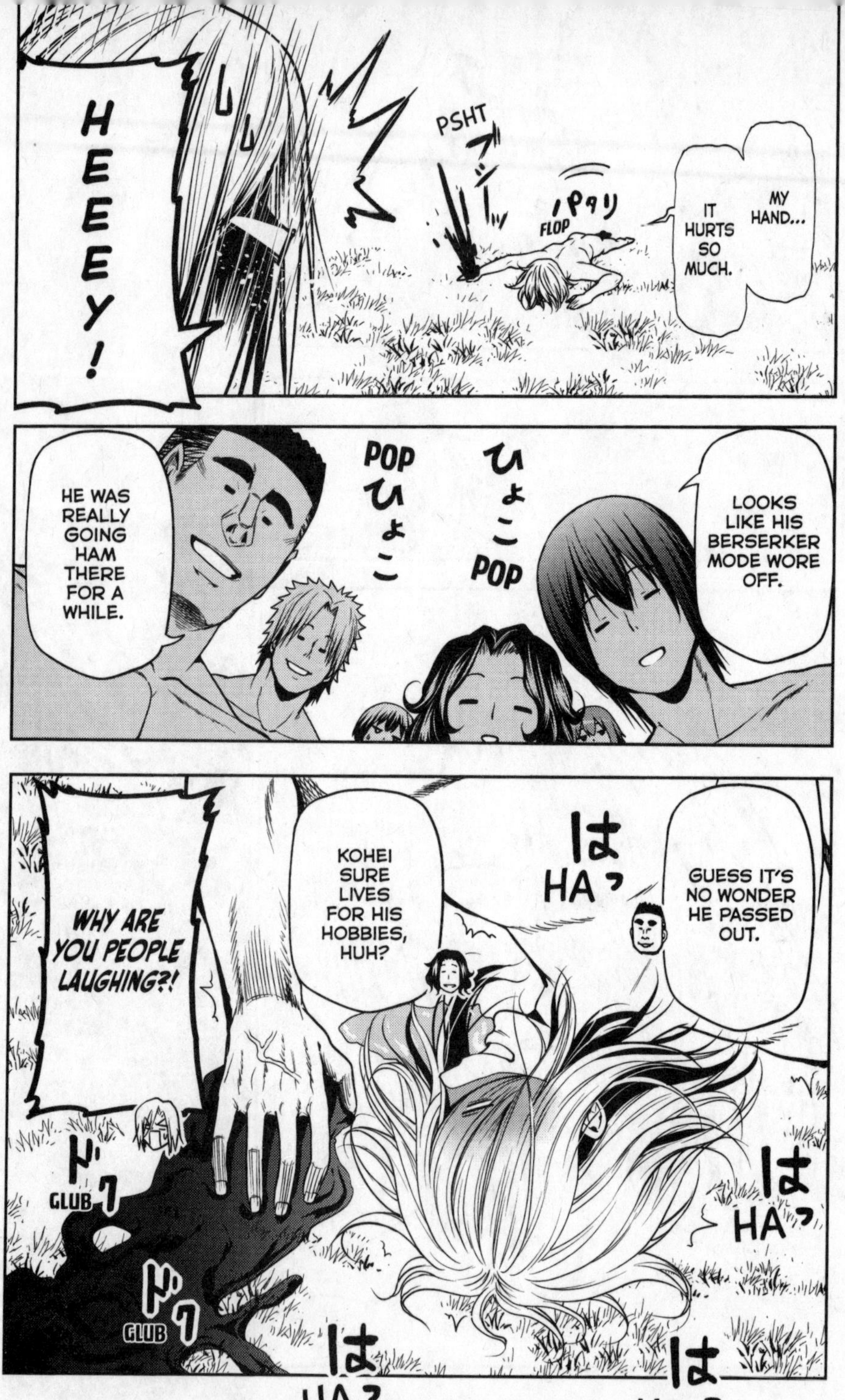
MY HAND... IT HURTS SO MUCH.
PSHT
パタリ FLOP
HEEEY!
LOOKS LIKE HIS BERSERKER MODE WORE OFF.
ひょこ POP
ひょこ POP
HE WAS REALLY GOING HAM THERE FOR A WHILE.
GUESS IT'S NO WONDER HE PASSED OUT.
はっ HA
KOHEI SURE LIVES FOR HIS HOBBIES, HUH?
WHY ARE YOU PEOPLE LAUGHING?!
はっ HA
ドク GLUB
ドク GLUB
はっ HA
はっ HA

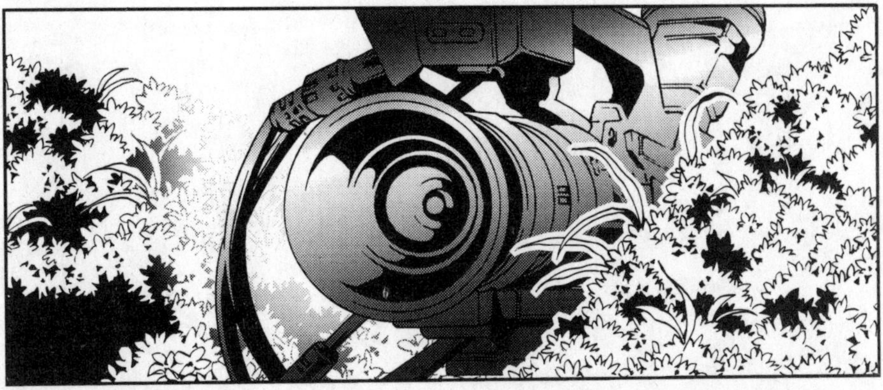

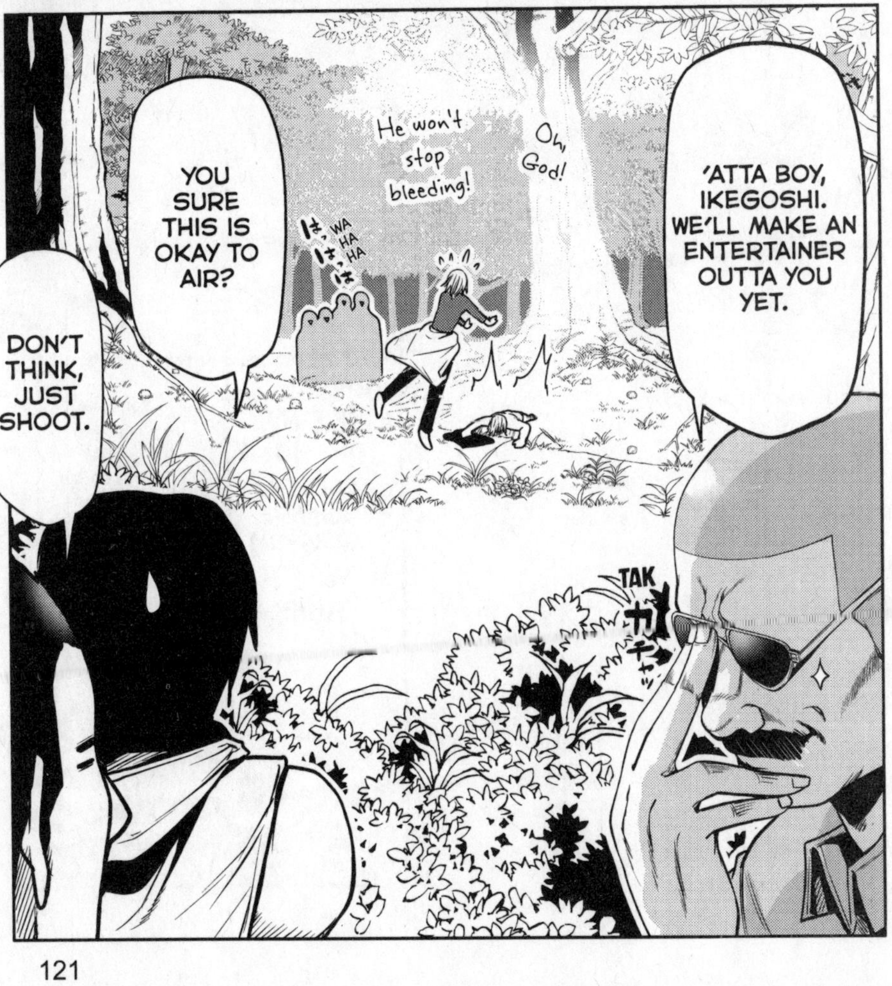
'ATTA BOY, IKEGOSHI. WE'LL MAKE AN ENTERTAINER OUTTA YOU YET.
Oh, God!
He won't stop bleeding!
は、は、は
WA HA HA
YOU SURE THIS IS OKAY TO AIR?
DON'T THINK, JUST SHOOT.
TAK
カチャッ

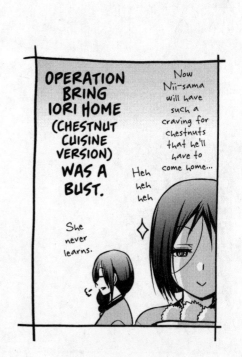

Now Nii-sama will have such a craving for chestnuts that he'll have to come home...
OPERATION BRING IORI HOME (CHESTNUT CUISINE VERSION) WAS A BUST.
Heh heh heh
She never learns.

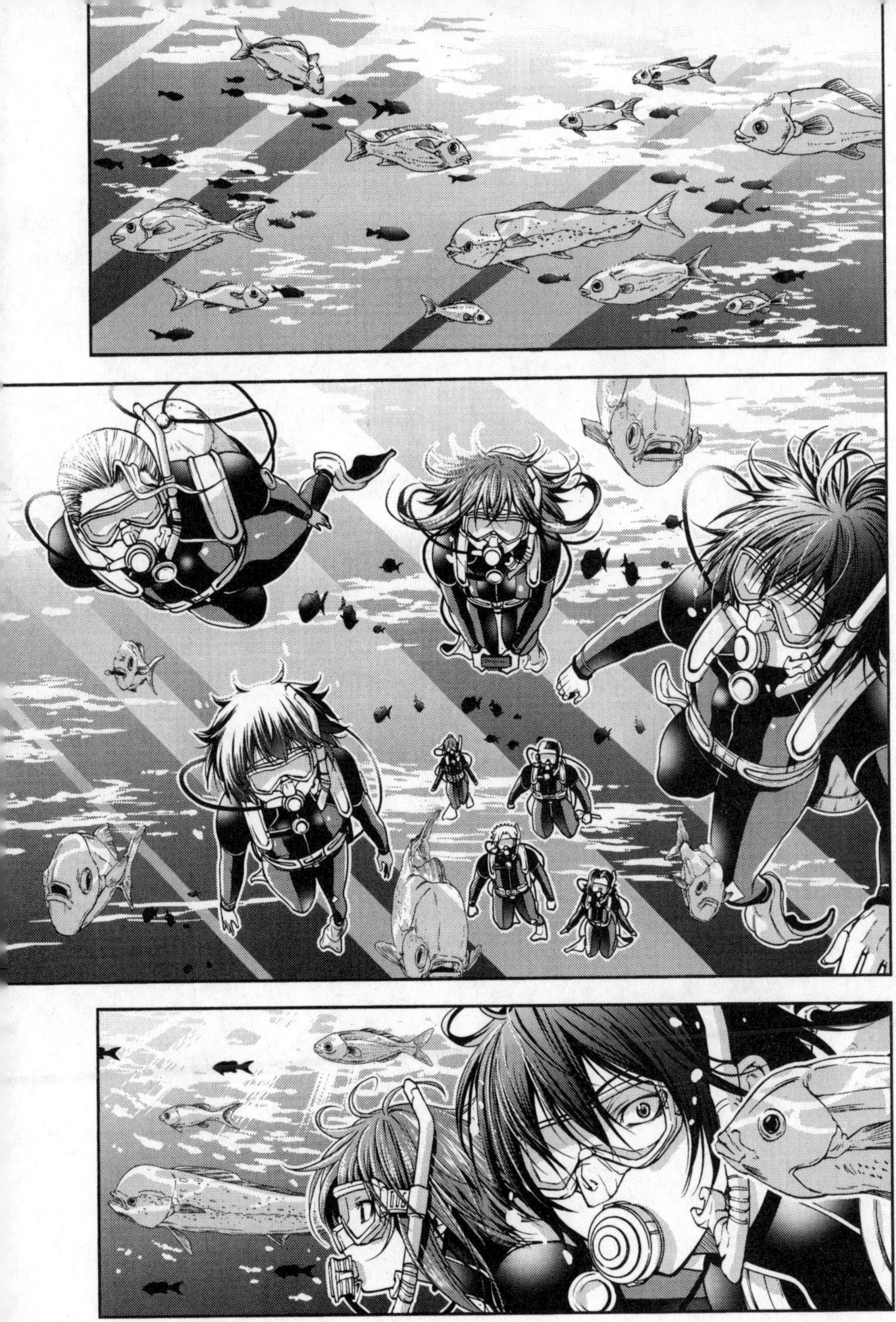

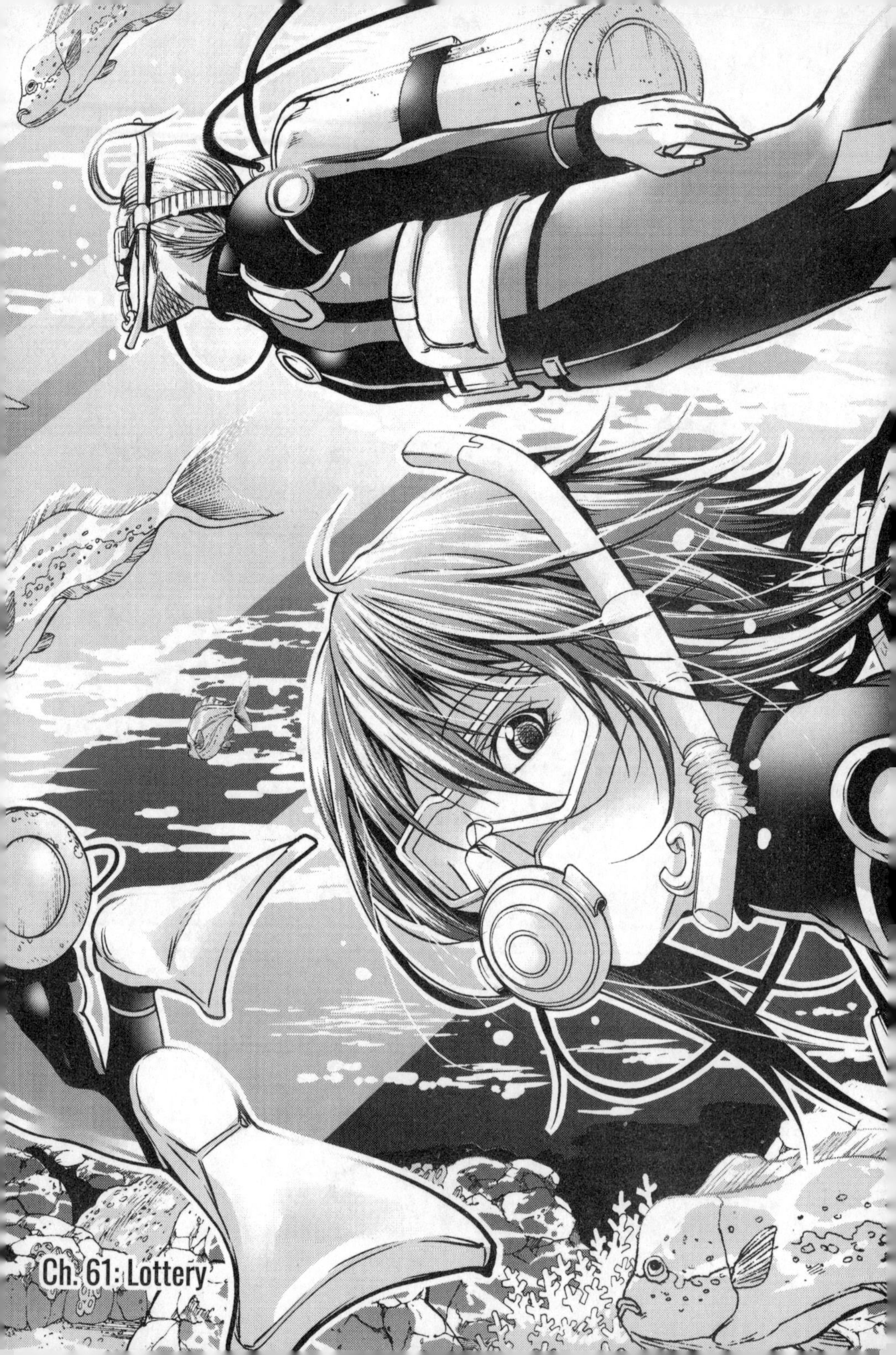
Ch. 61: Lottery

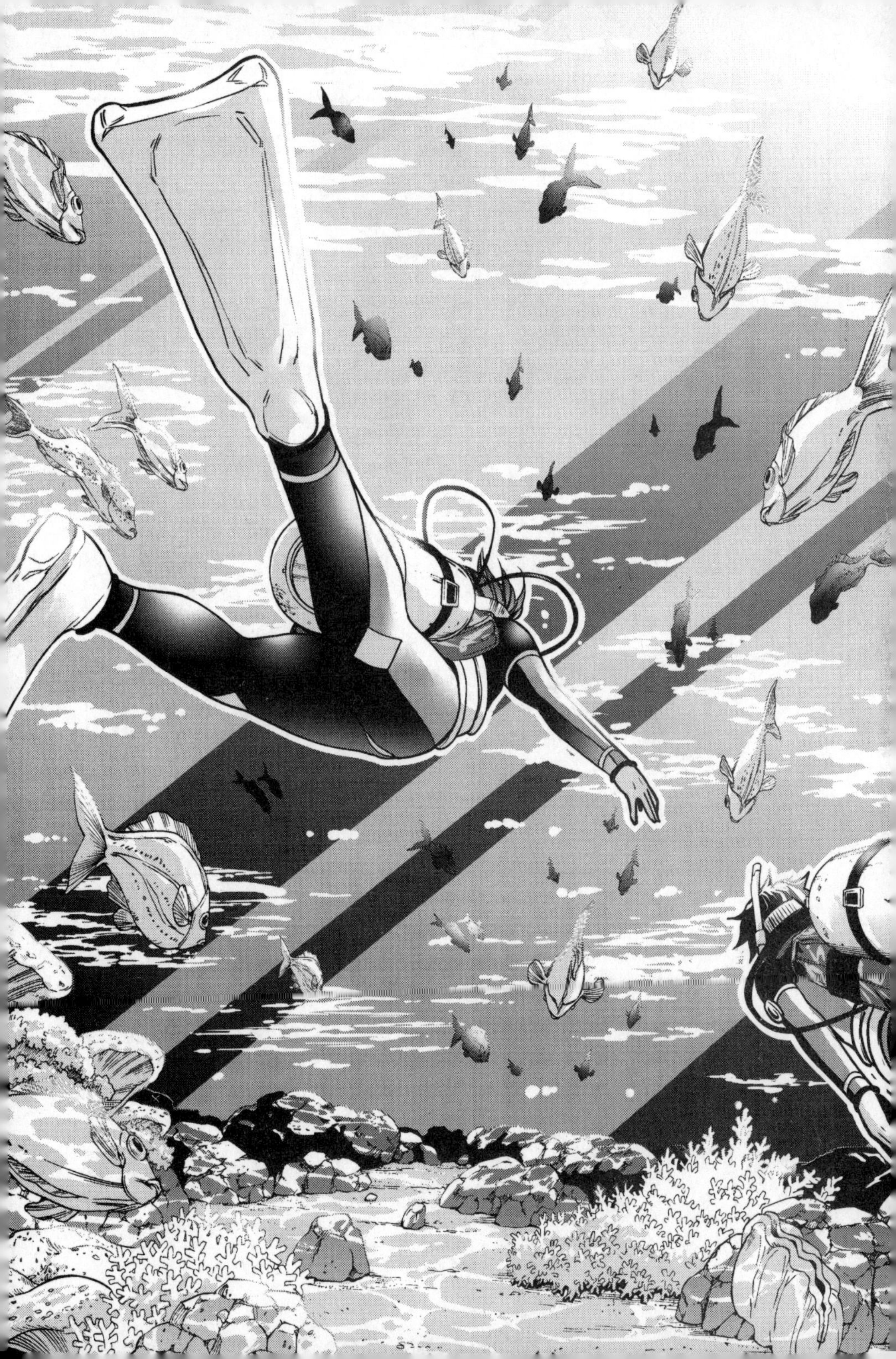

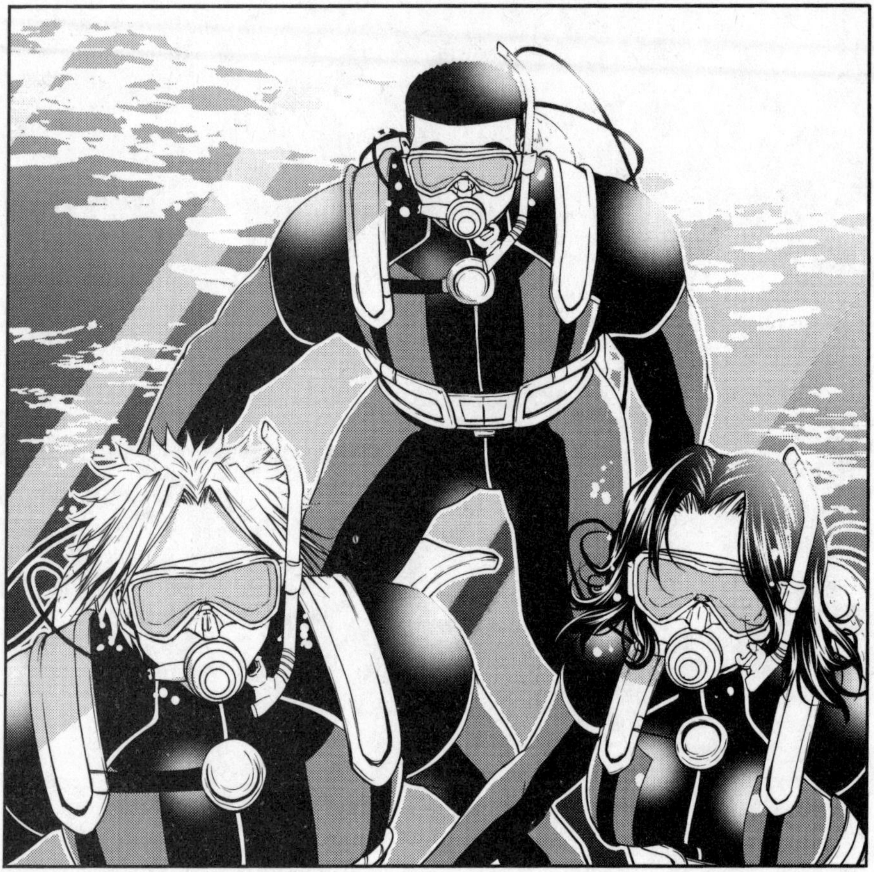

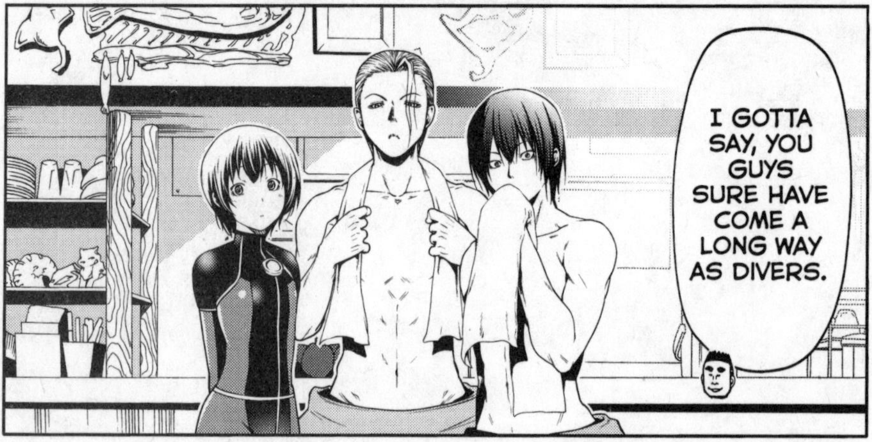
I GOTTA SAY, YOU GUYS SURE HAVE COME A LONG WAY AS DIVERS.

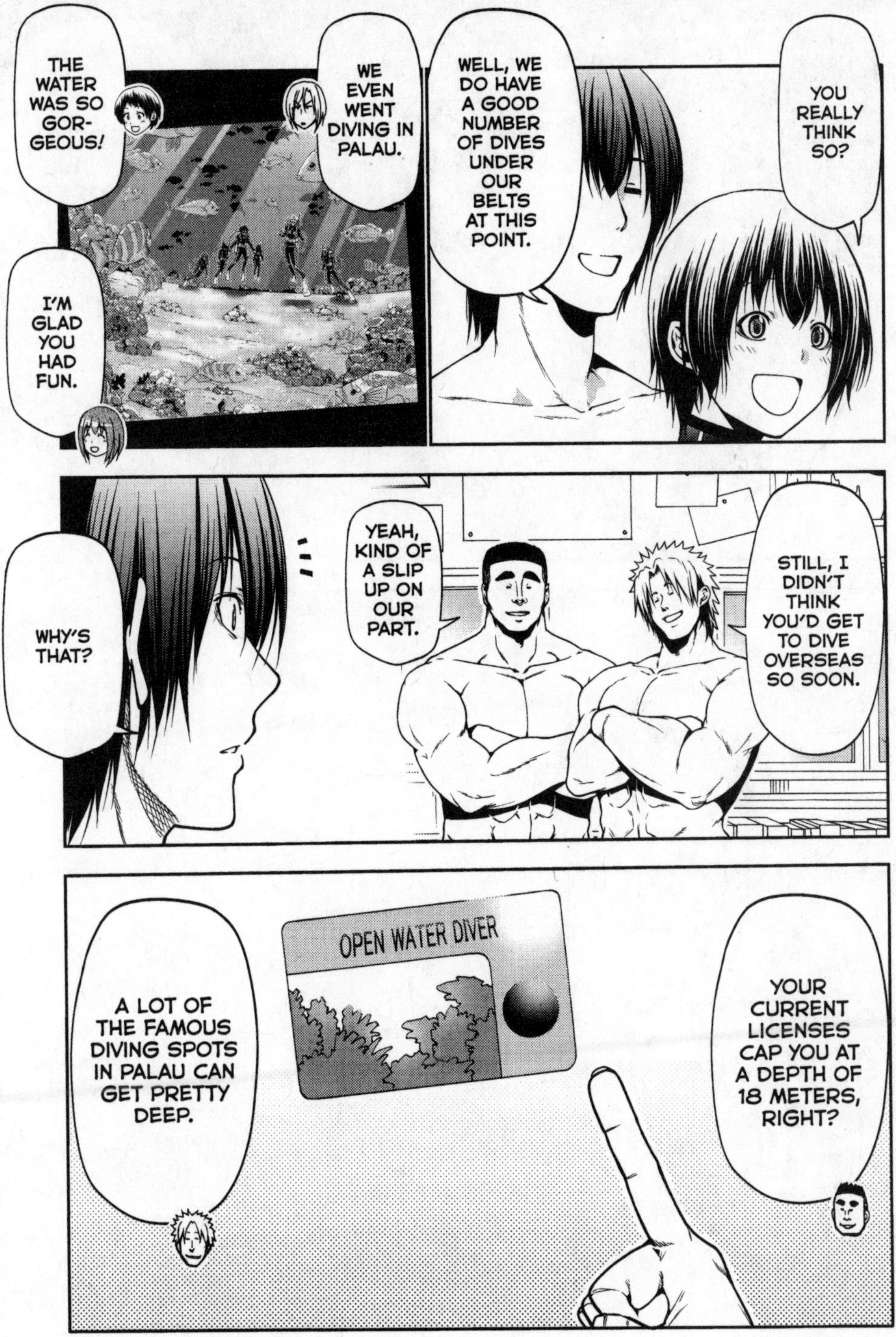
YOU REALLY THINK SO?
WELL, WE DO HAVE A GOOD NUMBER OF DIVES UNDER OUR BELTS AT THIS POINT.
WE EVEN WENT DIVING IN PALAU.
THE WATER WAS SO GOR-GEOUS!
I'M GLAD YOU HAD FUN.
STILL, I DIDN'T THINK YOU'D GET TO DIVE OVERSEAS SO SOON.
YEAH, KIND OF A SLIP UP ON OUR PART.
WHY'S THAT?
YOUR CURRENT LICENSES CAP YOU AT A DEPTH OF 18 METERS, RIGHT?
OPEN WATER DIVER
A LOT OF THE FAMOUS DIVING SPOTS IN PALAU CAN GET PRETTY DEEP.

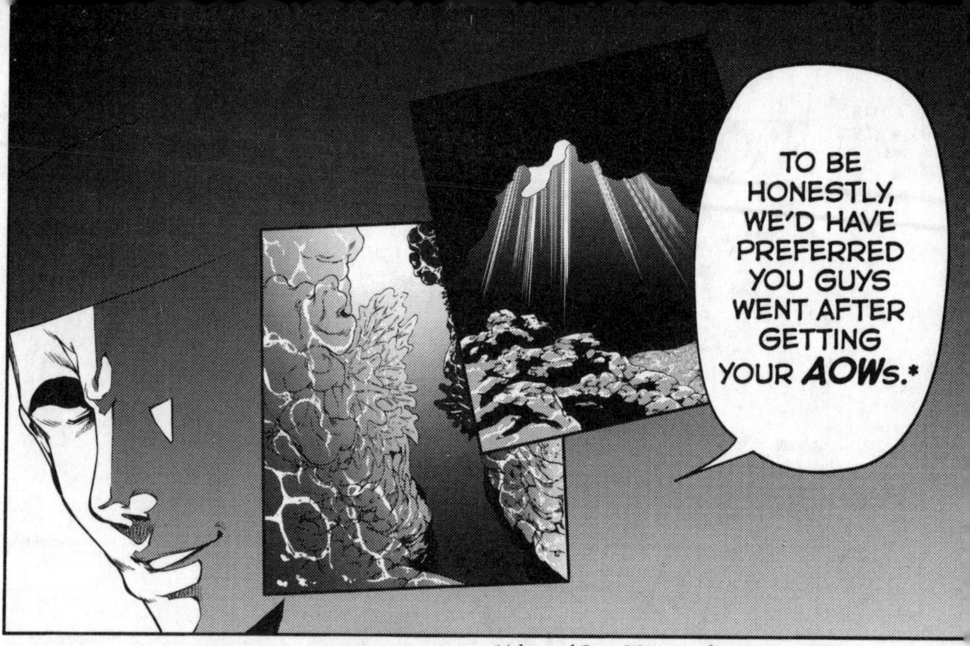
TO BE HONESTLY, WE'D HAVE PREFERRED YOU GUYS WENT AFTER GETTING YOUR AOWs.*

*Advanced Open Water certification.

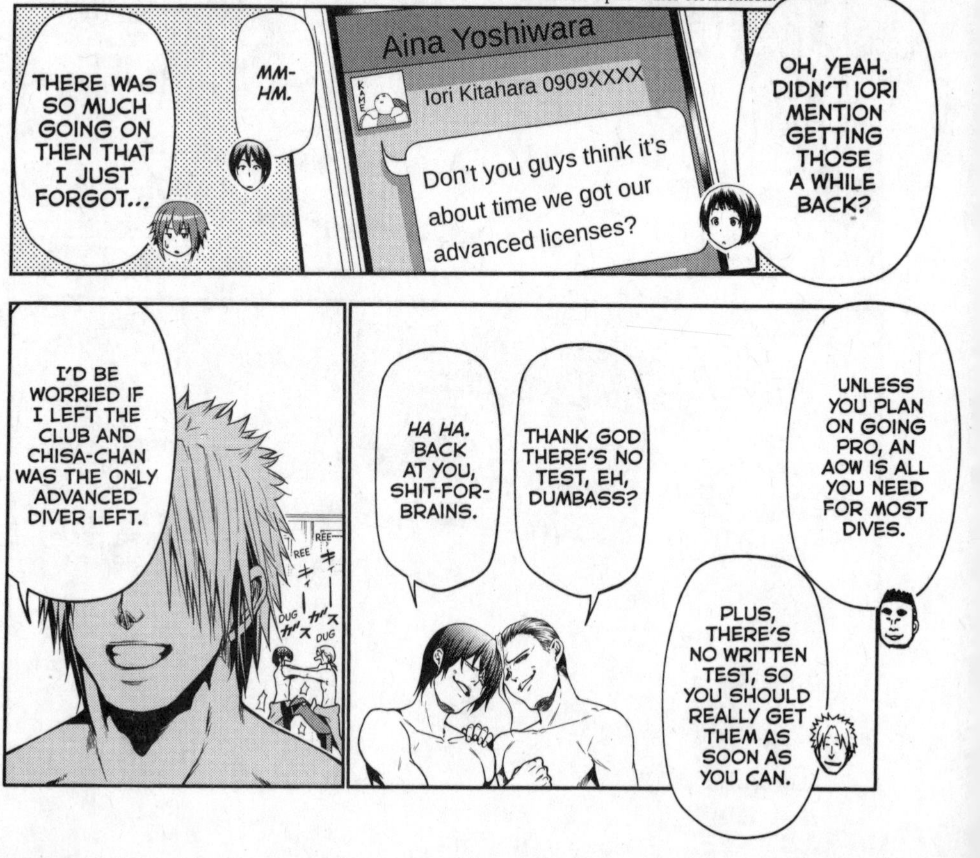
OH, YEAH. DIDN'T IORI MENTION GETTING THOSE A WHILE BACK?
Aina Yoshiwara
KAME
Iori Kitahara 0909XXXX
Don't you guys think it's about time we got our advanced licenses?
MM-HM.
THERE WAS SO MUCH GOING ON THEN THAT I JUST FORGOT...
UNLESS YOU PLAN ON GOING PRO, AN AOW IS ALL YOU NEED FOR MOST DIVES.
PLUS, THERE'S NO WRITTEN TEST, SO YOU SHOULD REALLY GET THEM AS SOON AS YOU CAN.
THANK GOD THERE'S NO TEST, EH, DUMBASS?
HA HA. BACK AT YOU, SHIT-FOR-BRAINS.
I'D BE WORRIED IF I LEFT THE CLUB AND CHISA-CHAN WAS THE ONLY ADVANCED DIVER LEFT.
REE キィー
REE キィ
DUG ガス
DUG ガス

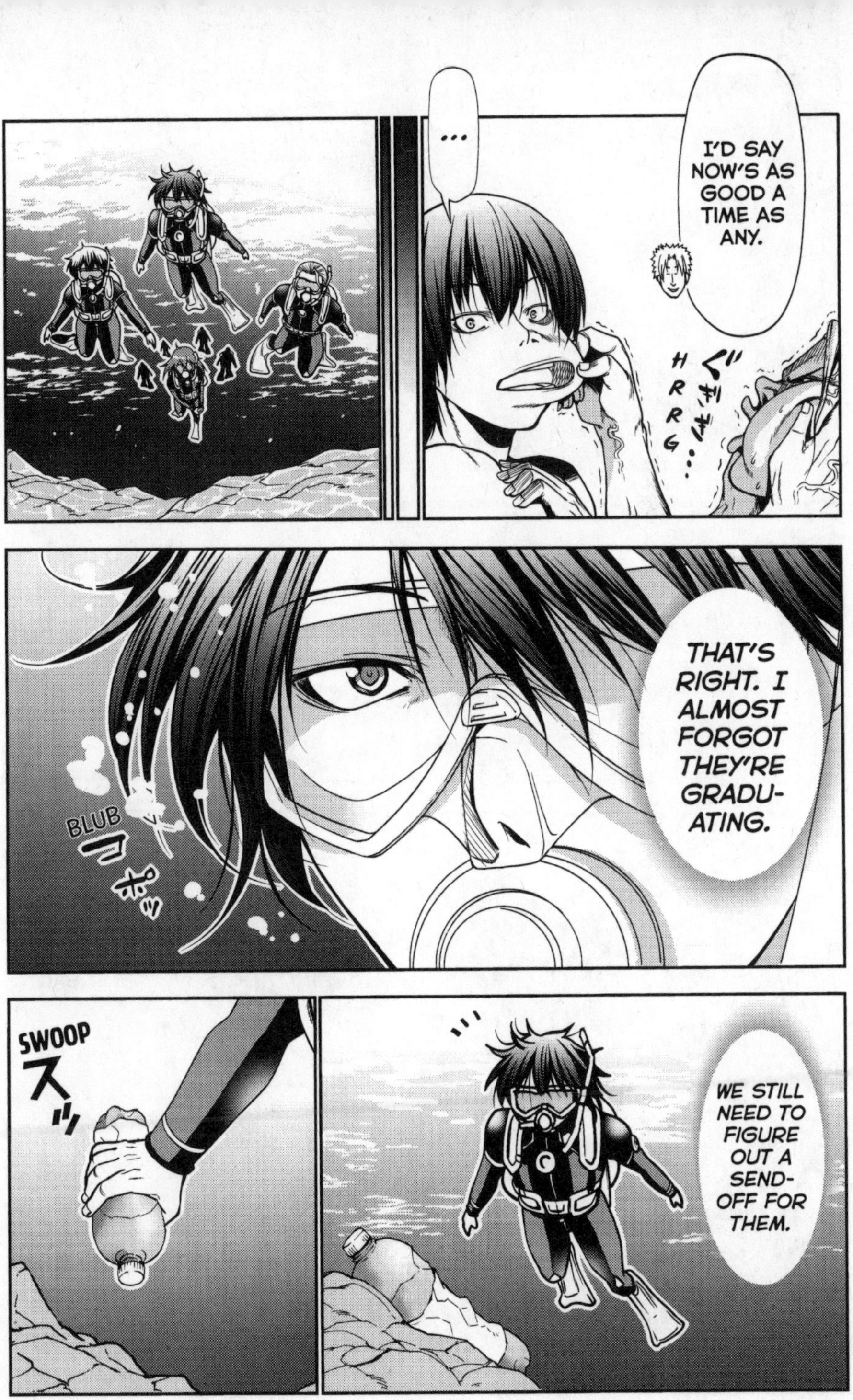
I'D SAY NOW'S AS GOOD A TIME AS ANY.
HRRG
...
THAT'S RIGHT. I ALMOST FORGOT THEY'RE GRADUATING.
BLUB
WE STILL NEED TO FIGURE OUT A SEND-OFF FOR THEM.
SWOOP

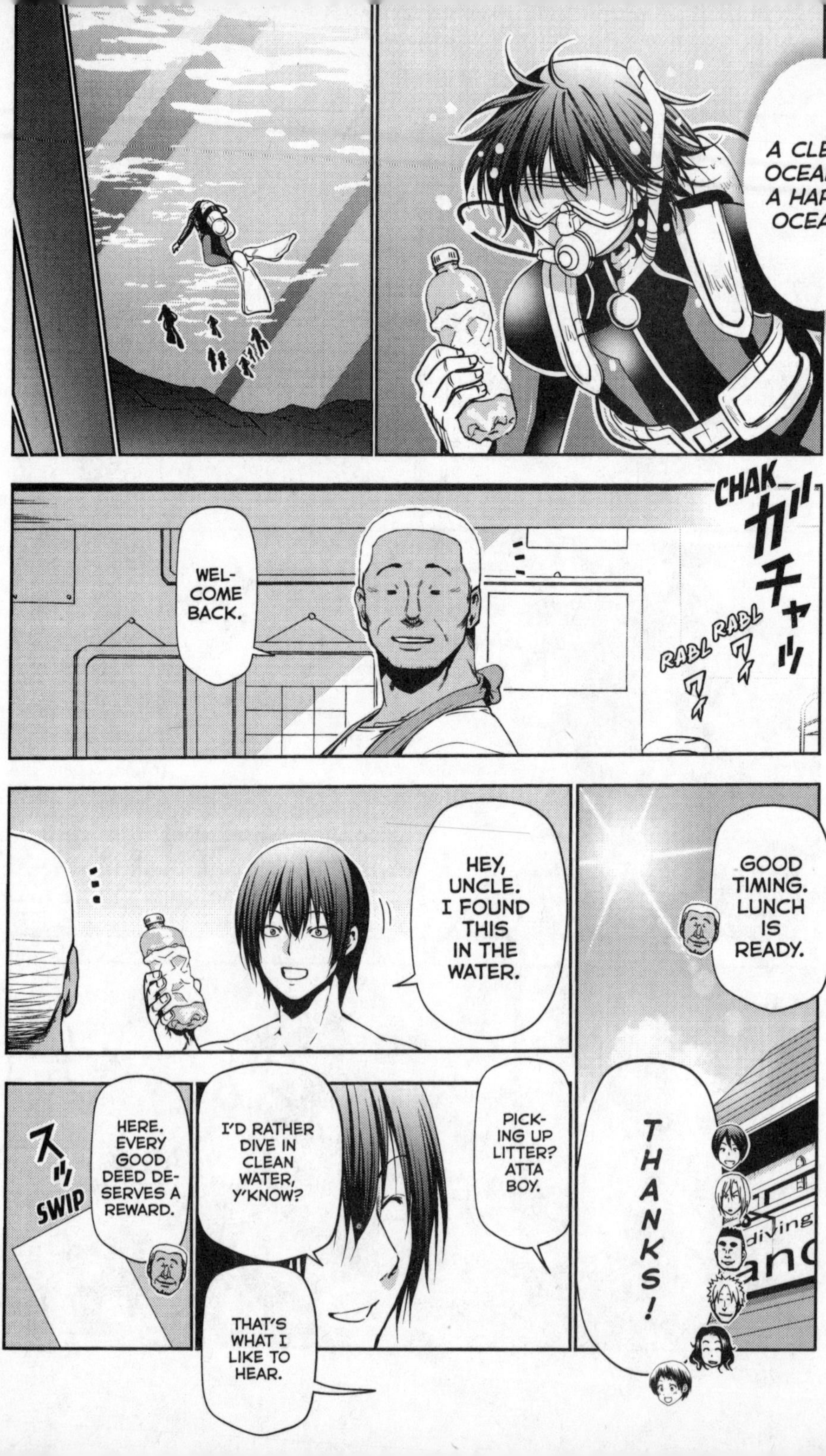
A CLEAN OCEAN'S A HAPPY OCEAN.
CHAK
ガチャッ
RABL RABL
ワイワイ
WEL-COME BACK.
GOOD TIMING. LUNCH IS READY.
THANKS!
HEY, UNCLE. I FOUND THIS IN THE WATER.
PICK-ING UP LITTER? ATTA BOY.
I'D RATHER DIVE IN CLEAN WATER, Y'KNOW?
THAT'S WHAT I LIKE TO HEAR.
HERE. EVERY GOOD DEED DE-SERVES A REWARD.
スッ
SWIP

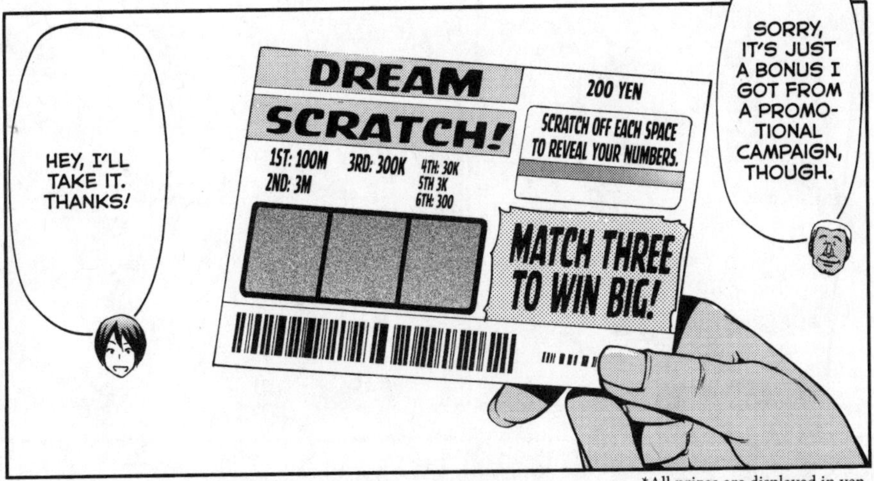
SORRY, IT'S JUST A BONUS I GOT FROM A PROMOTIONAL CAMPAIGN, THOUGH.
DREAM SCRATCH!
200 YEN
SCRATCH OFF EACH SPACE TO REVEAL YOUR NUMBERS.
1ST: 100M 2ND: 3M 3RD: 300K 4TH: 30K 5TH 3K 6TH: 300
MATCH THREE TO WIN BIG!
HEY, I'LL TAKE IT. THANKS!

*All prizes are displayed in yen.

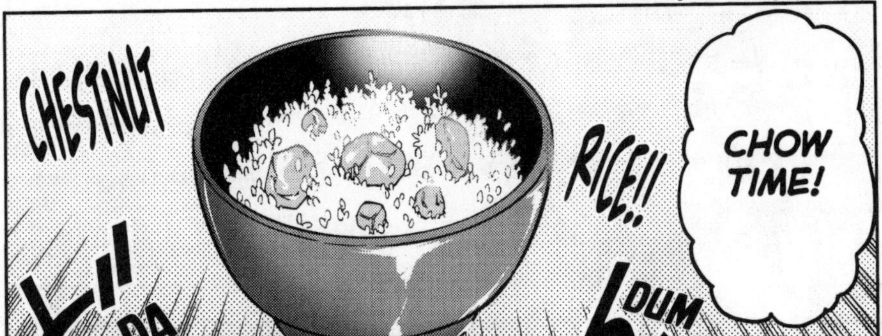
CHOW TIME!
CHESTNUT
RICE!!
DUM
DA

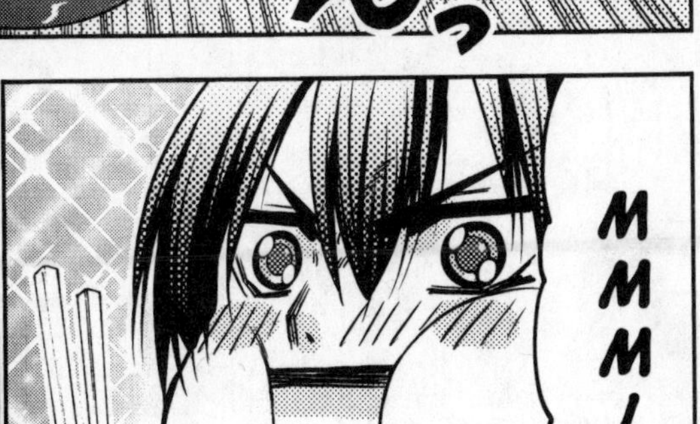
MMM!

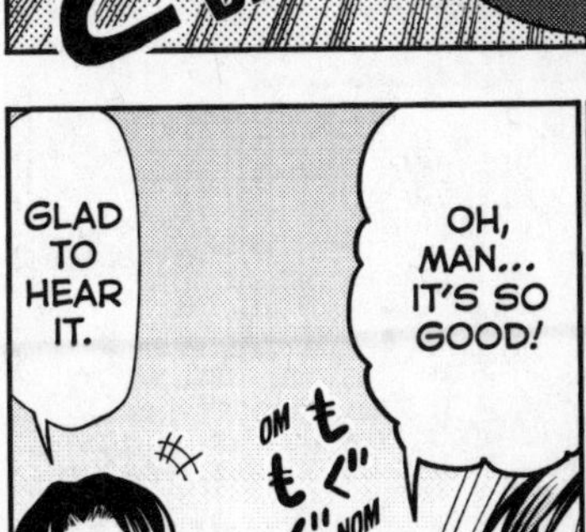
OH, MAN... IT'S SO GOOD!
OM NOM
GLAD TO HEAR IT.

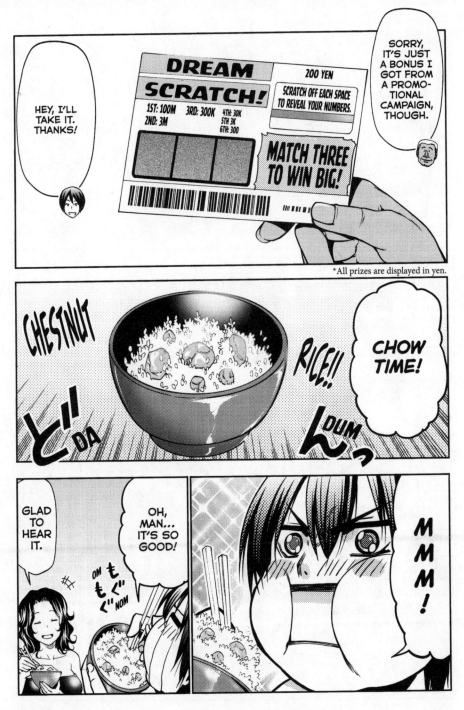

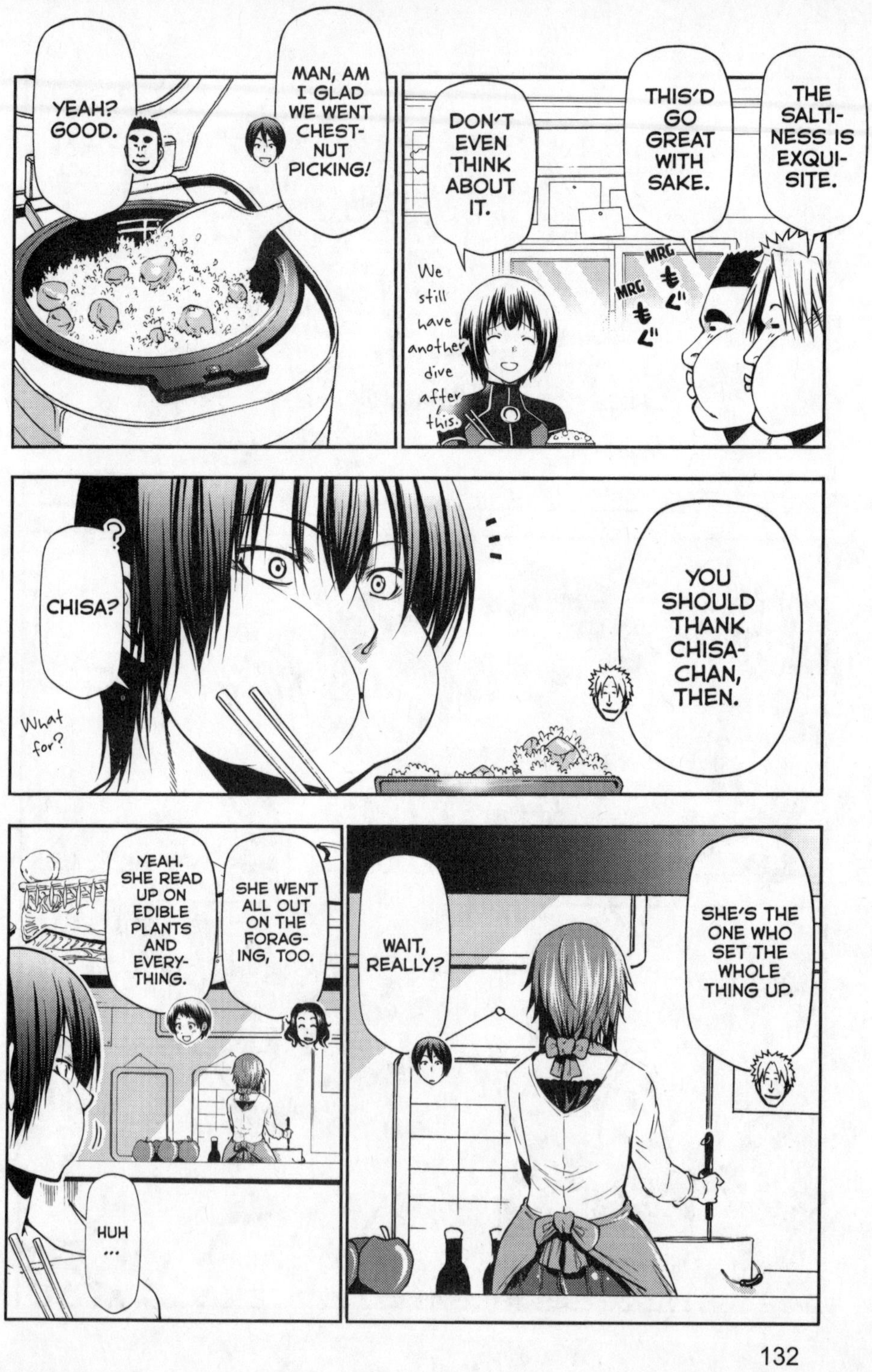
THE SALTINESS IS EXQUISITE.
THIS'D GO GREAT WITH SAKE.
MRG もぐ
MRG もぐ
DON'T EVEN THINK ABOUT IT.
We still have another dive after this.
MAN, AM I GLAD WE WENT CHESTNUT PICKING!
YEAH? GOOD.
YOU SHOULD THANK CHISA-CHAN, THEN.
CHISA?
What for?
SHE'S THE ONE WHO SET THE WHOLE THING UP.
WAIT, REALLY?
SHE WENT ALL OUT ON THE FORAGING, TOO.
YEAH. SHE READ UP ON EDIBLE PLANTS AND EVERYTHING.
HUH ...

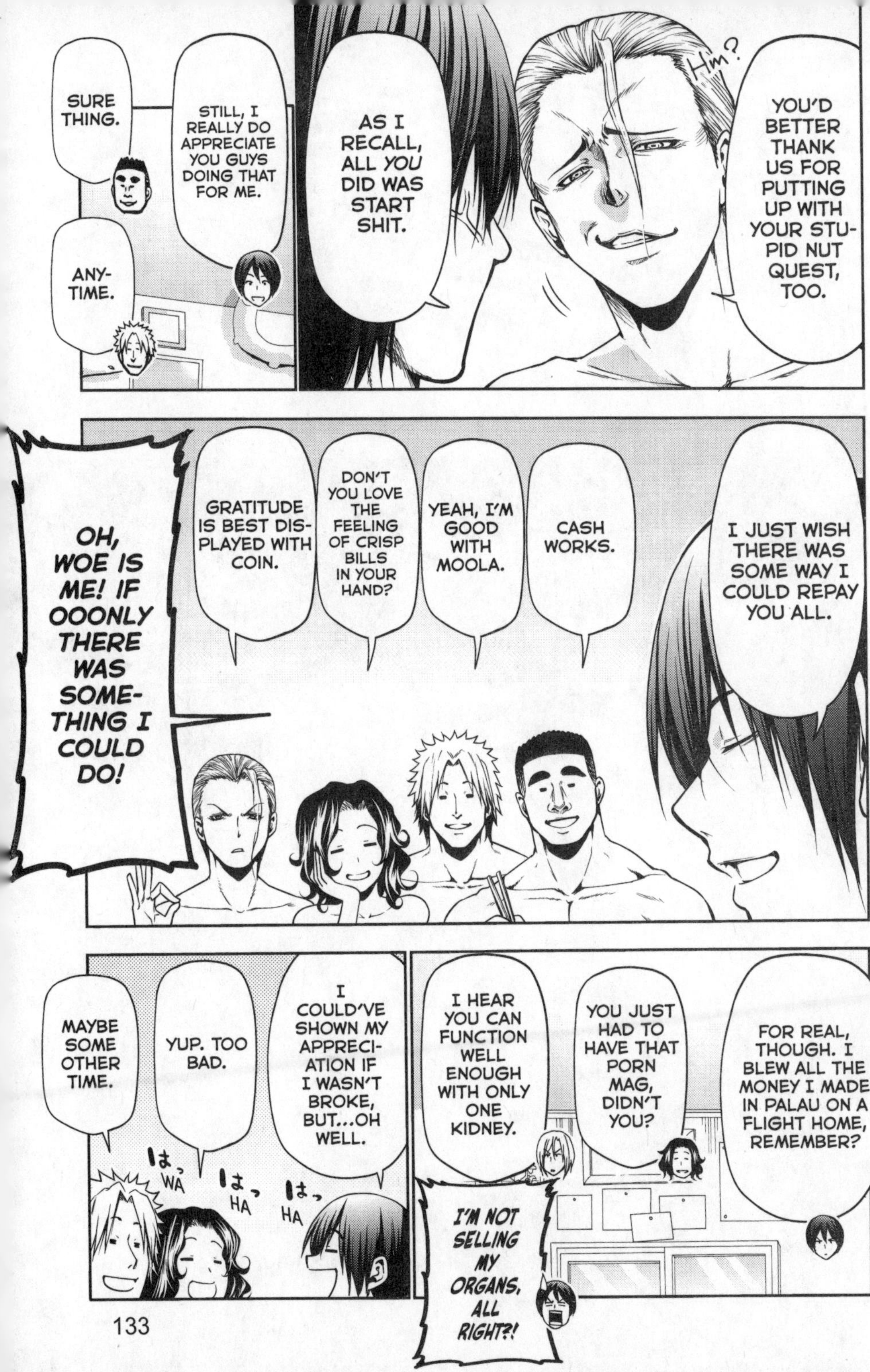
Hm?
YOU'D BETTER THANK US FOR PUTTING UP WITH YOUR STUPID NUT QUEST, TOO.
AS I RECALL, ALL *YOU* DID WAS START SHIT.
STILL, I REALLY DO APPRECIATE YOU GUYS DOING THAT FOR ME.
SURE THING.
ANY-TIME.
I JUST WISH THERE WAS SOME WAY I COULD REPAY YOU ALL.
CASH WORKS.
YEAH, I'M GOOD WITH MOOLA.
DON'T YOU LOVE THE FEELING OF CRISP BILLS IN YOUR HAND?
GRATITUDE IS BEST DISPLAYED WITH COIN.
OH, WOE IS ME! IF OOONLY THERE WAS SOMETHING I COULD DO!
FOR REAL, THOUGH. I BLEW ALL THE MONEY I MADE IN PALAU ON A FLIGHT HOME, REMEMBER?
YOU JUST HAD TO HAVE THAT PORN MAG, DIDN'T YOU?
I HEAR YOU CAN FUNCTION WELL ENOUGH WITH ONLY ONE KIDNEY.
I'M NOT SELLING MY ORGANS, ALL RIGHT?!
I COULD'VE SHOWN MY APPRECIATION IF I WASN'T BROKE, BUT...OH WELL.
はっ HA
YUP. TOO BAD.
はっ HA
MAYBE SOME OTHER TIME.
はっ WA

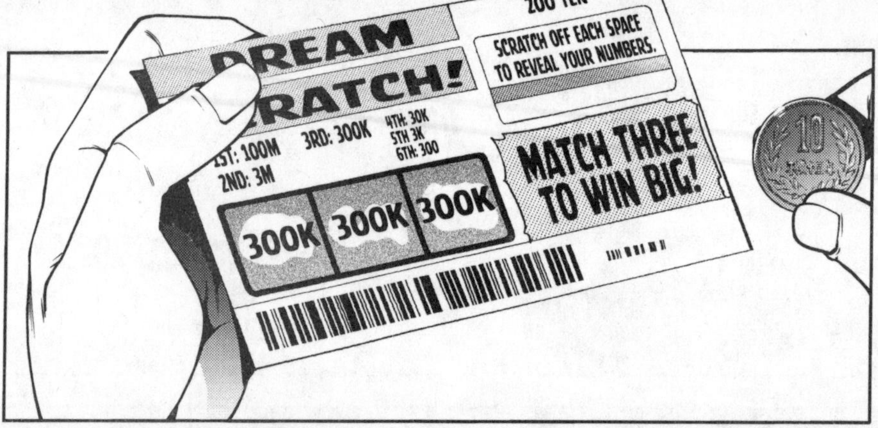
DREAM
CRATCH!
200 YEN
SCRATCH OFF EACH SPACE TO REVEAL YOUR NUMBERS.
1ST: 100M
2ND: 3M
3RD: 300K
4TH: 30K
5TH 3K
6TH: 300
300K
300K
300K
MATCH THREE TO WIN BIG!
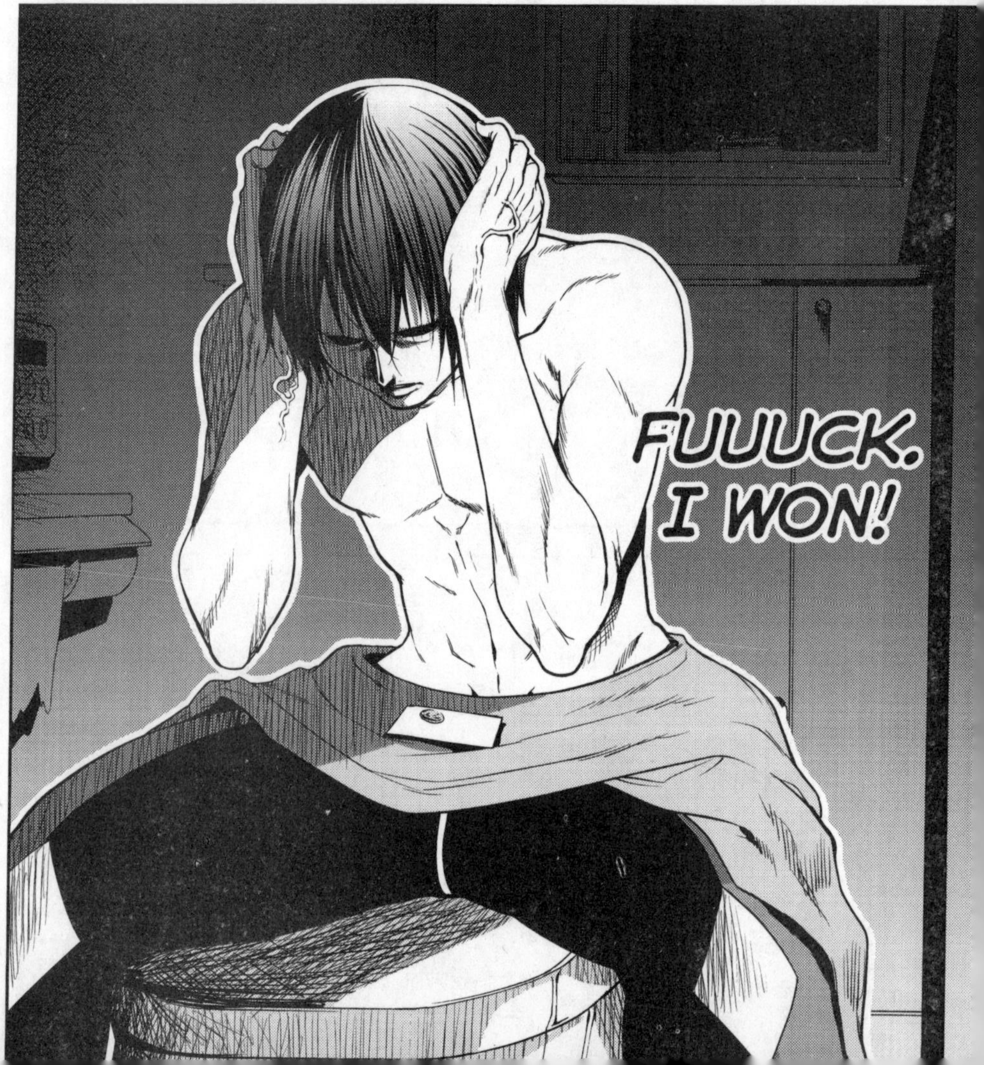
FUUUCK. I WON!

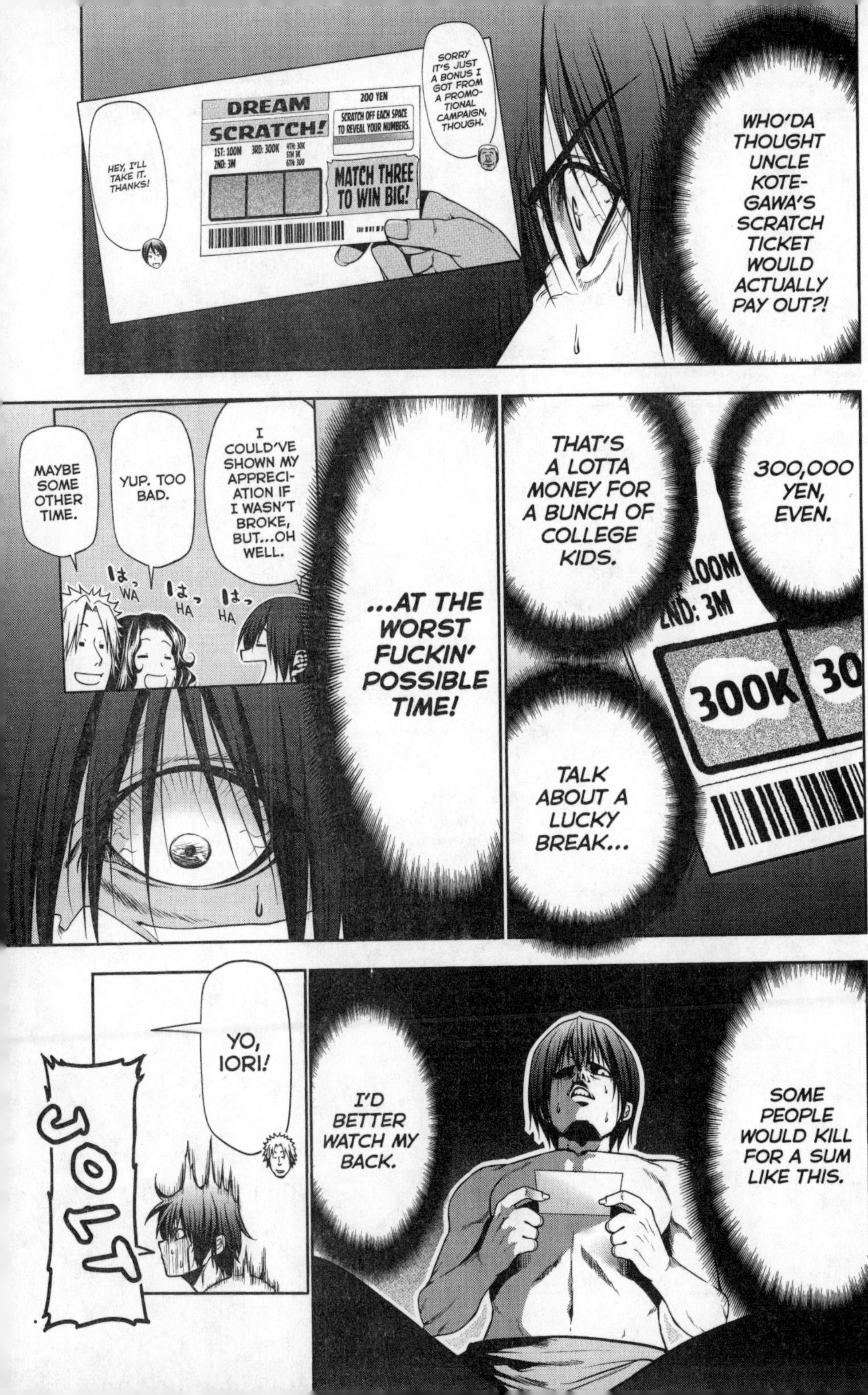
WHO'DA THOUGHT UNCLE KOTE-GAWA'S SCRATCH TICKET WOULD ACTUALLY PAY OUT?!
SORRY IT'S JUST A BONUS I GOT FROM A PROMOTIONAL CAMPAIGN, THOUGH.
DREAM SCRATCH!
200 YEN
SCRATCH OFF EACH SPACE TO REVEAL YOUR NUMBERS.
1ST: 100M 2ND: 3M 3RD: 300K 4TH: 30K 5TH 3K 6TH: 300
MATCH THREE TO WIN BIG!
HEY, I'LL TAKE IT. THANKS!
300,000 YEN, EVEN.
THAT'S A LOTTA MONEY FOR A BUNCH OF COLLEGE KIDS.
100M
2ND: 3M
300K
TALK ABOUT A LUCKY BREAK...
I COULD'VE SHOWN MY APPRECIATION IF I WASN'T BROKE, BUT...OH WELL.
YUP. TOO BAD.
MAYBE SOME OTHER TIME.
はっ HA
はっ HA
はっ WA
...AT THE WORST FUCKIN' POSSIBLE TIME!
SOME PEOPLE WOULD KILL FOR A SUM LIKE THIS.
I'D BETTER WATCH MY BACK.
YO, IORI!
JOLT

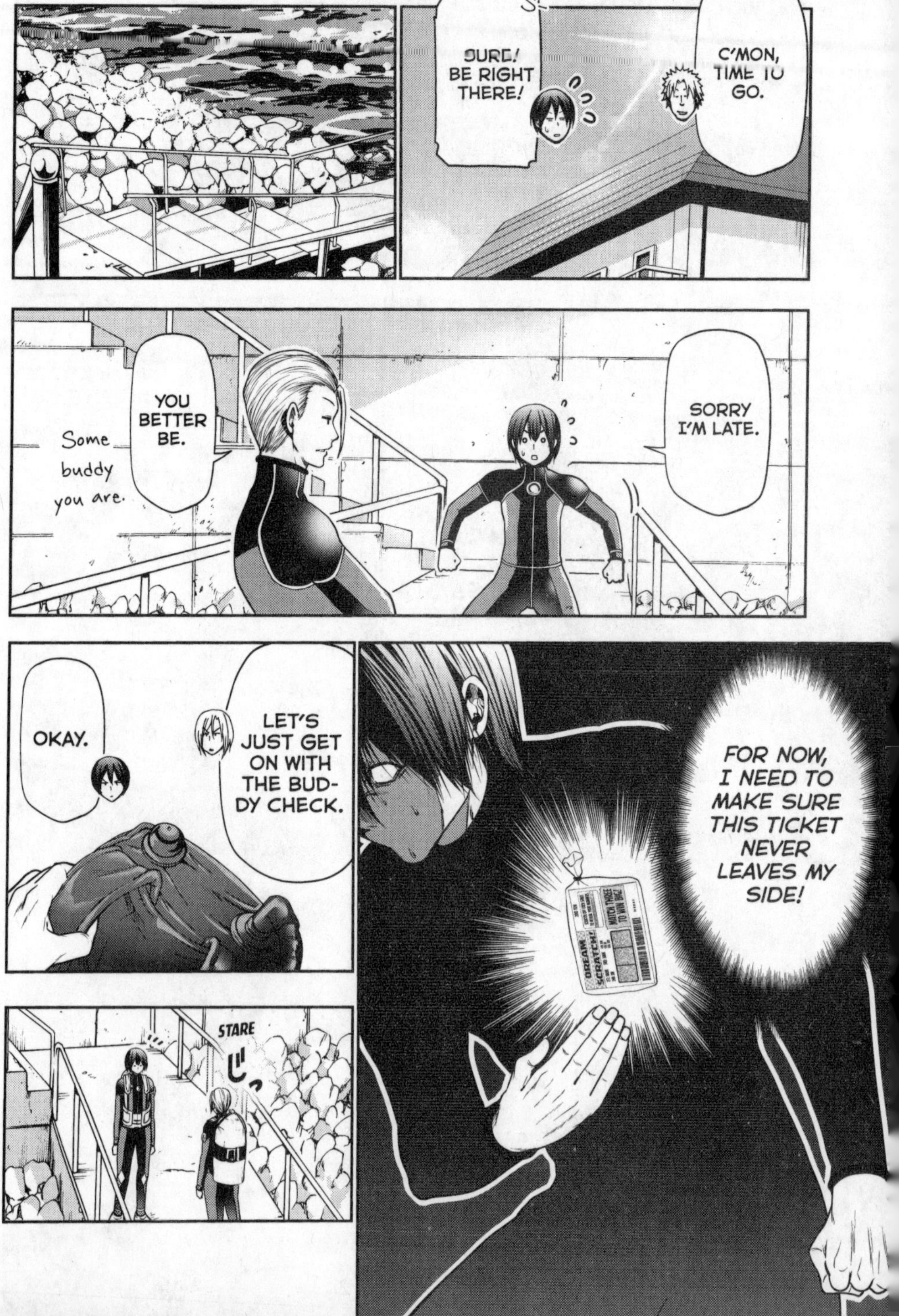
C'MON, TIME TO GO.
SURE! BE RIGHT THERE!
SORRY I'M LATE.
YOU BETTER BE.
Some buddy you are.
FOR NOW, I NEED TO MAKE SURE THIS TICKET NEVER LEAVES MY SIDE!
DREAM SCRATCH!
MATCH THREE TO WIN BIG!
LET'S JUST GET ON WITH THE BUDDY CHECK.
OKAY.
STARE
じっ

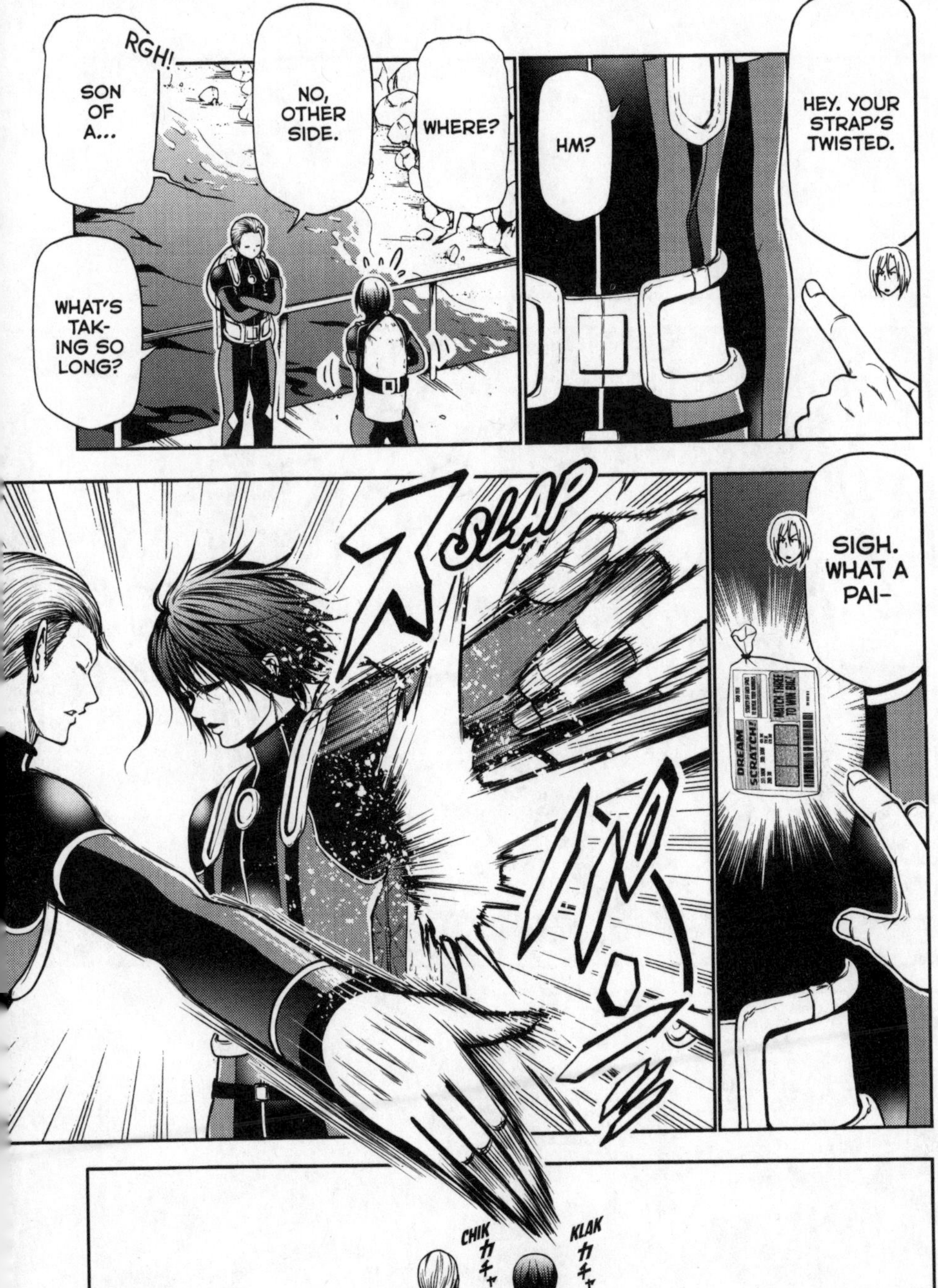
HEY. YOUR STRAP'S TWISTED.
HM?
WHERE?
NO, OTHER SIDE.
RGH!
SON OF A...
WHAT'S TAK- ING SO LONG?
SIGH. WHAT A PAI-
DREAM SCRATCH!
MATCH THREE TO WIN BIG!
SLAP
CHIK
カチャ
KLAK
カチャ

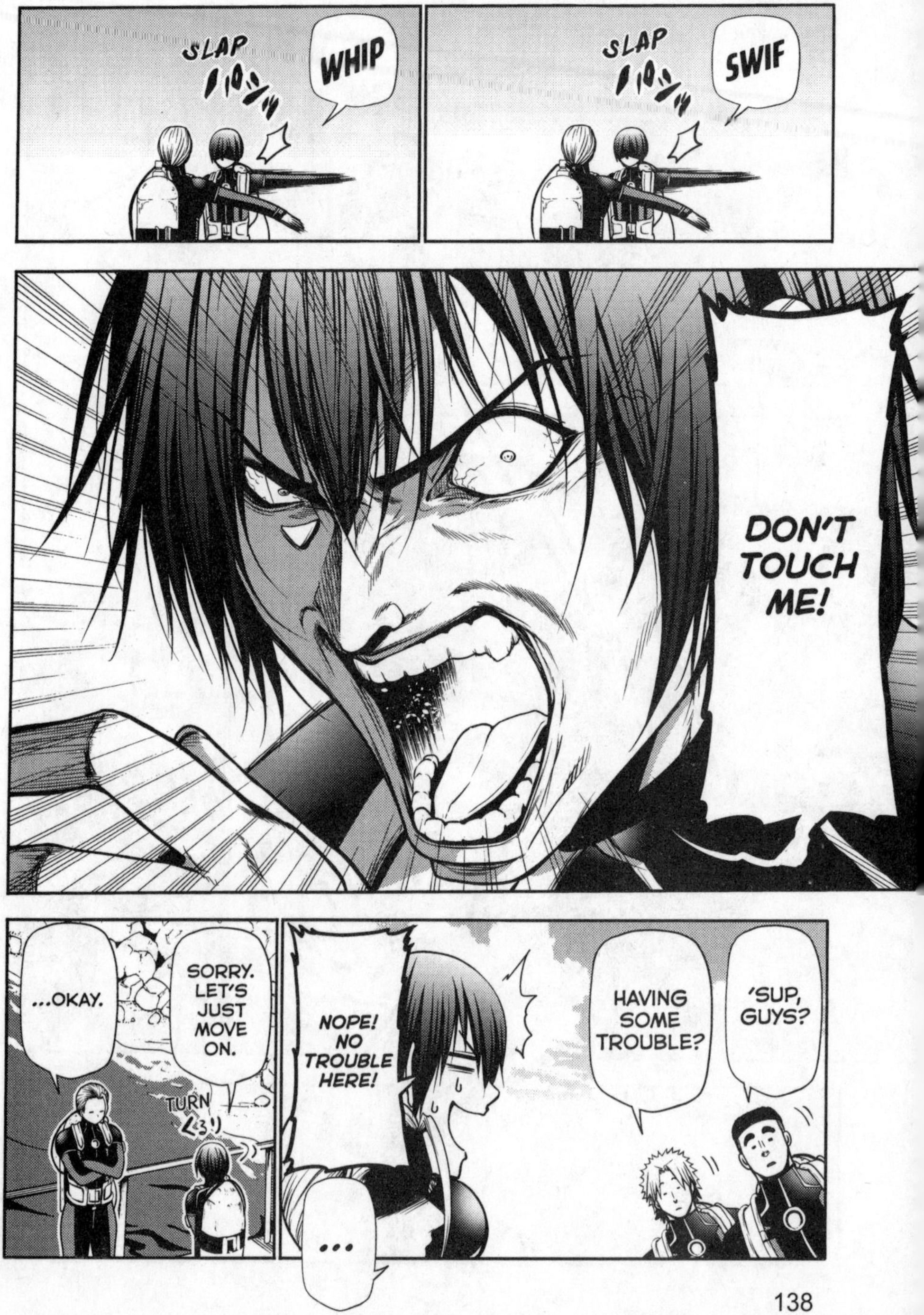
SLAP
SWIF
SLAP
WHIP
DON'T TOUCH ME!
'SUP, GUYS?
HAVING SOME TROUBLE?
NOPE! NO TROUBLE HERE!
...
SORRY. LET'S JUST MOVE ON.
TURN
くるり
...OKAY.

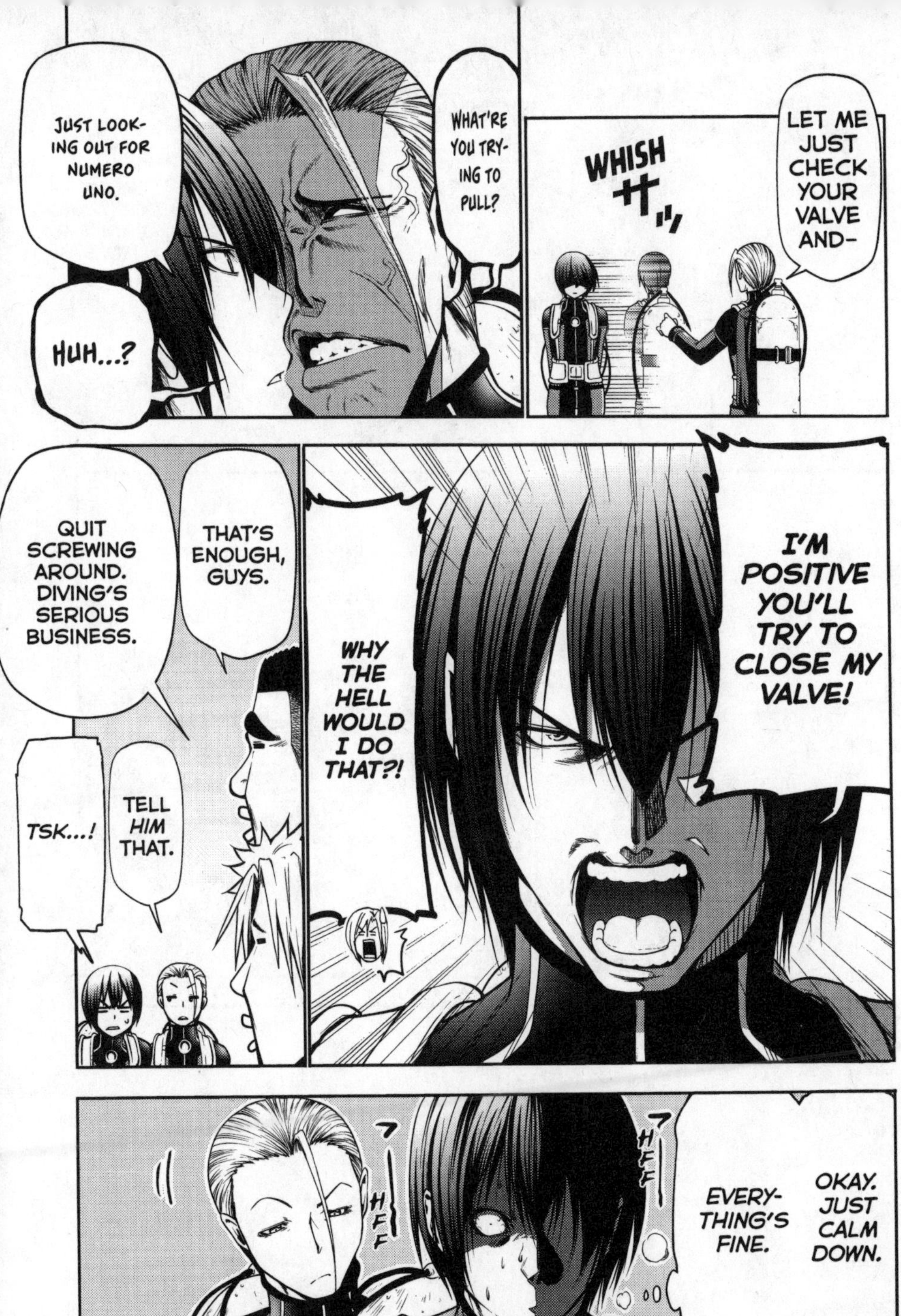
LET ME JUST CHECK YOUR VALVE AND-
WHISH
WHAT'RE YOU TRYING TO PULL?
JUST LOOKING OUT FOR NUMERO UNO.
HUH...?
I'M POSITIVE YOU'LL TRY TO CLOSE MY VALVE!
WHY THE HELL WOULD I DO THAT?!
THAT'S ENOUGH, GUYS.
QUIT SCREWING AROUND. DIVING'S SERIOUS BUSINESS.
TELL HIM THAT.
TSK...!
OKAY. JUST CALM DOWN.
EVERYTHING'S FINE.
HFF
HFF

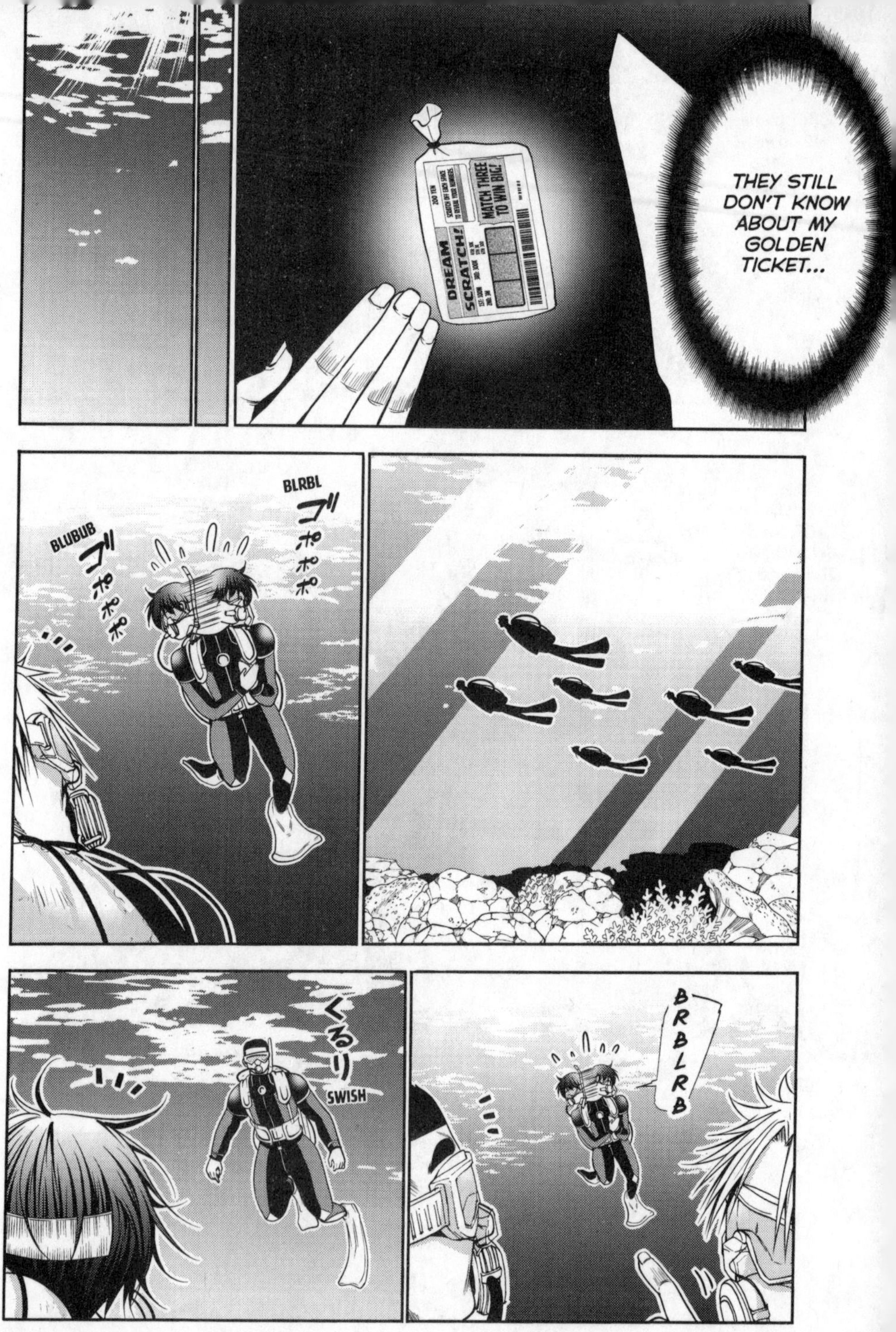
THEY STILL DON'T KNOW ABOUT MY GOLDEN TICKET...
DREAM SCRATCH!
MATCH THREE TO WIN BIG!
200 YEN
BLRBL
ゴポポポ
BLUBUB
ゴポポポ
...
BRBLRB
...
くるり
SWISH
...

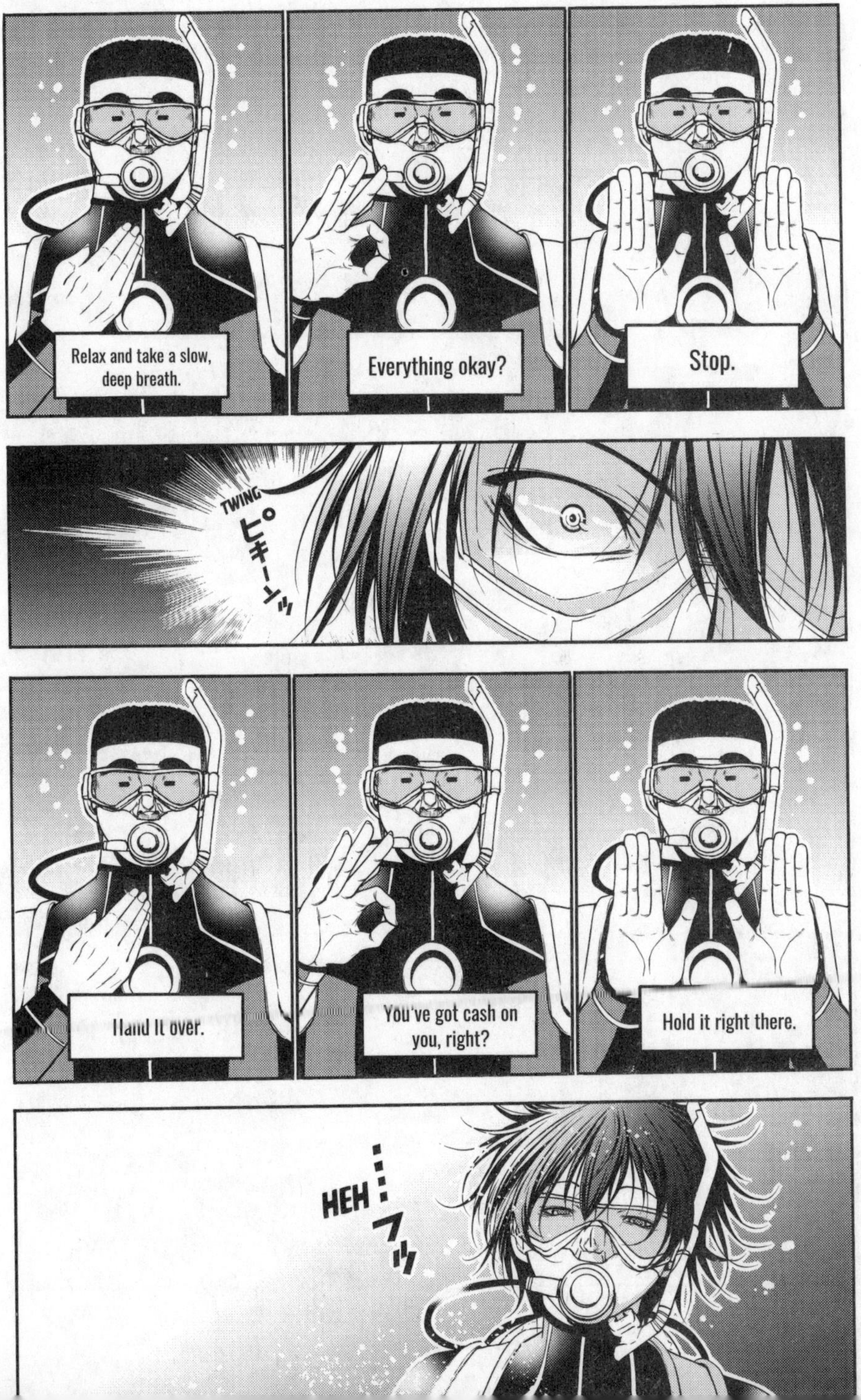
Stop.
Everything okay?
Relax and take a slow, deep breath.
TWING
ピキーンッ
Hold it right there.
You've got cash on you, right?
Hand it over.
HEH
フッ

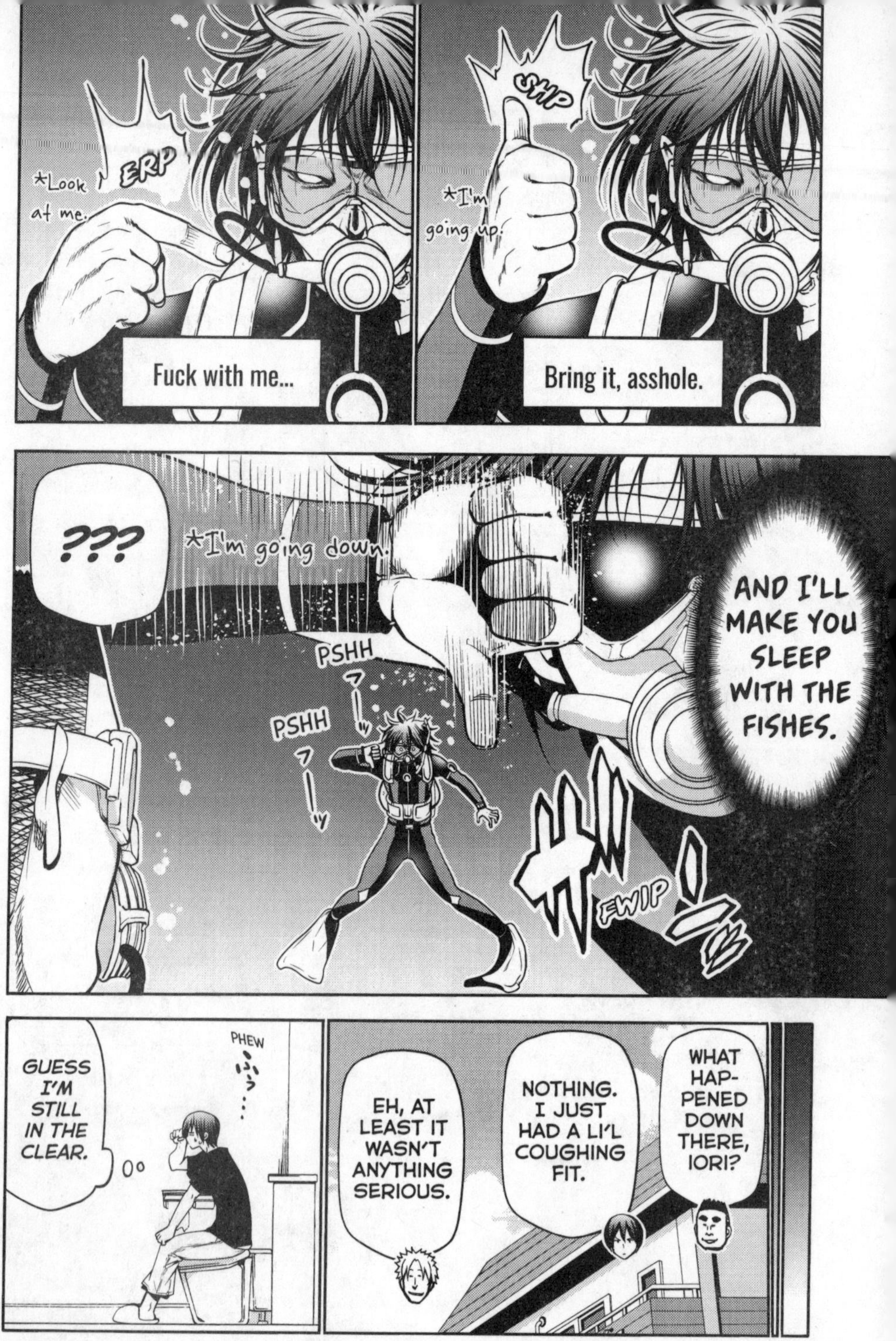
SHP
*I'm going up.
Bring it, asshole.
ERP
*Look at me.
Fuck with me...
AND I'LL MAKE YOU SLEEP WITH THE FISHES.
FWIP
PSHH
PSHH
*I'm going down.
???
WHAT HAP-PENED DOWN THERE, IORI?
NOTHING. I JUST HAD A LI'L COUGHING FIT.
EH, AT LEAST IT WASN'T ANYTHING SERIOUS.
PHEW
GUESS I'M STILL IN THE CLEAR.

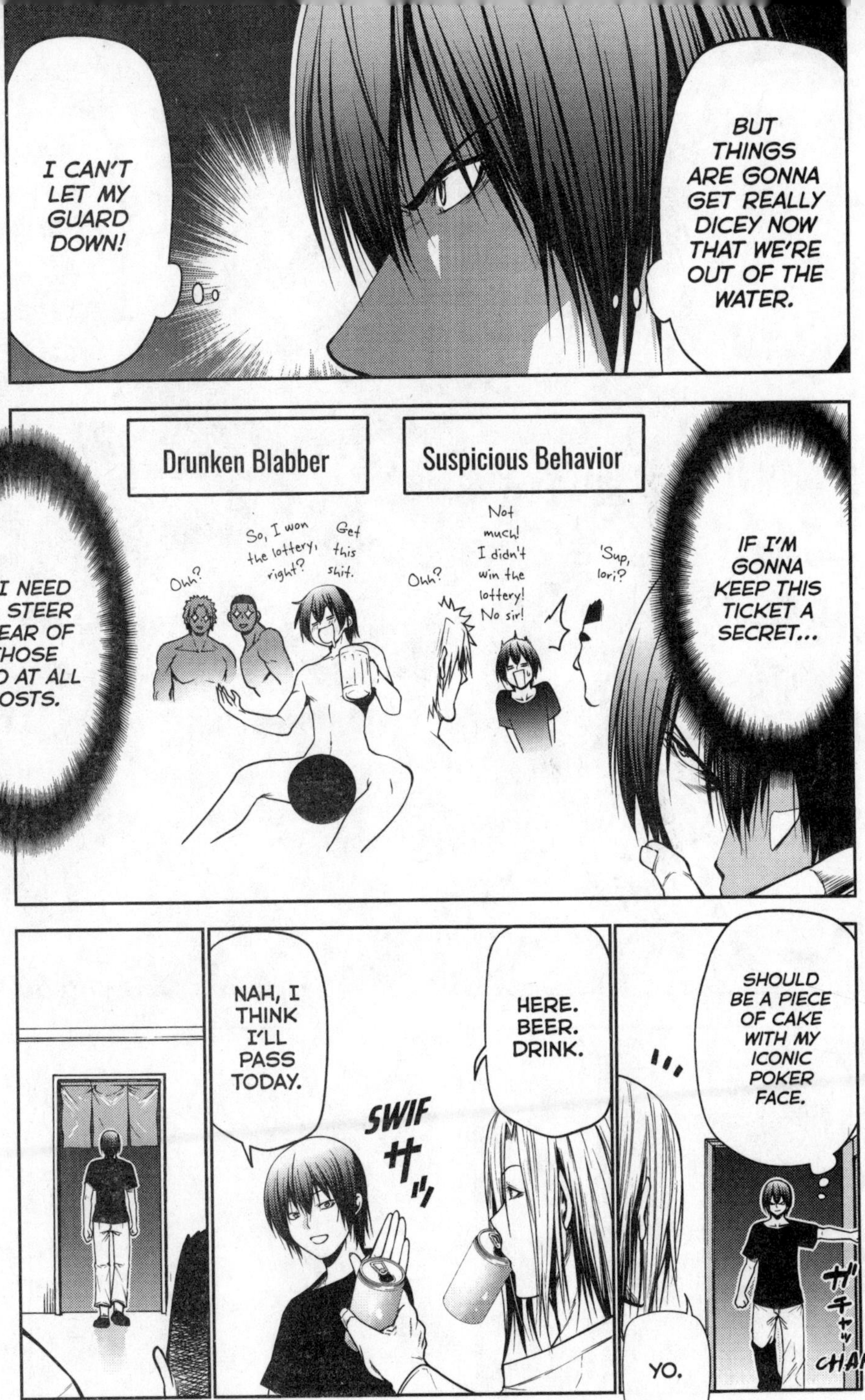
BUT THINGS ARE GONNA GET REALLY DICEY NOW THAT WE'RE OUT OF THE WATER.
I CAN'T LET MY GUARD DOWN!
IF I'M GONNA KEEP THIS TICKET A SECRET...
Suspicious Behavior
'Sup, Iori?
Not much! I didn't win the lottery! No sir!
Ohh?
Drunken Blabber
Get this shit.
So, I won the lottery, right?
Ohh?
...I NEED TO STEER CLEAR OF THOSE TWO AT ALL COSTS.
SHOULD BE A PIECE OF CAKE WITH MY ICONIC POKER FACE.
CHAK
YO.
...
HERE. BEER. DRINK.
NAH, I THINK I'LL PASS TODAY.
SWIF

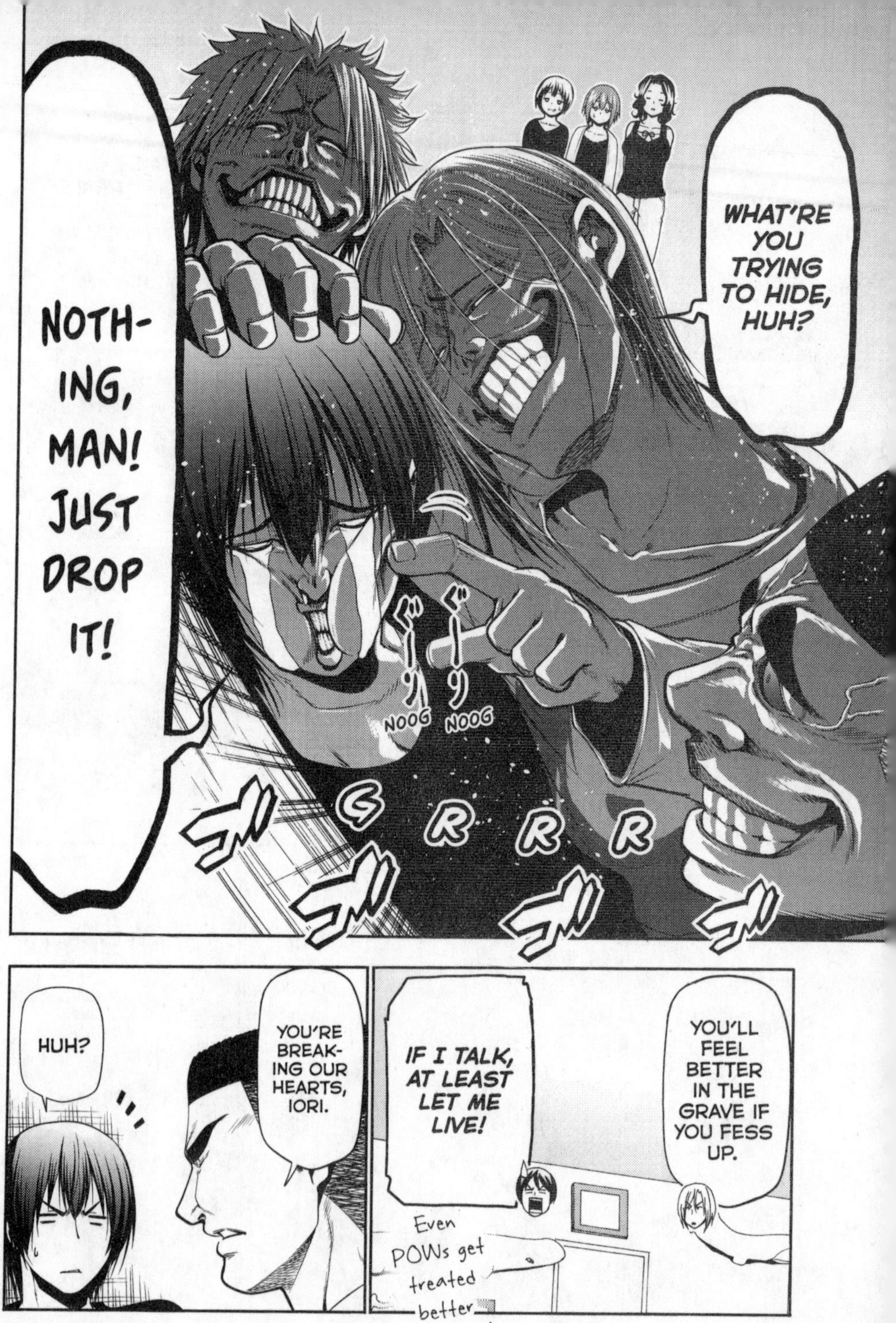
WHAT'RE YOU TRYING TO HIDE, HUH?
NOTH-ING, MAN! JUST DROP IT!
NOOG NOOG
GRRRR
YOU'LL FEEL BETTER IN THE GRAVE IF YOU FESS UP.
IF I TALK, AT LEAST LET ME LIVE!
Even POWs get treated better than this!
YOU'RE BREAK-ING OUR HEARTS, IORI.
HUH?

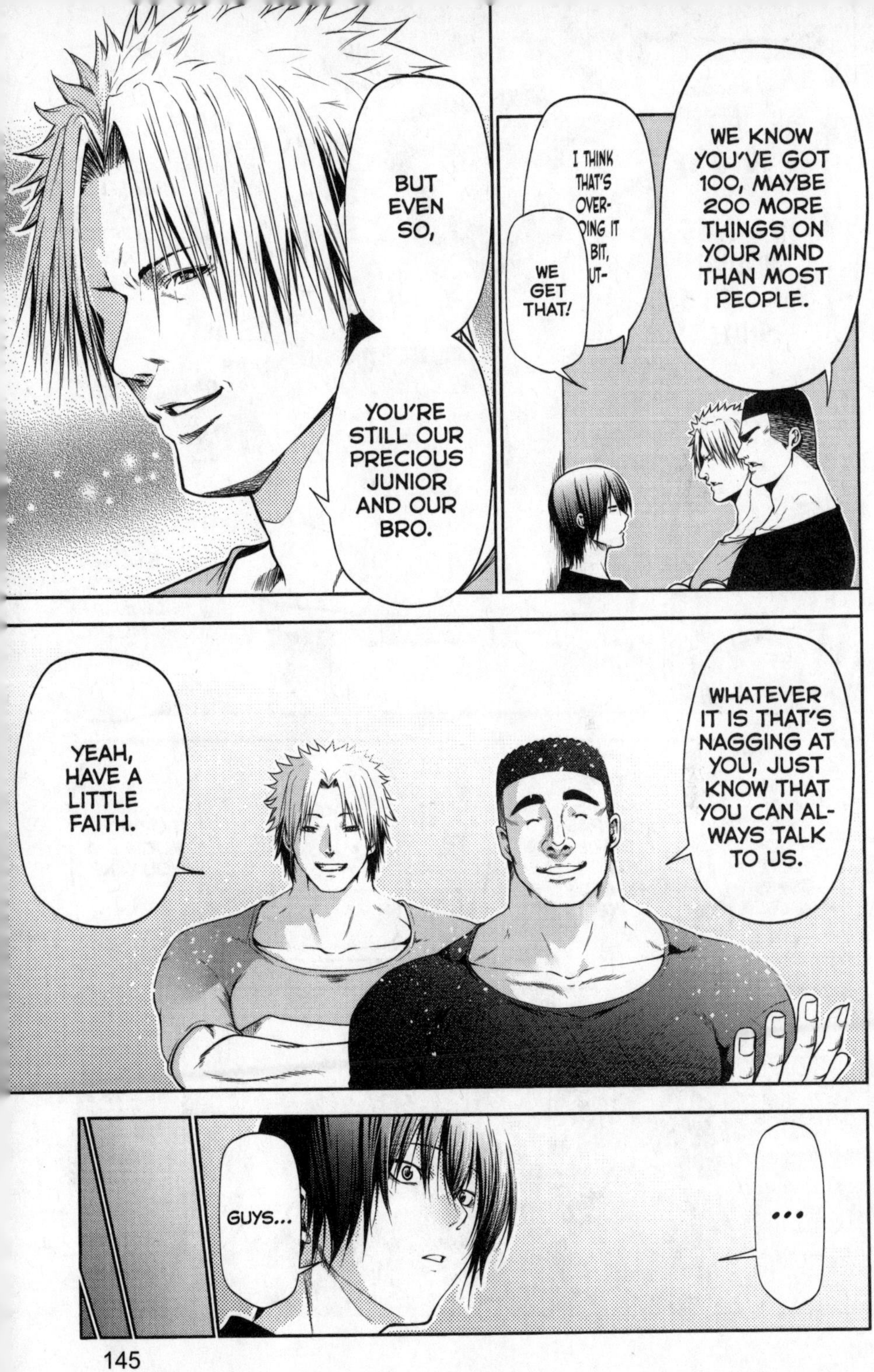
WE KNOW YOU'VE GOT 100, MAYBE 200 MORE THINGS ON YOUR MIND THAN MOST PEOPLE.
I THINK THAT'S OVER-DOING IT BIT, UT-
WE GET THAT!
BUT EVEN SO,
YOU'RE STILL OUR PRECIOUS JUNIOR AND OUR BRO.
WHATEVER IT IS THAT'S NAGGING AT YOU, JUST KNOW THAT YOU CAN AL-WAYS TALK TO US.
YEAH, HAVE A LITTLE FAITH.
...
GUYS...

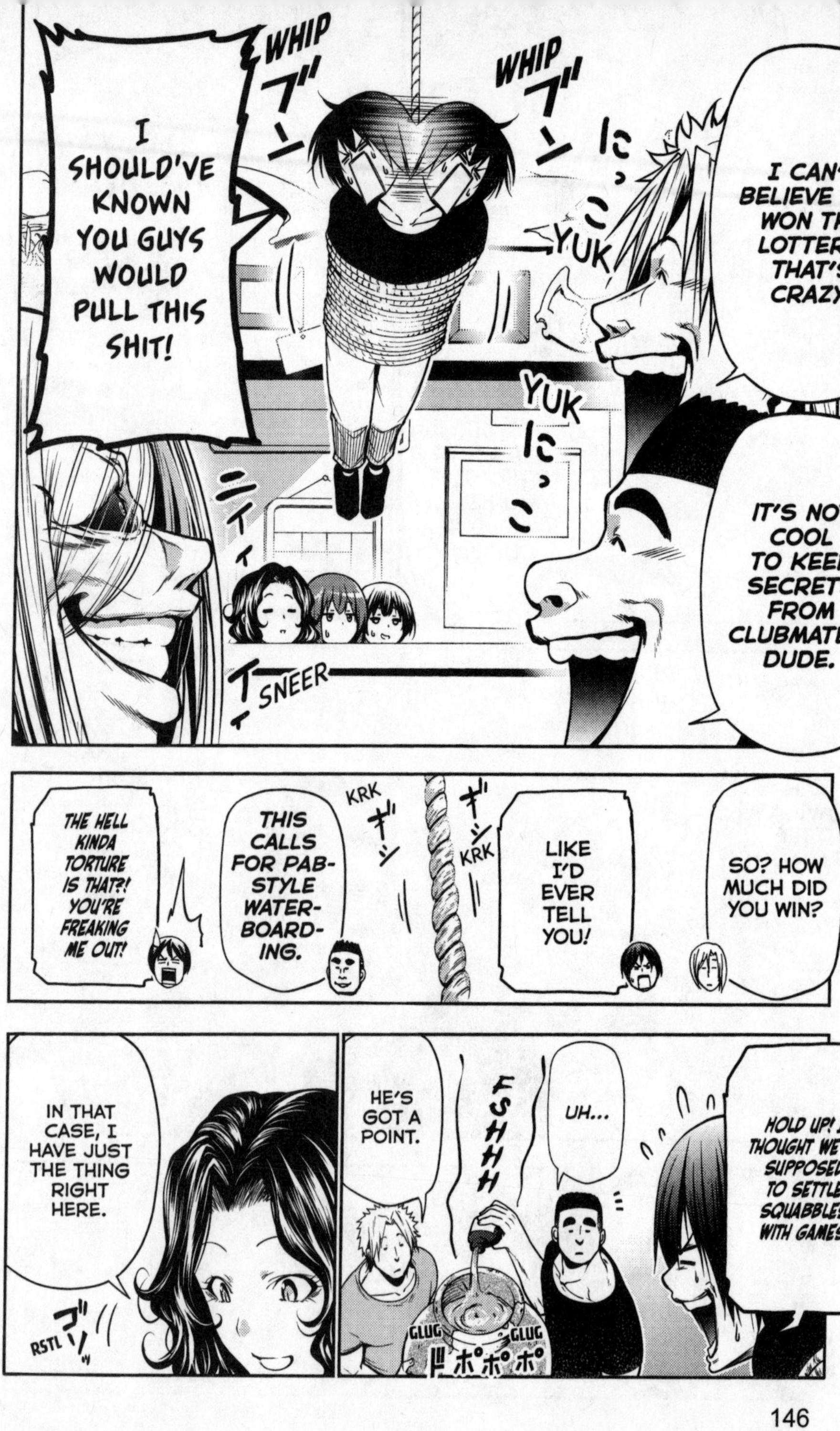

WHIP ブン
I CAN'T BELIEVE YOU WON THE LOTTERY! THAT'S CRAZY!
にっこ YUK
YUK にっこ
IT'S NOT COOL TO KEEP SECRETS FROM CLUBMATES, DUDE.
WHIP ブン
I SHOULD'VE KNOWN YOU GUYS WOULD PULL THIS SHIT!
ニィイ SNEER
SO? HOW MUCH DID YOU WIN?
LIKE I'D EVER TELL YOU!
ギシ KRK
KRK ギシ
THIS CALLS FOR PAB-STYLE WATER-BOARDING.
THE HELL KINDA TORTURE IS THAT?! YOU'RE FREAKING ME OUT!
HOLD UP! I THOUGHT WE'RE SUPPOSED TO SETTLE SQUABBLES WITH GAMES!
UH...
FSHHH
HE'S GOT A POINT.
GLUG GLUG ドポポポ
IN THAT CASE, I HAVE JUST THE THING RIGHT HERE.
RSTL ゴソッ

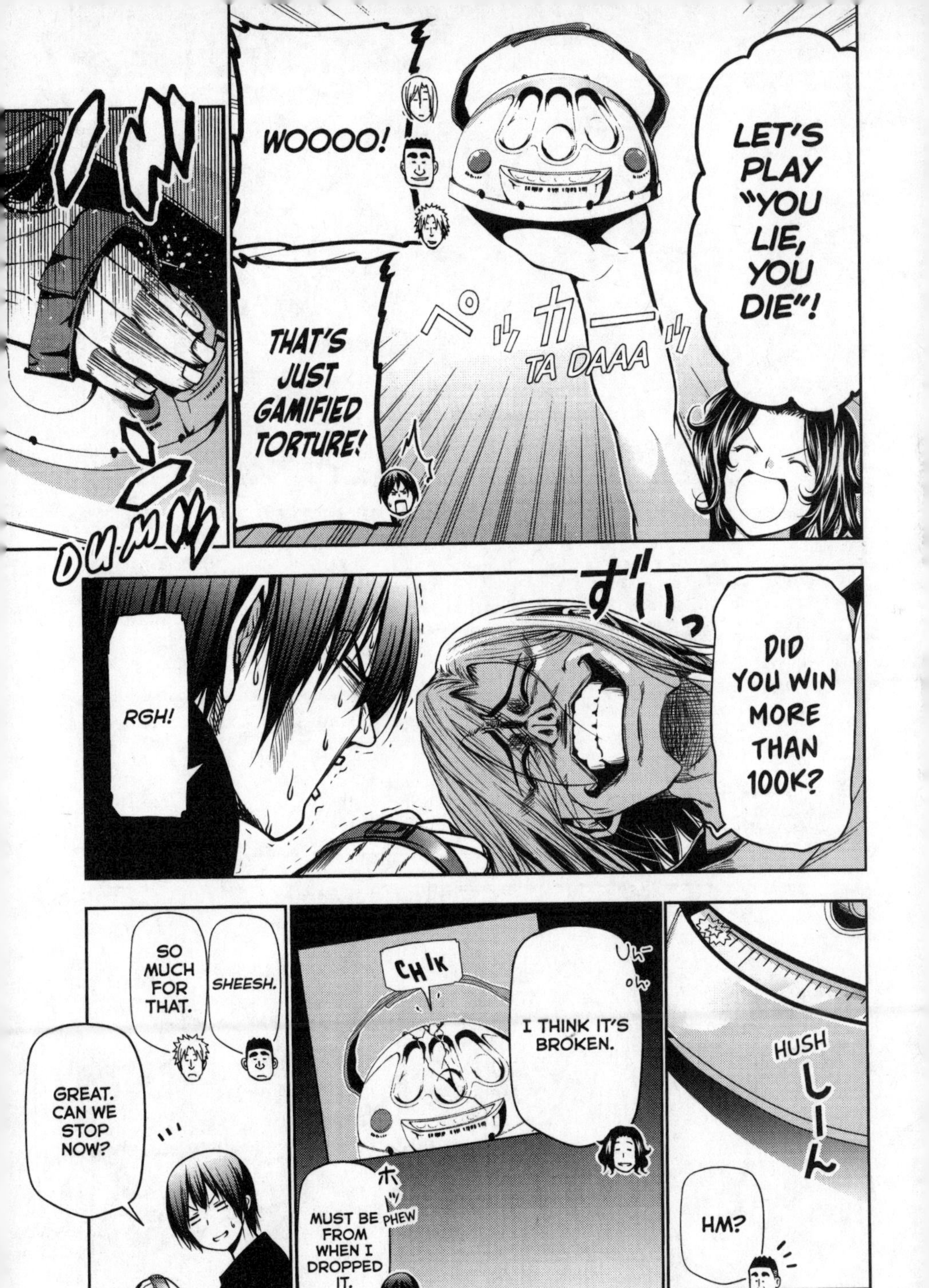
LET'S PLAY "YOU LIE, YOU DIE"!
TA DAAA
WOOOO!
THAT'S JUST GAMIFIED TORTURE!
DUM
DID YOU WIN MORE THAN 100K?
RGH!
HUSH
HM?
CHIK
I THINK IT'S BROKEN.
PHEW
MUST BE FROM WHEN I DROPPED IT.
SHEESH.
SO MUCH FOR THAT.
GREAT. CAN WE STOP NOW?

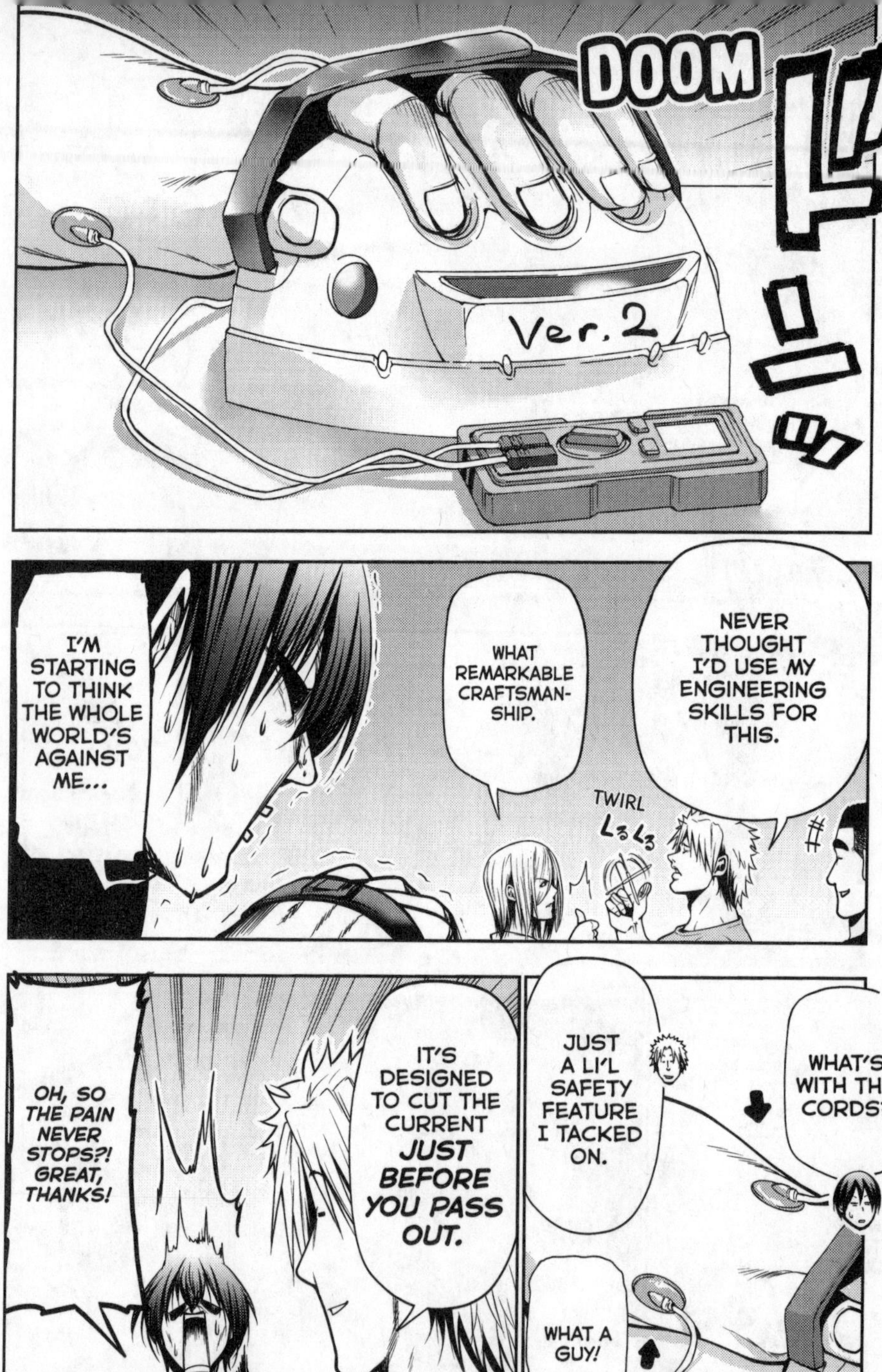
DOOM
NEVER THOUGHT I'D USE MY ENGINEERING SKILLS FOR THIS.
WHAT REMARKABLE CRAFTSMAN-SHIP.
TWIRL
I'M STARTING TO THINK THE WHOLE WORLD'S AGAINST ME...
WHAT'S WITH THE CORDS?
JUST A LI'L SAFETY FEATURE I TACKED ON.
WHAT A GUY!
IT'S DESIGNED TO CUT THE CURRENT *JUST BEFORE YOU PASS OUT.*
OH, SO THE PAIN NEVER STOPS?! GREAT, THANKS!

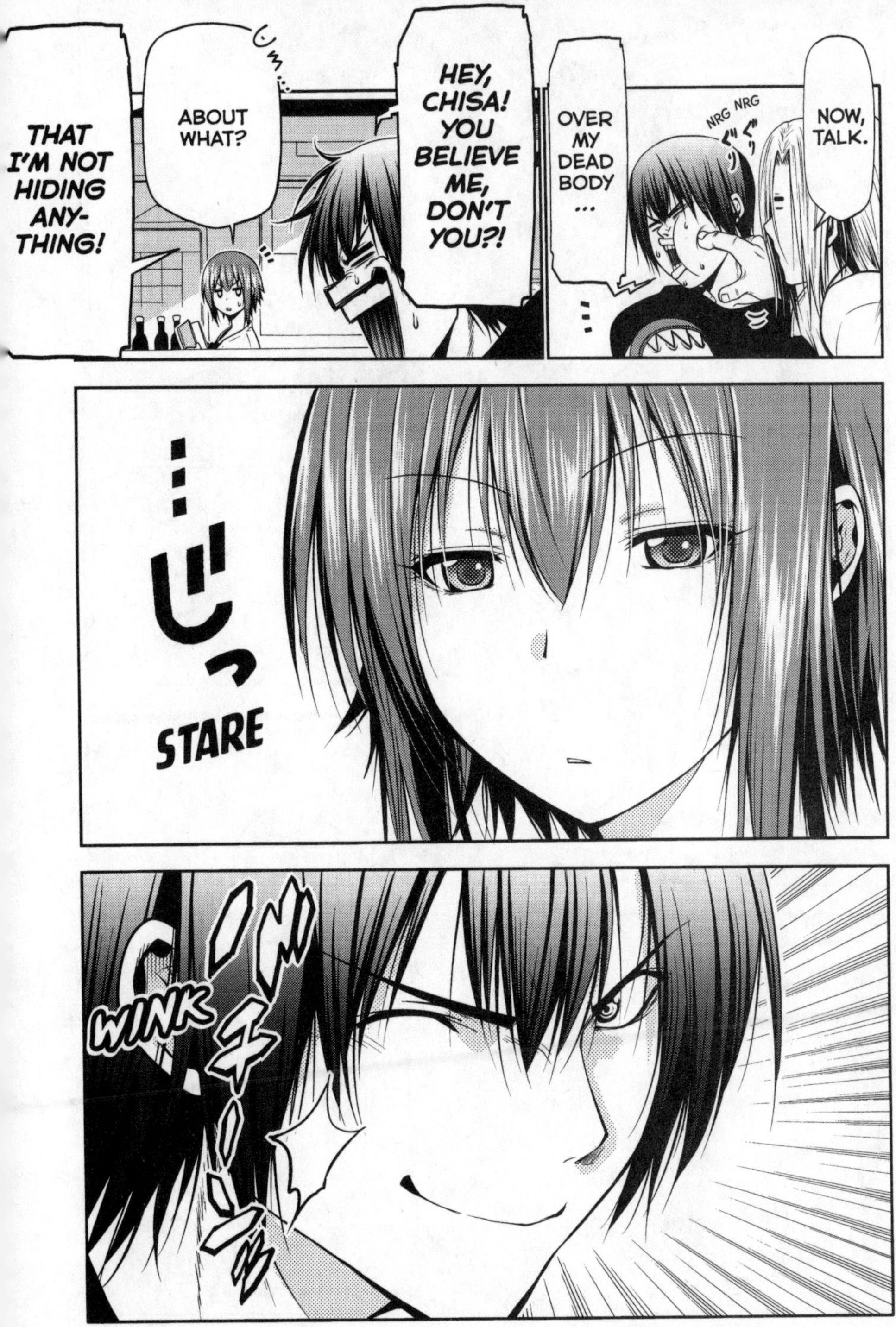
NOW, TALK.
NRG NRG
ぐぐ
OVER MY DEAD BODY ...
...
HEY, CHISA! YOU BELIEVE ME, DON'T YOU?!
ABOUT WHAT?
THAT I'M NOT HIDING ANY-THING!
...
じっ
STARE
WINK

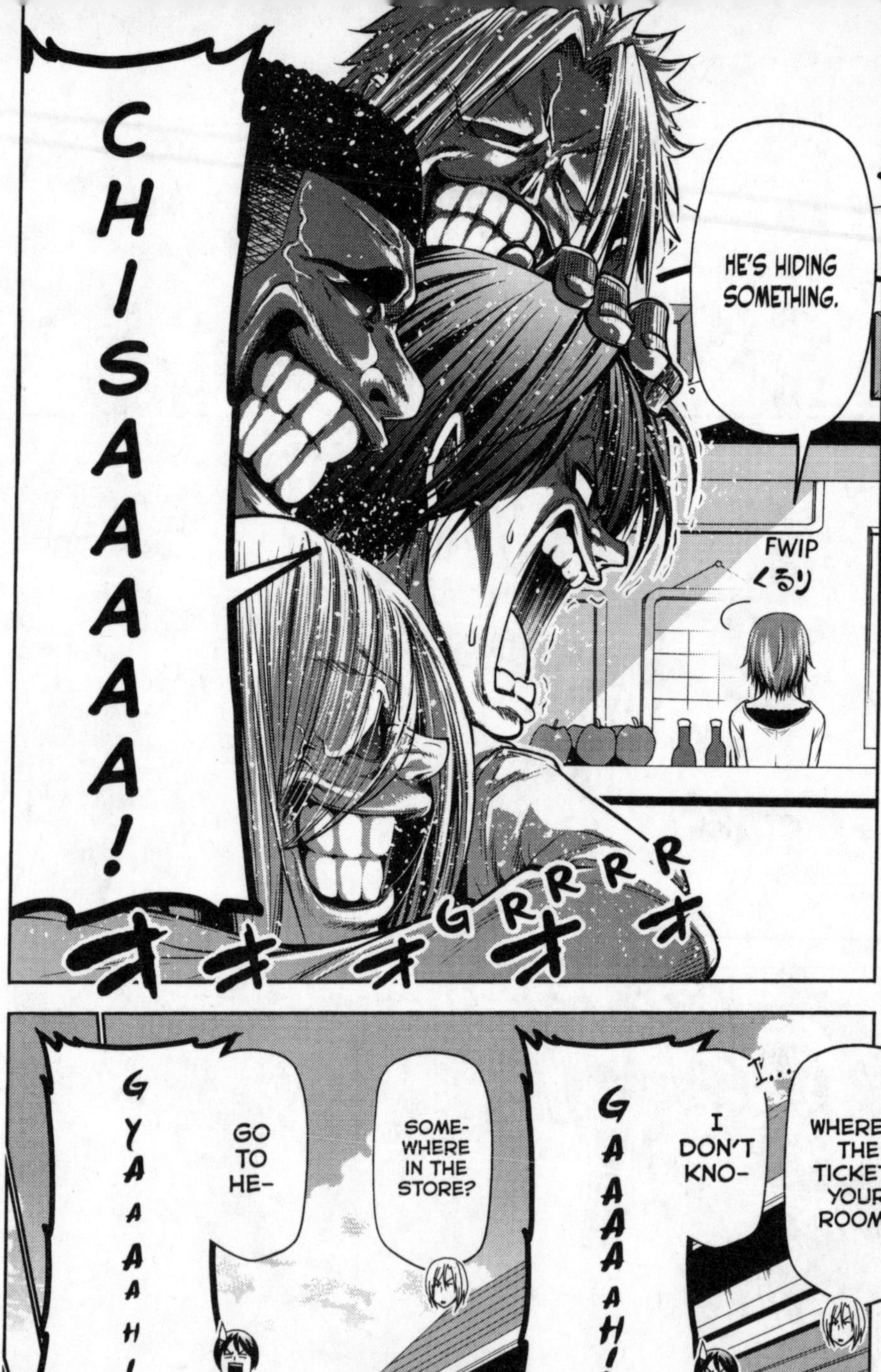
HE'S HIDING SOMETHING.
FWIP
くるり
CHISAAAAA!
GRRRRR!
オオオオオ
WHERE'S THE TICKET? YOUR ROOM?
I...
I DON'T KNO-
GAAAAAH!
SOME-WHERE IN THE STORE?
GO TO HE-
GYAAAAH!

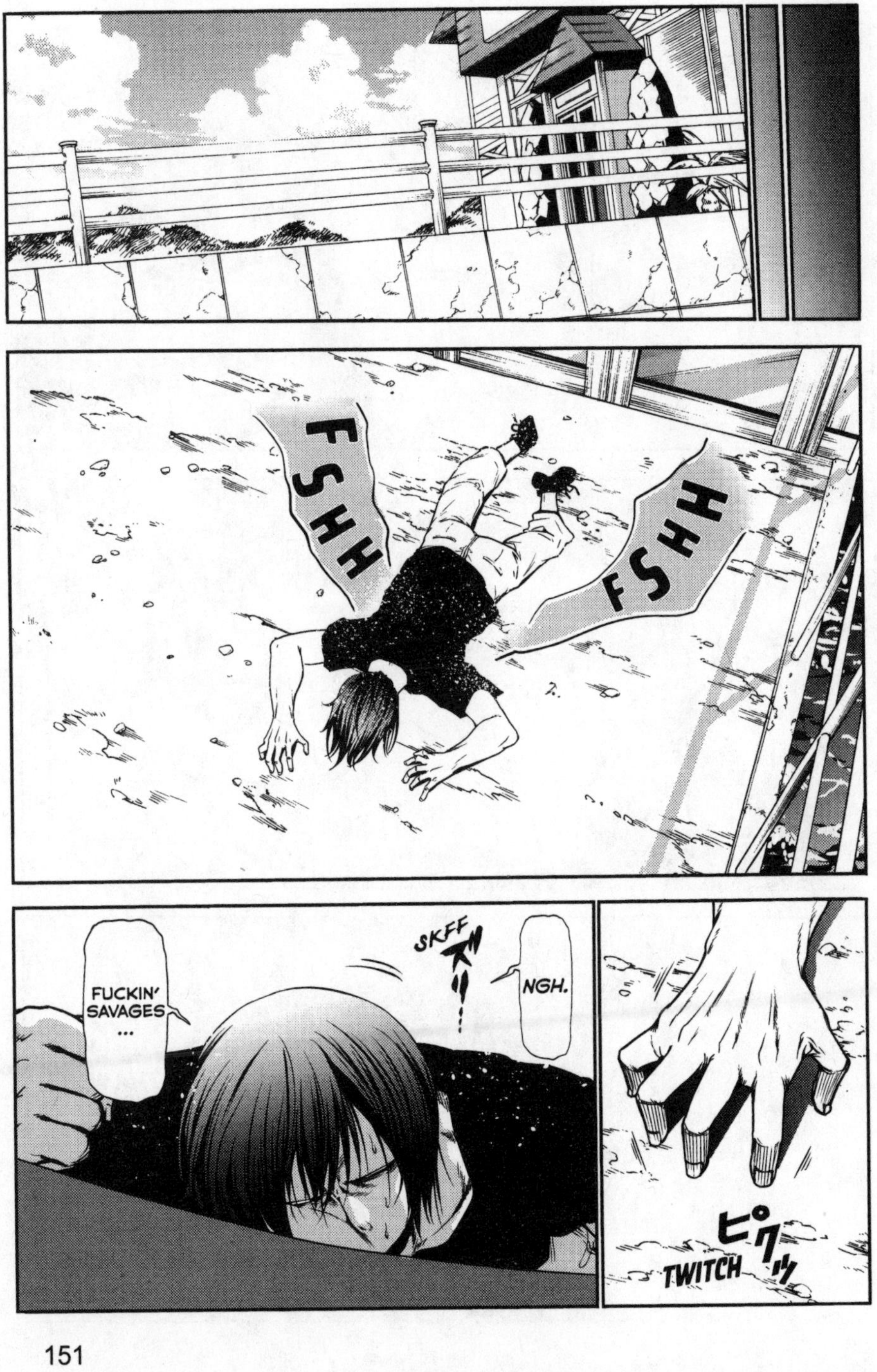
FSHH
FSHH
TWITCH
NGH.
SKFF
FUCKIN' SAVAGES...

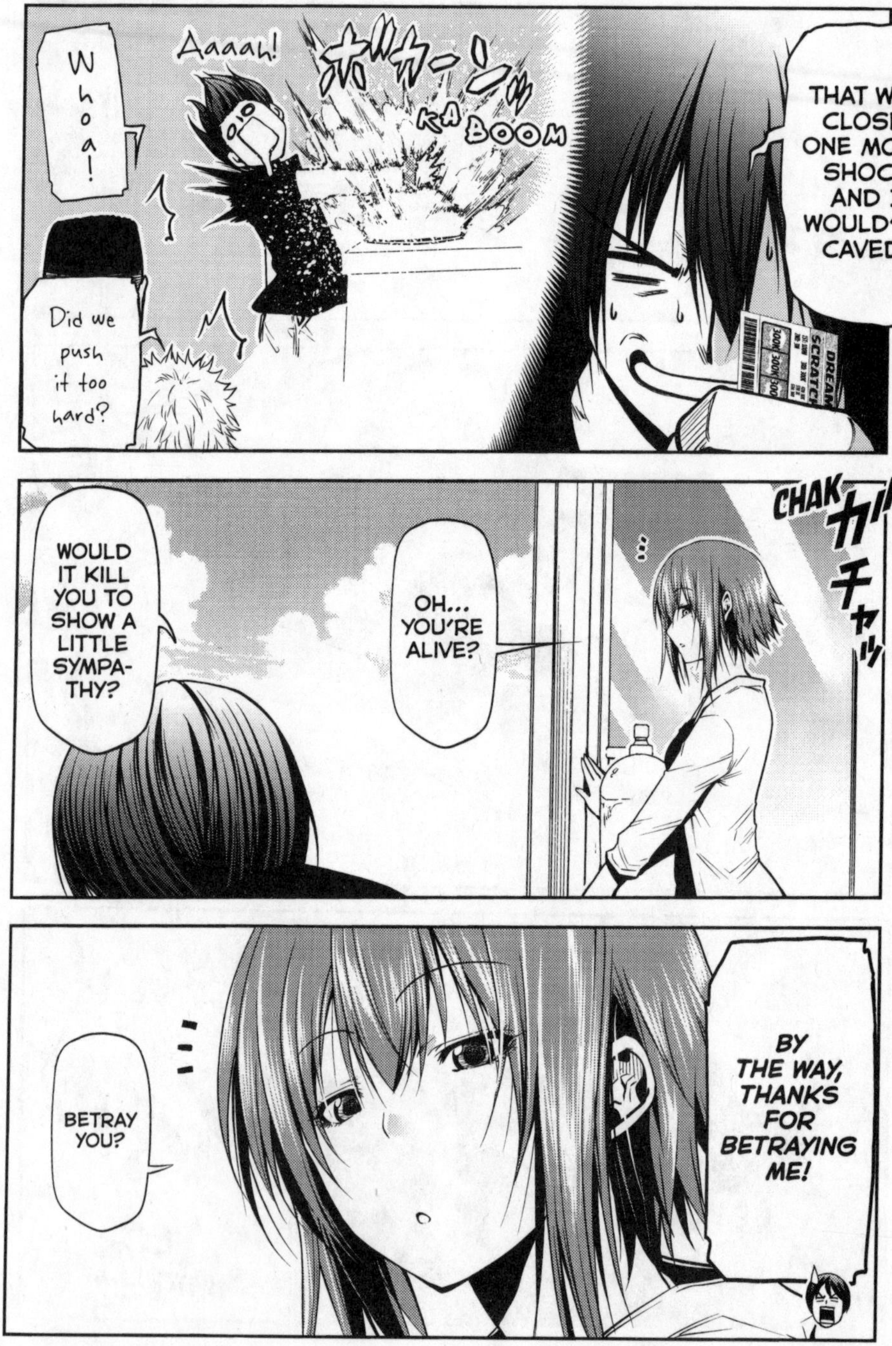
THAT WAS CLOSE. ONE MORE SHOCK AND I WOULD'VE CAVED!
KABOOM
Aaaah!
Whoa!
Did we push it too hard?
CHAK
...
OH... YOU'RE ALIVE?
WOULD IT KILL YOU TO SHOW A LITTLE SYMPATHY?
BY THE WAY, THANKS FOR BETRAYING ME!
...
BETRAY YOU?

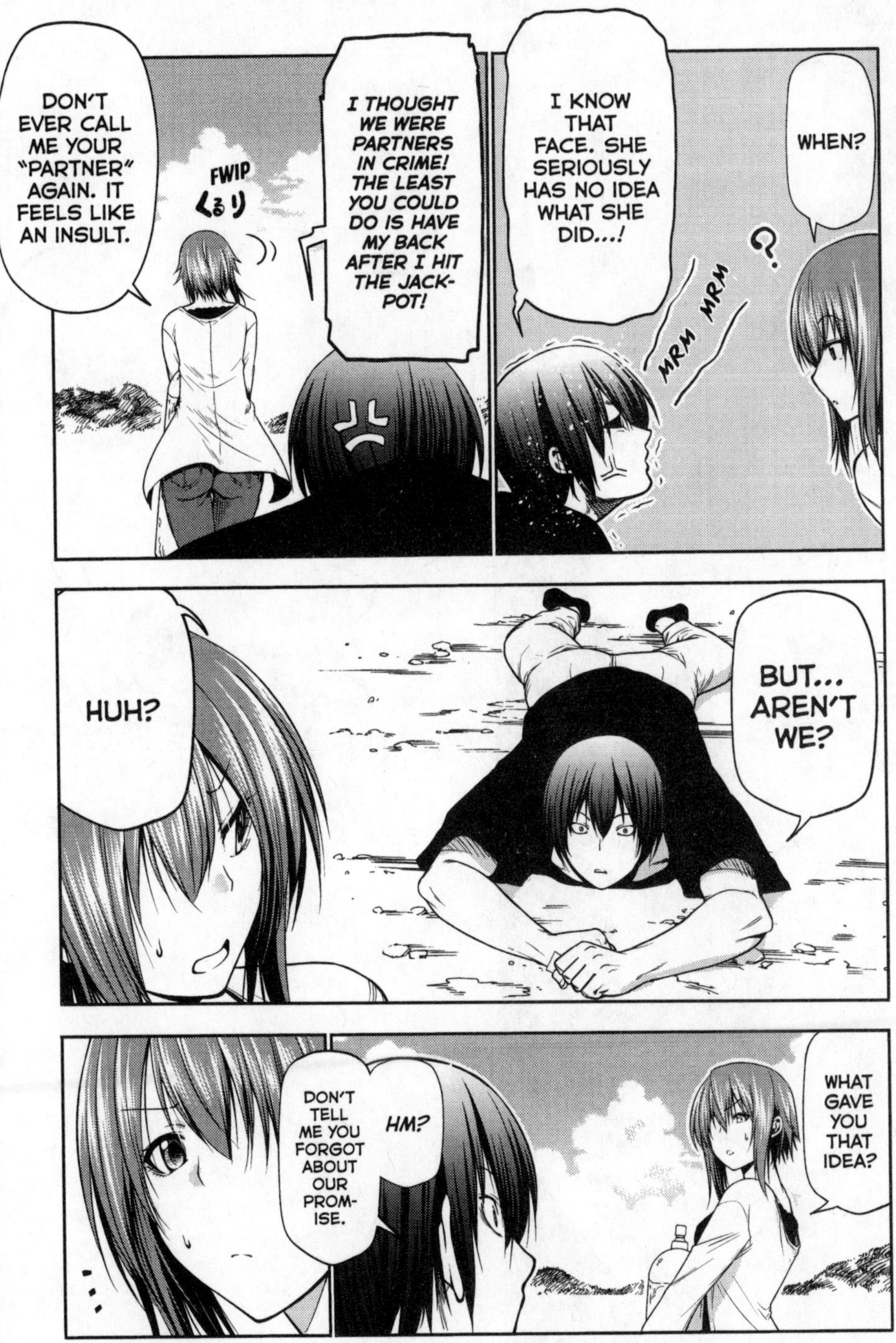
WHEN?
?
I KNOW THAT FACE. SHE SERIOUSLY HAS NO IDEA WHAT SHE DID...!
MRM MRM
I THOUGHT WE WERE PARTNERS IN CRIME! THE LEAST YOU COULD DO IS HAVE MY BACK AFTER I HIT THE JACK-POT!
FWIP くるり
DON'T EVER CALL ME YOUR "PARTNER" AGAIN. IT FEELS LIKE AN INSULT.
BUT... AREN'T WE?
HUH?
WHAT GAVE YOU THAT IDEA?
HM?
DON'T TELL ME YOU FORGOT ABOUT OUR PROM-ISE.
...

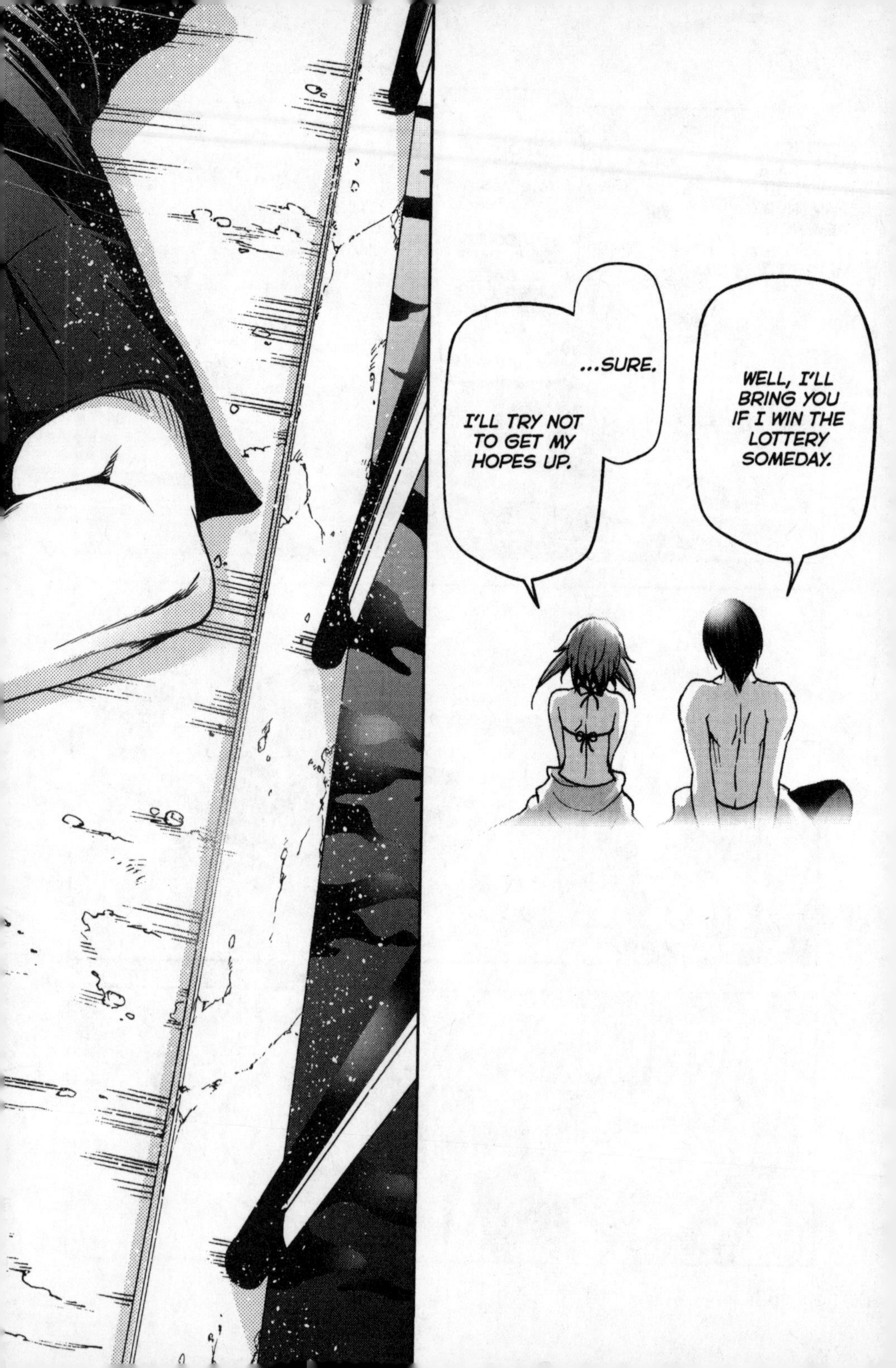
WELL, I'LL BRING YOU IF I WIN THE LOTTERY SOMEDAY.
...SURE.
I'LL TRY NOT TO GET MY HOPES UP.

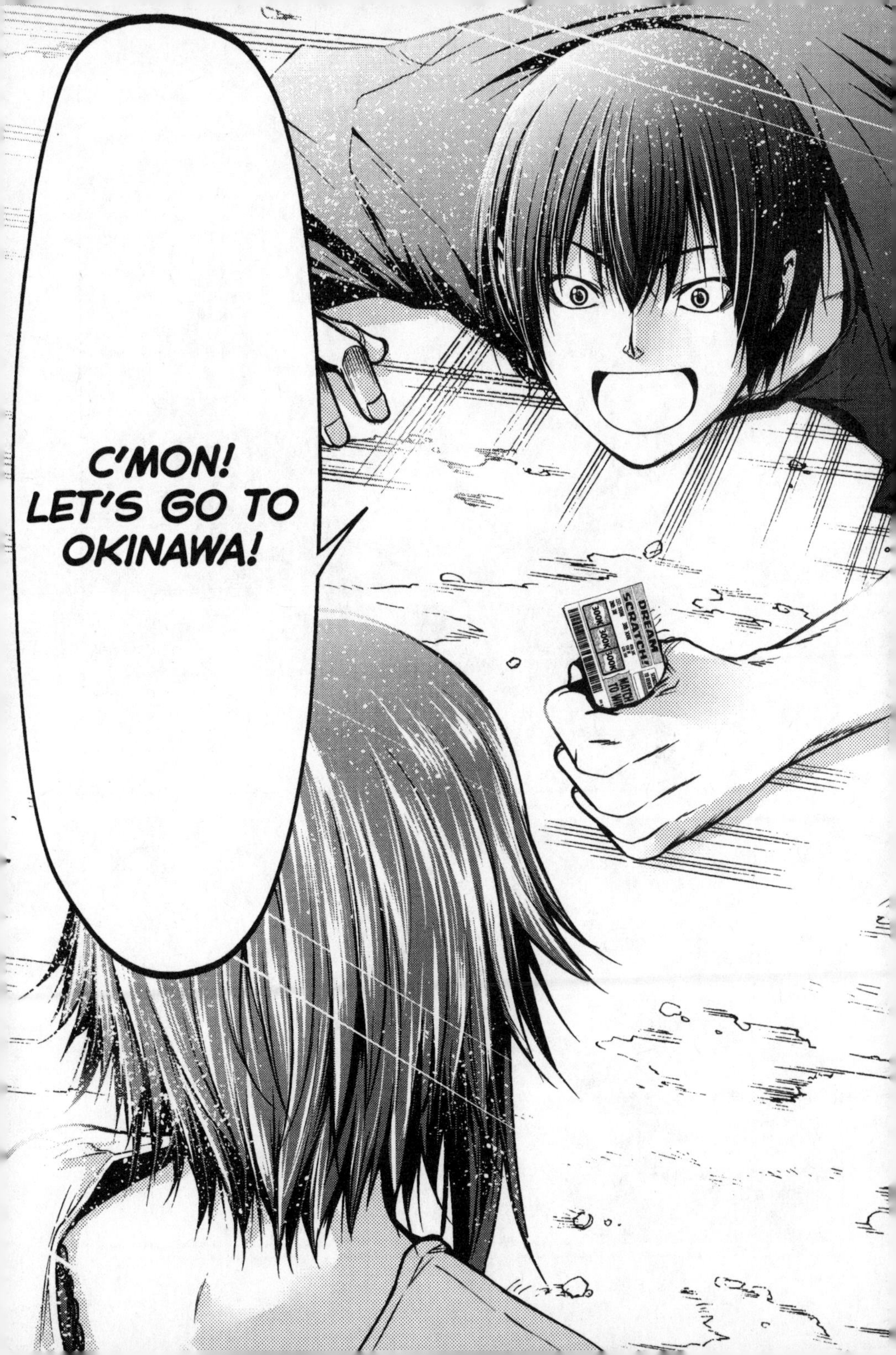
C'MON! LET'S GO TO OKINAWA!
DREAM SCRATCH!
300K 300K 300K

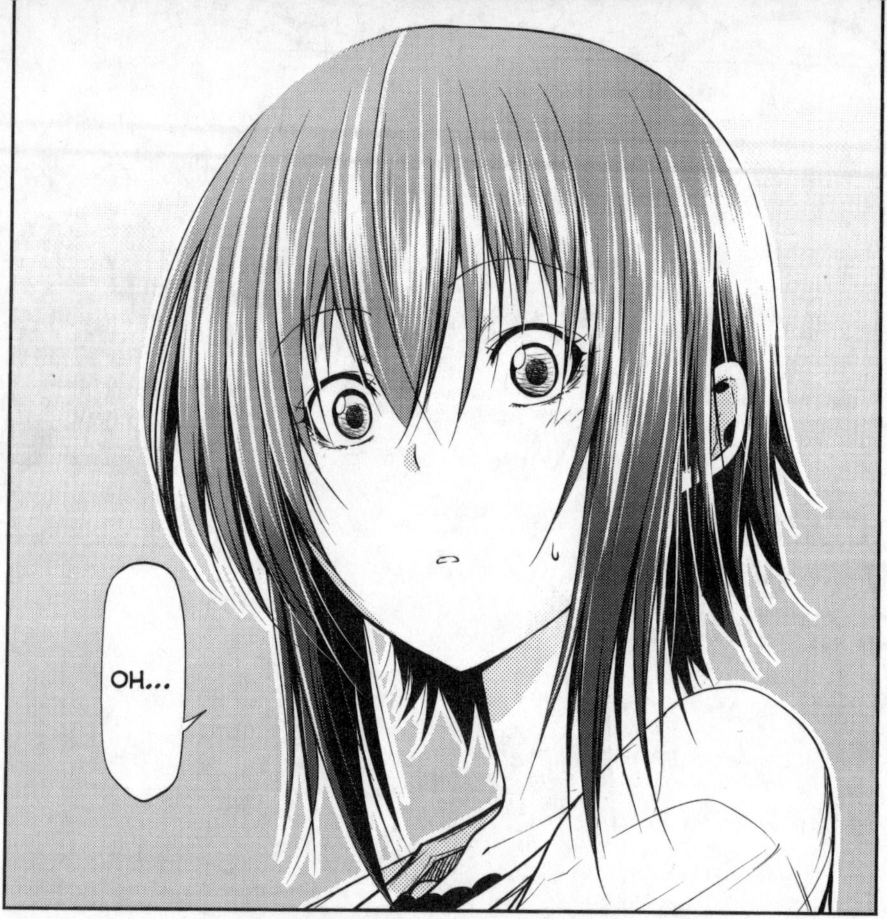
OH...

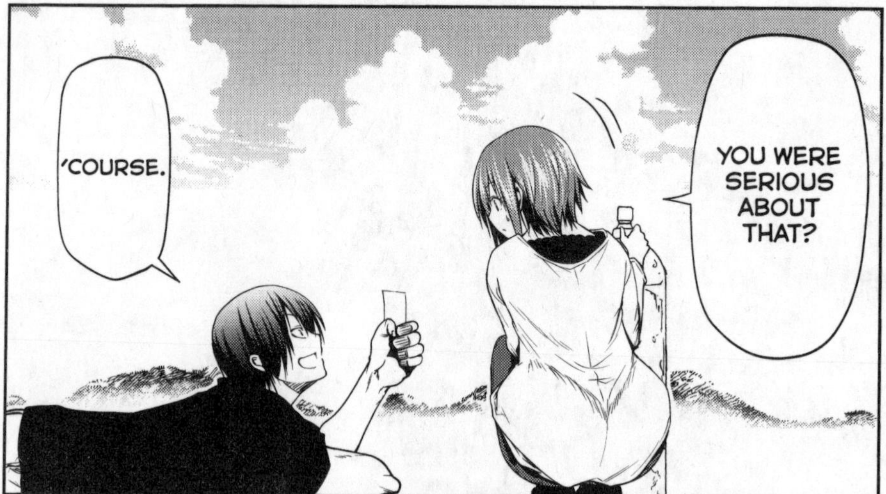
YOU WERE SERIOUS ABOUT THAT?
'COURSE.

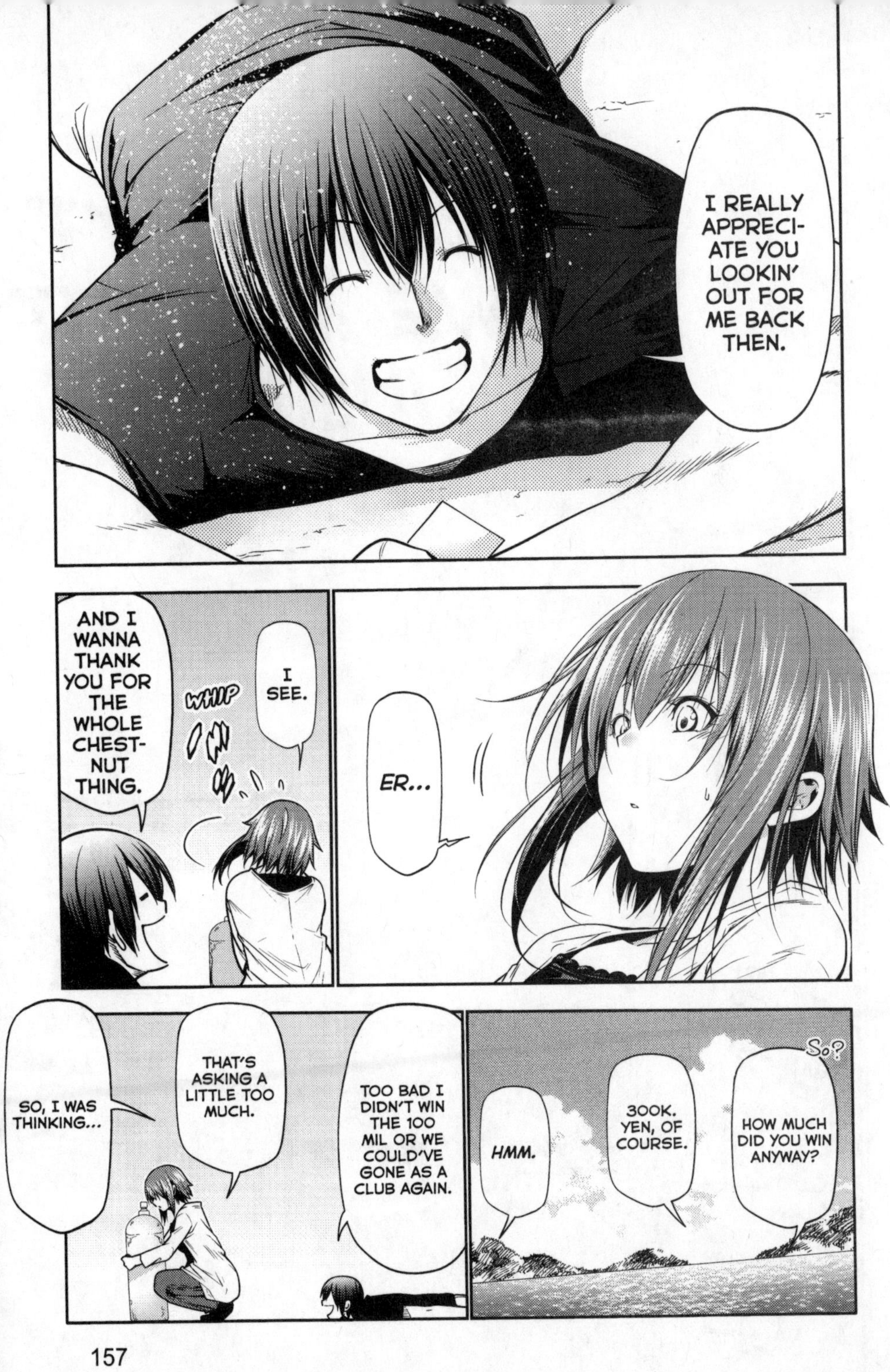
I REALLY APPRECIATE YOU LOOKIN' OUT FOR ME BACK THEN.
ER...
I SEE.
WHIP
AND I WANNA THANK YOU FOR THE WHOLE CHESTNUT THING.
So?
HOW MUCH DID YOU WIN ANYWAY?
300K. YEN, OF COURSE.
HMM.
TOO BAD I DIDN'T WIN THE 100 MIL OR WE COULD'VE GONE AS A CLUB AGAIN.
THAT'S ASKING A LITTLE TOO MUCH.
SO, I WAS THINKING...

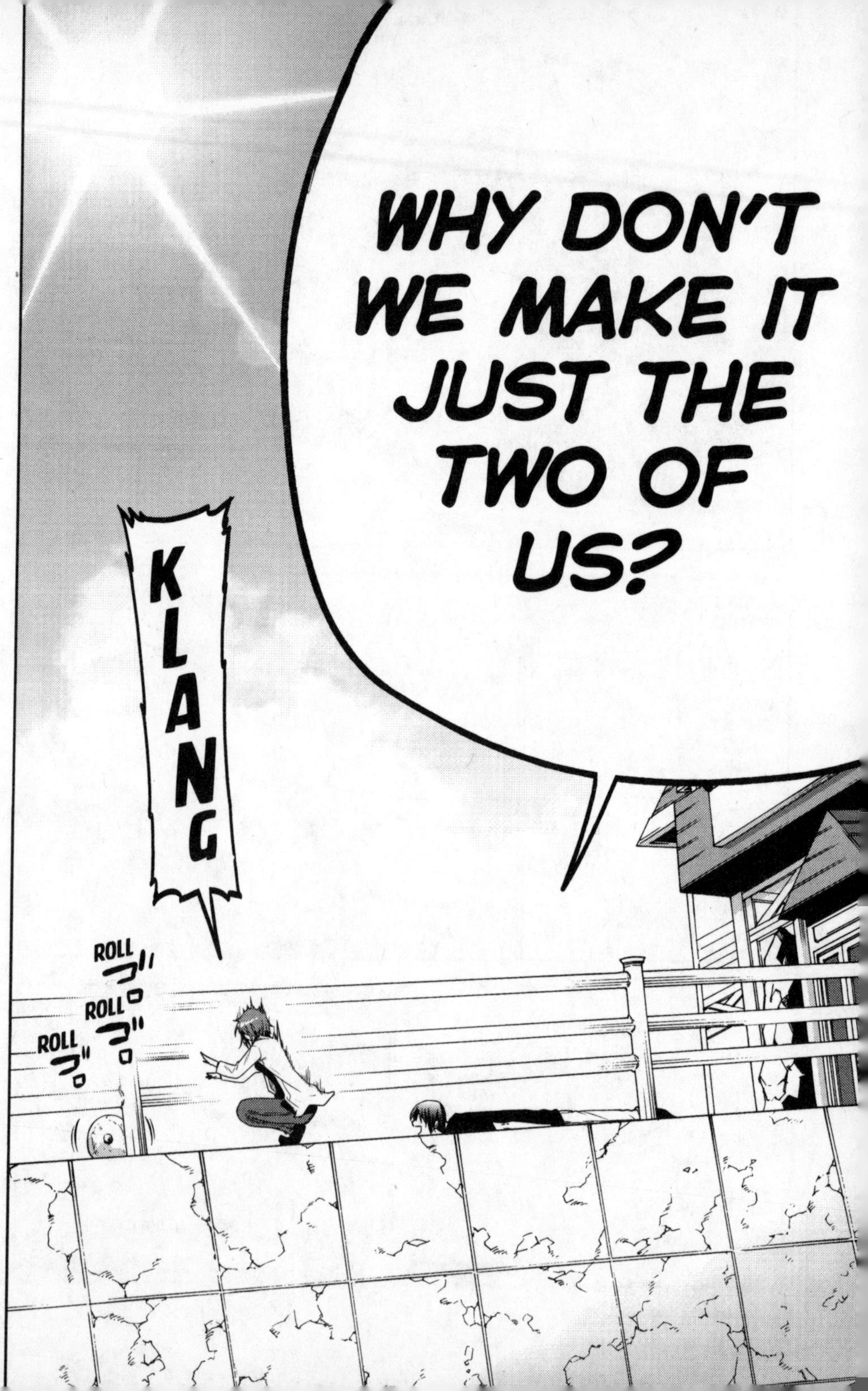
WHY DON'T WE MAKE IT JUST THE TWO OF US?
KLANG
ROLL ゴロ
ROLL ゴロ
ROLL ゴロ

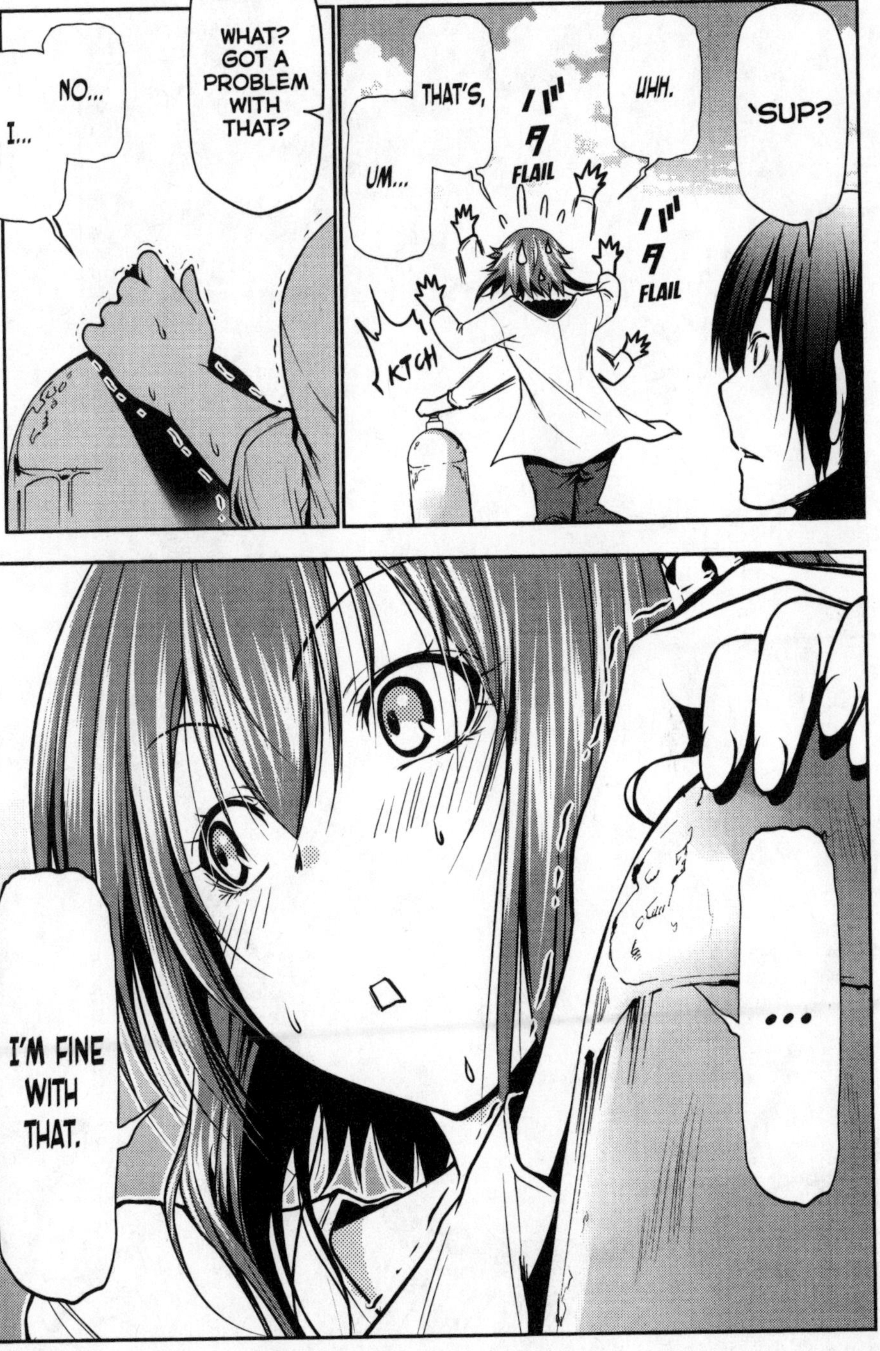
'SUP?
UHH.
バタ
FLAIL
バタ
FLAIL
THAT'S, UM...
KTCH
WHAT? GOT A PROBLEM WITH THAT?
NO... I...
...
I'M FINE WITH THAT.

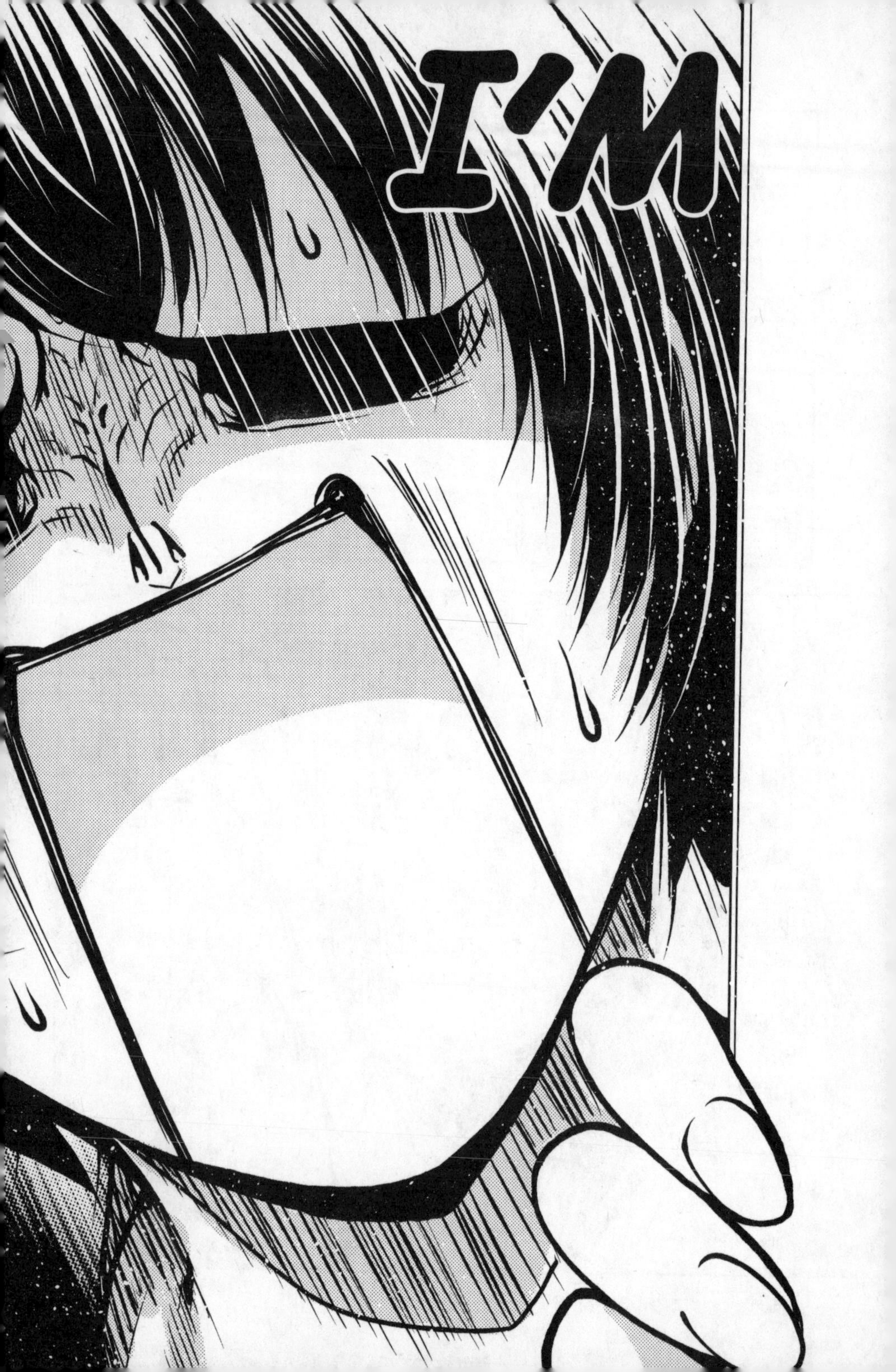
I'M

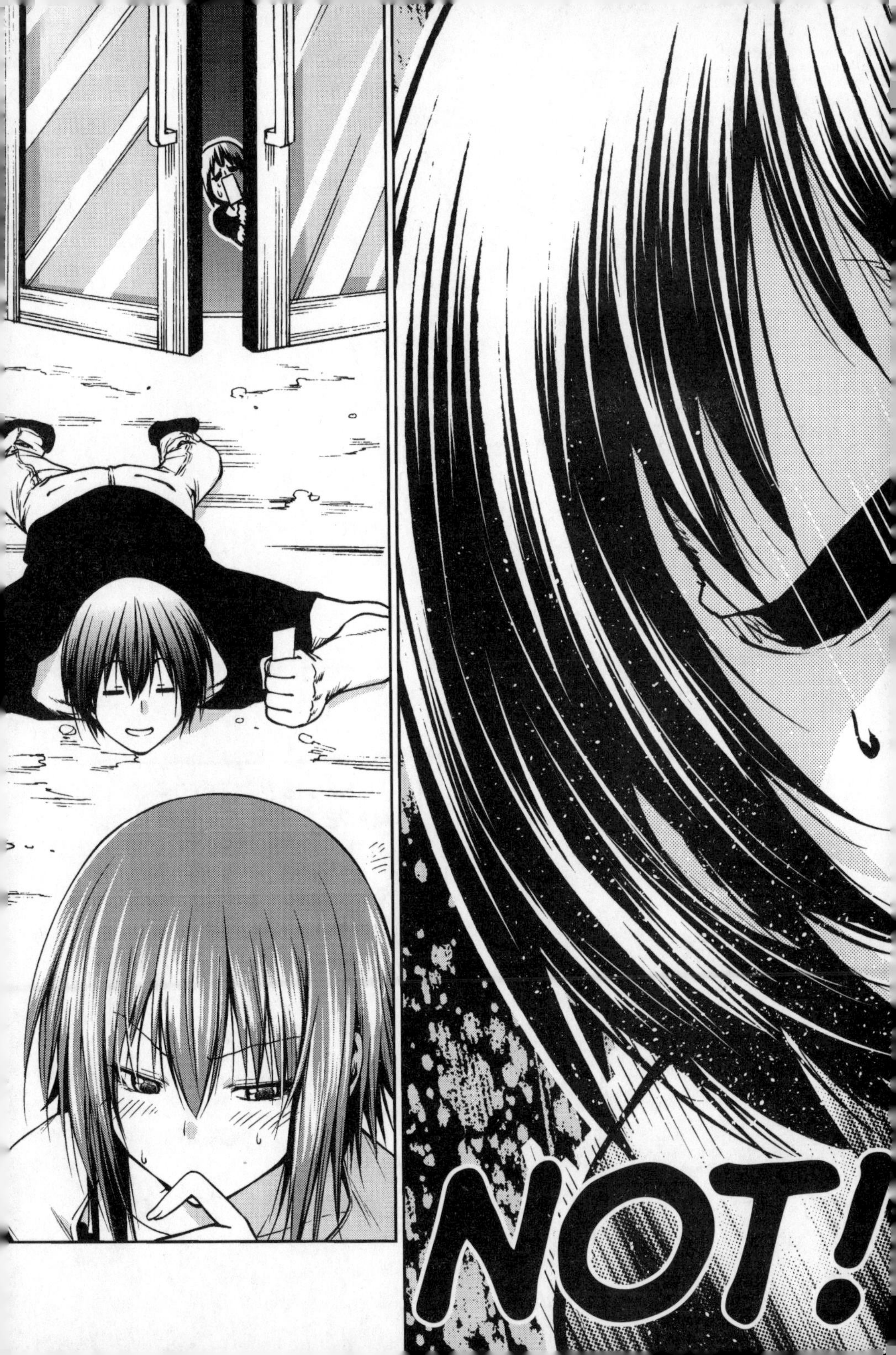
NOT!

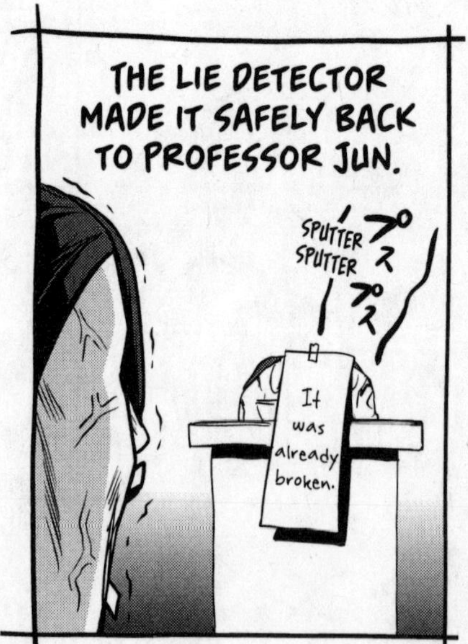
THE LIE DETECTOR MADE IT SAFELY BACK TO PROFESSOR JUN.
SPUTTER SPUTTER
プスプス
It was already broken.

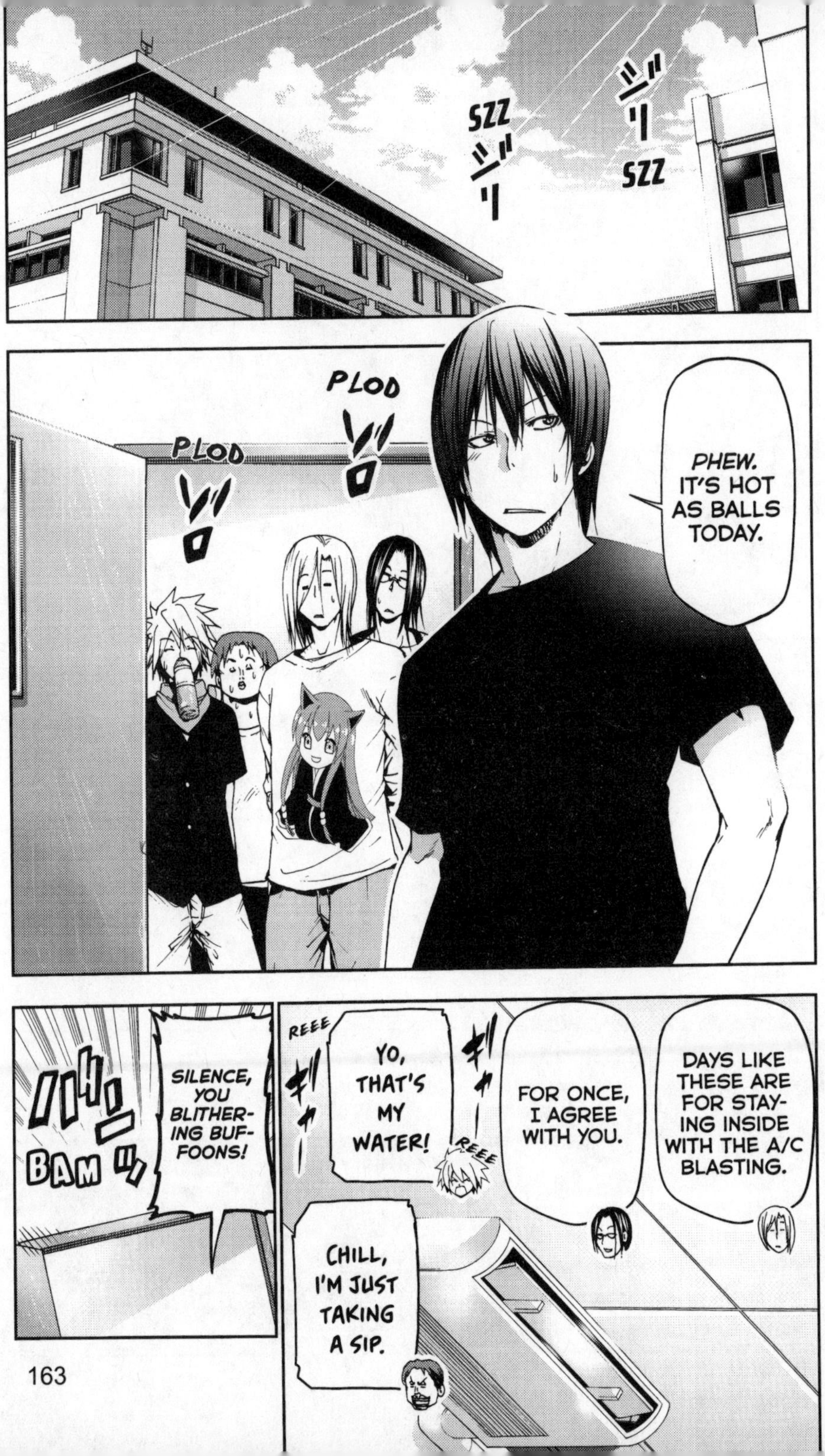
SZZ
SZZ
PLOD
PLOD
PHEW. IT'S HOT AS BALLS TODAY.
DAYS LIKE THESE ARE FOR STAYING INSIDE WITH THE A/C BLASTING.
FOR ONCE, I AGREE WITH YOU.
REEE
REEE
YO, THAT'S MY WATER!
CHILL, I'M JUST TAKING A SIP.
SILENCE, YOU BLITHERING BUFFOONS!
BAM

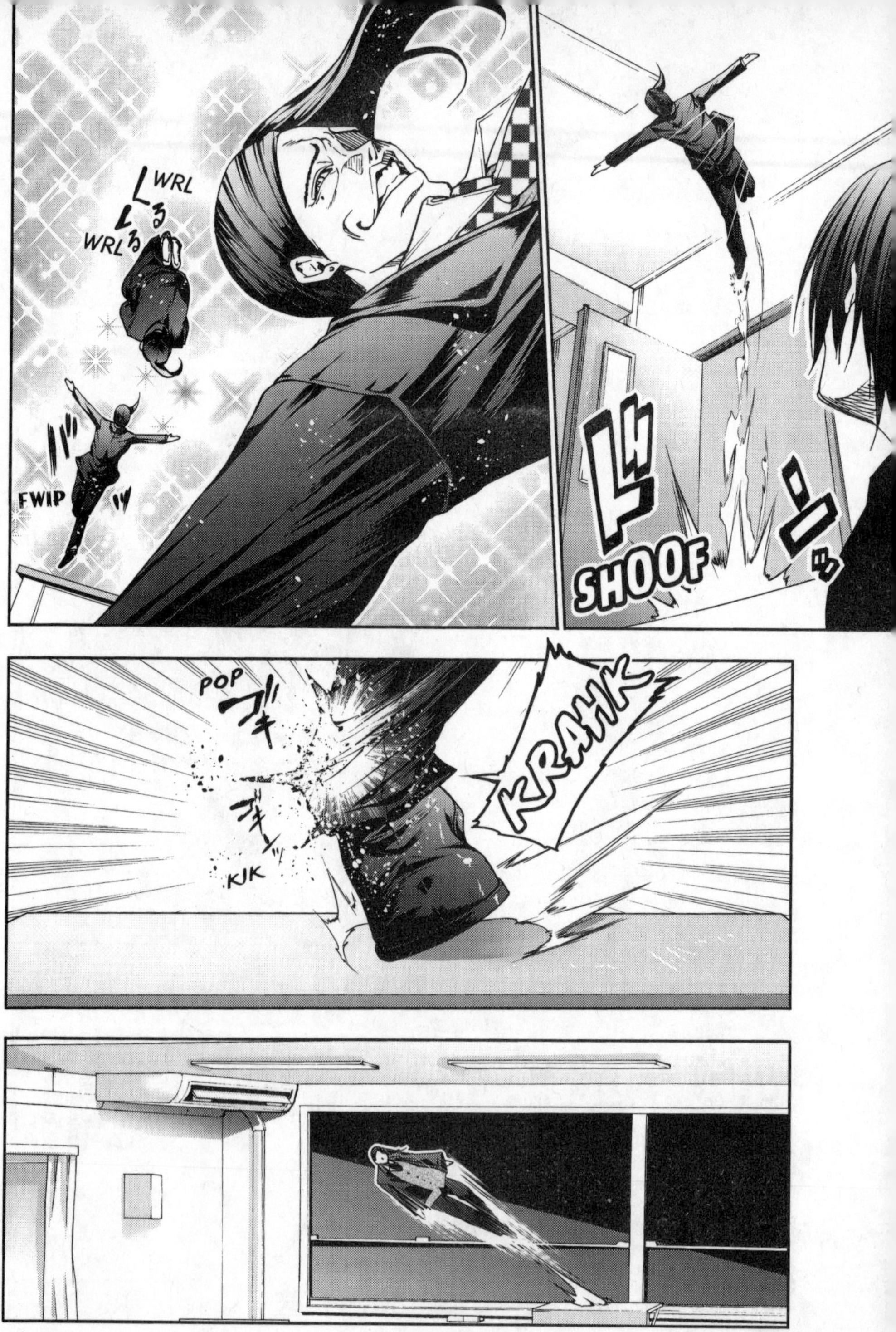
ドン
SHOOF
WRL
る
WRL
る
バッ
FWIP
KRAHK
POP
ゴキ
ゴキンッ
KJK

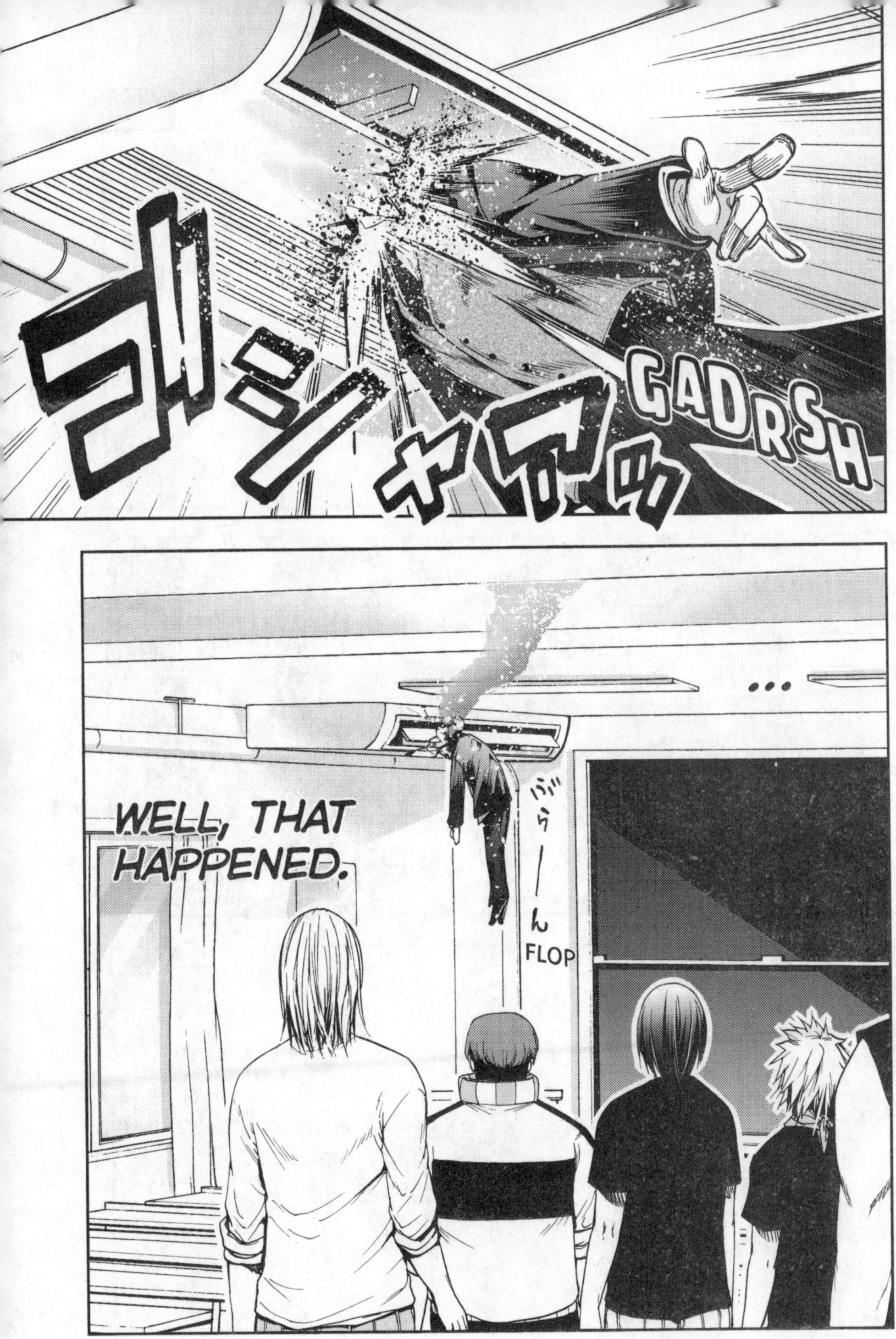
GADRSH
...
ぶらーん
FLOP
WELL, THAT HAPPENED.

Side Story: The Art of Escape

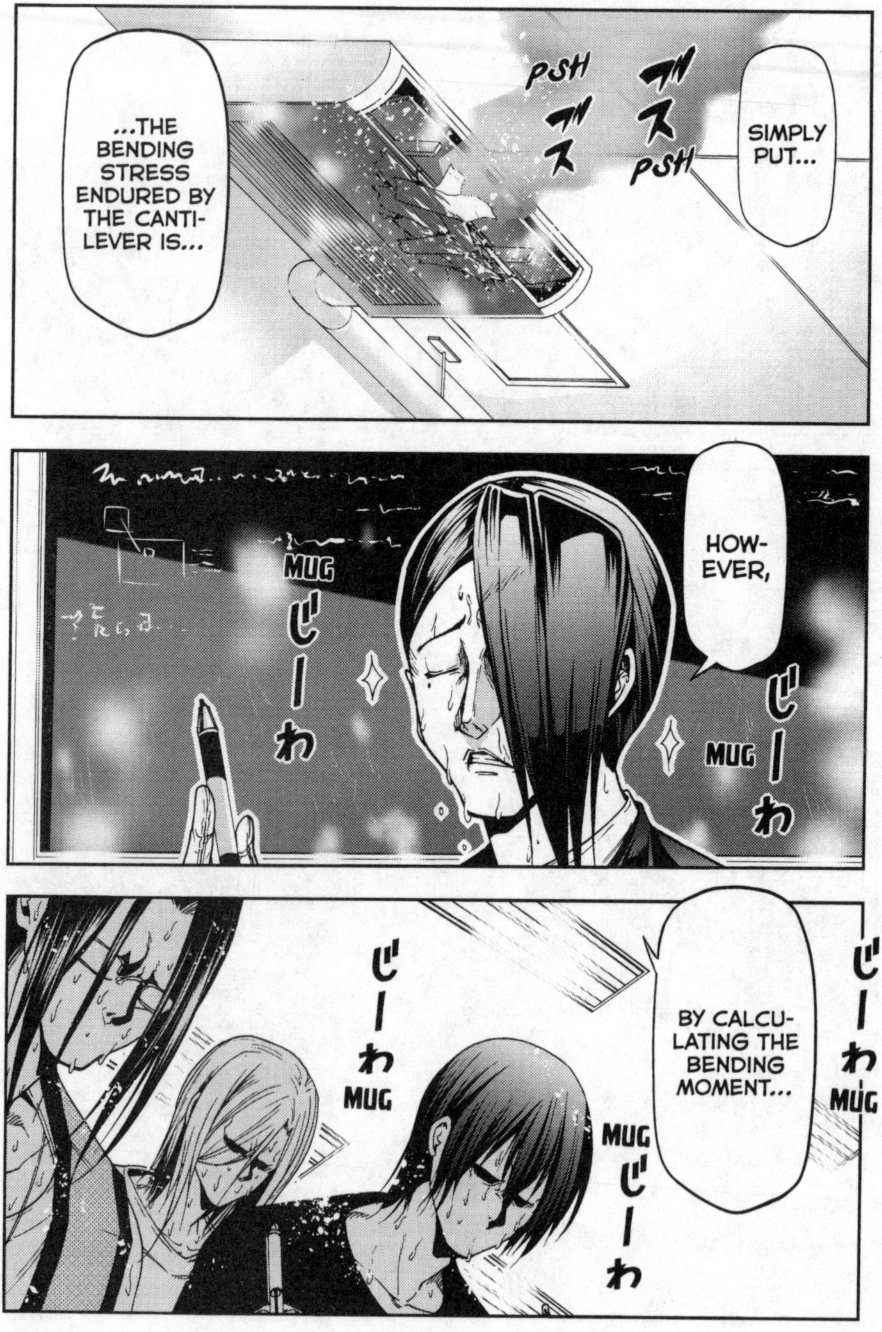
SIMPLY PUT...
ブス PSH
ブス PSH
...THE BENDING STRESS ENDURED BY THE CANTI-LEVER IS...
HOW-EVER,
じーわ MUG
じーわ MUG
BY CALCU-LATING THE BENDING MOMENT...
じーわ MUG
MUG じーわ
じーわ MUG

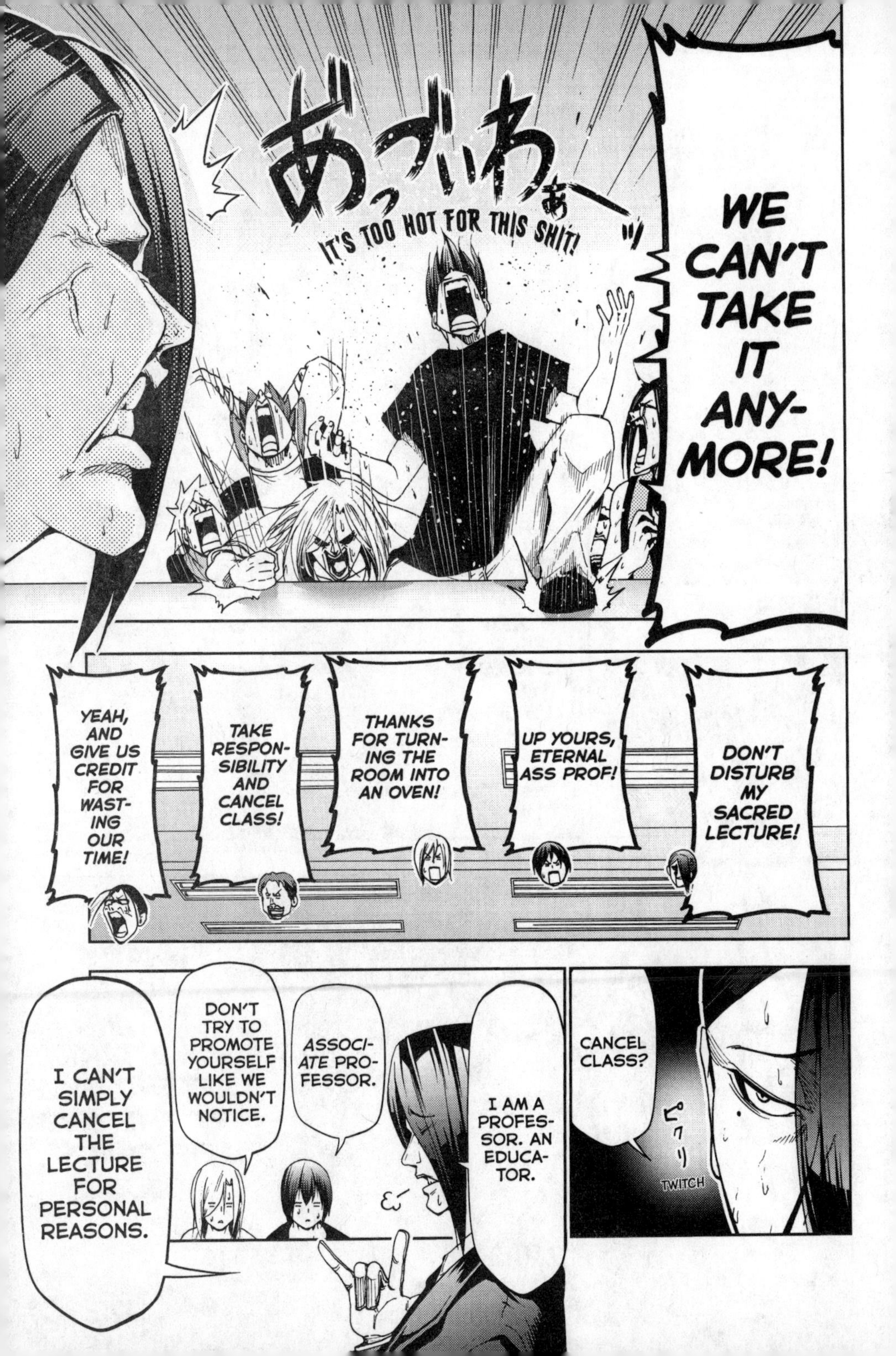
WE CAN'T TAKE IT ANYMORE!
あっづいわぁーッ
IT'S TOO HOT FOR THIS SHIT!
DON'T DISTURB MY SACRED LECTURE!
UP YOURS, ETERNAL ASS PROF!
THANKS FOR TURNING THE ROOM INTO AN OVEN!
TAKE RESPONSIBILITY AND CANCEL CLASS!
YEAH, AND GIVE US CREDIT FOR WASTING OUR TIME!
CANCEL CLASS?
ピクリ
TWITCH
I AM A PROFESSOR. AN EDUCATOR.
ASSOCIATE PROFESSOR.
DON'T TRY TO PROMOTE YOURSELF LIKE WE WOULDN'T NOTICE.
I CAN'T SIMPLY CANCEL THE LECTURE FOR PERSONAL REASONS.

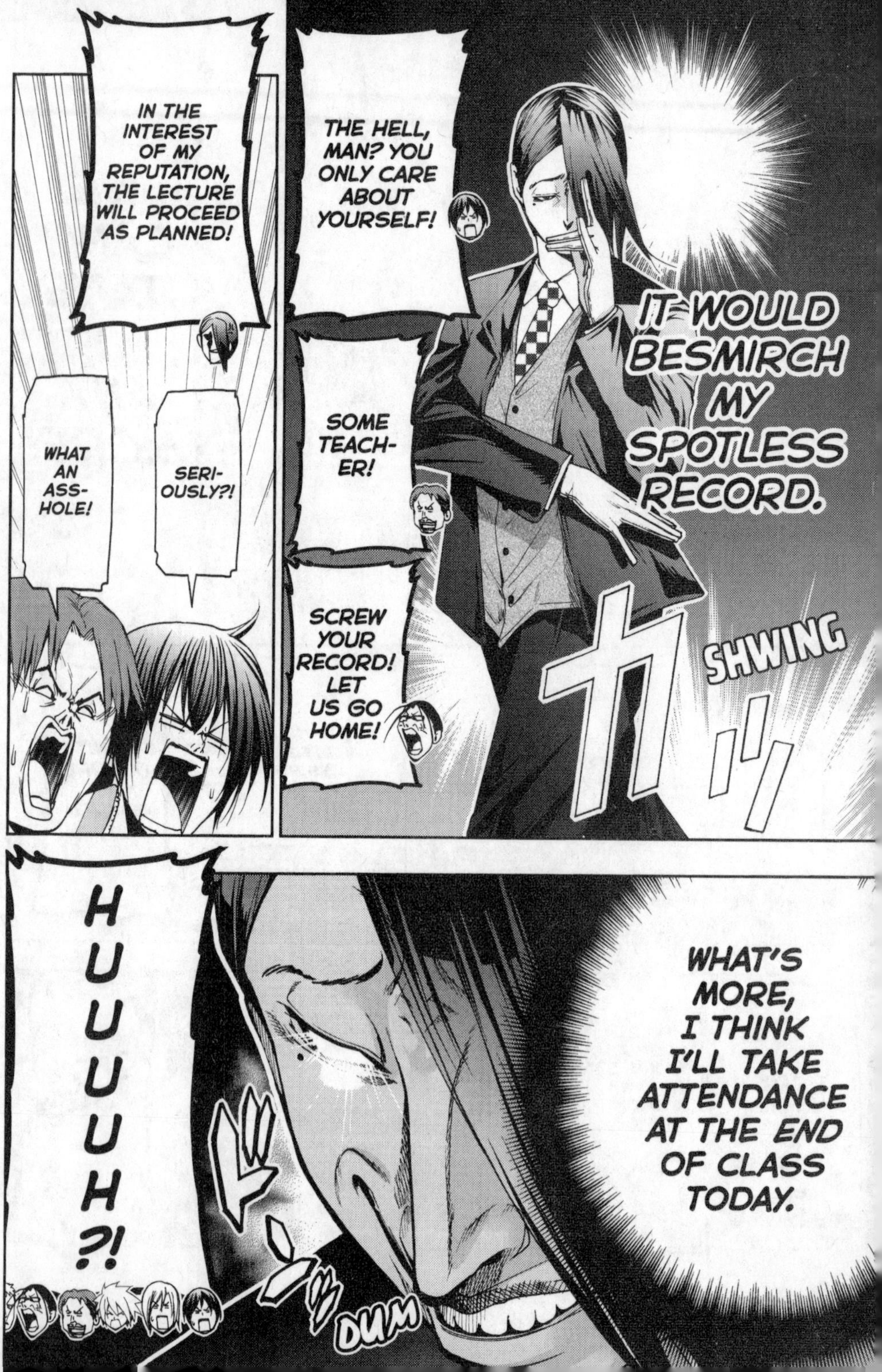

IT WOULD BESMIRCH MY SPOTLESS RECORD.
SHWING
カッ
THE HELL, MAN? YOU ONLY CARE ABOUT YOURSELF!
SOME TEACHER-ER!
SCREW YOUR RECORD! LET US GO HOME!
IN THE INTEREST OF MY REPUTATION, THE LECTURE WILL PROCEED AS PLANNED!
SERI-OUSLY?!
WHAT AN ASS-HOLE!
WHAT'S MORE, I THINK I'LL TAKE ATTENDANCE AT THE END OF CLASS TODAY.
HUUUUUH?!
DUM

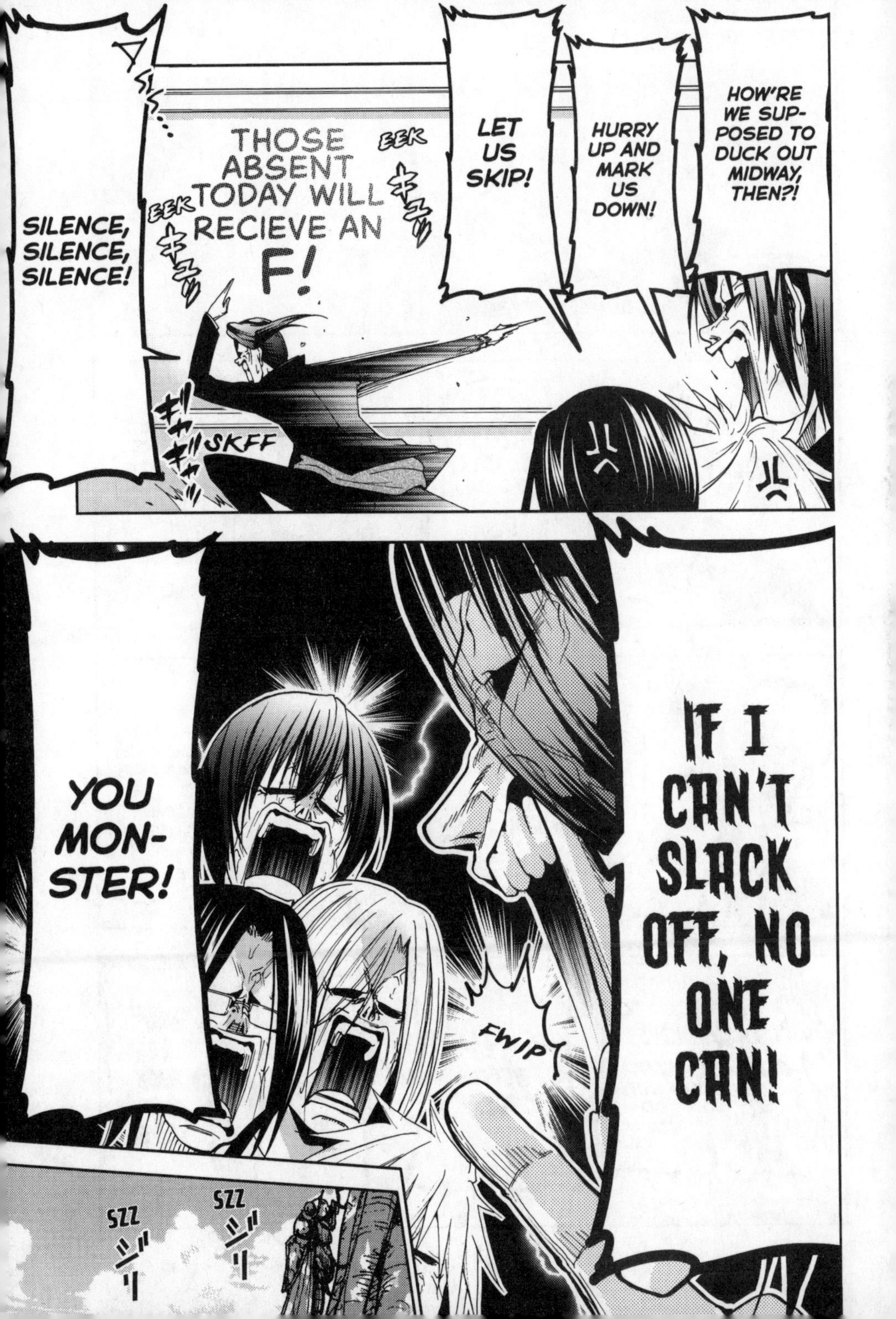
HOW'RE WE SUP-POSED TO DUCK OUT MIDWAY, THEN?!
HURRY UP AND MARK US DOWN!
LET US SKIP!
EEK
THOSE ABSENT TODAY WILL RECIEVE AN F!
EEK
SILENCE, SILENCE, SILENCE!
SKFF
IF I CAN'T SLACK OFF, NO ONE CAN!
FWIP
YOU MON-STER!
SZZ
SZZ

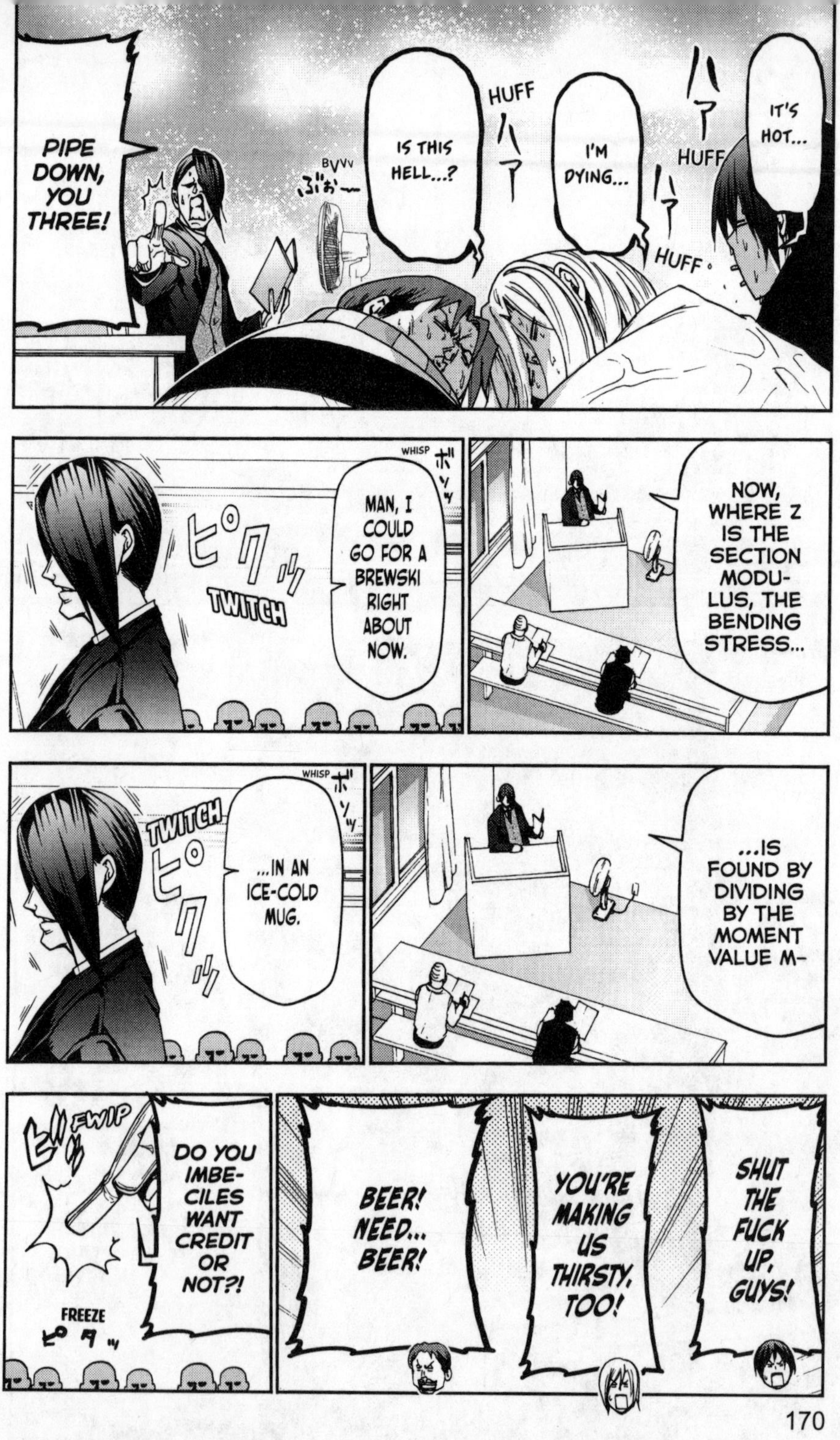

IT'S HOT...
HUFF ハア
HUFF ハア
I'M DYING...
HUFF ハア
IS THIS HELL...?
BVVV ぶぉ〜〜
PIPE DOWN, YOU THREE!
NOW, WHERE Z IS THE SECTION MODULUS, THE BENDING STRESS...
WHISP ボソッ
MAN, I COULD GO FOR A BREWSKI RIGHT ABOUT NOW.
ピクッ TWITCH
...IS FOUND BY DIVIDING BY THE MOMENT VALUE M-
WHISP ボソッ
...IN AN ICE-COLD MUG.
TWITCH ピクッ
SHUT THE FUCK UP, GUYS!
YOU'RE MAKING US THIRSTY, TOO!
BEER! NEED... BEER!
DO YOU IMBECILES WANT CREDIT OR NOT?!
FWIP
FREEZE ピタッ

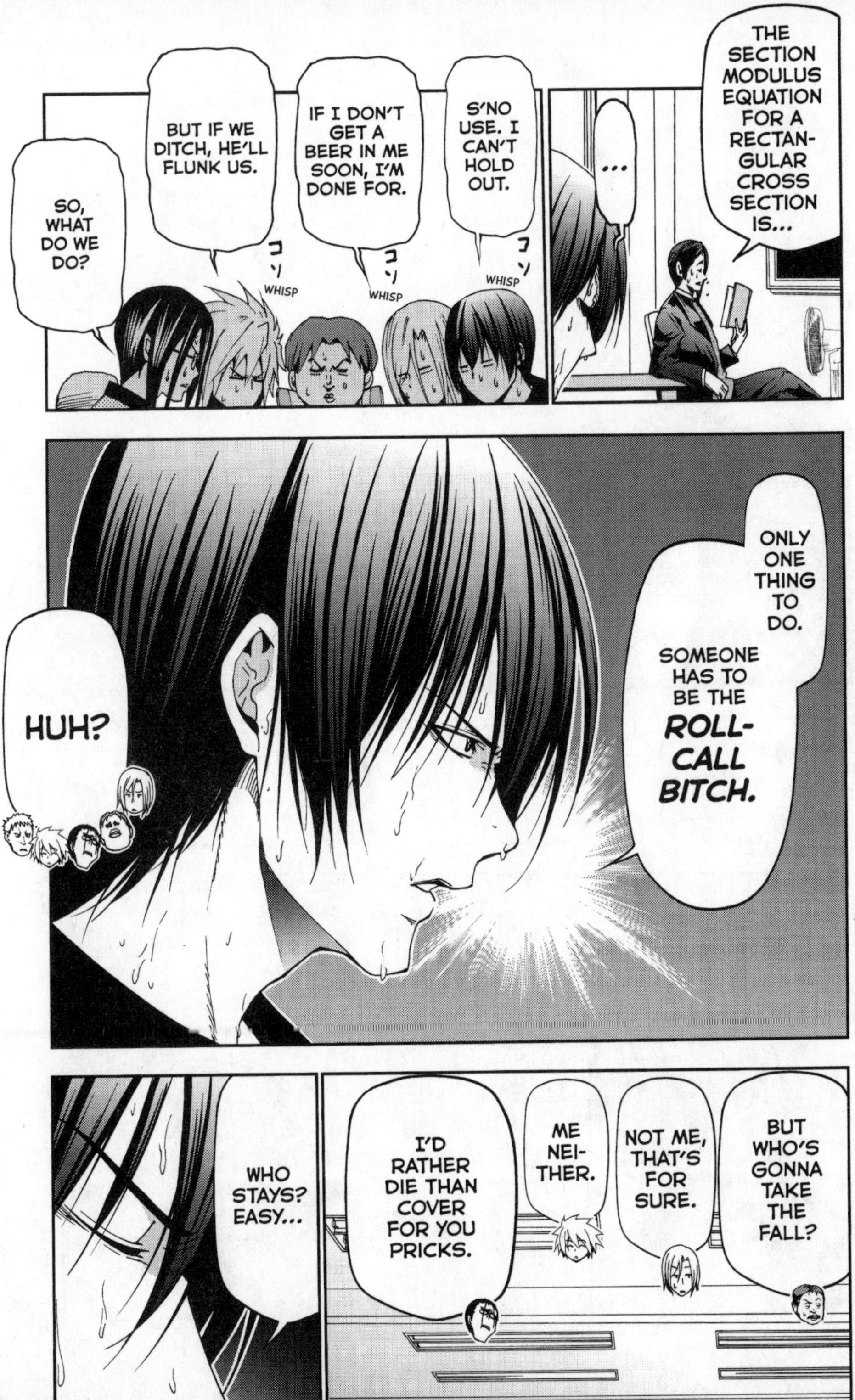
THE SECTION MODULUS EQUATION FOR A RECTANGULAR CROSS SECTION IS...
...
S'NO USE. I CAN'T HOLD OUT.
コソ WHISP
IF I DON'T GET A BEER IN ME SOON, I'M DONE FOR.
コソ WHISP
BUT IF WE DITCH, HE'LL FLUNK US.
コソ WHISP
SO, WHAT DO WE DO?
ONLY ONE THING TO DO.
SOMEONE HAS TO BE THE ROLL-CALL BITCH.
HUH?
BUT WHO'S GONNA TAKE THE FALL?
NOT ME, THAT'S FOR SURE.
ME NEITHER.
I'D RATHER DIE THAN COVER FOR YOU PRICKS.
WHO STAYS? EASY...

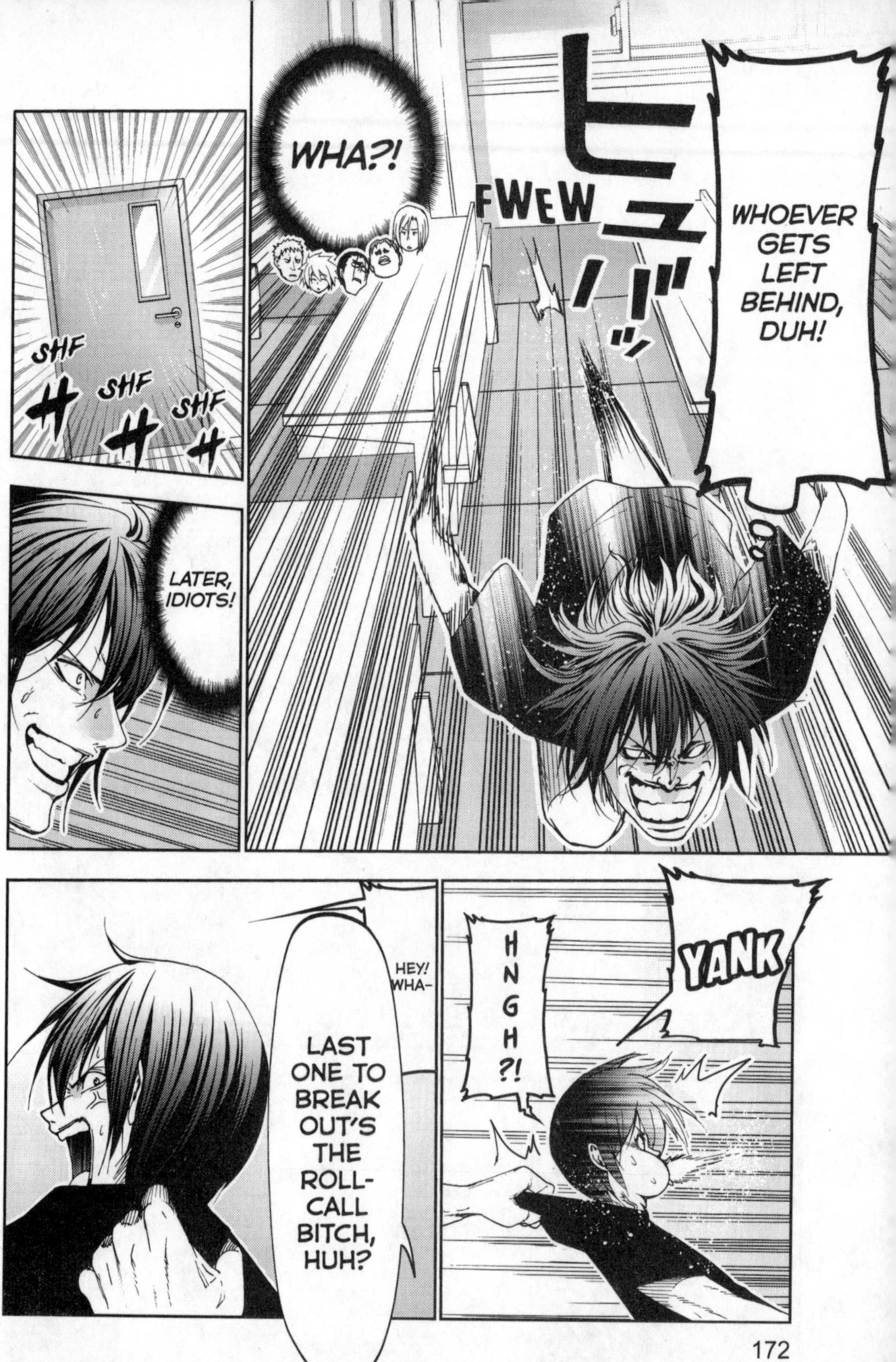
WHA?!
FWEW
ヒュバッ
WHOEVER GETS LEFT BEHIND, DUH!
SHF
SHF
SHF
LATER, IDIOTS!
YANK
HNGH?!
HEY! WHA-
LAST ONE TO BREAK OUT'S THE ROLL-CALL BITCH, HUH?

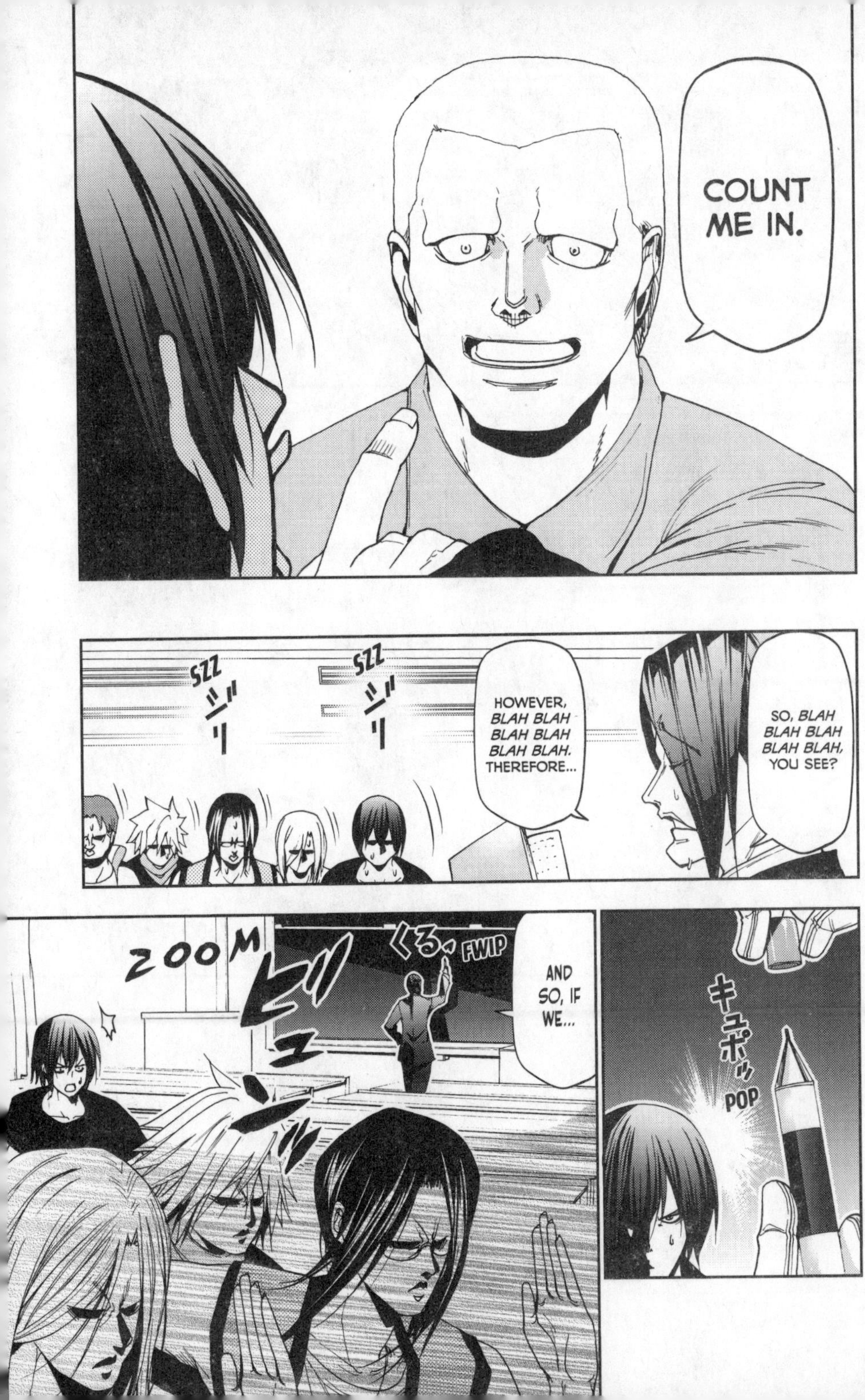

COUNT ME IN.
SO, BLAH BLAH BLAH BLAH BLAH, YOU SEE?
HOWEVER, BLAH BLAH BLAH BLAH BLAH BLAH. THEREFORE...
SZZ ジリ
SZZ ジリ
キュポッ POP
AND SO, IF WE...
くるっ FWIP
ZOOM ビュ

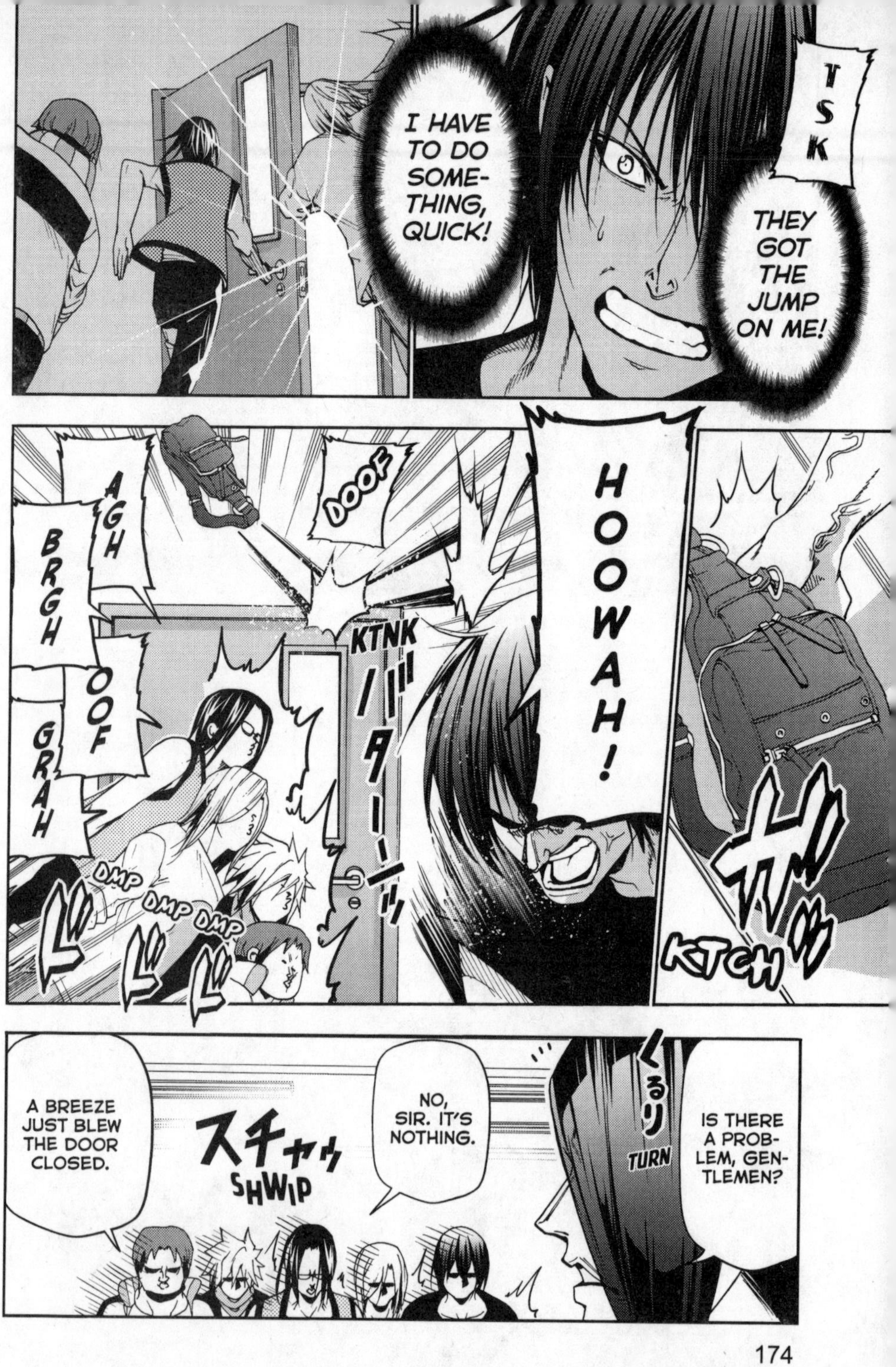
TSK
THEY GOT THE JUMP ON ME!
I HAVE TO DO SOMETHING, QUICK!
KTCH
HOOWAH!
KTNK
DOOF
AGH
BRGH
OOF
GRAH
DMP
DMP DMP
くるり
TURN
IS THERE A PROBLEM, GENTLEMEN?
NO, SIR. IT'S NOTHING.
スチャウ
SHWIP
A BREEZE JUST BLEW THE DOOR CLOSED.

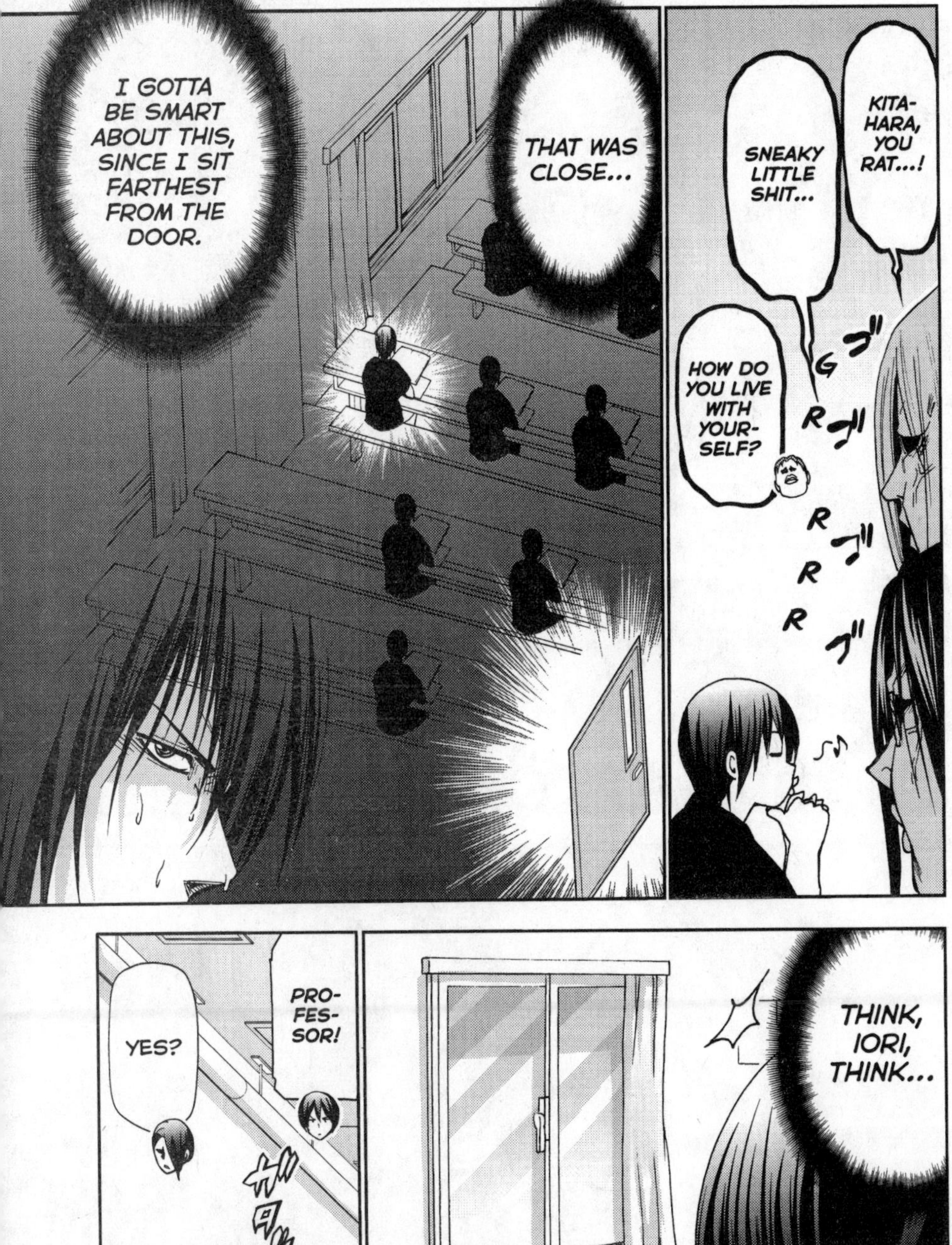
KITA-HARA, YOU RAT...!
SNEAKY LITTLE SHIT...
HOW DO YOU LIVE WITH YOUR-SELF?
GRRRR
THAT WAS CLOSE...
I GOTTA BE SMART ABOUT THIS, SINCE I SIT FARTHEST FROM THE DOOR.
THINK, IORI, THINK...
PRO-FES-SOR!
YES?
CLATR

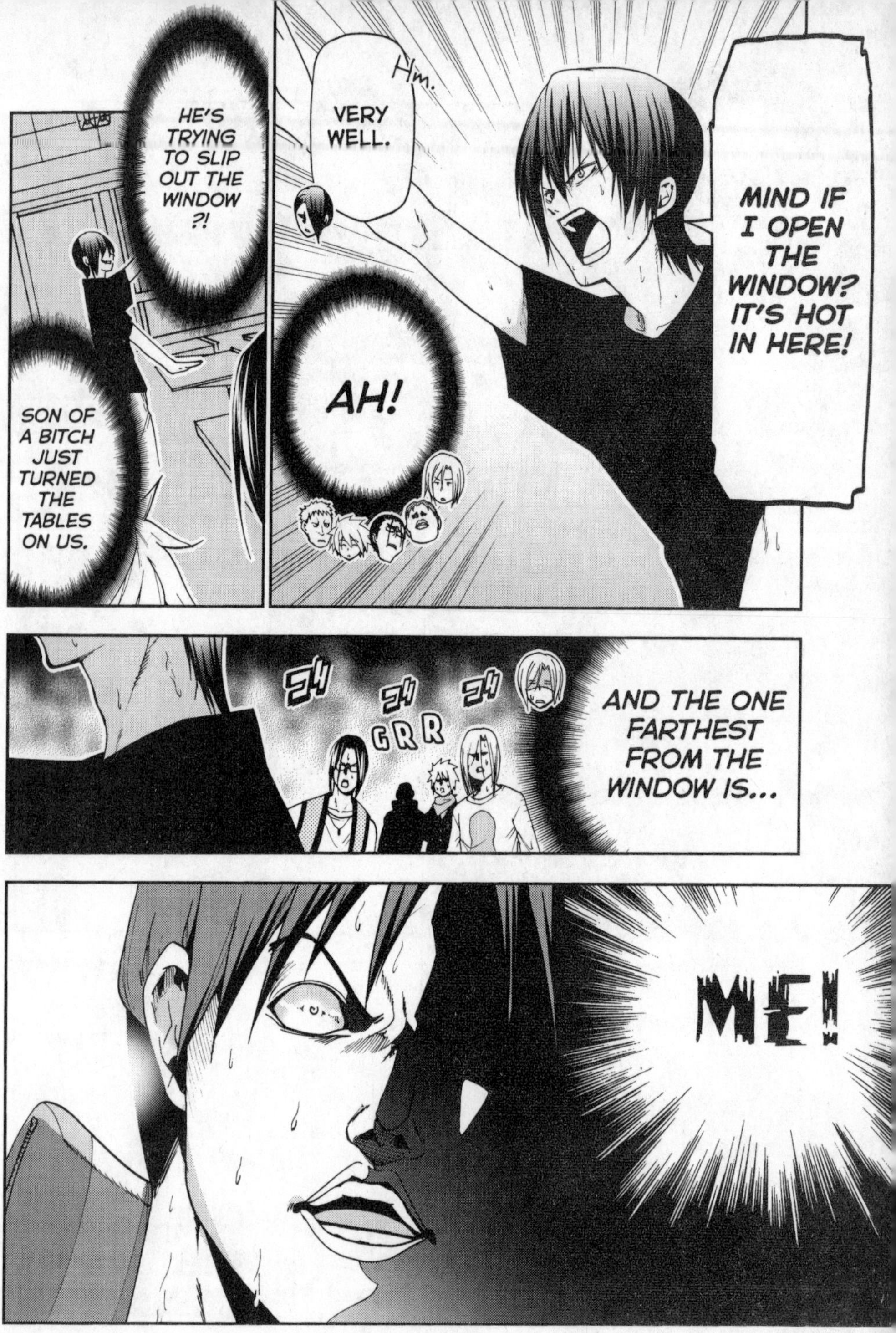
MIND IF I OPEN THE WINDOW? IT'S HOT IN HERE!
Hm.
VERY WELL.
AH!
HE'S TRYING TO SLIP OUT THE WINDOW ?!
SON OF A BITCH JUST TURNED THE TABLES ON US.
AND THE ONE FARTHEST FROM THE WINDOW IS...
GRR
ME!

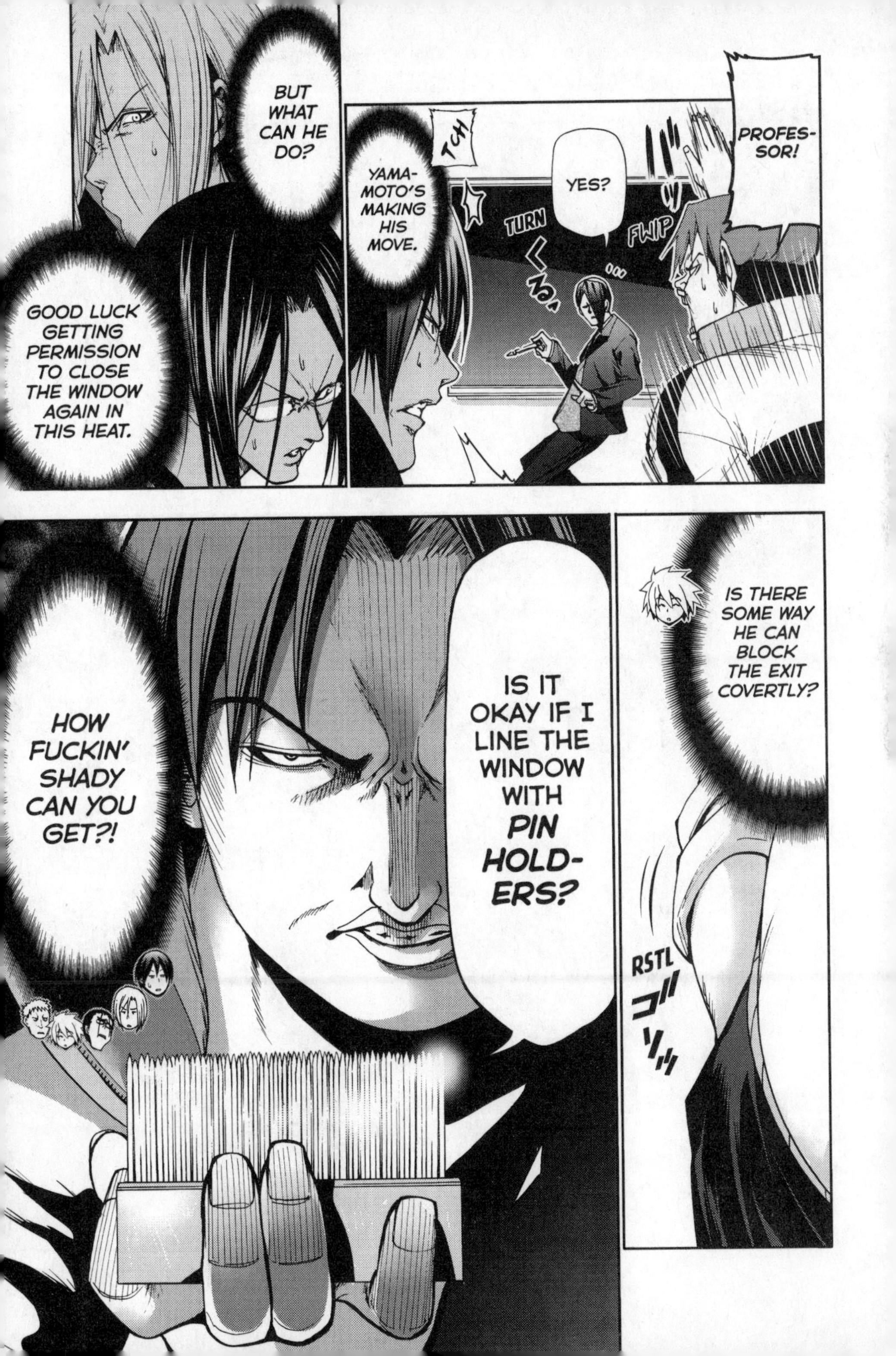
PROFES-SOR!
FWIP
YES?
TURN
...
TCH
YAMA-MOTO'S MAKING HIS MOVE.
BUT WHAT CAN HE DO?
GOOD LUCK GETTING PERMISSION TO CLOSE THE WINDOW AGAIN IN THIS HEAT.
IS THERE SOME WAY HE CAN BLOCK THE EXIT COVERTLY?
RSTL
IS IT OKAY IF I LINE THE WINDOW WITH *PIN HOLD-ERS?*
HOW FUCKIN' SHADY CAN YOU GET?!

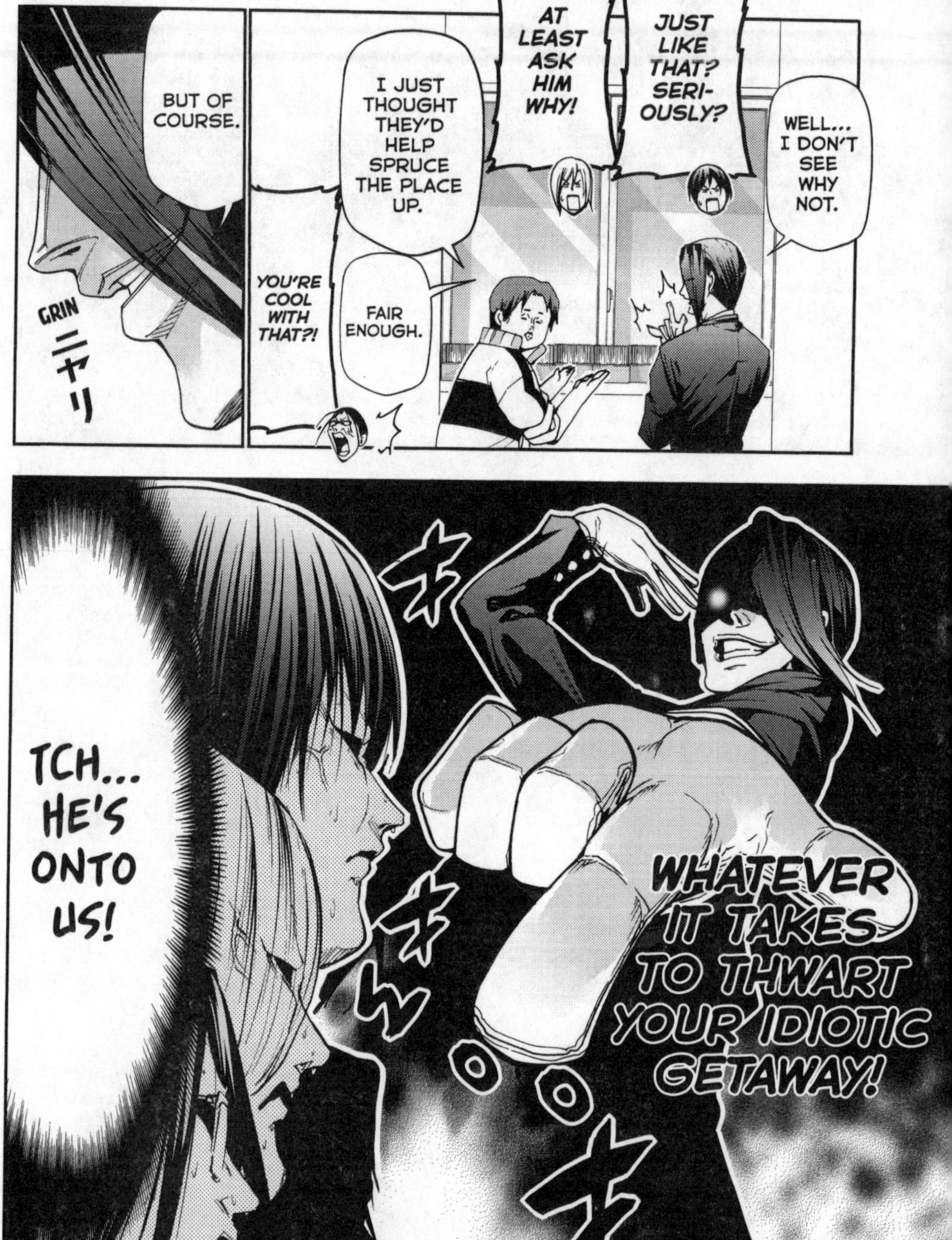
WELL... I DON'T SEE WHY NOT.
JUST LIKE THAT? SERIOUSLY?
AT LEAST ASK HIM WHY!
I JUST THOUGHT THEY'D HELP SPRUCE THE PLACE UP.
FAIR ENOUGH.
YOU'RE COOL WITH THAT?!
BUT OF COURSE.
GRIN
ニヤリ
WHATEVER IT TAKES TO THWART YOUR IDIOTIC GETAWAY!
TCH... HE'S ONTO US!

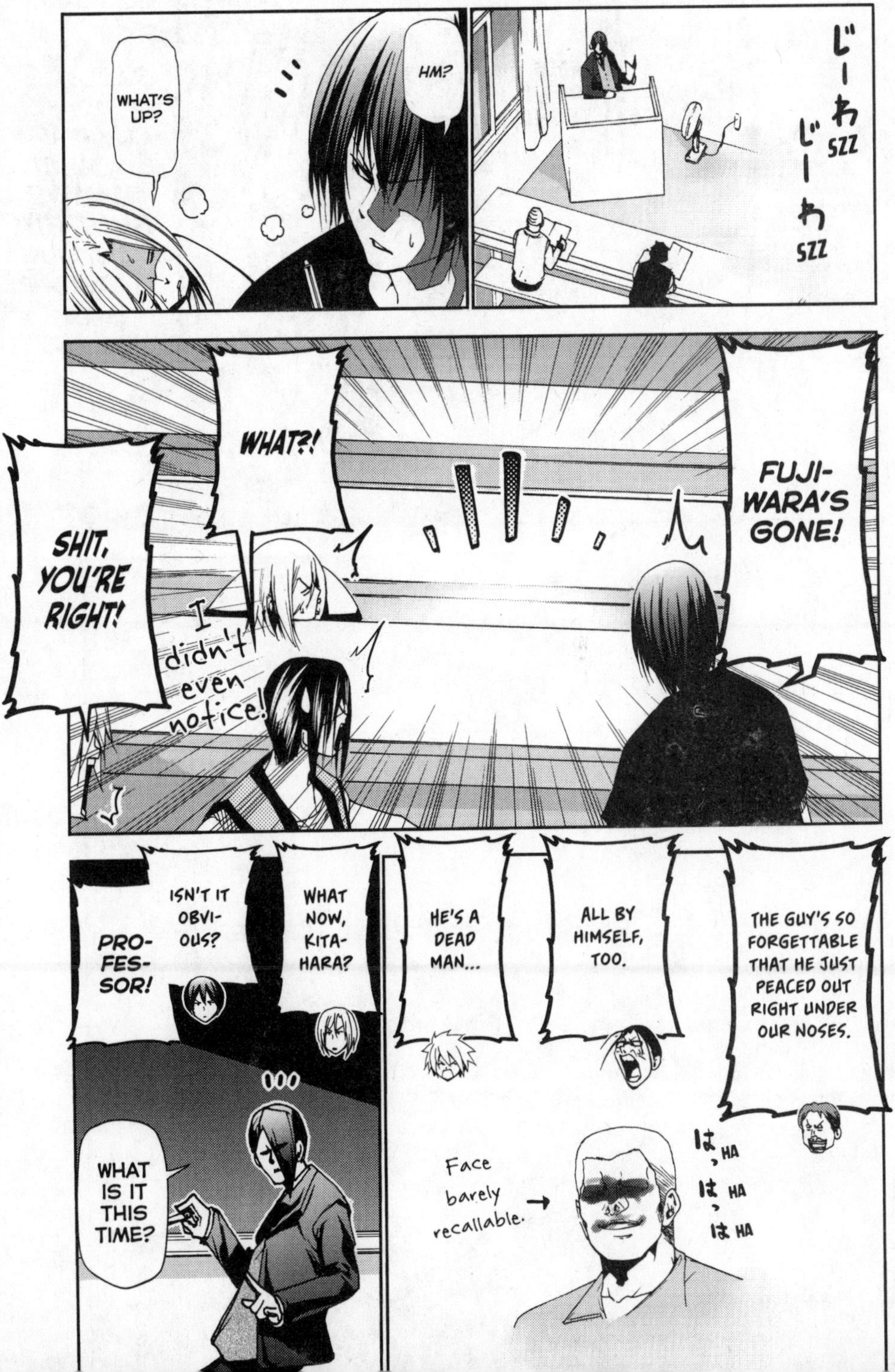
じーわ SZZ
じーわ SZZ
HM?
WHAT'S UP?
FUJI-WARA'S GONE!
WHAT?!
SHIT, YOU'RE RIGHT!
I didn't even notice!
THE GUY'S SO FORGETTABLE THAT HE JUST PEACED OUT RIGHT UNDER OUR NOSES.
ALL BY HIMSELF, TOO.
HE'S A DEAD MAN...
は、HA は、HA は HA
Face barely recallable.
WHAT NOW, KITA-HARA?
ISN'T IT OBVI-OUS?
PRO-FESSOR!
WHAT IS IT THIS TIME?

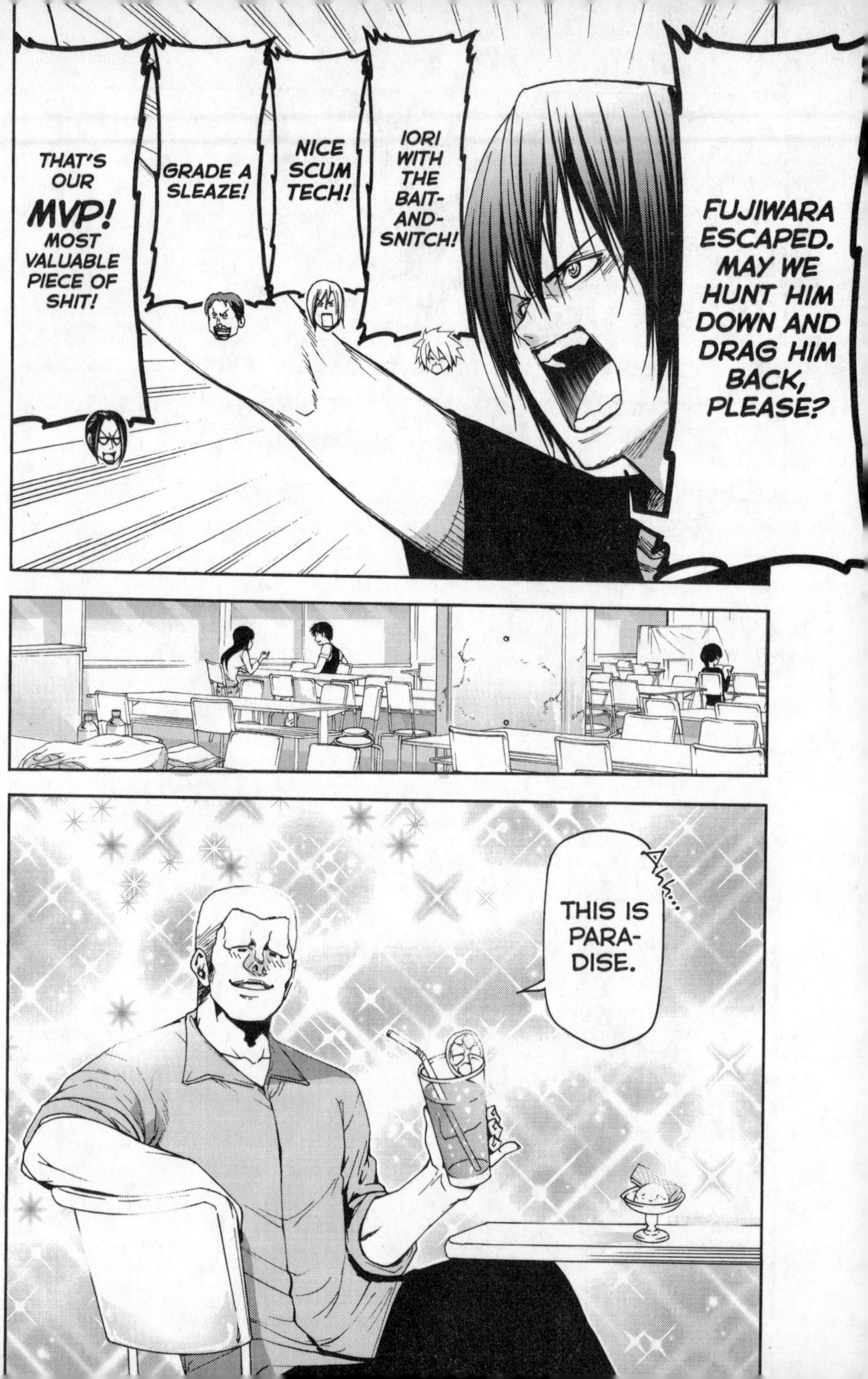
FUJIWARA ESCAPED. MAY WE HUNT HIM DOWN AND DRAG HIM BACK, PLEASE?
IORI WITH THE BAIT-AND-SNITCH!
NICE SCUM TECH!
GRADE A SLEAZE!
THAT'S OUR MVP! MOST VALUABLE PIECE OF SHIT!
Ahh...
THIS IS PARA-DISE.

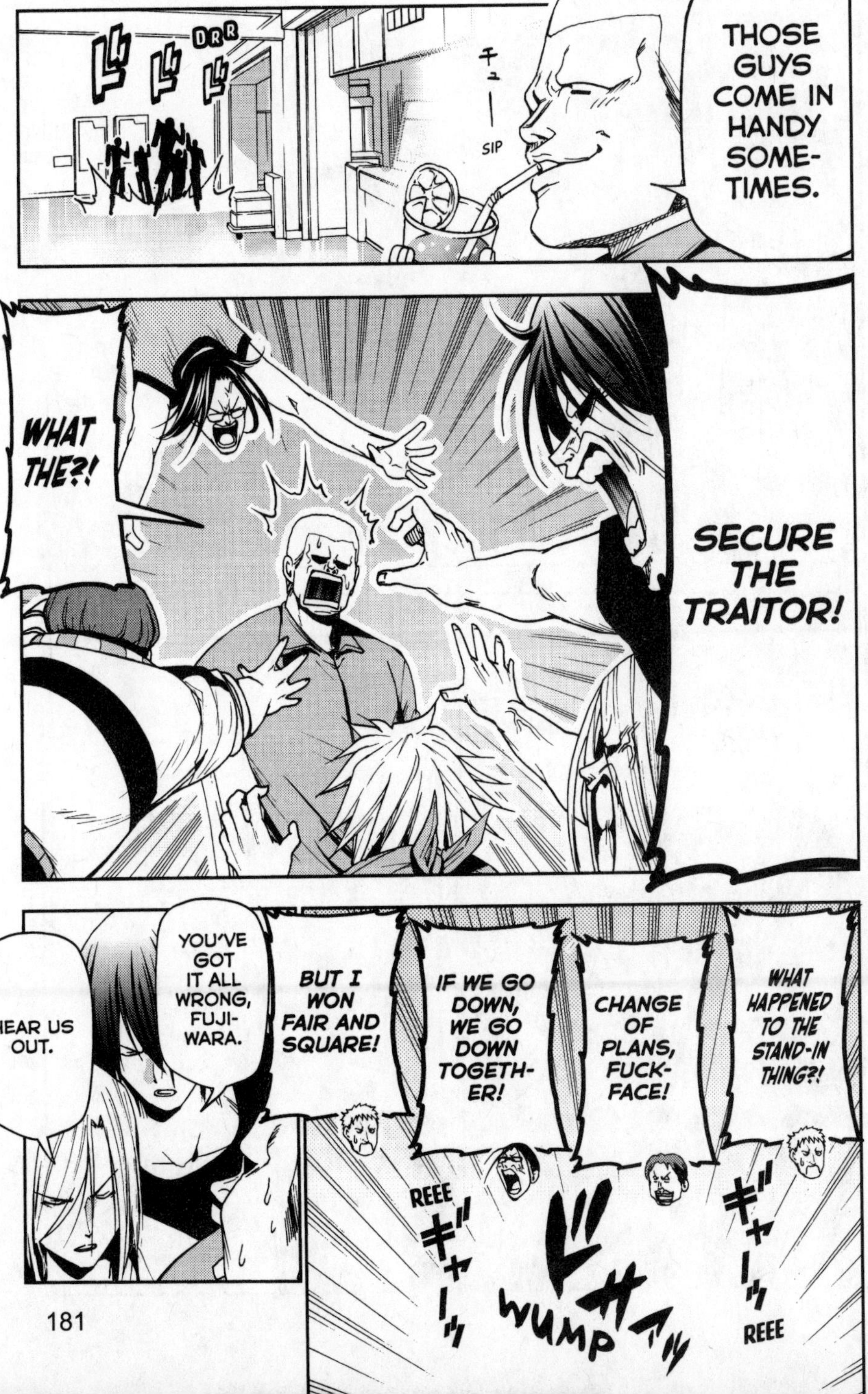
THOSE GUYS COME IN HANDY SOME-TIMES.
チュー
SIP
DRR
SECURE THE TRAITOR!
WHAT THE?!
WHAT HAPPENED TO THE STAND-IN THING?!
CHANGE OF PLANS, FUCK-FACE!
IF WE GO DOWN, WE GO DOWN TOGETH-ER!
BUT I WON FAIR AND SQUARE!
REEE
WUMP
REEE
YOU'VE GOT IT ALL WRONG, FUJI-WARA.
HEAR US OUT.

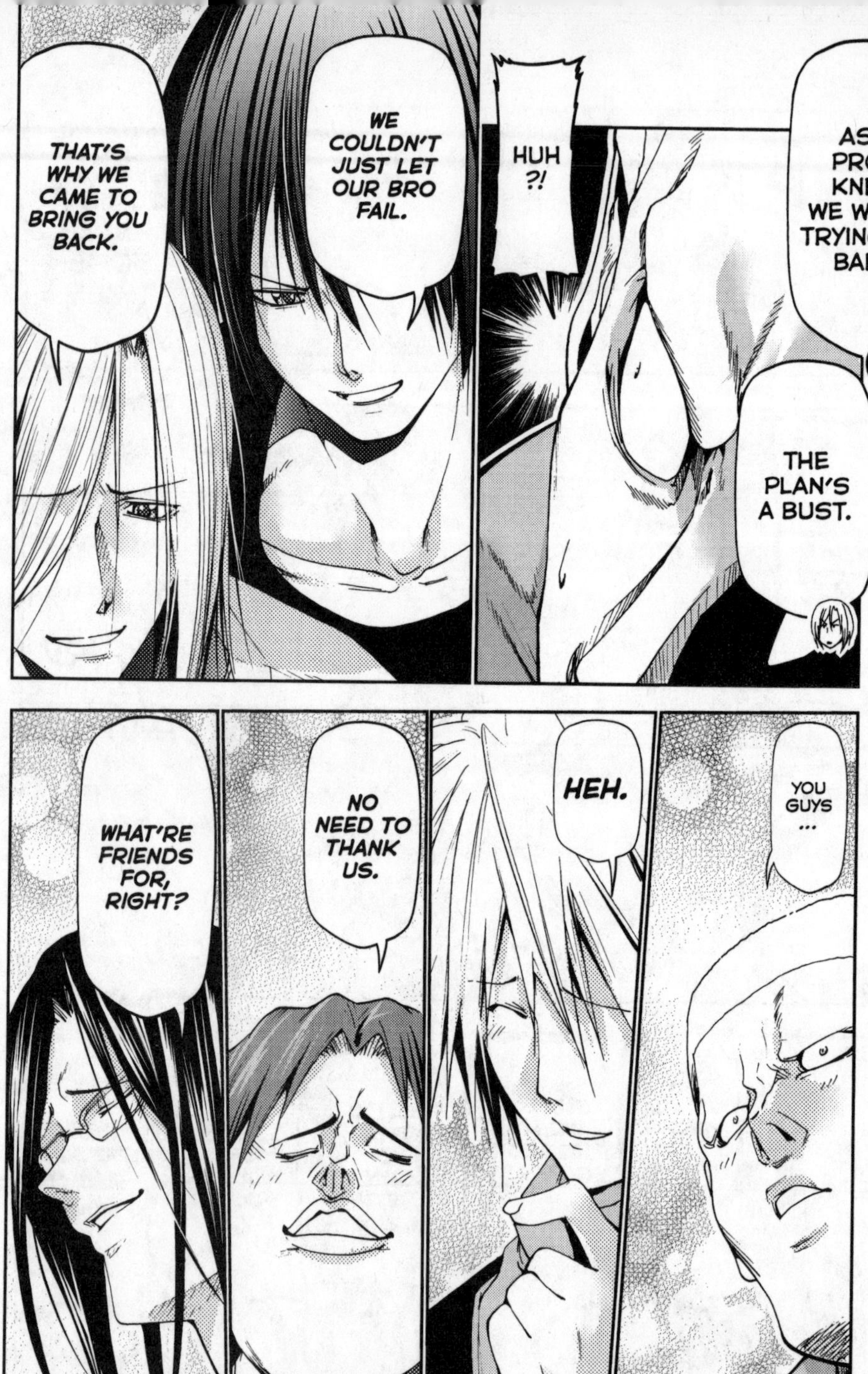
ASS PROF KNEW WE WERE TRYING TO BAIL.
HUH ?!
THE PLAN'S A BUST.
WE COULDN'T JUST LET OUR BRO FAIL.
THAT'S WHY WE CAME TO BRING YOU BACK.
YOU GUYS ...
HEH.
NO NEED TO THANK US.
WHAT'RE FRIENDS FOR, RIGHT?

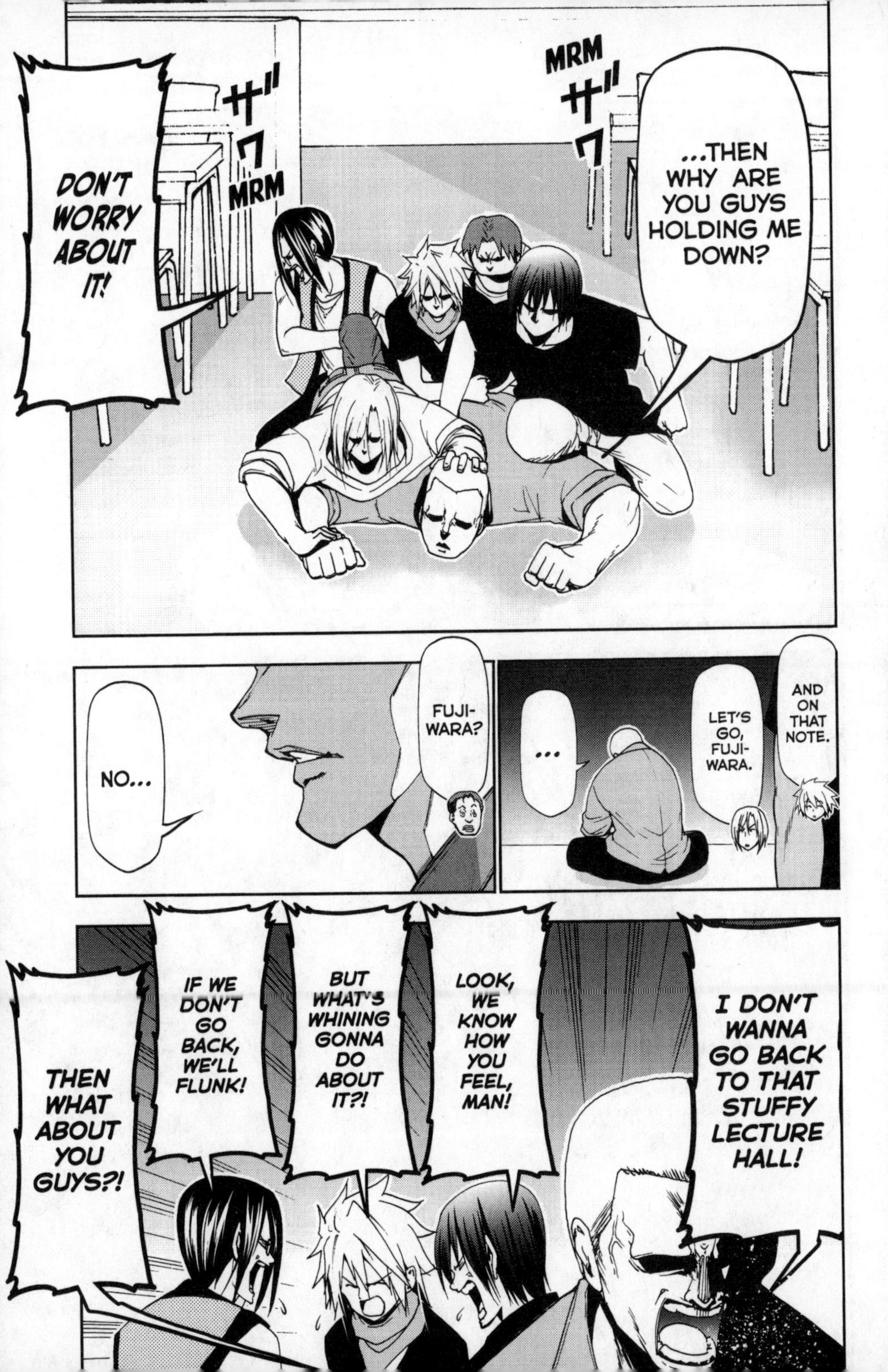
MRM
ザワ
...THEN WHY ARE YOU GUYS HOLDING ME DOWN?
ザワ
MRM
DON'T WORRY ABOUT IT!
AND ON THAT NOTE.
LET'S GO, FUJI-WARA.
...
FUJI-WARA?
NO...
I DON'T WANNA GO BACK TO THAT STUFFY LECTURE HALL!
LOOK, WE KNOW HOW YOU FEEL, MAN!
BUT WHAT'S WHINING GONNA DO ABOUT IT?!
IF WE DON'T GO BACK, WE'LL FLUNK!
THEN WHAT ABOUT YOU GUYS?!

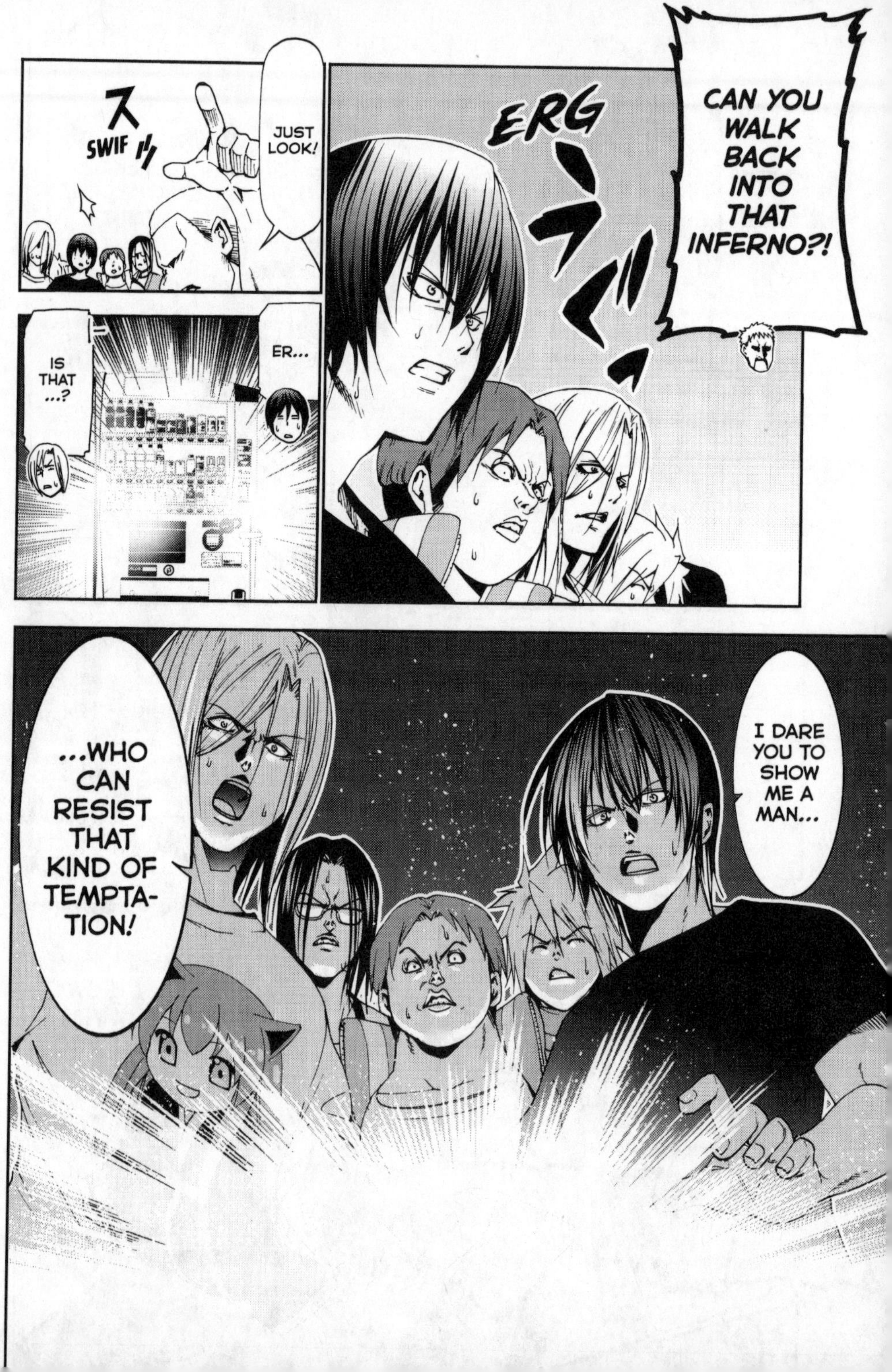
CAN YOU WALK BACK INTO THAT INFERNO?!
ERG
JUST LOOK!
ス
SWIF
ER...
IS THAT ...?
I DARE YOU TO SHOW ME A MAN...
...WHO CAN RESIST THAT KIND OF TEMPTA-TION!

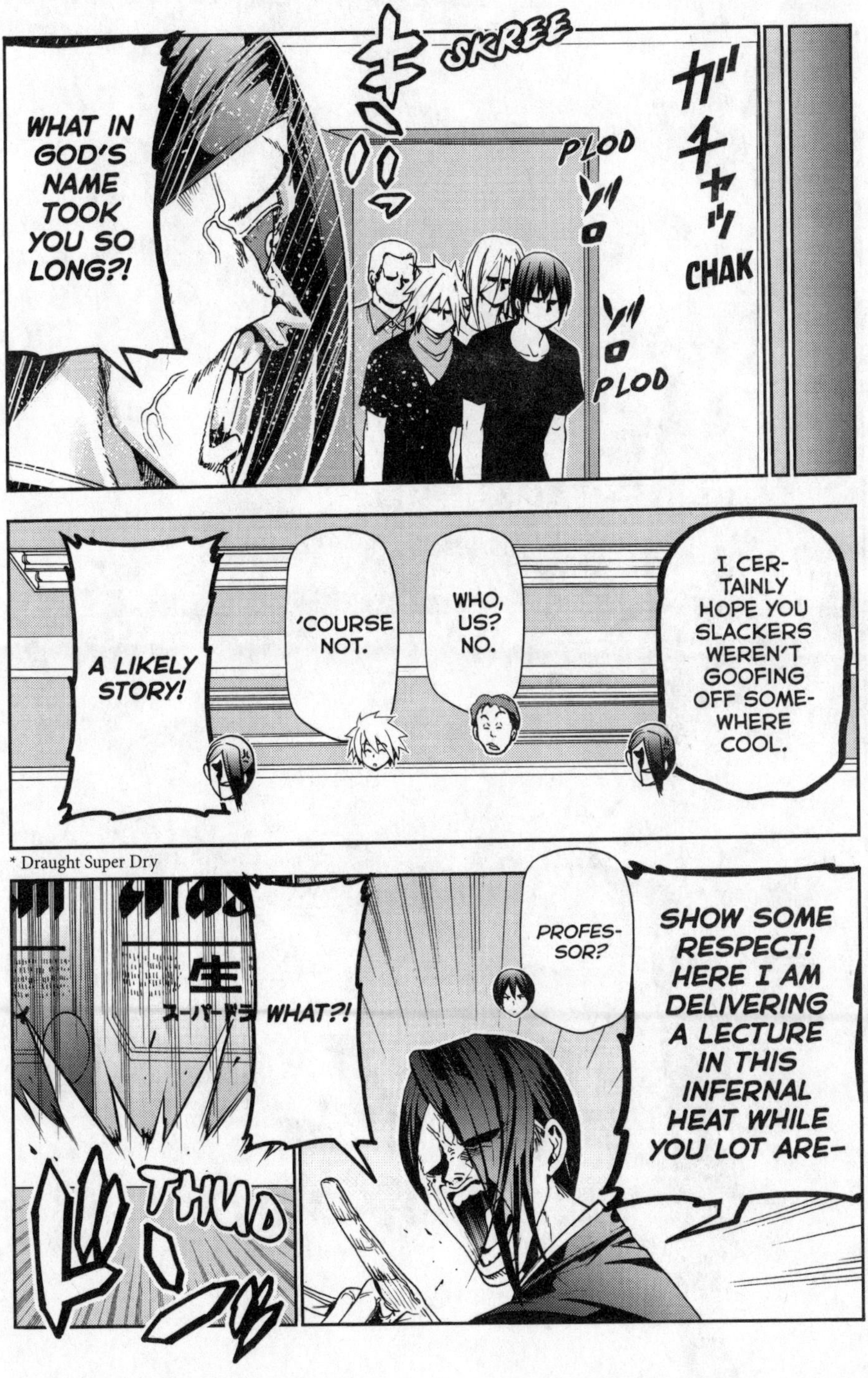
ガチャッ
CHAK
ゾロゾロ
PLOD
PLOD
キーッ
SKREE
WHAT IN GOD'S NAME TOOK YOU SO LONG?!
I CER-TAINLY HOPE YOU SLACKERS WEREN'T GOOFING OFF SOME-WHERE COOL.
WHO, US? NO.
'COURSE NOT.
A LIKELY STORY!
SHOW SOME RESPECT! HERE I AM DELIVERING A LECTURE IN THIS INFERNAL HEAT WHILE YOU LOT ARE–
PROFES-SOR?
WHAT?!
生
スーパードラ
ドンッ
THUD

* Draught Super Dry

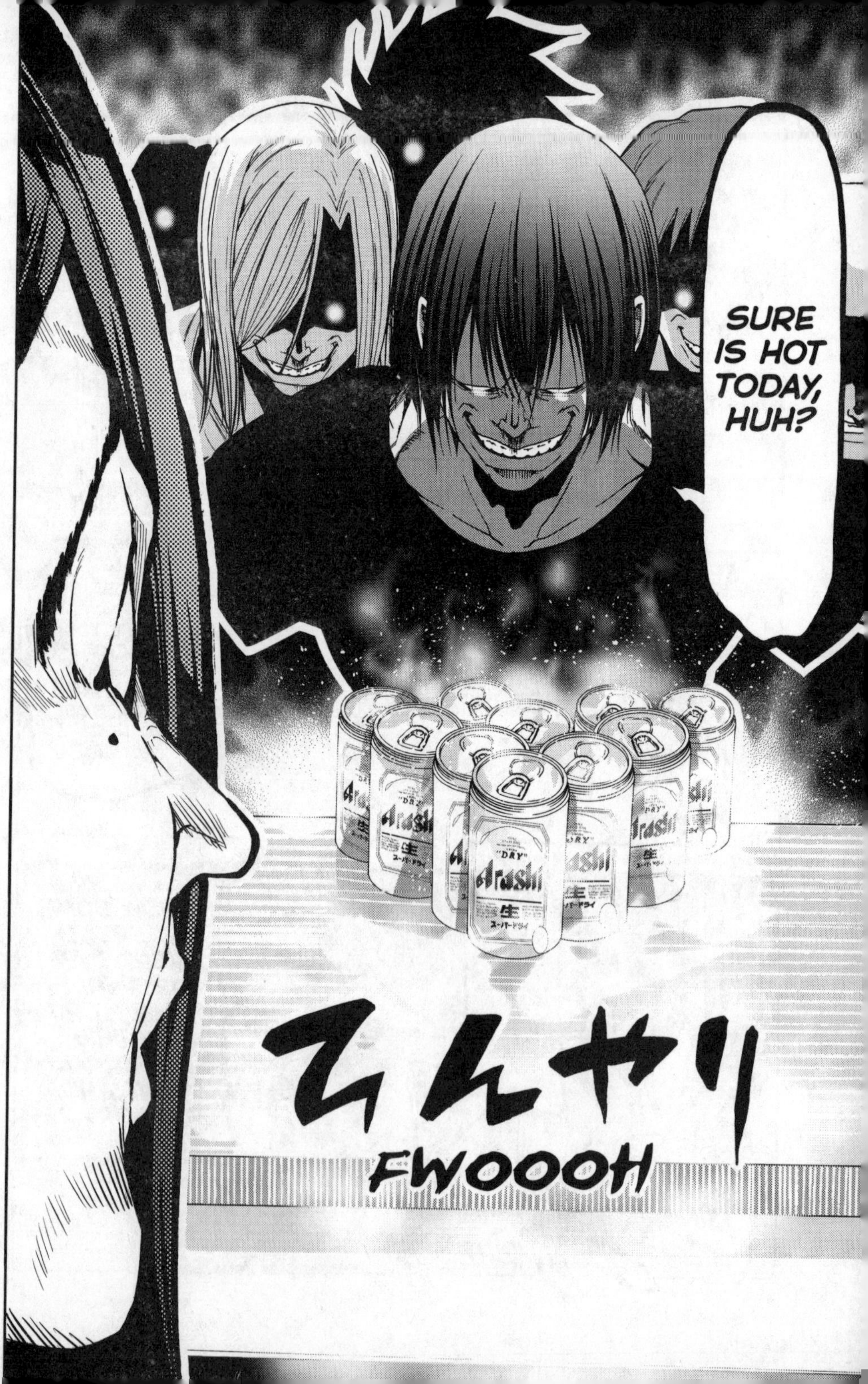
SURE IS HOT TODAY, HUH?
"DRY"
Arashi
生
スーパードライ
ひんやり
FWOOOH

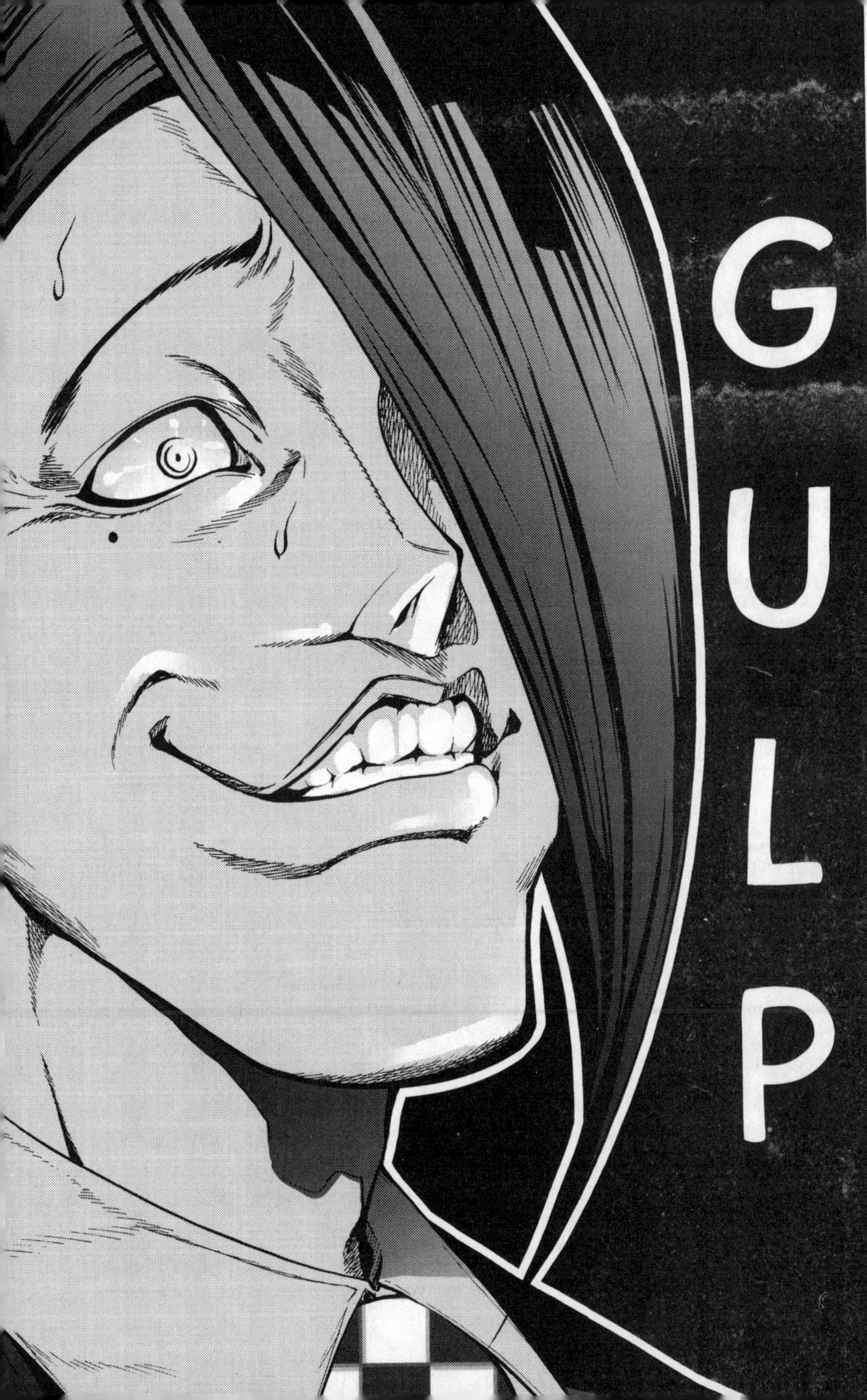
GULP

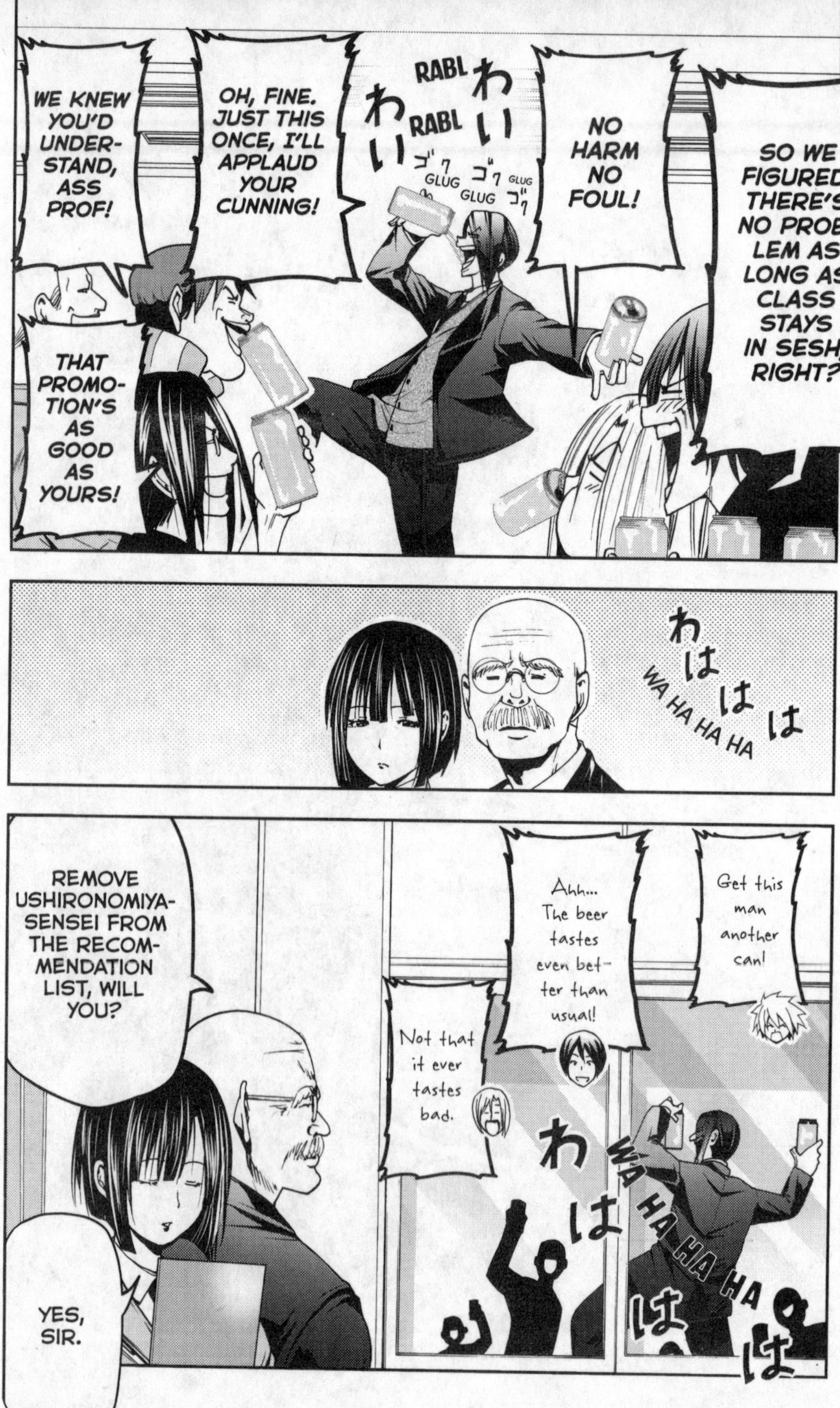
SO WE FIGURED, THERE'S NO PROBLEM AS LONG AS CLASS STAYS IN SESH, RIGHT?
NO HARM NO FOUL!
わい RABL
わい RABL
ゴク GLUG
ゴク GLUG
ゴク GLUG
OH, FINE. JUST THIS ONCE, I'LL APPLAUD YOUR CUNNING!
WE KNEW YOU'D UNDERSTAND, ASS PROF!
THAT PROMOTION'S AS GOOD AS YOURS!
わははは
WA HA HA HA
Get this man another can!
Ahh... The beer tastes even better than usual!
Not that it ever tastes bad.
わははは
WA HA HA HA
REMOVE USHIRONOMIYA-SENSEI FROM THE RECOMMENDATION LIST, WILL YOU?
YES, SIR.

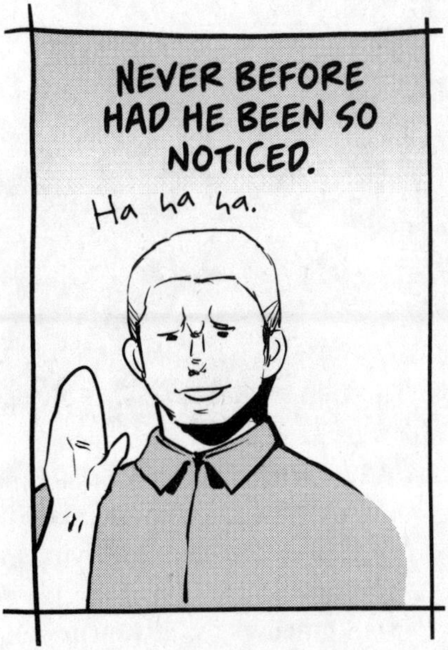
NEVER BEFORE HAD HE BEEN SO NOTICED.
Ha ha ha.

Young characters and steampunk setting, like *Howl's Moving Castle* and *Battle Angel Alita*

Beyond the Clouds © 2018 Nicke / Ki-oon

A boy with a talent for machines and a mysterious girl whose wings he's fixed will take you beyond the clouds! In the tradition of the high-flying, resonant adventure stories of Studio Ghibli comes a gorgeous tale about the longing of young hearts for adventure and friendship!

A SMART, NEW ROMANTIC COMEDY FOR FANS OF *SHORTCAKE CAKE* AND *TERRACE HOUSE*!

A romance manga starring high school girl Meeko, who learns to live on her own in a boarding house whose living room is home to the odd (but handsome) Matsunaga-san. She begins to adjust to her new life away from her parents, but Meeko soon learns that no matter how far away from home she is, she's still a young girl at heart — especially when she finds herself falling for Matsunaga-san.

A Kodansha Comics Trade Paperback Original
Grand Blue Dreaming 15 copyright © 2020 Kenji Inoue/Kimitake Yoshioka
English translation copyright © 2021 Kenji Inoue/Kimitake Yoshioka

All rights reserved.

Published in the United States by Kodansha Comics, an imprint of
Kodansha USA Publishing, LLC, New York.

Publication rights for this English edition arranged through
Kodansha Ltd., Tokyo.

First published in Japan in 2020 by Kodansha Ltd., Tokyo.

ISBN 978-1-64651-207-2

Original cover design by YUKI YOSHIDA (growerDESIGN)

Printed in the United States of America.

www.kodansha.us

1st Printing
Translation: Adam Hirsch
Lettering: Jan Lan Ivan Concepcion
Editing: Jordan Blanco
Additional layout and lettering: Sara Linsley
Editorial Assistance: YKS Services LLC/SKY Japan, INC.
Kodansha Comics edition cover design by Phil Balsman

Publisher: Kiichiro Sugawara

Director of publishing services: Ben Applegate
Associate director, publishing operations: Stephen Pakula
Publishing services managing editorial: Madison Salters, Alanna Ruse
Production managers: Emi Lotto, Angela Zurlo